Eric Pilon-Bignell, PhD

surfing rogue waves

A COMPASS TO NAVIGATING THE DISRUPTION OF THE FOURTH INDUSTRIAL REVOLUTION

How to paddle out into the 21st century

Ordering Information:
For details, contact eric@EricPB.me or visit www.EricPB.me

Cover artwork and design by BookBaby

Print ISBN: 978-1-09836-537-0
eBook ISBN: 978-1-09836-538-7

Printed in the United States of America on SFI Certified paper.

First Edition

Dédié à Angela. À toi, toujours à toi.

C'est toi, dont le regard éclaire ma nuit sombre;
Toi, dont l'image luit sur mon sommeil joyeux;
C'est toi qui tiens ma main quand je marche dans l'ombre,
Et les rayons du ciel me viennent de tes yeux!

—Victor Hugo

CONTENTS

PREFACE

Is it strange to think we are closer to 2050 than 1990? Is it weird to think about how we will experience more exponential change over the next 30 years than we did over the previous thirty? Or that we will experience more technological change in the next few years than the previous 100 years? Do you think about how you can influence and shape the next thirty years of your life or humanity's future? Most people do not have the luxury of philosophizing the future. They work jobs, have families, eat dinner, and scroll through social media. Most of us embrace the technology that is the result of the previous industrial revolutions without realizing we do not currently have the means to comprehend what is coming next.

Our political and social systems are outdated. General public trust in companies, governments, the media, and even science are all under attack. Your life, your business, companies, the world, governments—these things are all more complex than ever before.

Not complicated, complex.

Driving this complexity are technological changes that are fundamentally altering everything in our world. Our jobs, the way we live, the way we work, the way we interact with one another, and even us. The disruption we are facing is getting faster, bigger, and more complex than ever before. Our world is in hypermode, and we don't ever stop to notice we are transcending through a transformation unlike anything humanity has ever experienced before.

We have no way of predicting what is coming next—like waves on the ocean. All we do know, like the waves, is that it will eventually crash to the shore.

This book was born out of a sense of urgency and an inherent pursuit of purpose. A PhD is limited in its scope due to the required academic rigor and structure. The foundations of this book are rooted in my PhD thesis. I was happy with it, but it still felt incomplete as to its purpose in the world. I had focused my research on global leadership at the executive level. For my dissertation, I created a theoretical framework that applies to much more than global executives in organizations. After five years and completing my doctorate, I spent the next two years updating this research and framework to apply to leaders and apply to you, the CEO of your life.

To apply to all as we battle and surf both our professional and personal daily lives, I remodeled this theoretical framework into a surfing framework to serve as a compass, to help us identify, address, and engage the future so that we can surf the onslaught of increasing change and disruption we continuously take on in our daily lives. Surf that is transitioning from regular waves of disruption to never-before-seen monstrous rogue waves.

This book was also partly born out of excitement and fear. How do we get more people involved in the most critical discussions in human history? Platitudes aside, the future of humanity very much depends on you. In this book, I explain and answer how humans still fall victim to misinformation despite our human intelligence. Forget *fake news* for a moment; what about our *fake fears*? What is after our fake fears? How do we proactively address these ethics of tomorrow, today, and why is it essential to do so?

We have entered the Fourth Industrial Revolution. The most exciting time in human history in which we will regularly solve and achieve impossible feats.

But with more rewards comes more risk. We will be faced with the craziest rogue waves of disruption humanity has ever faced. Our past only sets the foundation for our future, which will be nothing like our past. This book presents a surfing framework, built on sound research and theory, for immediate and pragmatic application. This era of technological advancement will be fundamentally different than any other time in human history, and it will come faster than any of us think. The ethical discussions necessary for us to proactively build the world we want to live in are not happening at the scale we need them to happen at. These discussions will be key to understanding how we will reshape our industries, societies, and day-to-day lives. We will experience the disruption of not only how we interact with the world and the industries that create most of our jobs, but also the disruption of our biological selves and the one thing that makes us fundamentally human, human-level intelligence.

The surfing framework I present in this book works as a tool to equip the readers with a practical understanding of how to leverage the scientific and technological progress of our near future to create an outlook of this world that is all around better, safer, and more robust than the one we reside in today.

This book addresses the changes we will face in the next decade or two, all augmented by advancing these converging megatrends like AI, but it does not philosophize of a world in which AI reaches human-level intelligence, or if such a level is even possible. For now, AI lets us do more with less; it is a tool we can control, and, for now, the reward outweighs the risks. What happens when this is no longer the case? When AI becomes something more than a tool? Or if the risks are far heavier than the reward?

How does that future play out for humanity? Not 100 years from today, but over the next few decades? If we don't pay attention, we will wake up in a world of consequences without ever recognizing the changes as they happened. The decisions we make today will shape our near future, helping us to navigate this change tomorrow and the day after that. Ironically, our superior intelligence will decide if we remain as the superior form of intelligence on the planet.

This book was born out of a time in which the world hunkered down as COVID-19 blindsided our societal, governmental, and economic systems. Disruption can be good and bad. COVID-19 highlighted the power of rogue disruption and how pathetic our rigid, archaic systems are when they are called upon to adapt to global initiatives and problems. Our inability to address this change in an agile manner highlights the even greater need to create more all-encompassing, robust, and sustainable global systems. The potency of these rogue waves building along the horizon of our not so distant future carries a risk of being much more damaging to humanity than an infectious disease.

Humanity never voted for braces, or the internet, or IVF, or smartphones—they just happened. Our brains are what most differentiates us from the rest of mammalian life on the planet. As we continue to alter the one thing that makes us fundamentally human, we will be redefining what it means to be human. Advancements in the form of artificial, biological, and neurological technologies must be at the forefront of our discussions, as they will continue to redefine our understanding of what it fundamentally means to be human. Our surfing framework works to create a way to understand and navigate this discomfort as we paddle straight into these *barrels* of disruption, which are ironically key to our adaptation, growth, success, and survival.

We live in a time of enormous uncertainty, insecurity, and exponentially increasing change. It's terrifying unless we have a different way to think about and comprehend what is here today and coming tomorrow. This book is made up of five parts. It begins by surfing through *Yesterday* (Part 1), addresses *Today* (Part 2), introduces and explains the *Surfing Framework* (Part 3), which helps us understand *Tomorrow* (Part 4). From there, we look at the deeper questions on the horizon in *The Swell* (part 5) and how quickly the day after tomorrow will be here in *Epilogue: Pragmatic Dreams* (Part 6).

In the time I finally hit "publish," and when you read this, the world might have changed twice over. This is a crowdsourced book in a way, using many individuals' efforts to allow for the creation of something grander. Knowledge happens by recombining previous knowledge and ideas to create something new. This book is the result of the sound and rigorous research and knowledge from over 750 sources (listed in the notes section at the end of the book) that were used to build and inspire this creation. I want to thank everyone who produces incredible research, books, and content. Especially my editor Dave, who not only took a risk on a first-time author but did not hesitate to paddle out into uncertainty as we improvised our way to a tight deadline. I want to thank my friends and colleagues for unknowingly helping me shape this book. I would like to thank my family and my late father, who inspired me in ways they will never know. Without all of these people in my life, this book would not have been possible.

This book is also for you. For anyone interested in how the future is unfolding today. No more standing around watching from the shore. We must all jump in, paddle out, and start surfing the greatest waves in human history. No more excuses. Our decisions and actions today, small and big, will determine the fate of humanity. We must not fight the waves of advancement and progress; we must use them to our advantage and surf them. We must surf and navigate our way to a flourishing future that is more ethical, all-encompassing, and sustainable. This book aims to raise awareness of the speed of the rogue waves of disruption we are paddling out into, so we can be rational yet excited about what the future holds. Surf's up.

SURFING

True life is lived when tiny changes occur.

—Leo Tolstoy

Why is it that we only notice a change after it happens? We never really had a say in how the internet was shaped or planned the way smartphones worked their way into our lives. Connecting an entire house to Alexa? Who let that happen? All of these changes just kind of *happened*.

Do we not notice these changes because we don't know they are happening? Or do we just not know what to look for?

This was on my mind as I sat on a beach in the Gold Coast of Queensland, Australia. It was early in the evening, and the sun began to set over the city skyscrapers in the distance; before me, I watched the perfectly formed rows of waves roll over the ocean and crash onto the beach. I felt like I had just flown a million miles. I may as well have—hopping international flights from Dallas, Texas, to Sydney, to Brisbane, before driving the last stretch to the Gold Coast.

It had been a long day, but the fresh ocean air rejuvenated me. The ocean always looks perfect late in the afternoon; the lull of the waves caressing the shore beckoned me to go for a surf. It was the jetlag talking. I was exhausted, and surfing these waves would have likely resulted in drowning.

So, I sat with my toes in the sand, content with studying the rhythmic waves from the shore.

I love to surf, but I am a terrible surfer. Home, in Canada, was far inland and didn't leave me the means to practice with any regularity. But here, staring into the emerald sea, I honed my attention and thought about how and where the best waves would emerge tomorrow when I was rested and ready for them. Still, I couldn't help but zone out at the soothing sounds of the waves rolling against the beach.

I watched as a seal drifted among the waves. Then the seal grew arms. How jetlagged was I? Upon closer observation, I realized the seal was a surfer gracefully paddling out into the ocean. After a few moments, she sat up on her board, and, like me, she stared off into the great blue infinity. With each wave, she bobbed up and down, seemingly lost in an oceanic daydream. She was probably a local surfer, at one with her board and completely at home in these waters. She jumped up and easily caught a quick wave before pulling herself back onto her board. That maneuver alone meant she was a better surfer than I could ever dream of being. There she was again, sitting on her board, rising and falling with each wave. What was she staring at? Her eyes were fixed beyond the horizon at something I could not see.

She was relaxed, fluid as the ocean; waves rolled up under her, lifting her board, her legs, her back and shoulders. Every few rolls, she would tense her body just so and pop up slightly on her board, as if she saw something out past the next wave that would tell her something about the wave after that, and the one after that, before she sat back down on her board.

What was she looking for? No two waves are the same, but most waves follow a collective pattern. Every wave breaks roughly in the same spot, at roughly the same speed, and with roughly the same force. Would this surfer know the difference between roughly the right wave and exactly the right wave? Maybe I was too focused on trying to predict the right wave while she was assessing each wave? Maybe I was too impatient for this sport?

Come on lady! These waves are perfect, and the sun is setting. Go already!

What was she waiting for? What was she looking for? What did she know that I didn't know? After a few minutes of observing her intense focus, it arrived. A perfect set of waves formed as if rising out from nowhere. The best waves I've ever seen, appearing while I just sat on the Gold Coast, and they were converging on her exact position. I didn't even realize that I had gotten to my feet as I intently watched with anticipation for what was coming. She seemed unfazed; she didn't even flinch. I wanted to yell at her, to make sure she knew what was coming her way. But she just sat on her board, and bobbed over the first of the perfect waves. She didn't even seem to care that she was in the ideal position to capitalize on them. My mood shifted. This woman was insane.

Or maybe she was blind?

I started to feel bad for her, for the opportunity she was missing. Oh well, her loss. I sat back down on the sand and again focused on the waves I would be chasing tomorrow.

How do I say this next part?

Well, for one, the words "holy shit" left my lips.

From that perfect set of waves emerged a rogue *monster*. Not only was it the biggest wave I had seen while sitting on the beach that day, but it was perfectly shaped in every way. And she was still in the perfect position to ride it. I jumped back to my feet, nearly stumbling in the sand over my excitement. I looked up as she turned and dialed in. With a surgically methodical precision of efficiency, she jumped on it. Like some type of unnamed mythical predator, she became laser focused on every decisive paddle, her strokes and motions executed perfectly. She was in full stride, charging the wave to the point of no return. She wasted nothing. Her head snapped back and forth as she stalked the wave, hunting it down with commanding perfection.

What had started as a tranquil evening of watching waves had exploded into an incredible swell of energy and tension. There was no more calm ocean; I could feel ferocity building in this wave. The surfer came to life with the power of a sprinter to match the wave's building force. She was locked in. With a fluid, ninja-like yoga grace, she was on her feet, releasing built-up tension in a detonation of calm—she wasn't destroying this wave, but dancing in perfect unison with it. Like how a painter approaches a canvas, she created her own brush strokes with the turns and lines she carved with her board into the wall of the wave. Incredible.

Watching her masterful execution, I could feel the tension creeping back in. The wave was catching up to her, the foaming white wall ready to obliterate anything it ingested. Inevitable wipeout. The tension returned stronger and faster than before. Her every movement and position placed with dire perfection as the wave slowly gained on her. I thought to myself, *She should get out of there, pull off the wave, and claim victory on the best and biggest wave of the day.*

She was unfazed. There was no way she was backing down from this wave. She crouched down and vanished into the barrel of the wave.

I held my breath. Everything went quiet; everything froze. I scanned my eyes up and down the barrel of the wave, but no surfer. The wave had not yet spit her out the end, even though it had started to break down and close out its barrel. Time was running out.

In an explosion of mist and seafoam, she blasted out the end of the barrel with effortless control and style in what was the greatest in-person exhibition of surfing I have ever witnessed.

It was incredible.

It took me a moment to regain my composure. What did she know about the waves that I didn't? How did she know to wait for, and stalk down, that perfect wave? As she sat patiently on the water, passing up one great wave after another, what did she know to look for? Was she considering and calculating all the interdependencies and connectedness of every variable in the world to discover somehow the exact moment a perfect wave would emerge? How else did she know to put herself in such a perfect position to execute the barrel?

And how did she know what skills she needed to ride it? Was she a gifted physicist capable of processing real-time super-intelligent computations *in her head*? Did she calculate the wave's height and speed and force against her body's mass and the water's friction against the board as all of these variables shifted thousands of times per second? No two waves are ever exactly the same, so how did she surf that particular wave with such precision? The slightest error in placing her board or body could have spelled catastrophic failure, yet she consistently adapted to the evolving wave as though it bored her. She didn't try to fight or control the wave; she used every variable to her advantage, even though no single part of the ocean can be predicted in any way.

She did all this with perfect composure, style, and grace.

Jetlag aside, what was I missing? I have some surfing experience, but that wave would have crushed me. I wouldn't be here writing this if I had tried it. The surfer was not bigger or stronger than me, although she was most likely in better shape. But it wasn't her physical nature that made her a successful surfer; she was operating on a wholly different level. Inside her calm, patient mind was the mental framework of a surfer at play. A framework that not only helped her know when and where to catch the perfect wave, but how to ride the shit out of it.

Looking back out onto the water, I figured she would come running to shore, screaming in delight as she looked for someone to brag to about the performance she'd put on. Instead, all I saw was a subtle fist pump as she looked up into the sky and momentarily closed her eyes. After this, she simply turned back and paddled out to wait for her next wave.

Sitting in the sun-warmed sand that evening, watching a masterclass in surfing unfold on the waves in front of me, I wanted to know more about the mental framework that allowed the surfer to glide through such commanding waves. Yes, of course, I wanted to be something other than an embarrassment on the surfboard, but I was also curious to see if it could help how I approached other things.

I wanted to see if the surfing framework, the mindset that allowed one to stay standing while a million variables consistently changed, could help with how I lived my *life*.

Why is it we don't notice changes as they happen? How is it we don't look for the shifting tidal patterns or changing weather or developing and emerging waves of life thrown our way? Regardless of how well you ride a surfboard, we have all surfed through life in one way or another for many years now. Life, now more than ever, is composed of so much complexity, it'd be like counting the waves that crash on the beach. When we think about everything that must happen to make our lives' progression possible, being able to surf upon waves is nothing short of magical.

There is something wonderous about the expansive ocean's perpetual cadence. So many of us are drawn to it—the ocean's amazing ability to roar with a breathtakingly violent energy that can cause catastrophic damage. Yet, it does so with a constant, ever-changing rhythm dotted with seemingly random, cyclical patterns of lifelike pulses that give it a sense of peace and tranquility, where everything emerges as a place where time and space seem to have no hold. The ocean is the world's greatest mystery, its last frontier, and we have yet to explore it fully. We cruise along the surface on boats, we ride the waves on surfboards, and we sit on beaches to watch the surf crash onto the shore. It is crazy to think, for the most part, that we cannot build on the ocean, and it will remain a boundless open space perfect for contemplation.

How is it we have mapped every last square meter of the globe's dry surface, yet the oceans cover 70% of our planet and we have only significantly explored maybe 10% of it? Apart from the limitless cosmos above us, which we know virtually nothing about, the oceans off our shores hold untold mysteries about who we are. While they may seem unrelated, our cosmos and the oceans are heavily dependent and connected. Consider the vast emptiness of an ocean as it glimmers under the light of the moon. The tides rise and fall from the combined effects of the sun and moon's gravitational forces in conjunction with Earth's rotation. The moon's gravitational pull generates tidal forces, causing Earth, along with all its water, to bulge out on the side closest and farthest from the moon. These bulges are what we call high tides. While tides are usually the largest source of short-term sea-level fluctuations, there is much more than celestial gravity that affects our oceans.

The ocean levels and waves are also susceptible to changes in the wind and barometric pressure, resulting in the storm surges prominent in shallow areas and near coastlines—often making for excellent surfing conditions. The complex tidal phenomena are not just limited to the oceans; this emergence also alters other systems whenever a gravitational field varies in time and space. That is: the shape of the solid part of the Earth is affected slightly by the Earth's tide. These changes happen over long periods and are not as quickly seen as rising tides or waves from the shore. We may not see it, but it still very much affects surfers.

Half a century ago, American President John F. Kennedy said, "Knowledge of the oceans is more than a matter of curiosity. Our very survival might hinge on it." Humans are often so busy that we forget how interdependent and interconnected we are to space, Earth, the oceans, and even surfing. For example, our agricultural practices produce an excess of methane. Our use of fossil fuels like coal, oil, and gas creates CO2. The resulting greenhouse gases contribute to the smog and air pollution that directly impact respiratory diseases in every living being. Greenhouse gases have other far-ranging environmental impacts augmented through the complex, interconnected relationships between Earth and the cosmos. They trap more energy from the sun, which results in the oceans absorbing more heat, which increases the ocean's surface temperatures and sea levels. The changes in oceanic temperatures affect the currents, which further lead to alterations in climate patterns worldwide. Yet somehow, through the emergence of a biological, evolving, single-celled organism, a mammalian brain, and the human cortex, developed the ability to understand all of these interconnected complexities and the ability to surf through them.

To keep the analogy straight: Every interconnected thing that happens in our world causes a wave of change. The life we live is little more than how we choose to surf a certain wave. Or waves. Or one long, constant, barrel of a wave we know as "life." The waves are getting bigger, more complicated, and more relentless—yet we only have a surfboard at our disposal to ride it with.

Off the shores of Nazaré, Portugal, you can watch waves climb to over ten stories high. If you happened to be there over the past decade, you might have watched Garrett McNamara surf one of these 100-foot beauties. Insane. To put this in context, these waves at Nazaré hold enough energy to power over 30-million smartphone batteries *in each wave*. Imagine the power of one wave producing enough energy to power every Canadian smartphone? Ten of these waves would power a cell phone for every American. We all know how much energy this spot alone produces, and the ocean creates much more than ten waves a day. The impact of our oceans varies depending on if you view them from a macro or micro level. From space, looking down on our planet, our oceans appear a stagnant place. Standing on the shore tells a different story, a story wherein the ocean is in continuous motion. At a micro level, the ocean is a molecular soup of absolute pandemonium. From these views, we understand how our oceans are propelled worldwide through sweeping currents, how waves transfer energy across entire ocean basins, and how tides rise and drop every day.

In a way, unlike light or sound waves, the ocean waves are easy for us to understand. In the ocean, we can see the properties of the waves with our own eyes. If we look out to the horizon, we can estimate the amplitude (height) of a wave. We can roughly calculate its wavelength (the distance from the peak of one wave to the next), as well as the frequency (the number of waves that pass over a specific period). So, in a way, surfing is really that simple. Just by understanding the inner complexity of space and Earth, some basic understanding of wave propagation, and how waves carry energy as they move across the ocean floor, we need to capture this energy to stand up and balance on a board. The better we understand physics, the better we should be at surfing. Since surfing is just a mix of buoyancy, surface tension, mass, shape, and hydrodynamic forces all acting together—why aren't more physicists pro surfers?

Can an understanding of scientific principles make us better surfers? For sure. But it will not make you any better at standing up on your board. The science helps to understand what waves are, how they are made, and where they come from—all of which gives us a much better idea of what good surf should look like. But this is only half the cocktail. Once you are in the water, the name of the game is improvisation and using snap judgments through your conscious and unconscious decisions and actions to keep you upright and on the board. In our pursuit of surfing the perfect wave, science points us in the right direction, like a compass. The knowledge of science alone will not make you a good surfer. But physical training and practice in the form of real-world surfing, augmented with science, might.

As we know it today, the skill of surfing seems to emerge naturally over time with more experience in the water. Each wave you attempt to ride is a unique, one-time experience built on how the surfer's manipulation of the board and the wave emerging from a world where everything is affected by everything else.

Maybe this is why so many of us sit on the beach and stare into the sea, mesmerized by the rhythmic flow of the waves? Are we lost in meditative thought? Or are we unconsciously taking in all of the complexity in the world, studied through waves?

The Tides are Changing

You never really know what's coming. A small wave, or maybe a big one. All you can really do is hope that when it comes, you can surf over it, instead of drown in its monstrosity.

— Alysha Speer

We only notice change after it happens. Unlike surfing, we are not studying waves to see how their disruption will develop and emerge. We are not actively focused on looking for areas of change and building of tension in our lives. We are not actively considering the reasons for the building of these waves of disruption in our everyday lives. These disruptive waves can be either good or bad, but they have a place, and an influence, in our lives regardless. Unlike surfers who learn from each wave they catch, most of us are not learning from previous changes that have crashed into the shores of our lives. Each change and transition is very different; we fail to view life like a surfer watches the waves. Every wave a surfer catches is like starting over, and every wave is uniquely different. The difference between someone's first time out on the water and a seasoned surfer with a collection of wetsuits is how quickly they can adapt to the unique conditions of each incoming wave. Learning from past experiences allows us to prepare for the unexpected events coming down the pike—like the spontaneous emergence of a rogue wave that could either knock us off the board, or give us the ride of a lifetime. Further to the point, surfers are not merely preparing for rogue waves; they are actively hunting them. They *dream* about them.

Why not take this mindset into our everyday life? Not only should we prepare for the rogue waves of disruption, but we should continuously seek them out, dream of them, and hunt them down. We can either engage with the change or let it show up as a wipeout surprise. Without preparation, the only option is to run from the rogue waves before they annihilate us, leaving us vulnerable to the next giant wave building in the distance. Some people aimlessly drift through life, trying not to drown, while others prepare themselves to have the time of their lives surfing the shit out of rogue monster waves.

In the ocean of our lives, we are experiencing rogue waves building in a full-on mode of complex hyper-disruption. All the changes in our world feel less predictable, more relentless, and more catastrophic than ever before. We should be concerned, as these changes will transform everything we know about our world and ourselves. We will never be sure how all of this disruption and change will transform our lives, but we know change is happening. For the first time in human history, there are technologies of exponential capacity that are starting to crash into one another, creating an explosion of amplification of how each technology makes rogue waves. And the frequency of these collisions will only increase in the coming years, reshaping our lives every time. While we may start to see how these changes happen, there are still countless unseen revolutions happening in distribution, transportation, finance, real estate, retail, education, advertising, food, health, manufacturing, entertainment, and many other industries.

How do we prepare for changes we can't even see?

As our technologies get faster and develop more rapidly, the collisions get exponentially more catastrophic and impact our day-to-day in further-reaching capacities with less predictability. We don't know much, we can't see into the future (yet), but we do know that forecasts have advancements in robotics, virtual reality, augmented reality, digital biology, and sensors slamming directly into 3D printing, blockchain, global digital networks, and AI to create an explosion of rogue disruption, unlike anything we have ever seen.

And here you are. You need to buy milk and get to work on time and make sure you have an internet connection that is fast enough to stream your favorite shows. But these disruptions will only move the daily life of all humanity into uncharted, unexplored oceans, and we will be forced to reimagine the world. Not only will we be presented with technological and systematic challenges, but we will also be forced to rethink everything we know from the human experience, from aging and happiness to artificial human augmentations. These rogue waves of disruption are already making us reconsider how we raise children, how we govern our cities and nations, and how we care for this planet. What does it mean to be human? Or to have morals and ethics? Whatever the answers, one thing is for sure: we all have to stop watching from the shore and start learning to surf the greatest waves humanity has ever experienced.

PART 1: YESTERDAY

Those who do not remember the past are condemned to repeat it.

— George Santayana

It seems like only yesterday, most of our problems seemed so far away. This reminds me of a famous Beatles song, called "Yesterday". Honestly, though, how far ahead of their time were The Beatles? Maybe Paul and John were trying to tell us something when they wrote this song, like how the things we worry will happen in the future, have a way of just *happening*. Much like how we only tend to notice a change *after* it takes place. Then, after the change happens, we often forget it happened as we become enamored with the new changes in front of us.

To fully comprehend how much change we have experienced, we need to go back to the beginning, the *real* beginning, to see the incredible complexity that results in creating the modern-day Homo sapiens. Humans have never been the strongest or fastest species around, and we aren't the only species capable of thought. But we do have a brain region that is uniquely human in that it is linked to processes of higher thinking and cognitive powers. We are the only species on Earth that is capable of *thinking about thinking*. We formed a base of knowledge from thinking about thinking, which led to science and technology and our eventual dominance over the planet. Over millions of years, this happened slowly, yet we didn't notice all of these interdependent and connected changes as they happened. Looking back, we can now understand how these changes progressed and how they gave us the tools to see the direction we are heading.

The Beginning of Theory

Complexity is not a new concept; it has been around since the beginning of time. In prior times, we had a habit of repeating our mistakes and seeing history repeat itself time and again. Things were simpler then. Today, our world is becoming so complex that not only will we never make the same mistake twice; we won't even have time to recover from the errors or learn that they were mistakes in the first place. To understand how the world came to be, we have to know where it all started. Understanding our past is essential not only to understanding the present but also in shaping our future.

Go back to the real beginning, as far back as we can mentally comprehend, to when our planet was created out of complexity. The story starts about 14 billion years ago, when all the space, matter, and energy of the known universe would fit, as Neil Degrasse Tyson puts it, "in a volume less than one-trillionth the size of the period that ends this sentence." Small. Then, an explosion occurred, one that we knew little about until we met a Belgian named Gilles Lemaître in the early 1900s. He observed how neighboring galaxies were moving farther away from us, giving him the grounds of the expanding universe theory. Lemaître later proposed what most of us know today as the "big bang theory" to explain the universe's origin. Ironically, in addition to being a noted mathematician, astronomer, and physics professor, Gilles was a Catholic priest. Unlike other Catholic tendencies, Gilles didn't proclaim much of anything. There was no "Big Bang Proclamation," but a theory. Modern science, even in the earliest days, was built on the persistent testing of theories.

Theories rely on testing to deem their accuracy. Therein, a theory needs to be established in a way it can be routinely tested against numerous variables. The more times the theory is proven correct, the stronger it tends to be. It turns out this Gilles guy was pretty *bang* on with his theories and calculations, but sometimes we need to see things with our own eyes to believe them—which is exactly what happened. Shortly after Lemaître proposed his theory, another scientist confirmed it through physical observation. You know this other scientist as Edwin Hubble, the famous American astronomer after which the Hubble Telescope would later be named. Additional scientists who came to support Father Lemaître's big bang theory include other familiar names, like Albert Einstein.

Einstein used *Thought Experiments* to explain and prove phenomena through mathematics. In 1916, Einstein published a paper with a theory that would forever change our understanding of the universe. This theory outlined the detailed mathematical calculations about, well, essentially how everything in the universe moves by the influence of gravity. This theory explains "our modern understanding of gravity, in which the presence of matter and energy curves the fabric of space and time surrounding it," as Tyson would say with convincing simplicity.

Again, theories are made to be tested. In the early 1900s, what Einstein proposed must have seemed beyond absurd. His calculations and theory claimed that it should precisely bend the light from another star due to the sun's gravitational pull, causing an eclipse that could be calculated with exact precision. On May 29, 1919, a group of English scientists trekked over West Africa to see if they could witness a total solar eclipse predicted with Einstein's theory. As the haters and critics gathered and waited to scoff at the failed results, they were all terribly disappointed to see that the eclipse's measurements revealed that Einstein's predictions were correct with incredible precision. Since that day, the smartest minds in the world have challenged, attacked, and rigorously tested this law of General Relativity. The more they fail, the more it strengthens our view of the universe's theory and understanding. This was a theory devised in a person's mind, proven through math, about things they had no way of testing or seeing at the time. Yet it has somehow stood the test of time for over a hundred years now. Every day in labs around the world, the smartest scientists with increasingly precise technology and instruments further test and experiment with this theory. We tested this theory on everything, including variables we didn't know existed in 2019, never mind 1916. As we continuously test and accurately predict outcomes explained by the theory, our confidence in the theory is reinforced. This is what makes science so great: Opinions do not matter unless we can test them. On the other hand, even if a theory holds up and is strengthened by testing a thousand variables against it, the entire theory can fall apart if even *one* test fails.

Complexity explains emergence, but we see and experience emergence at macro and micro levels differently. Take the example of our cosmos timeline, which we all know starts with a bang, but then not many observable things happen. At the micro level, electrons start fusing to protons. Temperatures drop below 100,000,000 degrees Kelvin. Protons and neutrons get jiggy with it and form a universe made up of a nuclei breakdown of 90% hydrogen, 10% helium, and trace amounts of other stuff. Not much happens for the next 380,000 years—particles just rip about doing whatever. Eventually, things cool down to 3,000 degrees Kelvin and the particle party comes to a halt. All the free electrons mate with nuclei, creating light at the macro level! Light is essential because it gives us the start of the permanent ledger in our history. The light we see at night from stars represents time—and the arrival of light provides us with a recording of where all of the matter in the universe was at a specific time.

Skipping ahead 9,000,000,000 years or so, after all this micro-level complexity, we arrive at the Virgo Supercluster and within it, the Milky Way. While there may not be anything objectively special about the Milky Way galaxy, there is a tiny location within this galaxy, also not unique or special, called the Orion Arm, where an exceptional star was born. Well, exceptional to us, as it is our Sun!

Skipping a few hundred million years, a planet forms under fortunate circumstances and locks into orbit with this star (our Sun). This planet is primarily made up of liquid, which would have evaporated if the planet had been closer. Any farther away, and it would have frozen solid. In this perfect balance and dance with the Sun emerges a planet we know as "Earth," now primarily made up of the liquid we call oceans.

Without wandering down the complicated path of evolution, we can know that the newly cooled, liquid Earth is home to tiny, single-celled organic molecules that can self-duplicate. While the simple anaerobic bacteria did not require oxygen to do their thing, they did produce a fair amount of oxygen as a byproduct of their replication. At this point in our history, the Earth's atmosphere was mostly carbon dioxide. As these simple anaerobic bacteria replicated, they created more oxygen until there was enough for aerobic organisms to emerge.

From here, we start to see more complex-celled organisms capable of breathing air. They start to reproduce. The planet now had organisms roaming about both land and water. Another neat takeaway from all this oxygen production? The creation of our atmosphere, which would serve to protect us from the constant barrage of ultraviolet photons (or "sunshine," as you may know it) that would otherwise roast us to death. Even here, with breathing creatures and atmosphere, we are still a long way away from what we know as humanity.

In the meantime: enter the dinosaurs! There isn't a child alive who, at one point, hasn't loved dinosaurs, so it only makes sense to give them a shout-out. As we rip through the next billion years or so, the Earth continues to develop increasingly complex organisms and lifeforms such as grass, trees, weeds (unfortunately), flowers, reptiles, mammals, and of course, dinosaurs.

Sadly, the dinosaurs exit the story just as quickly as they entered it. Looking back at the scale of the last 14 billion years, dinosaurs roamed the Earth for less than the time you took to blink just now. As we continue to fast-forward through our timeline, we pause around 75,000 years ago. By now, primates, a sub-branch of mammals, have developed frontal lobes. A subdivision of these primates experienced a genetic mutation that would allow for speech, ultimately resulting in what we know as Homo sapiens.

We know, for sure, that something wiped out the dinosaurs. Then, something else nearly wiped out Homo sapiens—we almost shared the same fate, as though history were repeating itself. Right at this point in our history, Indonesia exploded. Like, as a region, it just...*exploded*. One of the Earth's largest-known eruptions—we are talking about a *super*volcanic eruption, the biggest volcanic event in the last 25,000,000 years—took place. If you were around then, it would be the eruption you talked about for the next 75,000 years, *assuming you survived.*

This massive and incredible explosion spewed a thick curtain of dust, junk, rubble, smoke, and ash that covered the skies and blocked out the sun for thousands and thousands of kilometers. This eruption was so violent that an estimated 2,793 cubic kilometers of dirt exploded into the air, covering massive parts of India and Malaysia in 30 feet of deep volcanic ash. The parts not buried in volcanic ash likely suffocated under an enormous blanket of deadly, poisonous smoke and dust. Suddenly, most of the planet was not what our ancestors would have called pleasant. If you weren't buried in volcanic ash, or choking to death on a thick poisonous cloud, or melted alive from a sudden and sharp rise in temperatures, then you lived in complete darkness for a long time.

If that was not bad enough, there was a drastic dive in temperatures because of the blackout clouds, giving the planet a "volcanic winter."

I'm from Canada, so I don't think winters are too bad. But this was not a Canadian winter. This volcanic winter was so bad that it killed off most plants and animals across the planet, causing most humans who survived the blast to starve and die. The few who survived did so by running from the death cloud and retreating to less-affected areas where life was slightly more fruitful. Estimates claim that only about 2,000 humans remained after the eruption, the equivalent of a large lecture hall in a university. Billions of years of history and complexity, creation, and survival against all the odds, more or less reduced to the population of a small village. Humans had to defy the odds again and repopulate the planet—which it did, topping nearly 8 billion people in the span of 75,000 years.

How do we know this happened? What makes this point in our history different from a fictional movie? Because we have theories that can be tested. Without going into extensive details and explanations on these theories, I found that Michio Kaku, one of the great physicists of our time, explains it nicely. He references strong evidence about this catastrophic event in our genetic code. The advancement of genetic studies has shown how all humans have almost identical DNA. Sure, this could all just be a *bloody* coincidence that we cannot explain, but it does support the theory that all humans came from that tiny group of 2,000 survivors. This also helps explain how the entire human race has less genetic variation than what we find between any two chimpanzees on Earth. Various other scientists have explained other theories that give mathematical support to this theory, which leads us to the same conclusion and point in time, further reinforcing this catastrophic event that nearly caused the extinction of the human race.

Feel special; your ancestors were the ones who somehow survived the most miserable period in history and saved the human race against all odds. Humanity spent the next several thousand years multiplying, adapting, and inhabiting nearly every region around the globe. It isn't until this point that we finally meet our story's hero: the present-day human surfer.

What happened before this? What happened before the beginning? That is an excellent question that can lead to philosophical, spiritual, and religious debates, none of which have theories that can currently, consistently, or confidently support a specific scientific scenario. We know that the sciences have done a great job explaining how we came to be (present day), from this point referenced as "the beginning." We also know that the development of our brains has led us to be the only species on the planet to understand where it is we've come from. We aren't just human, we are...

Uniquely Human

Intelligence is based on how efficient a species became at doing the things they need to survive.

— Charles Darwin

Before we dive into another history lesson, a word on "complexity." There is a complete section later dedicated to defining and diving into the nature of complexity. As a temporary, working definition, it is the **interactions, emergence, dynamics, self-organization**, and **adaptation** of, well, everything. Throughout this book, "complexity" works better as an adjective than a noun.

As I was saying before: Compared to the complexity of the universe and the history of our planet, humans are just as, if not more, complex. Our brains bear intelligence and, in turn, the ability to surf (among other things). Understanding how we formed our intelligence might help us understand how it will evolve next.

The story of our intelligence starts in a world capable of programming the type of information that brought about human evolution. This evolution began with increasingly complex molecules (specifically tiny carbon atoms), which created fruitful informational structures by connecting in various directions. We understand these structures through chemistry, which, thankfully, some people enjoy studying by *choice*. Over the next billion years, complexity went beast mode and, through its emergent nature, created a molecule that could precisely encode lengthy strings of information. These encoded strings resulted in the generation of organisms—all of them from what we call DNA. These organisms developed decision networks and communication channels at an ever-increasing rate through the self-organizing and emergent nature of complexity, which ultimately created the first nervous system. Through this nervous system's interconnectedness, organisms gained the ability to coordinate their progressively complex behaviors and body parts to adapt to their surroundings advantageously.

Just having a brain, on its own, isn't terribly special. Most animated creatures on this planet have one. The human brain, however, is the only one capable of hierarchical thinking. Again, this isn't terribly special because this limits our ability to comprehend nonhierarchical systems like complexity. Nonetheless, our hierarchical thinking allows for the understanding and assembly of various elements. We organize these elements into patterns represented with symbols, which are then used to create more complex configurations—we know this as language. All of this happens in our neocortex, unique to the mammalian brain, and the thing that allows us to have ideas. Building ideas upon other ideas is what gives us "knowledge," something which appears to be, so far, uniquely human.

In the beginning, it was all about physics. This all spawned from something the size of a decimal on this page, and 14 billion years later, we have the complexity of the world around us. It started with physics, evolved into chemistry, then biology, and neurology—atoms to DNA to brains. We were lucky—or so we'd like to believe—to gain a neocortex out of this. It's what allows us to dominate as the top species. The neocortex is only about the thickness of a decent, quality sheet of paper (2-4 mm thick, made up of six layers). While the neocortex in smaller mammals, such as rats, is smooth, in larger mammals it is folded with grooves (sulci) and wrinkles (gyri) to significantly increase the surface area. For humans, the neocortex comprises around 76% of our brain and is made up of billions of cells (100 billion neurons), which each have thousands and thousands of synapses. This means this particular region of our brain has about a hundred trillion connections—the equivalent of packing 300,000,000 feet of wire down into the volume of two clenched fists. That's dense.

As much as we claim to know about our brains, there are likely an infinite number of mysteries left to uncover. The world's leading neuroscientists are racing to better understand the human brain, each offering different opinions and views on what might be taking place in our skulls. Everyone seems to agree that the mind, our consciousness, is in no way separate from the brain. The research shows the interconnectedness of billions of ordinary cells in the brain is the physical basis for the entirety of what makes us human. This physical basis of the brain refers to our agreed understanding of its physical properties and how specific regions work. The brain's physical, structural science explains the basis for all of our thoughts, aspirations, language, sense of consciousness, moral beliefs, and much more. Despite what we might have been raised to think, these things are not controlled or created by anything other than our own physical wiring. Meaning, in time, science will eventually help us understand every one of these connections.

The physical structure is one thing, but how about *feelings?* Like love? Many of us grew up with the idea that love is feeling from the heart. Most individuals agree they "can feel" love, and we can type a heart-shaped emoji on our phones. Love, therefore, must come from the heart, yes? Most of us are fortunate to have experienced the feeling of love. It's important to the human experience. Many would argue love is the foundation for the amazing wealth of art, poetry, music, paintings, and dances, just to name a few. Love is also responsible for terrible things: like romantic comedies and 90% of the pop music sung to at karaoke bars.

Ray Kurzweil's book *How to Create a Mind* explains how we currently understand the biochemical changes that happen when we "fall in love." This happy, warm, tingly feeling we get is simply a release of dopamine in our brains. We get a massive spike in norepinephrine, which significantly increases our heart rate, leaving us with a feeling of excitement and euphoria. In addition to phenylethylamine, these chemicals produce an increase in energy levels that increase our attention, decrease our appetite, and create the overall need for the "thing" or "person" we desire. Some interesting university research also shows that serotonin levels go down in parallel with all of this happening—not unlike what happens in those with obsessive-compulsive disorder and what we know as "puppy love."

When we are "falling in love," testosterone and estrogen have an essential part in establishing sexual instincts. The thing we call "love" is just the romantic process of partnership bonding. If the only purpose of feeling love was sexual reproduction, there would be no reason for two individuals to create an emotional attachment. Love would be as useful as the Tinder app. After the early phase of "falling in love," we move onto an attachment and longer-term bond with our loved ones. Again, this does not just happen miraculously; our brains release vasopressin and oxytocin that create this feeling. If Tinder and lust are all we need to assure reproduction, why did we evolve this thing called "love"? It turns out that mature, long-lasting love creates a bond conducive to creating a stable and secure environment for children to develop their neocortices. Your neocortex developed "love" to give your offspring the best chance to learn and grow in their youngest years. Oxytocin and the vasopressin hormone are a large part of what drives the vital bond between children and their parents. For example, my mother's favorite child is my youngest brother, a big-time "mama's boy," and their bond clearly produced much more oxytocin and vasopressin hormone in him than in the rest of us. I swear, I'm not bitter about this.

It's not just our physical biology. Our cultural surroundings are invested in programming the idea of love into our lives. Children are more likely to develop into healthy, working adults when raised by parents versus when they raise themselves. In the days of yore, young children would become farmers, who would produce food for society and spur the next round of reproduction and development essential to their society's future. This is where the ideas of marriage come from, and they have remained relatively unchanged throughout humanity. In days of yore, life expectancy was far shorter, and "till death do us part" usually meant "about twenty years." Now that we live much longer, "till death do us part" is a far healthier commitment than twenty years, for better or worse.

The wants and needs of humans change faster than what our evolution can keep up with, and we can see this through how the purpose and function of love has changed throughout history. Today, most of us fall in love for every reason *but* reproduction. It is even rumored that humans can have sex without worrying about making babies. We also can create babies without having sex. These developments are common today, even though they were unheard of a mere hundred years ago. We're one of the few species that copulate for reasons other than reproduction; we're the only ones who can reproduce without copulation—it is unique to us, but it is only the beginning of what makes us uniquely human.

Intelligent to Rational

The pessimist complains about the wind; the optimist expects it to change; the realist adjusts the sails.

— William Arthur Ward

Our brains are a supercomplex system of billions upon billions of nerves that communicate with the rest of our bodies within fractions of seconds. This system can arrange patterns that systemize our emotions, behaviors, and thoughts, both consciously and unconsciously. Our brains necessitate higher sensory perception functions, motor commands, spatial reasoning, and language—another uniquely human thing. Do we fully understand, structurally, how billions of loosely coupled neurons, firing around on synapses, give rise to these incredible functions? In some cases, yes. In others, not so much.

Intelligence in the human brain is not centrally driven in any way. It is not predesigned, preplanned, or predetermined. Intelligence is a decentralized emergent phenomenon. The brain's left side tends to be more numeric and logic-based, while the brain's right side is associated with creativity. Associating the brain's left and right parts exclusively to certain behaviors and actions is clearly a misnomer, but it helps us visualize the structures. The metaphor of numeric vs. creative largely refers to tasks predominantly accomplished by one side of the brain over the other. Science shows us how the brain is more complicated than a simple right side/left side division. However, we do understand how specific tasks, like problem-solving, reside predominantly in certain regions of the brain (neither right nor left). We often need very little of our brains to complete most tasks. Scientists were able to remove up to 90% of a rat's brain without causing significant deterioration in its ability to problem solve and navigate through a maze. Does this mean we only need 10% of our brain for problem-solving and navigation? Not exactly. We should keep the remaining 90% of our brains in case it is useful in the future for other things, like love, or to read books about how to become better surfers.

Our brains allow our intelligence, and this intelligence created our scientific mind. Science is proven through reliable and repeatable experiments. It does not rely on speculation or consider hearsay, nor does it build any of its foundation upon what your friends post on social media. When it comes to being "most correct," science has significantly outperformed all other methods, like opinions, anecdotes, religion, and practically everything else in the world. Through science, we now know how modern-day humans came to be. Evolution and our brains' development help us understand how humans developed into the dominant race on Earth.

From science, we know that if you are reading this book outside, there is light created by the sun's chemical reactions that bounces off your book's pages. From this light emission, some of the photons reflect into the pupils of your eyeballs and hit your retinas. The energy from these photons stimulates neural impulses transmitted to your brain in the area responsible for visual processing. At this moment, in near real time, your brain performs a series of mechanical and chemical operations to process and rebuild the data into a 3D model of the words on a page in this book. From this, you confidently know you are looking at a page in this book. This is not magic; we understand how it happens. Through similar means, we can also comprehend the best way to think that accurately aligns what we think to the reality around us, and which thinking methods do not work.

This is why an optical illusion can trick a young child or an animal; they only believe what they see. Their brains have not developed to the point where they understand their visual cortexes. Human adults are aware they have eyes, which makes them aware that they do not need to believe everything they see with their eyes. Most adults are rational enough to question things they see that do not mirror the world's realities. This is how science works. Science is consistently rethinking the reasoning behind our brains to comprehend a better way of accurately understanding the world. We use science to understand the world and create experiments to invalidate some theories while strengthening others. Science advances our species by reinforcing rationality. Science is the process that helps us best connect our brains to reality so we can do things, like surfing.

What makes us different from apes is that animals do not think about science, which may very well be why animals do not have science (sorry, Dr. Zaius). Although both animals and humans have flawed brains through which we view reality, only humans are aware of it. Since humans understand our brain's flawed nature and are aware of these flaws, we can identify these systematic errors and biases and apply a secondary review to correct course. The collaborative effort is by no means perfect, but it is by far one of the most powerful advantages we have over every other living thing on Earth.

Understanding all this, we can look inward at what doesn't work and how to enhance what does. Those with a properly functioning arm made of muscles, ligaments, and tendons can quickly learn to raise their hand (and arm) to ask a question. Humans with functioning, non-damaged cortical and subcortical areas can train their brains how to think, much like how you can train your muscles to move, flex, and react (muscle memory!).

Centuries of human evolution hardwired our most important physical instincts to survive through ancient times. For example, we just know to get out of the way of a falling object that might hit us. We do not consciously think through the process of engaging our muscles and tendons at the risk of avoiding injury or death; we just know to move out of the way. This is not unique to humans; most animals do the same. But it was not our physical attributes that allowed humans to maintain dominance over other species.

Like our muscles, our brains are not as uniquely human as we think, since animals also have them. What is uniquely human is a part of our brain that makes us aware *that we have a brain*, which gives us the ability to use it better. This concept of accurately controlling our brains, thinking how to think, is a more recent development than when humans learned to control bodily movement, making it a far more difficult process. As Chris Stapleton croons, "the hard roads are the ones worth choosing." We can train our brain the same way we learned to raise our hands. Understanding our shortcomings lets us be more rational and better understand the truth.

Humans make mistakes. One-off mistakes are usually due to insufficient data or knowledge needed to make a decision—it happens, but these aren't the kinds of mistakes we need to worry over. After all, these are the types of mistakes where we can gather new information and make better decisions and fewer errors in the future.

For example, imagine we were washing freshly picked apples from a barrel. You reach into the barrel and pull out an apple because that's all you think is in the barrel. You could believe that there are only apples in the barrel. But as you pulled out more items, you find that there are also potatoes in the barrel. With this new information, it would be rational for you to no longer conclude that there were only apples in the barrel.

But we must be careful. There are traps! There are situations where more information could make your prediction worse. This happens when we learn from biased methods. For example, statistical bias: the more you learn from wrong information, the worse your prediction ends up being.

Imagine once again using our example of the apple and potato barrel. Instead of a small barrel, we have a large deep barrel. Imagine again we had the huge barrel filled with water to soak 100 apples and/or potatoes. Now picture that you were asked to reach in above your head, so you cannot look into the barrel, and pull them out one at a time and guess the makeup of apples versus potatoes left inside. At first, you would pull out an apple, but being aware that more information is more accurate, you proceed to pull out another forty apples in a row. You would likely conclude with confidence that the barrel is made up entirely of apples.

This is a systematic error in which the sample is significantly underrepresented in a specific direction. What you fail to understand is that apples float, and potatoes sink. There could very well be many more potatoes than apples in the barrel, but after pulling out 30 or 40 apples in a row, you may as well believe the barrel is mostly made up of apples because you couldn't reach any potatoes.

This is the value of peer-reviewed research in rigorous and proper science. Peer-review identifies and corrects biases in data, vastly different from most of the claims being reposted and shared by your friends on social media. Reminding ourselves of these biases helps prevent us from falling into these traps in our real-world, everyday lives when assessing new information.

Humans are fallible to far more than just data-based traps; others come from the very architecture of our brain. Human minds are famous for having cognitive biases. Unlike random, one-off errors from having limited information or misusing data, cognitive biases are functional errors in how we think and draw us further away from the truth. Worse yet, we learn our cognitive biases; it is not the result of our evolution.

Understanding and knowing *truth* has never been essential to our survival; some would argue governments and religions intentionally promote non-truths as a way to control populations. Historically, as individuals, it was more important to believe what others believed so we could get along in our communities, regardless of what may or may not have been true. Understanding cognitive biases is essential, especially at the speed our world is moving and changing, to determining where we might end up. Biases may have mattered less in the snail-paced, linear world our ancestors lived in, but accurately mapping our actions and understanding of today's real world are now more important than ever.

The context of a cognitive bias in sciences should be noted differently from the bias of individual experiences. A cognitive bias in science is not the same as learnings from false beliefs. Learned false beliefs are simply wrong and could very well be called "errors" or "mistakes," not biases. Learned false-hoods are easy to correct; we may have once believed in ghosts, monsters, fairies, and Santa Claus. We stop believing once we recognize the mistake— at least, a rational adult would.

Rationality is not new, many of humanity's greatest thinkers worked with the idea for generations. By definition, rationalists like Rene Descartes asserted that certain rational principles exist in logic, mathematics, ethics, and metaphysics that are so fundamentally true that denying them causes one to fall into contradiction. Rationality is, if nothing else, a test of our knowledge and our ability to test our knowledge. Through a meticulous and systematic approach, rationality has helped us understand our mechanical blind spots and the blind spots created from made-up, bad, or even a lack of philosophy.

So how do we define being rational?

A rational person believes dropping a thirty-pound cinder block on their foot is a bad idea. They believe this because they know the block, driven by gravity, will smash their foot. An irrational person might say: I will drop the cinder block at night because, at that point, I am technically upside down from the sun, and the cinder block will not fall toward my foot (although, it may strike them in the face?). Humanity needed to be rational to advance our species. It is not rational to use scientific knowledge selectively. You cannot get a flu shot, then use your smartphone (invented by science) to post that COVID-19 is not real.

It is best to look at rationality in two concepts, epistemic rationality and instrumental rationality. Epistemic rationality is when we work to improve the accuracy of our beliefs systematically. The art of believing informs our new beliefs based on new evidence. Think of this as upgrading how our beliefs can most closely match the truth—they attempt to map our beliefs to the realities of the world. Instrumental rationality is when we systematically achieve our values. This is the art of choosing actions that lead to outcomes and then ranking these actions higher in our preferences.

Rationality is about forming and using our beliefs to make decisions that most accurately reflect what will happen in the real world. Think of this as an attempt to increase our *chances* of being correct, without necessarily always *being* correct. We can never know with 100% certainty that dropping a cinder block will crush our foot, but we do know with very high certainty it will. People are always entitled to their own opinions, as long as those opinions are not fundamentally and factually wrong. Irrational and wrong opinions are, in a way, immoral to present and push onto other people. They can even be dangerous, if not lethal, to act upon.

Our rationality defines the decisions we make and the actions we take. Living in a world of constant flux, we no longer have the luxury of a fixed, controlled environment to analyze our options before acting. The way we address our challenges today is vastly different from how previous generations tackled them. Today we are in a constant state of improvisation as we attempt to keep up with the onslaught of disruptions and changes that persistently emerge as rogue waves of life. The increasingly interconnected and interdependent world is driving such rapid change that we stand little chance of surviving without considering how complexity impacts us. We need a modern-day, theoretical framework to make optimal, everyday decisions while also developing longer-term strategies. I refer to this theoretical framework as the *surfing framework* that will serve as a compass to help navigate where we are going and how we might best get there. The *surfing framework* is a compass; it is a tool to help us navigate the waves of change now arriving on the horizon.

Go Big or Go Home

You miss 100% of the shots you don't take.

—Wayne Gretzky

Right now, as you read this any time after the year 2020, you are at a point of change beyond what your linearly assembled brain can comprehend. In the span of one minute, 208,333 participants join a Zoom meeting, 41,666,667 messages are sent on WhatsApp, $239,196 worth of payments go through Venmo, Amazon ships 6,659 packages, Instagram users post 347,222 stories, and 404,444 hours of video is streamed through Netflix. In just one minute, every minute. In 2020, sales on Amazon Prime Day amounted to an estimated 10.4 billion US dollars over forty-eight hours. They estimate one million dollars is spent online every minute, meaning e-commerce brings in $1.44 trillion a day.

In 1995, Clifford Stoll of *Newsweek* printed the truth about *Why the Web Won't Be Nirvana*. "The truth is no online database will replace your daily newspaper, no CD-ROM can take the place of a competent teacher and no computer network will change the way government works," Stoll wrote in an article that has since been saved on the internet. "How about electronic publishing? Try reading a book on disc," Stoll continued. "Yet Nicholas Negroponte, director of the MIT Media Lab, predicts that we'll soon buy books and newspapers straight over the internet. Uh, sure." Seventeen years later, *Newsweek* terminated their print publications. You can *only* read Stoll's op-ed online. This is an example of how ill-prepared most of us are at surfing the waves of emerging complexity and change.

No risk, no reward. Catching the best waves brings the greatest joy and the best stories. As we continue to push the limits and ride better and bigger waves, the potential and result of failure is more catastrophic. The more we keep pushing the limits, the higher the rewards, but the greater the risk. The 21st century will produce bigger, more incredible waves, forcing us to reach heights humanity could never before imagine. We will be pushing beyond the limits of what is possible as we change more than ever, go faster than ever, and experience higher levels of adrenaline than ever before.

Do we ride it? Or should we brace for a total wipeout?

PART 2: TODAY

Live as if you were to die tomorrow.
Learn as if you were to live forever.

— Mahatma Gandhi

In 1975, while working for Kodak, Steven Sasson created the world's first digital camera. This was in the days when your treasured memories were stored on film and paper; that's just the way things were. Sasson's innovation suggested the process of creating and saving images could be digitized, but the first working device was a beast. It took twenty-three seconds to produce a .01 megapixel image—a fraction of what the first iPhone could create in an instant. While Sasson's device was unlike anything anyone had seen at the time, it wasn't impressive enough for Kodak to pursue. Over the next twenty years, competitors would develop other digital cameras—Sony launched their first in 1981 with .72 megapixels (on a floppy disk!), and Canon sold their first digital camera in 1986 for $3,000.

Even with these innovative devices hitting the market, film cameras still maintained the lion's share of the market, and Kodak figured they didn't have anything to worry about. However, by 1988, the digitization of images was widespread enough to meet media standards—and the first .jpg format was set to determine compression rates. Then, in 1996, Sony released the first of their Cybershot cameras. The 2001 release of the Cybershot DSC-f55—which shot at 2.6 megapixels and retailed for under $400—was a death knell for the point-and-shoot film market. The consumer market for rolls of film and developing tools vanished almost overnight, and Kodak found itself in a nosedive. Kodak's coffin was sealed six years later with the first iPhone release—why bother with a camera when you had a smartphone? Today, with the wide availability of affordable smartphones, coupled with any number of free photo-sharing applications and websites, sharing images has become fast, free, and completely democratized.

We no longer have "Kodak Moments." For the moment, we "do it for the 'Gram."

The waves of disruption we experience today are nothing like what we were facing a few centuries, or even just a decade, ago. Not only are we finding ways to capture images in higher megapixels than ever before, but we are finding ways to put them in smaller devices that are more affordable, accessible, and practical to the everyday consumer. Those who were alive a century ago would have no idea how to manage the pace of change and innovation we are experiencing today. Inversely, you and I will have almost no idea how our children will manage the choices and changes their generation will be faced with.

We have to deal with these changes, but we don't notice them until after they happen. The changes Kodak had to face were with Sasson's first presentation of his invention, but they didn't recognize the potential changes until it was far too late. We live in a world engulfed in complexity and exponentially rapid change. We don't notice these changes because exponential and linear trajectories look very similar at first but diverge and end in very different results. Linear growth happens in a progressive, additive manner, while exponential growth is a beast of compounded doubling—vastly different growth. After only thirty intervals, the linear example is at thirty. The exponential example, over the same period, grows to one billion. It feels simple, but it is so commonly misunderstood and underestimated—yet it is the foundation of how technology impacts our everyday lives. This is how the Six Ds of Exponentials ultimately work their way into and disrupt even the most stalwart institutions. Exponential growth begins when a process transitions from physical to digital, at which point it becomes exponentially empowered. Kodak didn't see this change happening, and they went from controlling 85% of the camera business to unprofitable and eventually bankrupt.

The power of exponential systems is in their foundational frameworks, free of limited growth restrictions. Limited resources control the past's linear systems; an assumption of abundance governs exponential organizations. Kodak was limited by the raw materials and production processes behind film and paper. Digital cameras bring a potentially infinite capacity. Midway through 2007, Apple released the first iPhone. Less than six years later, more people have access to a mobile phone than a toilet. As we unconsciously and continuously adapt to technologies like our smartphones, we must shift our global mindset to a more exponential way of thinking. How is it we can make a better iPhone every year, but a third of the world doesn't have enough to eat? It could be due to the old-school, linear way of thinking many of our bureaucratic, hierarchical systems still adhere to, that impede the pace of the advancements and improvements required to solve the world's biggest problems.

Summarizing the Six Ds

> *The Six Ds are a chain reaction of technological progression, a road map of rapid development that always leads to enormous upheaval and opportunity.*

— Peter Diamandis and Steven Kotler

Throughout the book, we will reference exponential complexity and disruption. This is easily understood at a high level through a quick summary of the Six Ds of exponential growth highlighted below.

Digitalization – For anything that can go from the analog, tangible, physical realm and into the digital ones-and-zeros format of the computerized world, the potential for exponential growth is infinite. In a way, it leaves the bounds of physical reality, and its potential becomes unlimited.

Deceptive – Exponential complexity doesn't grow very fast…at first. The .001% difference doesn't seem like much. Neither does .002%. Exponential growth doubles quickly. Soon, .002% is 2%, then 4%, 16%, and so on. Once it hits this point, the competition doesn't stand a chance.

Disruptive – Every time, digital companies and products can outrun and outstrip the tangible, linear markets. Why buy camera film, twenty-four frames at a time, when you can shoot 10,000 pictures on your cell phone?

Demonetize – New, expensive technology is released every year. This means the generation of tech before it is less costly to produce and distribute. With applications on your phone, you can access a near-infinite amount of information for next to nothing. As technology improves, operating costs decrease.

Dematerialize – As technology improves, the physical medium is rendered obsolete. There was a decrease in the amount of plastic needed to produce DVDs versus VHS tapes. Even fewer components are required today, as you can stream just about any media to the device of your choice.

Democratize – As products are digitized, more people get access to them. Studio-quality movies are being shot on iPhones in suburban basements. As increasingly powerful technologies make their way into the hands of everyday people, the expanse of the imagination opens up for the next round of exponential growth.

How did this play out for Kodak?

Digitalization – Sasson creates the first digital camera, allowing the light-based optics to store their mediums in a new format.

Deception – Kodak didn't see the potential in a slow, .01 megapixel camera. They also didn't notice when it doubled to .02 MP, then .04. After all, the digital wasn't producing anything close to what their film business was earning them across their broad customer base.

Disruption – Truth is, disruption always follows deception. By the time you are facing disruption, it is too late. Kodak didn't invest early enough, but other companies did. When the Sony Cybershot entered the market, it was basically over.

Demonetization – Kodak becomes unprofitable and eventually goes bankrupt.

Dematerialization – With digital shooting and storage, there was no longer a need for the physical medium of prints and film. Everything about the photo process was on digital screens.

Democratization – Cell phones put a camera in everyone's pocket, letting them capture any image at the push of a button. Free photo editing, storage, and sharing apps meant you could spread your images to any market. Instagram meant you could become a world-famous photographer without ever setting foot in a studio, developing bay, or gallery show.

The Surfing Mind and Mindset

Exponential empowerment first happens when we transform physical goods and offerings into digital ones. Although this might seem crazy, even irresponsible, the most extraordinary minds of our time are working on precisely this idea, by transitioning the physical brain into a digital one.

Who wouldn't love this? We would gain all the benefits of exponential thinking while shedding all the linear problems holding us back! Alas, if only it were so simple. It's equally dangerous to just assume that once something is digitized, it is automatically rendered exponential. Exponentiality and complexity only happen when it is *empowered* to do so. The exponential value of digitization only creates the ability to shift our mindset to be more efficient.

Since we can change our mindset, we may not have to physically alter our brains or upload them onto a computer to gain exponential benefits. At least, not anytime soon. Fixed mindsets are those who believe one's traits cannot change—the kind of people who say, "It is what it is." They believe talent and intelligence are traits one is born with and not something that can be improved upon with enough hard work. They believe in overnight successes, so why bother putting effort into anything?

A linear mindset is slightly different than a fixed one. While linear mindsets can focus on improvement, they can only do so in an additive or incremental manner. Work twice as hard, be twice as successful. But what if you want to become 100 times more successful? Could you work 100 times harder? A linear mindset may be short-sighted, but it makes sense for someone whose mind can only think as far ahead as they can see.

A growth mindset, in a way, is the opposite of a fixed mindset. A growth mindset views talent and intelligence as something developed through learning, dedication, and hard work, not something you are born with.

An exponential mindset is fundamentally different from all other mindsets because it does not just look to improve but rather to make something completely different. They don't want to grow twice as fast; they want to be a hundred times faster. A thousand times faster! They learn from the past to leverage their success and momentum on not just progressing into but also accelerating their future.

Transitioning to the digital empowers the ability to create exponential value. This value is only identified and leveraged when the world around it is also viewed with an exponential mindset. Otherwise, you're more or less a digital guy in an analog world. In the past, we focused on creating solutions with the technology available to increase efficiencies and economies of scale. Once we can transform these offerings into the digital space, these models use what Ray Kurzweil defines as the "laws of accelerating returns." These laws are essential because exponential thinking does not often give you instant returns. Those who get frustrated with the slower, earlier stages of growth often fall back on their incremental and linear way of thinking.

Just as the digital camera was deceptive in how it crept up on Kodak, every exponential enablement's results are slow to start.

Consider Moore's Law. In 1965, Gordon Moore noticed the number of transistors per square inch of integrated circuits doubled every year. Moore predicted this doubling trend would continue every year for the foreseeable future. Recently, his law was amended to reflect how the doubling occurs every eighteen to twenty-four months. Moore's Law also implies that the total number of transistors on an integrated circuit for the same price will increase exponentially. This had held true ever since 1958, when scientists built the first integrated circuit of two transistors, for which they won a Nobel Prize. From 1971 to 2011, a single transistor's price dropped from one dollar to about $0.0000001, while also producing a 100-billion-fold improvement in quality, correctly predicted by Moore's Law.

Models like Moore's Law use network effects to generate returns at an accelerating scale. Computational exponential growth has gone through five different paradigms before finally ending with Moore's Law, which is only one subset of broader exponential principles explained through the Law of Accelerating Returns (LOAR). The first paradigm was electromechanical computers, the second was relay-based computers, the third was vacuum-tube based computers, the fourth was transistor-based computers, and the fifth was the integrated circuits of Moore's Law. LOAR is an evolutionary progression that is continuously accelerating due to the growing power of technology. With increasingly powerful technology, humans have the tools and knowledge to create and design the next tech evolution and apply exponential doubling to areas beyond transistors. We see exponential growth in smartphone technology and industries such as fiber-optic throughput, optical networks, wireless communications, bits per dollar, magnetic storage, digital cameras, DNA sequencing, pixels per array, hard drive storage, bandwidth—all of which creeps into the everyday world you and I experience.

All of this is possible because of digitization. Once a mechanical technology can be programmed into ones and zeros, it is no longer constrained to the limits of the physical world and is subject to the potential of Moore's Law and LOAR. Yes, of course, there is a *physical* limit to how small circuits can get, but the slowing of Moore's Law does not decrease the acceleration of exponential change all around us. Once an exponential technology reaches the end of its useful life, it is replaced by other technology looming on the horizon. It was one thing to have early-stage transistor technology develop at this speed, but we now have some potent technologies about to join the party. Technologies like quantum computing, robotics, nanotechnology, biotechnology, various material sciences, networks, AR, VR, blockchain, sensors, 3D printing, and AI—each capable of doing amazing things on their own, and exponentially impressive things when combined.

While we know what is on the horizon, we still can't predict what changes will happen even though we have the framework that just about every exponential growth follows. It's not a matter of if, but when, and the when will likely be here far sooner than you think.

Hell, it might be here right now.

The Industrial Revolutions

> *Science ... has no consideration for ultimate purposes, any more than Nature has, but just as the latter occasionally achieves things of the greatest suitableness without intending to do so, so also true science, as the imitator of nature in ideas, will occasionally and in many ways further the usefulness and welfare of man,— but also without intending to do so.*
>
> —Friedrich Nietzsche

Thirty years ago, in 1990, a CD player cost about $200. Nothing special about it—something you plugged into your receiver. It shared space with your turntable and tape deck. It wasn't portable, and it wasn't compatible with your car (remember skipping?). In 1990, computers could do a fraction of what they can do today, but they cost exponentially more. Today, CDs are nearly obsolete, and the entire world is connected. In just thirty years. Hell, even twenty years ago, some of us were only starting to use computers for the first time ever. Our grandparents lived through far less technological innovation. Every generation is now feeling speed and change, unlike anything the previous generation could imagine. Now, as this book is coming to light, we're about to do it all again exponentially faster as we progress into the Fourth Industrial Revolution. And like the revolutions before it, there will be no "start time" or opening day party. It will just *happen*.

Compared to the fourteen-billion-year scale of the universe, human evolution happened within the last few million years. It goes quick; blink and you'll miss it. Humans went through many anatomical changes, such as our upright posture and opposable thumb that lets us grip and manipulate tools like our precious smartphones. While other mammals and primates also have opposable thumbs, none can move their thumbs as far across the hand as humans can. This was important a few hundred million years ago; we started using our thumbs to manipulate stone tools to build and kill things far beyond most other mammals' capability at the time. Our physical evolutions pale compared to the minor change in the neurological arrangement and slight size increase of our brains. These minor changes in our brain structure were the step-change of our cognitive abilities needed to fully separate us from all other living creatures. These minor neurological anomalies allow us to think, communicate, and understand abstract and complex concepts, create tools, and document information to pass down to future generations.

As humans, our initial growth rate was so slow that it took one million years for our ancestors to create an economy capable of sustaining one million humans at the basic standard of living. That is: food, water, shelter, protection, society, and so on. During the agricultural revolution, around 5000 BC, the growth rate exploded—we could sustain another million people in just 200 years. Today, the global economy can accommodate another million humans every nine minutes—we're changing and growing faster than ever before.

Shifting into the early modern period, our ancestors leveraged great inventions and exploration as they instinctively pushed for a global network and discovered the unknown. The printing press allowed our ancestors to stay relatively up to date about explorations into the new world. Christopher Columbus's little voyage in 1492 likely yielded him a level of fame on par with whatever the Kardashians did last Tuesday. He was big.

Oh, who am I kidding? Nothing in humanity's history is anywhere nearly as perplexing, complex, and mind-boggling as our ability to manically follow lives as mundane as the Kardashians'.

Within the last 200–300 years, we start to see the previous three industrial revolutions' progress. Each revolution brought incredible change, each foundationally driven by technological inventions. Every innovation brought the emergent nature of complex social and political systems, the creation and end of specific industries, and a shift in how humans related and interacted with each other and the entire world beyond them.

This starts with the invention of machines that could spin thread from wool and cotton. In Europe during the 1700s, this invention would redefine numerous industries with the idea of machine tooling. This led to mechanical gears and the steam engine, steel manufacturing, and railways—dawning an era of transit and connectedness. This all happened within 100 years, and it would be the foundation of how we did things for the next two centuries. It would eventually bring about advancements in physics and science and the eventual birth of Instagram's grandfather, the photograph.

The First Industrial Revolution brought about significant wealth. But all wealth comes at a cost. In this case, it was colonialism and the environmental degradation of the planet. Klaus Schwab, a German engineer and the founder and executive chairman of the World Economic Forum, highlights how even the wealthiest countries before 1750 (Britain, France, Prussia, the Netherlands, and the North American colonies, to name a few) only had an average growth of about 0.2%. During this time, inequality was worse than today, and the average income put the average person in extreme poverty. However, due to the impact of technology over the 100 years of the First Industrial Revolution, annual growth rates of the previously mentioned countries grew by 2–3%, increasing the average citizen's income with it.

The late 1800s marked the end of one era and the birth of the Second Industrial Revolution. Nikola Tesla and Thomas Edison drove a massive transformation with discoveries in electrical power generation and distribution. Entire new industries sprung up as humans moved from candles to electrical lighting in their homes, workplaces, factories, and streets. This brought in an influx of inventions like the telephone, the radio, home appliances, and television. Then came the internal combustion engine and the automobile and all of the connected sectors required to support the automobile. The onset of aviation allowed our ancestors to connect by water, land, and air. Every innovation in this industrial revolution drives a massive demand for labor to work in factories and to develop infrastructures like roads and other services. New factories and infrastructure eventually breed new technology that furthers the cycle of needing new labor and infrastructure. Every scientific breakthrough brought the creation of new materials, improvements, and processes. This era saw advancements in fertilizers to increase farming production and improve public health conditions by developing clean drinking water and ample sewage disposal. Better health and increased labor demand brought about an explosion in population and the eventual foundation of our modern world. The end of this era would overlap in the 1950s with the older part of a generation we know as the Baby Boomers.

The Third Industrial Revolution would again change the structures of the world's economic and social systems. The technology was the driving force behind this transformation, propelled by breakthroughs in semiconductors, mainframe computing, personal computing, and the internet. Advancements in information theory and digital computing are why many call the Third Industrial Revolution the *digital* revolution. The ability to digitally convert, store, process, and circulate media disrupted just about every existing industry while creating entirely new industries and completely changing everything about everyday lives. The momentum of these three industrial revolutions has created enormous amounts of opportunity, wealth, and riches—assuming you were fortunate enough to reside within a developed nation and control the means of production.

Every news outlet makes as much money as they can trying to tell you how depressing the world is. Yet more people than ever are living during the greatest time in human history. The OECD (Organisation for Economic Co-operation and Development) represent about 80% of the world's trade and investment, but only make up 17% of the world's total population—mostly in Europe, North America, and a few other regions. Citizens of these regions had their lives transformed by the industrial revolutions and, on average, live significantly longer lives than our ancestors did. In all OECD countries, life expectancy from birth nearly doubled by the third revolution. We have better health, more economic security, and nowhere near the chance of dying a violent death than our ancestors did. Better yet, you're making about 2,900% more income than what you might have made a few hundred years ago. Complain all you want, but the data says your life is pretty damn good.

So, what next? Understanding the previous revolutions gives us a lens to try and see what the next leap in industry might be. Whatever comes next will inevitably be a drastic change that will bring out changes and infrastructure, unlike anything we can imagine. It will also likely lead to an existential crisis unlike anything we've ever known. If not done well, the Fourth Industrial Revolution could very well be our last.

The Fourth Industrial Revolution

*The Fourth Industrial Revolution represents a fundamental
change in the way we live, work, and relate to one another. It is a
new chapter in human development, enabled by extraordinary
technology advances commensurate with those of the first,
second, and third industrial revolutions.*

— 2020 World Economic Forum

Change is a thing to study. It is something for after the fact, to look back
upon. We have never before been able to notice changes as they happen,
only after they have altered the course of human history. Yet, today, with the
tools we have available, there is no reason why we can't anticipate change
and ride the benefits while it is happening.

There is no reason we can't benefit from the change while also mitigating
the negative drawbacks it inevitably instigates.

It's hard to say what the Fourth Industrial Revolution will bring us, but
there is an underlying fundamental difference compared to the previous
industrial revolutions. In the past, we enhanced our human and mammalian
strength through mechanical power, increased connectivity, and the introduction of computational speed. We are now approaching a tipping point
where the acceleration of these exponential technologies converges and will
ultimately create an explosion of progress that will completely reshape and
redefine every industry and society over the following decades. In previous
industrial revolutions, we invented new "things" and made "things" better.
In the Fourth Industrial Revolution, the "thing" we are reinventing is *us*,
the human. We are already well underway in this era of augmenting and
enhancing human cognitive output. This means our brains will be able to
do more at a different level than we've ever seen before because we have no

other choice. For the first time in human history, it is not something else that we will be innovating or making better; we will have to improve human capabilities to maintain pace with the innovations of the world around us.

The speed of innovation we're about to experience in this Fourth Industrial Revolution will be unlike anything ever experienced before. Consider the telephone, which is without a doubt, a technology that transformed the world. It took seventy-five years for 100 million users to adopt the phone as a standard technology. In 2016, *Pokémon Go* reached that many users in less than a month. In his book *Shaping the Future of the Fourth Industrial Revolution*, Schwab explains how the technological revolution currently underway is "blurring the lines between the physical, digital, and biological spheres." These blurred boundaries between the physical, digital, and biological world are megatrends that have a foundational element in common: They harness the exponential power of digitization, information, and technology. The innovations we are seeing and ones emerging are possible through the augmentation of this digital phenomenon. You can see this in seemingly unrelated fields like gene sequencing, which was impossible without the aggressive increase in computational power and Big Data and analytics advancements. Similarly, all the amazing advancements in robotics wouldn't have happened if not for artificial intelligence, which is influenced by the exponential increase in computing power.

Research findings from the World Economic Forum detail many of the physical megatrends driving this Fourth Industrial Revolution, such as autonomous vehicles, 3D printing, advanced robotics, and new materials. Any one of these megatrends will easily have a major impact and change the way we live our everyday lives. These trends tend to be the easiest for us to identify since they are tactile and physically visible. Autonomous vehicles have not only already made headlines, but they are good at dominating our attention. Elon Musk has a gift—or curse—of making the most noise, which gave his Tesla automobile line room to pave the way for the future of electric and autonomous cars by disrupting antiquated car manufacturing giants.

Although gaining some mainstream popularity, autonomous vehicles of all kinds are an industry still very much in its infancy. While less prevalent in traditional media, autonomous boats and water vessels already have various applications and help play a critical role in helping us learn, understand, and protect the oceans. These autonomous water vehicles can go long, high-risk distances at relatively low costs, allowing them to collect large amounts of valuable research data. Aside from consumer applications and progress in autonomous cars and trucks, there are endless other applications for autonomous land vehicles in everyday life. Obvious military applications would reduce human casualties while the agriculture industry uses various forms of autonomous irrigators, tractors, and carriages to manage land. We see commercial applications of autonomous vehicles used in mining and industrial settings to reduce the risk to human life. Each day, this automation creeps more and more into our lives.

The military's use of unmanned aerial vehicles (UAV) gives us an aircraft without a human pilot on board for combat and reconnaissance missions. When it comes to autonomous aerial vehicles, many of us envisioned a future like the Jetsons' world, where we call for unmanned flying taxis instead of ground-based Ubers. Fortunately, Uber is working on it and plans on having flying car options for you to summon within the next ten years. For now, drones are making some of the biggest advancements in this space. In the defense sector, which has always been a driver for technologies that eventually become everyday applications, the US military spending on drones grew from $4 billion in 2014 to $9 billion in 2019. As of 2019, nearly one hundred countries have some level of operational military drone technology, but even more are using drones for emergency response, humanitarian aid, and disaster relief. Unmanned aircraft help agencies monitor and combat forest fires through specialized imaging that can detect abnormal forest temperatures and identify troubled areas long before the fire ignites. Drones were leveraged in 2017 to mitigate the aftermath of Hurricane Harvey in Texas to restore power to damaged areas and survey high-risk and flooded areas for search-and-rescue operations.

The demand for this kind of technology is growing. Every company knows that the "human" in "human resources" are the most expensive and valuable to keep up, and every insurance agent knows humans are the unpredictable factor. Anytime you can remove the human element, costs and risks ultimately go down. In 2019, the Department of Defense made an official request to deploy drones during natural disasters to distribute food and water to affected areas. In the conservation arena, drones currently help address poaching, track and monitor endangered species, and address climate change initiatives. The applications across every industry are endless.

Another growing physical megatrend is 3D printing, which is exactly what it sounds like. In the case of 3D printing, you would send the file to the printer, and it would print a physical product in an additive manner—a direct opposition to traditional manufacturing, which uses a subtractive method, where pieces are removed until we have the desired shape.

3D printing can make small, customizable, complex items on demand. Although most of its applications are currently within the automotive, aerospace, and medical space, the adoption is set to increase as the costs continue to decrease. As technology continues to improve, it will produce more complex products like detailed electronic computer components and even human cells and organs. Eventually, 3D printing will disrupt every physical supply chain on the planet. No longer would we need to ship products, just the product information. Our at-home printer could create whatever we needed. Anywhere you can put a 3D printer, you would be able to create anything. A 3D printer on Mars can simply print the food, equipment, pipes, or building materials space explorers might need. No need for the pizza delivery guy. Instead of cooking, we would watch the printer layer dough, tomato sauce, pepperoni, and mushroom of our favorite pizza. Just bake at 375 for twenty minutes! Maybe not yet the epicurean delight some of us love, but it could revolutionize how we address world hunger. Once the technology becomes cheap enough and can run on solar power, an autonomous drone could drop-ship an entire nutritional food supply to anywhere in the world. Simply print and eat on demand.

Can we talk about the near future and not discuss robots? Maybe your idea of a robot is Chappie or WALL-E. If you're older, maybe you think of Transformers, RoboCop, the Terminator, Johnny Five, or R2-D2. If you are really old or really hardcore about robots, you think of the mechanical characters in Isaac Asimov's old books. Boston Dynamics's famous robot, Atlas, always trends on YouTube whenever the development team releases another video of the bot ripping through an obstacle course while doing parkour and backflips. Every year, the robot does something more incredible due to the exponential advancements of sensors. Faster and more sensitive sensors allow robots like Atlas to adapt and adjust to their environments swiftly. Now that robots can wirelessly connect to the cloud, they can access much larger networks and space to compute their robotic brains' commands. Everything that used to slow the robots down in those old-school, blooper-reel demonstrations is getting lighter, faster, and more accessible—meaning the idea of robots is becoming more widespread. It's beyond evident that robots may be adapting to their new environments faster than humans have adapted to theirs.

The thing is, robots are already around you, and with you, every day. They just don't look the way we think they should. What happens when we say, "Alexa, please order more Pure Maple Syrup?" Alexa, our new friend—a disembodied robot? - whom many of us speak to more than we do another living human, has our back. Instantly, Alexa connects through the cloud to her autonomous robot friends on the fulfillment floor at Amazon to fill your order. More than 200,000 mobile robots are running throughout the Amazon warehouse network, but they do not work alone. Inside Amazon fulfillment centers, robotic arms with small drive units work alongside hundreds of thousands of human workers. The human-robot collaboration is designed to maximize shipping speeds through inventory efficiency optimization, all resulting in your timely, competitively priced, and well-delivered

Pure Maple Syrup. This only starts with our need for more syrup—the applications are endless.

We will see further robotic advancement in muscle-mimetic, self-healing, and hydraulically amplified actuators. Scientists at the University of Colorado have successfully developed a series of extremely low-cost artificial muscles that can lift 200 times their weight and can heal themselves. Impressive, but we also see significant advancements in self-assembled nanoscale robots from DNA - tiny, flexible, nanoscale robots made of your own DNA! In 2018, German researchers built the first remote-controlled DNA robotic arm controlled by an external application of electrical fields. Exoskeleton robots in the workplace prevent personal injuries, they also can help injured or paralyzed people walk again. These exoskeletons are not necessarily like the large, bulky metal suits Ripley wore in Alien. Rather, they are soft exoskeletons made from specially designed textiles and actuators that hug the human they encase.

These advancements are possible because of lighter, stronger, adaptive, and often recyclable materials coming out of labs and into the market. We even have smart materials that are self-healing and even self-cleaning. New types of metal that are plastic-like have a kind of memory, letting them return to an original shape after being deformed. New nanomaterials, such as graphene, is harder than diamonds, 200 times stronger than steel, a million times thinner than a human hair, capable of conducting heat 1,000 times better than copper, and is currently the best-known conductor of electricity at room temperature. We are in an age where we can synthesize any material to do whatever we want—we just have to know what we want. The only inhibitor is the economic cost. Yet the near-daily breakthroughs across the industry mean they're getting cheaper and more available by the day, and my dream of owning a graphene surfboard, essentially indestructible and lighter than air, might happen in my lifetime. Today, such a surfboard would cost about seven million dollars—three million in materials alone. The trends show that graphene will soon drop below the price of silicon—meaning the material will be available to every single sector dominated by silicon, such as computing, chip manufacturing, sensors, solar cells, and most importantly: surfboards.

Considering everything we have in play, how do we connect the vast future with the everyday labors that most of us know? The Internet of Things (IoT) is at work on this, quietly, in all of our lives. The IoT is the system of inter-related complex connected relationships between computing, mechanical, and digital devices that are all capable of transmitting data over a network without human or computer interaction—and we're all involved with it. The smartphone, tablet smartwatch, voice assistant, connected TV, Nest Thermostat, a doorbell camera, and refrigerator that talks—all a part of the IoT. Most of us want to be in denial about this change, but the billions of devices currently connected to the internet tell a different story. We are more connected than ever before, and these connections only stand to increase from the billions into the trillions. We use apps to redirect us around accidents and track our packages, groceries, and food deliveries in real time. We can change our house's temperature with our phone before viewing another app showing how nicely our dog is behaving while home alone. The list goes on, but this connectedness is why it often seems like the Googles, Apples, Facebooks, and Amazons of the world know what we want before we do.

To cover all the trendy buzzwords: blockchain. An "open, distributed ledger that can record transactions between two parties efficiently and in a verifi-able and permanent way." Blockchains create trust at a low cost by allowing secure collaboration without any central authority. You'd be surprised at how much money you pay for the sense of trust. Think of your money, the cash in your wallet or checking account. We use the money to buy things because we trust the banks and governments will honor the currency—which is little more than a piece of paper. This trust comes at the cost of central controls, bank fees, and taxes. Cryptocurrencies like Bitcoin offer all the same securities without a central bank. The encryption also makes it possible to remain anonymous. All currency, no matter what it is, is built on trust. The difference with cryptocurrency: the value isn't impacted by human emotion. A toppled regime or greedy oligarchies aren't going to impact the everyday value of blockchain ledgers. These digital trends are already reshaping finance, contracts, governments, healthcare, supply chains, and many more industries and functions in our world.

Tom Goodwin wrote in 2015: Uber, the world's largest taxi company, owns no vehicles. Facebook, the world's most popular media owner, creates no content. Alibaba, the most valuable retailer, has no inventory. And Airbnb, the world's largest accommodation provider, owns no real estate. This article was quoted and shared approximately 18.7 trillion times on LinkedIn and was included in every single business motivational speech for the next two years. Approximately. But Goodwin's point: Digital platforms reduce the transactional and frictional costs of doing business and further divide the cost and tasks of doing business into very small increments, allowing for economic gains to all users involved at all levels of the offering. These digital platforms have virtually zero additional marginal cost. Meaning for them to produce more or add to their customer base, they do not need to expand investment into costly overhead to see rapid userbase growth. Unlike the linear systems of the generation before us controlled by limited resources, present-day exponential organizations are governed by an assumption of abundance. Think Blockbuster vs. Netflix.

To this point, we have been dealing with economies and productions and materials. But the promise of the Fourth Industrial Revolution—improving humans—is the hardest pill to swallow. Pun mostly intended. Biological innovations, understandably, tend to freak people out. This fear is older than Mary Shelley's *Frankenstein* novel of 1818. Did you trust a "doctor" in those days who used bleeding, leeches, and ether in their medical practice? Things have gotten comparatively better. In recent years, there have been incredible advancements in this arena of genetics. As the overall cost of genetic sequencing decreases, we have seen a rise in our ability to activate and edit genes. Many famous inventors, like Thomas Edison, invented and developed quickly because they had a machinelike army of engineers to do trial-and-error research for them. Technology is leveling the scientific playing field. Much like in Edison's way of working, the massive advancements in computer power allow present-day scientists to skip long periods of trial and error and focus their efforts on the specific problems they are trying to solve. What we ultimately do with our newfound genetic prowess is the root of intense debate. Most people readily and philosophically speak out against genetic modification. That is, until it becomes a personal matter. Anyone who has lost a loved one from a heart attack, or heart disease, or cancer, or a stroke would happily edit any gene to prevent it from ever happening again. Who would want to relieve unnecessary pain and suffering? Why not reprogram and edit cancerous cells to prevent the loss of someone we love and care for?

How would you modify your brain? Sure, research shows doing the crossword every day can delay the onset of Alzheimer's, but what if we could do more? While Elon Musk unveiled Gertrude, a pig with a coin-sized computer chip in her brain, to demonstrate his ambitious plans for mind control, there are many other exciting advancements behind the headlines. Certain brain advancements help us better understand, and even fix, the impact of brain traumas, and how to prevent these traumas in the future.

Gene editing and neurotechnology, as a practice, leaves us asking where we should draw the line. What we consider ethical today is nowhere close to what we found acceptable a century ago, and this will likely change again in the next few decades. Every new advancement is a new opportunity, but it is also a chance for us to ask: what are we OK with? Today, it is common practice to inject embryos into a human through artificial insemination—unthinkable a century ago. Gene editing now gives us the ability to manipulate the human genome within embryos and possibly produce "designer babies" who have the parents' desired traits while making them resistant to specific diseases. Other advancements and developments in genetic engineering, like CRISPR, show incredible potential in revolution-izing research, transforming medical treatments, and changing the world. But this also exposes incredibly sensitive and ethically challenging issues that need discussion before they are widely implemented.

What do you think? Let's ask a few questions to get an idea of where you stand, or if you need to determine a position at all.

Question 1: Would you be for or against using gene editing to design babies who possess particular traits, natural abilities, and strengths while also making them resistant to many life-threat-ening diseases?

Question 2: If you knew your loved one would die within a year from a heart attack, heart disease, stroke, or cancer, would you be for or against using gene editing to remove the risk and have them live a long and fruitful life?

You probably were against the first question but more open to the second scenario.

Even if you were against a designer baby, you would be open to saving a loved one. It's the same question phrased in two different ways to prove a point: We haven't talked nearly enough about these advancements, and if we don't proactively address these questions, we may find humanity sliding down a slippery slope. All these scientific and technological advancements should inspire moral and ethical discussions against our stances. We will have to agree on how we proceed in certain areas universally. While this may seem philosophically obvious and simple, we have many countries that are just as divided on ethical and moral concepts now as they were fifty years ago.

Rogue Waves of Today

Big waves aren't measured in feet, but in increments of fear.

— Buzzy Trent

Imagine a freak wave, a monster wave, an episodic and killer wave—a rogue wave. Notorious in ocean-faring cultures as the unusually large and unexpected waves that emerge suddenly from the ocean, making them extremely dangerous—and not just to surfers. Rogue waves have taken out massive shipping vessels and ocean liners. Furthermore, rogue waves happen far more frequently than we initially thought, making them something more than the folklore of nautical Bigfoots told by sailors in coastal towns around the world. On January 1ˢᵗ,1995, a rogue wave struck the Draupner oil installation in the Norwegian North Sea. The ocean was rolling with big twelve-meter (thirty-nine feet) waves when the system recorded a high-resolution snapshot of a 25.6-meter (eighty-four feet) behemoth wave emerging from the ocean. Since then, researchers have concluded that rogue waves have claimed twenty-two supercarriers and more than 500 human lives over the back half of the twentieth century alone.

Well, now we are in the twenty-first century, and the Fourth Industrial Revolution is upon us, and we are about to ride technological rogue waves unlike we've ever imagined.

No longer a maritime myth, we are now aware of the beastly 100-foot killer walls of water that sporadically emerge from nowhere. The rogue wave phenomenon occurs from various means, like constructive interference or wave energy. In the event of wave addition, if swells travel at different speeds, eventually one overtakes another, combining the two for just a moment. If several swells happen to overlap at the same place at the same time, a rogue wave may appear. When rogue waves are created by swells combining in conflicting directions, they can emerge quickly, violently, and with incredible aggression and unpredictably—the more waves intersecting at once, the larger and more unpredictable the event.

We can't predict when these happen. But we can prepare for them, both on the ocean and in our everyday lives.

As we surf through the waves of disruption in our present-day world, we must be aware of the convergence of all the exponential technologies around. We cannot ignore the dangers lurking in the waters around us. The convergence of disruptions will create more rogue waves in our technological advances. Unlike waves surfed previously by humans within and beyond our living history, we will experience considerably more colossal, gigantic, unpredictable, and potentially dangerous rogue waves of exponential converging technologies.

When two waves converge in an additive manner, they produce a large rogue wave.

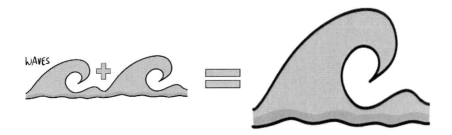

The figure above shows how rogue waves happen. The figure below maps this exponential rate of technological change back to the oceans of our world. We are experiencing something far grander than exponential change; these lanes of technological development are beginning to intersect, overlap, and collide. This convergence of overlap is where the technological rogue waves appear. They combine, one with the other, and present something far more than a doubling of their force and power. All this gives birth to radically new rogue waves that are creating new exponentially disruptive industries. So many contributing factors touch each potential wave and its exponential possibility, it is nearly impossible to predict when or where they will happen. Assume that in the chart below, along the x-axis is time. There is an incredible number of factors that could bend the curve earlier, shortening even our expected timelines for many of the products. Frank Diana accurately blended a futurist perspective with a pragmatic, actionable approach to create the chart below.

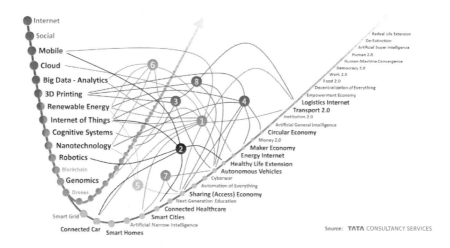

Surf is up. These rogue waves are just a warm-up to the tremendous rate of change on the horizon. Some waves are mellow and slow rolling compared to what is coming—and even those mellow waves can leave us feeling seasick. Although we cannot know precisely when the rogue waves of tsunami-like disruption are going to emerge, we can prepare ourselves as best we can for whenever they do appear.

Science, technology, and innovation are all highly interdependent and connected. They influence and build off of their respective foundations; there are no boundaries anymore. Everything they do is mixed into one big ocean, where one event or advancement affects every other. Change and the unknown can be scary, but it can also be exciting. These rogue waves are a reminder of how tomorrow will be nothing like today, and today is nothing like yesterday.

We can see technological change as exponential by analyzing the history of technology, contrary to our intuitive way of viewing history linearly. We also know we are sitting in the middle of a forecast with advancements in robotics, virtual and augmented reality, digital biology, materials, and sensors colliding directly into 3D printing, blockchain, global digital networks, and AI, which will create an explosion of disruptive rogue waves. Buckle up. The amplification of the waves from all this convergence will make for the craziest surfing condition humanity has ever faced. The time to surf is upon us.

Artificial Intelligence (AI)

Intelligence is evolving, and these changes are not strictly biological. Of all the megatrends that are advancing, AI stands out with particular importance. People seem to either love or hate talking about artificial intelligence. Yet, it's not up for debate. We need to acknowledge that AI already carries a heavy influence on our daily lives and shapes our future. Nonbiological forms of intelligence are all around us in our everyday lives whether or not we choose to accept it.

Having a habit of not noticing change until after it happens, we can usually detect the recent changes that have happened but have not yet leaked into the mainstream. We have all used video calling to exist in multiple different places at once. Surgeons use microscopic tools to perform surgeries through machines. None of this is "new" to us. In 2015, an organization planted microchips into their employees' hands. These chips housed the personal and security data that allowed them access to certain areas of the building, much like an internal keycard. The implanted chip, barely the size of a grain of rice, also granted the employee access to approved technology like the printers and vending machines, just by waving their hand. A cool party trick, sure. But what happens when we go beyond augmenting our technologies through the physical manipulation of our hands and connect these instruments directly to our minds? We mastered voice and touch commands; neural connectivity is the next logical step. In fact, it's kind of surprising we have this capability already in place today.

The US military has already implanted chips into human brains to advance our knowledge and understanding of how to treat and cure individuals suffering from combat trauma and post-traumatic stress disorder. In other studies, we have seen how doctors and researchers can cure acute depression by implanting electrodes directly in the brain of patients. These electrodes are controlled by a small computer embedded in the patient's chest. Signals from the computer send weak electrical transmissions to paralyze the region of the brain responsible for depression. While the science isn't perfect, in some cases, patients found that the dark, depressing void that haunted them for their whole life magically disappeared. Yet, in one case, months after the operation, a patient complained about having a complete depression relapse. It turns out the computer's battery had died. They replaced the battery and chased out his depression once again. Implanting electrodes into human brains comes with a laundry list of ethical restrictions, and for the most part, the research is very limited and only implemented in extreme cases.

The evolution of change is here, no longer a sci-fi concept we read about in books or saw in movies. Today, using just our minds, paralyzed individuals can move bionic limbs and operate computers. There are wireless remote-control technologies that allow individuals to control connected items in their homes through a "mind-reading" electric helmet-like device. No longer do we need wires to charge our smartphones or use earbuds, and this helmet-like technology requires no brain-wired implants. Just by scanning the electrical waves passing through your scalp, you can lock your door or change the thermostat or use any connected device.

Out of sight, out of mind? The wireless manipulation of things tends to feel less intrusive, and therefore many of us are not as opposed to it. As the convergence of technology and science advancements further our understanding of intelligence, we learn that our desires merely stem from how our neurons fire. If the pattern of our neurons firing changes our desires, does it matter how the neurons are stimulated in the first place? Our neurons could fire because they are stimulated by another neuron or stimulated by an electrode, and the result is the same. The research is already there; we have already altered and even removed complex emotions and feelings like fear, love, anger, happiness, and even depression by artificially stimulating the corrected regions of the brain. Scared is scared, regardless of how your brain created the feeling.

The US military is deep into wireless brain research at its Ohio Air Force base. They are testing wireless helmets to manipulate the focus and performance of soldiers. The buzz and rumor around these transcranial contraptions currently exceed their performance, as they are far less effective than physically wiring regions of the brains with electrodes. Nonetheless, they are seeing progress and breakthroughs in the enhancement of cognitive abilities of the soldiers who need to hold their focus over long periods. Sally Adee, a science and technology journalist, visited the military testing facility to give the helmets a try.

At first, she ran a simulation and was instantly overwhelmed by an onslaught of attackers who appeared at a faster rate than she could shoot them. Then they wired up her helmet and put her back into the simulation. She reported feeling incredibly calm as she easily picked off the virtual enemies, moving from one target to the next, in complete control. Suddenly, the lights turned on in the simulation room, and it was over. Sally, laser focused, didn't realize the seemingly shorter simulation had run for nearly twenty minutes.

She was equally shocked to hear that she had handled all the targets. All of this was in 2016, and transcranial stimulation has likely come a long way since then, especially as it collides with other exponential advancements.

All of this progress assumes the human biological brain will remain the central, controlling element of intelligence. Our organic brain has limitations, a limitation that nonbiological architectures can be designed not to have. Human intelligence has evolved over billions of years within our physical, biological constraints. Still, we can now work around these limits with intelligence systems capable of leveraging and residing in virtual and non-virtual worlds. In a way, we would be completely free of our biological limitations. We are creating forms that blend with human intelligence, and some that are completely independent. AI is not all doom and gloom. The godfathers of AI view the future of the field as an augmentation to our intelligence, not as a replacement for humanity. At least, that is how Yann LeCun, Yoshua Bengio, and Geoffrey Hinton all view artificial intelligence. And they might know, as in March 2019, they won the Turing Award. AI isn't coming; it's here.

Technology advancements are getting larger and happening at faster rates. Think of our lifetime: How on earth did we live without the internet? Or smartphones? Imagine what our parents' or grandparents' generations have seen? The average rate of advancement and change continues to increase, which means we advanced and changed significantly more in the last twenty years than we had in the twenty years before that. But it was not always that way. In the fifteenth century, not much changed over twenty years. When we look back at technological advancement through a historical lens, everything seems logical.

If the law of accelerating returns is accurate, then we have experienced the entire progress of the twentieth century between the years 2000 and 2014. In a few decades, we will experience all the progress of the twentieth century multiple times in a single year. If we go much further back in our history, human progression and advancement (change) that took hundreds of thousands of years is now matched during the course of years and months.

Understanding now that those exponential curves start out looking linear, this of course makes sense. If we look in the mirror immediately after going to the gym and expect to see results, we may conclude that working out does not work. When comparing immediately before and after a workout, we look the same. Not leaner or more buff, just the same. But if you photographed yourself today and then worked out regularly over two months, you might see the changes. We would be wrong not to believe in small unnoticeable changes that build up over time. If we use a myopic view of the world through our day-to-day timeframes, we could find peace of mind thinking that not much is changing. This mindset assumes we will advance on the same linear trajectory as the last 200 years, which will cause us to get blindsided by rogue waves of technological disruption.

I want to return for a moment to the evolution and advancement of intelligence, more specifically, nonbiological artificial intelligence. The term AI makes many people uncomfortable because of popular culture. Think of shows like *Westworld* and movies like *Terminator*. This type of entertainment often mimics human-level or superhuman-level artificial intelligence and humanizes AI so we can relate to them. The AI kicks humankind's ass and outsmarts us in every possible way. Yet in the end, we manage to outsmart the AI with our human intuition.

Sort of like how we battle ants. Not that most of us particularly care about ants or think about them much, but we can agree that humans (well, most humans) can outsmart ants. But now imagine, in this constant battle of getting their asses kicked by the uncaring humans, the ants magically started to outsmart us and kill us off. If we were ever to create a superintelligence, it would be like comparing our intelligence with an ant's intelligence. At this point, it is too late; there is no outsmarting the superintelligence. For now, there's not much use in anthropomorphizing AI or dreaming up life after the creation of a superintelligence. Instead, let us focus on today and mindfully think about how we navigate the future, as we are continually adapting and changing to our world.

Right now, the consensus is that we are in the evolutionary stage of what is being called Narrow AI. Artificial Narrow Intelligence (ANI) is usually programmed to do one task in real time. ANI is pointed through programming to retrieve information from a specific dataset and order. We all live in an amusement park of narrow forms of artificial intelligence. Amazon recommends our next purchases, our Nest thermostat self-adjusts the temperature, Apple makes recommendations based on our music preferences, Siri tells us the weather when asked, and WAZE navigates us to a destination with the fastest method, in real time. Netflix lines up the next show we most likely want to watch, and Google finishes typing most of our email sentences, often with more logic, completeness, and coherence than whatever it was you thought you wanted to write. AI decides for us when the antilock brakes should kick in. Self-driving cars are simply an ANI that ingests massive amounts of computational information in real time to adapt and react to the surroundings continuously. Some form of ANI is used across every industry and vertical. Retailers use it to price their offerings, and doctors use it to read imaging and suggest a diagnosis. Most of the US stock market is exchanged with high-frequency artificially narrow intelligent trading algorithms—all built by humans.

Every now and again, ANI encounters a situation we did not think to program. In the 2010 market flash crash, $1,000,000,000,000 of market value was accidentally erased because of ANI. It happened in a brief moment before the programmed "fail-safe" engaged. To this day, part of that trillion-dollar mistake was never recovered or reinstated. These forms of AI have absolutely annihilated and slaughtered humans in just about every game imaginable, from checkers and scrabble to *Jeopardy!* and Go. There was a point not that long ago when cocky humans claimed something would not be artificially intelligent until it was able to beat us at a knowledge game, like chess. Our parents' generation would have never believed they could lose to a machine. Now, after getting massacred by our computers in a game of pro-level chess, we still lean back and ask the computer if it can pass us our beer. And we think to ourselves, *Stupid computer, can't even hand me my beer.*

Narrow forms of artificial intelligence can't do anything outside of what they were programmed to do, functioning exclusively within predetermined and predefined parameters. Artificial narrow intelligence will never understand emotions, have self-awareness, or develop consciousness. ANI is the farthest from human consciousness you can get while still being definable as "intelligent."

> *"A computer would deserve to be called intelligent if it could deceive a human into believing that it was human."*
>
> — Alan Turing

However, Narrow Intelligence could evolve into Artificial General Intelligence (AGI). AGI, also known as Strong AI because of how it demonstrates humanlike intelligence, is what you see in movies like *The Terminator* or shows like *Westworld*. Characters like the T-800 and Dolores, with a human exterior and robotic operating system innards, have consciousness and are motivated by a sense of self-awareness. These fictional AGIs have intelligence equal to and indistinguishable from human intelligence, making them a strange beast to interact with. Again, I promised not to anthropize AI in this book. It would serve you best to not think of AGI as ever being a humanoid robot because it will likely never get to that state.

As fallible as humans are, why would something as intelligent as AGI want to take our form?

Unlike the movies, creating AGI is more complicated than working with ANI. A true Artificial General Intelligence can solve problems, strategize, think abstractly, make judgments, improvise, learn, innovate, imagine, and create, just like any human might. While machines can process external data faster than any human, they are by no means at our level of active intelligence. Yet.

When it happens, it will happen exponentially. Bostrom, a leading AI philosopher, theorized that we will be facing Artificial Super Intelligence (ASI) shortly after we achieve AGI. Bostrom defines this superintelligence as "any intellect that greatly exceeds the cognitive performance of humans in virtually all domains of interest." In other words, we are screwed. Humans will have effectively designed their replacements as the dominant being on the planet. When (or if; let's hope if) ASI occurs, it will surpass the smartest human to ever live in every single aspect of intelligence instantly. Just like our intelligence compared to that of an ant, we'd be crushed. Due to the exponential trajectory of ASI, our linear capacity of brain development would never catch up. Most likely, this will all happen by accident. Although many of the world's greatest minds debate the specifics of future AI, they would all, for the most part, agree when Elon Musk says, "AI does not have to be evil to destroy humanity—if AI has a goal and humanity just happens to be in the way, it will destroy humanity as a matter of course without even thinking about it, no hard feelings."

For those new to AI, *Our Final Invention* by James Barrat can be a sobering nontechnical read that puts perspective on the possible long-term realities of artificial intelligence. I connected with James to discuss how the same problems leading to potential disasters when he published his book in 2014 are still in place today. Not only are we facing the same problems with AI, they are likely more exasperated. James did not see the machine-learning revolution coming quite as fast as it has over the last five years. At the time of this writing, James is toying with the idea of writing a sequel to address his thoughts and opinions on the development of AGI and how past performance tends to predict the future. In this case, the results are not very rosy.

AI alone will not revolutionize everything overnight, but it will amplify other industries as its capabilities collide with other technological mega-trends. We laid the foundation today, and we'll see the changes tomorrow. Our cities will look nothing like they do now. Using data and the Internet of Things, city projects like the Hudson Yards in New York and Sidewalk Labs in Toronto are already putting in tomorrow's foundations. Although a "smart city" is not a new concept, these two projects start the cross-over between data and connectivity to make smart cities a reality in North America. It will not be one single technology that transforms our cities, but a confluence of technological waves all building off each other. The launch of 5G will drive greater connectivity for IoT devices and be further amplified by colliding with quantum computing fueled by AI. All of this allows for the analysis of trends from the incomprehensible amounts of data we are already collecting while decreasing the cost of renewable energy—all at once! Cheap power means we can further fuel this loop. This combinatorial effect is what brings about the rogue waves and a relentless onslaught of change. Much of this demand will be driven by self-driving cars; drones; and in-home, public, and environmental monitoring and security devices such as sensors and cameras. These accelerating megatrends of the Fourth Industrial Revolution will bring the reality of smart cities to us very soon. We will see the explosion of this inflection point of change with our own eyes, not sometime in the distant future, but starting tomorrow.

PART 3: THE COMPASS, A SURFING FRAMEWORK

Your surfing can get better on every turn, on every wave you catch. Learn to read the ocean better. A big part of my success has been wave knowledge.

— Kelly Slater

Can you imagine being one of the first big-wave surfers? Those founding fathers looked at giant waves from the shoreline and thought, "Let's ride that thing." They pushed the limits of what they thought possible and rode this menacing, unpredictable *thing*? Standing on the shores of Makaha in Hawaii, they had to imagine everything they knew about the ocean, the board—everything—and how to do it at an unimaginable scale. Equally exciting and terrifying, these surfers were not content staying in their comfort zones, as they heroically paddled out into a seemingly suicidal scenario just to see if they could do it.

Big-wave surfing has always been the kingdom of those who are never satisfied, those who push the limits of what is believed to be possible. Each new generation of surfers pushes the boundaries of possible a little further than those before them. This constant evolution, adaptation, growth, and progression are why bigger waves get surfed every year. We see a similar story in the history of humans.

As we shift our attention to surfing the biggest and baddest waves humanity has ever faced, we focus on the three surfing requirements: waves, a surfer, and a board.

How do we identify these barrels in our lives and future?

How do we improvise to stay in these barrels?

The foundation we must stand on to best improvise within a barrel.

Big-wave surfing has come a long way. Rarely do we learn something new from scratch—every one of us is persistently looking at and learning from mistakes, trials, and tribulations experienced by those who came before us. We look to this experience to use as the building blocks to help us reach new heights. We do the same with knowledge, building off the knowledge created by those before us.

The surfing framework is fashioned in the same way, built from the mistakes humans have been making for years and the knowledge we have created. Think of the surfing framework like a compass: It is designed to point to the magnetic north. It isn't a map or a GPS. A compass does not tell you where to step, which detours to take, or the obstacles you may have to overcome on the journey. A compass is simply a tool to guide, to point us in the right direction. We know we will encounter hurdles and setbacks as we go through life, which is why it is crucially important to understand the direction we're going in. Our goal is to understand where the greatest barrels of our life will form and how to position ourselves inside these barrels for the best surfing possible. This depends not so much on what we *know*, but how we *think*.

The surfing framework aims to help us determine the best data around us and turn it into information that becomes the knowledge that we make wise choices with. How do we make sound, rational actions or make decisions based on our experiences, knowledge, and good judgment by using the information we have? When should we be skeptical of what we know and what we're presented with? When should data convince us otherwise? Not only do we need to equip ourselves with the proper tools to find and understand objective truths, but we must also help others understand how to see this reality in our world. The less connected someone is to the objective truth, the less likely they are to map their actions and decisions to the realities of the world around them. Meaning it is less likely they will make decisions beneficial to their own selves, their loved ones, or even the future of humanity. Humans have created and developed tools to aid in our pursuit of consistently wanting more and getting better. Tools like science, which allows us to develop theories for how we view and understand the world. Do you believe in science? Of course you do. If not, let's pretend you do.

The great thing about science: it is true whether you believe in it or not.

The surfing framework trains the mind to reach new heights. Take flying, for example. We don't know exactly when humans began their aerial attempts, but we do know that early attempts were often foiled by gravity. Our ancestors likely saw what birds could do—traveling great distances quickly and descending down rock faces without impact—and mimicked them to get the same result. There were most likely scenarios where starving humans would chase a flock of birds off a cliff, only to follow them flapping their arms in desperation. It sounds ridiculous! But let's be real, you can probably find a YouTube video from 2020 of a human doing the exact same thing. As generations are born, died, and fell while trying to fly, trial and error brought about different methods that could lend themselves to flight. The common thought process for a while: birds flap their feathered wings, so must we. Over thousands of years, we have documented proof and recounted stories of individuals with human-made, feathered-covered wings leaping from the highest points they could perch upon. These short-lived entrepreneurs of flight jumped from cliffs and trees, mosques, cathedrals, castle walls, and towers—only to all suffer a similar fate. Hundreds, possibly thousands of people plummeted to their deaths in failed flight attempts before the Wright Brothers made the first successful flight in a small-engine plane in 1903. Their craft was a vastly different method from their feathered predecessors, but they achieved the same result as birds. In this case, the difference is between causality—what causes something to happen—and correlation, a connection between two things.

We witness the frequent correlation between flapping feathered wings and birds flying; no one can argue with that. Our aerial ancestors' struggle was developing a *theory* that would help them assess and understand causation versus correlation. They needed a theoretical framework built from principles of lift, gravity, thrust, and drag. Once we understood and applied this theoretical framework, we went from the correlation of wings and feathers to a causal mechanism of what causes flight. It wasn't the flapping of feathers alone that made the flight possible, but the thrust of a flapping wing certainly helped. Leveraging a sound framework helps us to navigate causation and correlation to our advantage and learn from the research and mistakes experienced by those who tried and failed before us.

Most of what you know right now is the result of a series of anecdotes you experienced or heard about. Much of what you consider "knowledge" is not grounded in anything that is necessarily true or reliable. Most popular thinking spawns from personal accounts, not facts or research. Addressing the complexity of everyday life requires extensive comprehension of the what and the why behind the things that happen. The solution you're after is rarely a single theory that can account for everything. Rather, it is a framework of several ideas and concepts that work together to provide us with accurate insights.

The surfing framework's goal is to focus on *how* change is happening in your life instead of simply relying on chance. Relying on our past knowledge means we rely on luck to move us forward—like riding a surfboard backward. Sure, you might be able to catch the odd wave, but you won't last long once you are on it. Without understanding where waves come from, you could paddle out only to sit in the middle of a glassy ocean and complain about how you never catch good waves. Or, you could use this surfing framework, built off scientific theory, to shape your future through intentional decisions so you can have the time of your life riding the best waves that come your way.

We will be unpacking this framework throughout this book. It is the tool we will use to investigate the future to understand better the forces that cause change and how to navigate these circumstances. When leveraged properly, this framework will lead the investigation of goal achievement and function as the foundational mechanism for the future development of change. It is designed for individuals who reside in various environments who experience change to investigate and explore a specific topic, situation, or decision. These changes aren't always global and drastic—like rapid technological changes. Sometimes, it is a simple everyday life change in how you balance your personal and professional life. Since change is constant, the framework needs to be flexible enough for a world of great complexity, so we can continually adjust, learn, and innovate.

In science and academia, this is known as a theoretical framework. Science and academia can tend at times to be terribly dry, and surfing involves getting wet. Although based entirely on sound theory, the surfing framework has been pragmatically designed to be applied in the real world, not in a theoretical world. Lastly, it is worth noting the surfing framework is built from an interdisciplinary perspective. Just as we can't use one theory to explain all of life's intricacies, we also can't rely solely on one subject's ideas (leadership theories only, for example) to develop a framework. The framework becomes far more flexible and useful by taking a multidisciplinary approach that accurately aligns appropriateness, application, and explanatory strength.

The Surfing Framework

A good decision is based on knowledge and not on numbers.

— Plato

Definition: Barrel

bar·rel/ˈberəl

> The cylindrical area created by a wave breaking. The ultimate
> move in surfing is to position oneself inside the barrel and ride
> the wave while it breaks.

To surf, we are reminded of three things: waves, a surfer, and a board. The
surfing framework is made up of these three things:

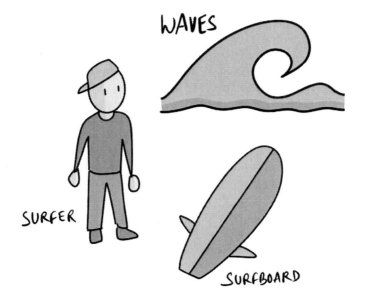

Waves – How do we identify these barrels in our lives and
future?

Surfer – How do we improvise to stay in these barrels?

Surfboard – The foundation we must stand on, to best improvise
in a barrel.

The surfing framework, at its core, challenges us to rethink thought. Much of what we think about is constrained by our past and present social systems and ideologies. By tracing our development through this world to right now, we understand what we need to break free of the shackles of the previous ways of thinking and rewire our brains to think faster and more creatively, especially about what comes next. Instead of being prescriptive in the steps required to succeed in the future, the surfing framework asks the opposite. It empowers you to lend way to creating your future by building from the realities of everyday moments. This isn't about predicting ideal situations or definitive scenarios, but rather opening up your mind to the endless potential that resides in the future shaping around us.

Keep in mind, being broad in your mindset can be just as damaging as being myopic. The endless possibilities will definitely confuse you. Every aspect requires your attention, but analysis by paralysis—overthinking everything—can be as damaging as not thinking at all. Both constructs create a state of inaction. Our surfing framework challenges us to move out of equilibrium. It forces action and uses knowledge to react in the moment. Overanalyzing waves and waiting for the perfect wave, or not believing in waves at all, results in the same outcome: nothing. Our surfing framework requires us to surf instead of falling victim to the modern-day traps of old concepts. Censorship used to be a matter of blocking information; now, censorship works by overloading us with irrelevant information. This creates division and leads people to spend their time analyzing and debating topics instead of taking action to address them.

Our surfing framework arms us with more than just knowing what to focus on; it lets us understand what is worth ignoring. In previous industrial revolutions, power was accessed through information and data. In the Fourth Industrial Revolution, having power is knowing what information to ignore. Human dominance of this planet is based entirely around one thing: intelligence. Artificial intelligence is here to be a direct competitor to human intelligence if we let it. Our brain's biology is by no means exponential, and falling behind AI only seals our fate. Once we're one step behind AI, we may as well be a million steps back. We'll never catch up, and every wave after that will only crush us.

More than ever, it's time to wax your board and embrace complexity.

Complexity creates the waves in our world, and through this complexity we identify the barrels we want to ride in life from the pressure between life's abstract and functional systems. The pressure in the space between abstract and functional is rather uncomfortable, and much like being in the barrel of a wave, it is equally exciting and terrifying. To remain in this barrel, the surfer must improvise by constantly reading and reacting to their situation in real time. What allows you to improvise your way into these barrels is the foundation you stand on, your surfboard. To ensure you remain in this barrel, you must rationally improvise. Your surfboard is the foundation to create your decisions and beliefs to accurately map back the reality of the world. This is how you create rational improvisation. The surfing framework helps you understand how these barrels will happen and when to lock in and surf them. It will also help you know when the tension you are feeling is not a barrel but just a riptide, and you should get out of the water.

Although our life will throw all kinds of waves at us, a particular wave of interest emerges between the abstract and functional systems of complexity in our world. We feel pressure in our lives as these two systems, consciously and unconsciously, create tension between one another. This tension is where disruption, transformation, and growth happen by creating a space we call the barrel. This is the area where we adapt, evolve, and grow while we embrace the tension. We instinctively react to this pressure, finding a need to shape it at the moment—we call it improvisation. Much like the accomplished surfer who continuously improvises while riding their board, improvisation in your daily life lets you ride the waves of pressure and disruption. Your surfboard is the rational foundation for your decisions and beliefs; you will surf the gnarliest barrels humanity has ever seen.

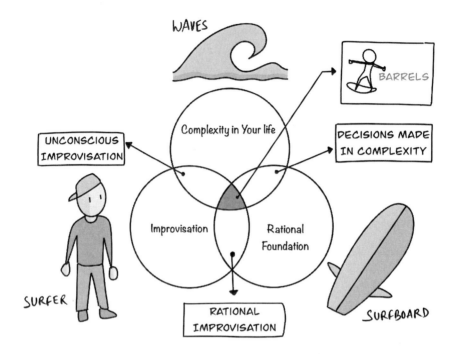

By leveraging rational improvisation, we can ride these barrels and create new disruptions, ones we can take advantage of as we map out the decisions we make. Despite the seemingly counterintuitive nature, we will hunt down the forming barrels of pressure and use them to propel ourselves forward instead of indefinitely running from it. With the surfer's mindset, we will paddle straight for the swell and ride these waves into, and through, the greatest period in the history of humanity.

WAVES: The Barrels of Complexity

I think the next century will be the century of complexity.

— Stephen Hawking

Why do we not notice changes until after they happen? For one, complexity. And the fact that changes are constant. So what, then, is complexity?

What is Complexity, and Why Does it Matter?

We like to frame our lives as being "complex." Maybe you have a lot of meetings to attend or an endless inbox or a bunch of birthday parties to go to on the same weekend, but this is far from what complexity can be. Your full calendar is thoroughly organized and predictable compared to the scale of what complexity truly is. How the earth was created and life as we know it is littered with complexity. Complexity is everything around us. It's not a result of a condition; it is everything. Complexity is not a goal or a state we are trying to achieve; it is merely the reality of the world we now live in.

We all regularly make complex decisions, but our instinct is to simplify things. As a result, we tend not to consider the complexity of the world around us consciously. The study of complexity science focuses on systems and challenges that are dynamic, unpredictable, and multidimensional by nature. Everything in complexity science looks at the interconnected relationships between everything. This is immensely helpful when looking at the exponential changes that happen when things are digitized—complexity science allows us to move away from our traditional, linear thinking. No more cause and effect, but rather a million effects that might lead to one cause you notice and a thousand you don't.

Complexity at a high level is made up of **interactions, emergence, dynamics, self-organization**, and **adaptation**. As in, true complexity is all of these things at once. If it is dynamic, but not self-organized, then it falls out of definition.

Imagine you get a nice high-end watch—maybe you got it as a gift, or you treated yourself to it. You wear the watch out to dinner with your friends, and they compliment you on how great it looks. Subconsciously, you map the connection: Wearing the watch brings compliments, and compliments make you feel good. But the watch is just a small piece of the complexity; all it did was surface how happy the interconnectedness of other people in your life could make you.

Expanding on this watch: There is an essential definition between complex and complicated. When you consider a real watch—the type of non-smart, analog watches that are meticulously designed with interconnected springs and gears that keep time with unimaginable, mathematical precision. These watches don't even require a battery—the coils within them wind and store kinetic movement energy so they can run even during static moments. The inner workings of a mechanical watch are incredibly complicated, but they are not complex. The components inside the device are interconnected and interdependent, but they are not diverse. The mechanical coils and gears within a watch operate in a fixed manner, are not adaptive, and rely on specific conditions to get a specific outcome. A watch is complicated, not complex; it cannot produce complex outcomes, build up large events, and or produce unpredictable outcomes. In fact, you buy a watch because it is the very *definition* of predictable. Despite how much cash you fork over for a Jaeger Lecoultre or Rolex, they are not robust. Watches cannot withstand small or large disturbances. In fact, a proper watch cannot withstand any kind of disturbance. If you were to remove even the smallest gear from a watch, the watch would no longer work, as it cannot adapt and operate without the missing gear.

Compare the workings of your expensive, complicated watch to your life. Things are constantly removed or added, but your life's overall system does not cease to exist based on the changing variables. You may remove money from your account, but you are not any less, as that money likely went to groceries or rent. Humans are some of the most complex systems, and we reside in incredibly adaptable and robust environments. We are the definition of complexity.

What is an entity? Consider the complexity of financial markets. Banks that employ bankers and traders who all adhere to governing bodies and government entities are interconnected through an interconnected and interdependent system. The behavior of one bank affects what other banks do, and vice versa. They all adapt based on the conditions the other banks and global environments present. Unfortunately, there are times when every bank adapts in the same direction and creates a large event, such as a bubble or a crash.

You and I? We're even more complex—infinitely more, even as individuals, especially as individuals. Every part of our lives interacts with everything else. Friends, family, coworkers all impact our lives and outcomes. Then there is everyone we know on our social networks or the internet. Combine all that with the human body's internal complexity; our brain is made up of tens of billions of neurons flying around and communicating via trillions of synaptic connections, some of which guide our thoughts and decisions. Amazingly, it all works together. Seriously, amazing.

The biggest byproduct of complex systems is their unpredictable nature—crashes, fires, wars, all the fun stuff. The unpredictability has an upshot, though, as complex systems are incredibly robust and can endure incredible damage and massive environmental change. In the last two centuries, industrial progress has trashed our environment, but the durability of complex systems meant we found ways to adapt (so far). Those who do not understand complexity fail to see how large events build into things like climate change. All of us think we have essential jobs, yet our job doesn't vanish when we call in sick for a day. When the president is hospitalized for a few days, the country does not shut down or collapse into chaos. Robust, complex systems always find a way to the next state of being.

If you live in a city, go over to the window and look outside. You will see a plethora of people coming and going, people riding bikes, cars, and buses driving around, delivery trucks stopping up traffic, the movement of endless ideas and goods all throughout the city. Somehow it all makes sense and works, yet there is no central planner for everything that is happening; it is not preplanned or managed from the top; the order of a city just emerges from the bottom up. Complexity systems can self-organize to create outcomes and spontaneous patterns without any guidance or planning. When we walk into our favorite coffee shop on our way to the office, we unconsciously get in line behind the nearest person. Twelve strangers walking into a room and naturally forming a line are obvious examples of everyday self-organization. We see this with swarms of insects, schools of fish, and flocks of birds throughout nature. Even in June, if you are in Canada, and you look closely enough, you will see cooling water droplets colliding together and freezing as they chaotically fall from the sky, creating big, beautiful snowflakes. Self-organization exists all around us in our lives.

It feels like magic. But magic and science aren't great bedfellows.

To truly understand the emergence's captivating complexity, we have to take very pragmatic considerations to unwrap the magical mystery. Like with any magic trick, the mystique vanishes once we understand what is happening.

We understand the world differently when we peel away the mystery, but the complexity still lends a sense of romanticism to it. Emergence shows how the micro differs from the macro. What our neurons do at a micro level is different from what is emerging at the macro level. Our brain is a great example. We have neurons that are individually very simple and straightforward at the micro level. On a macro level, as each neuron interacts with billions of others, we start to see intelligence, consciousness, and personality emerge. We see this everywhere. Watching a surfer ride smoothly is the macro emergence of thousands of things happening on the micro level. Or if we just consider water: at a micro level, the water molecule consists of two atoms of hydrogen linked by covalent bonds to the same atom of oxygen. While this molecule is water, it is not wet. At the macro level, when you compile these molecules together, you're soaked.

Emergence rises from the bottom up without any central control. Fish do not get together to discuss who is swimming in what order; it just happens. The neurons in your brain do not actively collaborate to ensure they fire properly to get you to read the words on this page. Likewise, you do not think of making your brain work to read this page at a macro level; it just happens. This is emergence; it is an incredible phenomenon we come to understand much of, but not all of, through complexity sciences. Stock market crashes, epidemics, flocking birds, and schooling fish are all things we can understand through complexity to see where the emergence comes from.

From a purely intellectual viewpoint, complex systems are fascinating to study as they produce bewildering novelties of unpredictability, large events, robustness, and emergence. From a pragmatic view, we have no choice but to be interested in emergence as a way to better understand complexity. We see complexity play out in market volatility, industry failures, warnings of ecological failures, and even regularly in our daily lives. Furthermore, complexity is getting faster by the day—this is neither good nor bad, neither a gift nor a curse, but simply the inescapable reality of the times. Not all complexity is the same; some situations are far more complex than others—neurons, people, snowflakes, species, countries, companies, natural phenomena, and surfing, just to name a few! How we choose to engage complexity, if we can even consider it a choice, can be a burden or a blessing, or both.

New paradigms require new ways of thinking and new tools to view and engage with our world, including the very paradigm of complexity. In the past, researchers sought out and built logical definitions, mathematical theorems, and formal models to use as paradigms for their day. This text will take more of a social-scientist approach, allowing us to use looser definitions while staying out of the weeds of computational tools and mathematical formulations. Once we understand the why, we can use it as a guide—a compass—to understand where we are heading.

Research and observation show us that high-level structures and patterns emerge from the bottom up and are in no way planned, predetermined, managed, or built. The world we live in, and life itself, is an example of an emerging phenomenon and a constant novelty source. Complexity is robust yet susceptible to large events—a disturbance can have next to no impact on a complex system. Yet, at the same time, a small miscalculation can escalate into the collapse of a financial market or a world war.

Much like the metaphors of a city teeming with life, the analogy of complex systems pulsing with life is metaphorically accurate. Complex systems are not in equilibrium; they are dynamic and, in a way, have a life of their own. They frustrate macroeconomists as they lack the balance of supply and demand. Complexity lacks structure, but it isn't necessarily chaotic. It occupies the unusual and uncomfortable space between order and chaos, which means that your beliefs' interconnectedness to the truth or your expected truth is all part of the complexity.

Is life more complex now?

Without a doubt, today is more complex than at any other point in our history. Ten thousand years ago, we were a global population of maybe ten million and largely just concerned with hunting and gathering the fruits in nature. We cared about the basics of survival and creating the next generation, not how quickly Netflix was buffering or two-day shipping. Go back 100 years, and humanity added farmers to the mix. Farmers belonged to communities and all generally did the same type of work and had the same skills. Farmers operated in isolation and would visit the nearest town once every few months to either pick up supplies or sell their crops. There was little diversity and interdependence for farmers. Plant corn, get corn. Aside from the odd bit of bad weather, the farmer's life was very predictable.

Today, vastly different. We live more in urban areas, and our skill sets are incredibly diverse. Yes, we still have a few farmers, but now we also have everything from engineers and researchers to lawyers and tradespeople, technicians, teachers, service industry workers, and doctors. Our work is more connected to the world beyond our immediate community, while our virtual connections are seemingly infinite. With no debate, we are the most connected era in human history.

Our actions are more interdependent. Our contribution depends on the value of others' work, such as colleagues, competitors, and clients. The modern knowledge worker is only as good as the team that surrounds them. The farmers from a previous era did not have this interdependency; they grew what they ate and got everything else through bartering or selling.

We are more adaptive with new organizations, new technologies, new jobs constantly appearing as things are made continuously better and faster. We have more information instantly available than ever before. Everything happens in real time; we want instant feedback for everything. No one wants to wait six months to know their sales performance—they can do their job better with real-time updates.

Why send a letter when you can FaceTime or text someone?

While living in the olden days may have been less interconnected and interdependent, it was by no means not complex. Populations exploded, only to be outpaced by the advancements in technology, both of which contribute to the increased complexity we experience today. This doesn't mean the past was more comfortable or that it was boring; it only claims that it was less complex. In the short term, complexity will continue to increase, but our world may be less complex in the distant future. Why we lose complexity is not easy to predict—likely to some sort of collapse that is completely incomprehensible to us today. But it could happen and would be explained through things like chaos theory, not complexity sciences. We've seen the disaster movies where electricity vanishes, and we all learn to read by candlelight and cook over campfires again.

But let us sit with the claim: Today's world is socially, economically, and politically more complex than it was in the past. We need new ways of thinking and tools of observation to comprehend what's coming. For example, the 1590 invention of the microscope brought about numerous revolutionary technological and scientific advancements. As our instrumentation gets better, we see finer details about naturally evolving biology. But we don't yet have the instruments to see the monumental advancements in bioengineering where the future will blur the known boundaries, adding to the complexity. The more we learn, the deeper we look, the more we understand through complexity the world within and around us, and the less we can ultimately understand with the old ways of thinking.

The ultimate byproduct of complexity? Disruption. Emergences of large events feel aggressive and catastrophic. Large events have large consequences, like political takeovers, stock market crashes, traffic jams, rogue waves, divorces, biological events like pandemics, or one of your apps on your smartphone crashing and wiping out your high score on *Candy Crush*. Remembering that complexity in our life is any system that is diverse, interconnected, interdependent, and can adapt. It is paradoxical to think that complex systems are robust and adaptive in one sense yet vulnerable to these large events in the other. Cities experience earthquakes, hurricanes, riots, and flash floods. Economies crash. Lives are upended with all manner of failures. Yet, we're still here. Unlike a broken watch, complex systems do not simply stop working when faced with disruption. From a purely pragmatic perspective, we *must* understand complexity as a way to build robust systems. We'd like to think that if we can identify the conditions that create large events, maybe we can prevent them from happening. The reality is that these events' pressure on our life is where we grow, adapt, and evolve—the moments we live for, getting deep in the barrel of these waves. We don't want to prevent them from happening, we want to exploit the chance to learn from the opportunity.

The Barrel

If there was no such thing as barrels I probably wouldn't even surf.

— Clay Marzo

Consider the two systems of complexity: abstract and functional. The abstract is where learning, creativity, innovation, and growth happen. The functional system pushes for standardization, formality, structure, and performance. These two systems are essential, as they help us identify complexity and help us understand when to use complexity to grow and transcend into our futures.

Our abstract system is the carefree side, where we take risks, get creative, dream, and envision our goals. This is where you roll the windows down, stick your head out, and ride along to wherever life takes you regardless of rules and regulations. The functional side keeps you in a job to pay bills and taxes, follow laws, save money, and plan for your future. Both systems are in constant competition, but we grew up learning the need to move our systems back into functional space as swiftly as possible and find a linear functional system that is easily understandable and predictable.

Children dream of their future. Adults want to be as carefree as possible while on vacation. Yes, we would all love to live hedonistic lifestyles and be carefree all of the time, but how would the bills get paid? Therefore, we have learned to find comfort when the functional system is in control. We are comfortable when we are at the polar extremes of these two systems but not in the middle, where the two systems conflict.

Yet, it is in this tension, this conflict, where life's disruptions happen. Michael Arena and Mary Uhl-Bien are responsible for much of the research behind complexity leadership theory and the space between these two systems. Understanding complexity leadership theory allows us to understand when we are in the "barrel" of the wave by embracing the dynamic tension between the two systems. For a long while, we should do whatever it takes to reduce or manage the conflict in our lives, especially between the functional and abstract systems. Our grandparents and parents worked tirelessly to bring equilibrium to their lives, but our goal is to embrace the uncertainty and complexity to amplify the significance of the change. We don't run away from big waves, the complexity, and the eventual disruption; rather, we hunt them down and surf the shit out of them.

The transformation we're after happens in the barrels of these waves. Residing in the extreme left of the abstract system is pure chaos, and pure order operates on the other extreme. You can never transform or transcend into the future if you are purely in order or chaos, meaning growth happens between the extremes. The barrel's tension that forms between these two systems is exactly where we want to be.

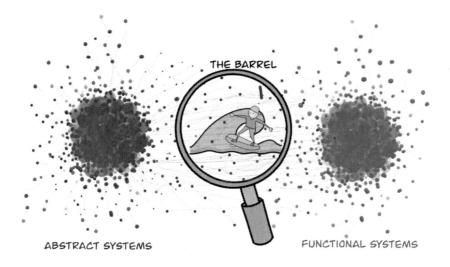

THE BARREL

ABSTRACT SYSTEMS

FUNCTIONAL SYSTEMS

Figure. A diagram of the barrel between the two systems of conflict in our lives.

Albert Einstein is quoted: "The definition of insanity is doing the same thing over and over again, but expecting different results." Insanity? Maybe not, but it does highlight a common trap most of us fall into: Humans are creatures of habit and often unconsciously stick to their routines. This is our functional system at work. Our evolution is based on primitive survival, making us naturally risk averse. Every new approach means an unpredictable outcome and a higher perceived risk. Conceptually, Einstein's quote is still correct; if we want different results in life, we must try different approaches.

The primary role of pressure in complexity is to move our system out of equilibrium. While we want to remain on the extreme end of the functional system, going fully to the extreme end of the abstract system is equally dangerous—you will be in chaos, which is not the same as complexity.

In speaking with Mary Uhl-Bien, I found the best way to identify the barrel in any system is to look for the pressure. The stress and tension we feel in our lives are often the footprints of complexity. Does this mean every time we feel the pressure, we are in the barrel? Not necessarily, but if we understand the correct type of pressure, we can take advantage of being in the barrel.

The barrel in our life is identified by four components of pressure:

1. A need for new and novel solutions. ("This is boring!" "Ugh, I just want to go somewhere else!")

2. New partnerships and relationships. (Like when Nike partnered with Apple, or Uber with Spotify.)

3. Healthy conflicting perspectives. (Feeling bored with the same old conversation? Competition and debates are a great way to spawn new ideas and increase the creative energy.)

4. Interdependence of working together as the only option for success. (i.e., when we have no choice but to work together—adapt or die.)

We have discovered what we call "the barrel" as the key to our ability to innovate and reinvent ourselves and take advantage of adaptive tension that produces new and creative outcomes through complexity theory advancements. But this means we must embrace these often-uncomfortable situations, as the purpose of these pressures is to move the system out of equilibrium. External and internal actions influence the pressures on our functional and abstract systems. If you believe your boss will fire you, you will start looking for a new job. This might bring you to get a better or worse employer. You didn't know that your boss was just having a bad day and had no intention of firing you. But you perceive a different reality that pushed you out of your functional comfort zone. This is why our rational beliefs and thoughts must adequately align with the truth of the world so we can optimally navigate these barrels.

How do we navigate through the barrel when we lack the information, facts, or data we need to act in the moment? Well, for starters: improvisation.

SURFER: Improvise Like Slater

In any moment of decision, the best thing you can do is the right thing, the next-best thing is the wrong thing, and the worst thing you can do is nothing.

— Theodore Roosevelt

The world in which we reside is complex, meaning it is diverse, interconnected, interdependent, and can adapt. The only piece we can control to a certain extent is how we adapt within all this complexity. We can identify specific situations, which we call *the barrel*, in which we must constantly adapt to keep our life's system in this space. But how do we do that? How do we keep ourselves in the barrel?

Why was Kelly Slater so much better at surfing than everyone else? Most surfing fans would agree that his flexibility, paddling strength and speed, and reach are nothing out of the ordinary or worth writing home about. Slater had "surfing sense." He could anticipate what was about to happen on the water and reacted to it faster than the competition. He could gather, process, and understand massive amounts of complex information instantaneously. Instead of seeing the linear connection of individual waves forming, Slater fluidly improvised on all his minor predictions of the formations, breakdowns, and re-formations of the patterns he saw. Being present in the moment, he would use the constantly evolving spatial and temporal relationships among his position, his board, the forming waves, the other surfers, and the waves' amplitude and speed to dictate his next thoughts and movements.

Like a musician playing jazz music, Slater would use a loose framework to dictate his next action in real time. This is not to say that Slater was also not a gifted and talented surfer or didn't put in an extensive effort to his sport. But on a world stage, competing with all the best surfers in the world, this is what set him apart. Slater could perceive many patterns to improvise minor adjustments through the unfolding complexity of the water. He could use his decisions and actions to shape the outcomes in his favor, often putting him in the right place at the right time. We see this everywhere in sports—highly paid athletes who always seem to be in the right place at the right time.

What we see in Slater is improvisation executed at the highest level. We have all, at some point, had to improvise. Are we aware when we are improvising? Do we know how often we do it? The research indicates that you might improvise more than you think. Turns out, about 90% of your daily decisions are improvised. Business leaders value people with agile and adaptive decision-making skills. Research shows that most plans fail because of the ever-increasing instability and uncertainty of our modern-day world. Only 11% of individuals are happy with the outcome of their planning efforts. Despite all of this, we still rely on traditional planning methods before we undertake a big task when we should use techniques that allow for improvisation when conditions change. And conditions always change, always. Studies already show that only 10%–30% of planned strategies are ever actualized; we're already improvising solutions.

The debate every MBA candidate endures: Plan or execute? The answer is both. Have a plan, but only as a framework to guide and direct the execution. Not unlike our surfing framework! Long gone are the days of overengineered business plans!

Strategic planning fails because of the unpredictability of the complex and ever-changing landscape—we have to improvise! Unfortunately, research shows that we don't know how to make the decisions we need to get the desired outcome. We will remain incapable of these decisions without a better understanding of improvisation. Since 75–90% of our daily choices are improvised, it is worth learning how to make off-the-cuff decisions. Doing nothing is worse than doing something, so why not learn how to do the most useful thing for our desired outcome?

Improvisation is making something from whatever resources or information are available at that moment. While this results in a spontaneous execution with no specific or scripted preparation, we can actually practice improvisation by leveraging our past experiences. Much like in jazz music, improvisation is rooted in exploration and discovery. Instead of being controlled or composed by an individual, jazz musicians use improvisation within a loose framework to create.

As controlled as we think the world is, improvisation is everywhere. Without it (and GPS), how would you navigate around a road closure on your commute to work? How would you debate with a friend? How do the random ingredients in your fridge turn into a last-minute meal at dinner-time? Anytime something does not go entirely to plan, you are improvising on some level. Yet we are often taught not to improvise or "wing it." Teachers want us to follow instructions or adhere to the structure of proven methods and strategies, blah blah blah. "Five-year plan" and all that. Furthermore, research shows improvisation leads to faster innovation and improved performance. Since the complexity in our lives is changing faster than ever before, improvisation is an essential skill to develop.

Awareness of the importance of improvisation has increased over the past two decades. Much of this interest stems from the hypercompetitive nature of our modern world. Things are changing faster than ever, thanks to technological and social innovations consistently emerging and bringing relentless waves of complexity. As we move deeper into the twenty-first century, structured planning may be worthless even to try, and we may be forced into improvisation.

The old days are gone. Competitive pressures everywhere around us are growing, further increasing our environment's volatility; this volatility increases forces for us to adapt. This instability increases uncertainty, which influences our decision-making process, which is impacted by globalization and new technologies that have created an exponentially growing amount of knowledge and information, requiring faster decisions than ever before. So how do we improvise? At the highest and most general level, there are four principles behind improvisational decisions:

1. Spontaneity: Go with your gut. Mention the first thing that comes to mind. Mistakes are opportunities to learn, which involves some rewiring of our brains. Yet most of us have been told to "think before you speak" since we were kids.

2. Say "Yes, and...": Always accept ideas. In the moment, as stupid as some of the ideas or suggestions might be from the group around you, do not shut them down. Instead, accept the idea and counter or build off it.

3. Always stay with the group and in the moment, constantly be listening and observing the environment.

4. Individuals within a team always work together to make each other look good. Our instinct might be to compete or cast blame for failures; we may want to remove ourselves from the uncomfortable experience. Don't. Stay in the moment, be with those around you, and work to make each other look good instead of leaning into your instinctive, competitive tendencies.

"People look at the ocean that don't know anything about it like that's crazy looking, but once you put yourself in this situation, you realize there's a flow to everything."

— Kelly Slater

Just like Einstein and insanity, we think things are less risky when we plan to do them the way we always have. But this is no longer the case. To best transcend our complex future, we need to keep our systems on tilt through our decisions and actions. We need to keep ourselves in the barrel and learn to make ad-hoc, improvisational decisions at the moment when insufficient information is available. Improvisation, the second pillar of the surfing framework, allows us to best leverage and surf the waves of complexity the world throws our way. The third and final pillar of our framework, decision-making, is what makes this possible. Understanding how our complex world and improvisation works are only useful when our beliefs and thoughts align with the truth of our world. Like any model or system, putting in bad information causes bad information to come out the other end.

Garbage in, garbage out.

It is not enough for us to just improvise; we need *rational improvisation.*

SURFBOARD:
Rational Decisions and Beliefs

That which can be destroyed by the truth should be.

— Patricia Christine Hodgell

Our decisions define who we are and what we ultimately become. The emergence of all cumulative decisions will define the future of humanity, so we'd do well to make the best decisions. The way we think and the beliefs we hold affect our choices, which affect our actions and how we improvise. With an influx of continually changing information, how do we filter through it all to make the best decision without outside influence or judgment? This final section rounds out our framework to help us do exactly this. As we navigate complexity and improvise our way through life, we need to understand why our decisions' shortcomings are so significant.

What is behind the spread of misinformation? Why does it feel impossible to understand the truth? Why do some people seem impervious to facts? This final section of this surfing framework will answer these questions by first looking inward at ourselves. Consider how often you make the right choice. In all of the decisions you have ever made, what percentage of the time have you been right? Whatever you think your answer is, you're likely wrong. Over fifty years of research has shown that human decision-making and judgment proves we are not as rational as we think we are. Without ever having met you, dear reader, I can assure you that you are nowhere near as rational as you think you are.

Human decisions tend to irrationally deviate from rational choice. We consistently overvalue irrelevant information, incorrectly overanalyze situational and contextual variables, and then we go to work on rationalizing our incorrect decisions. Not only are we irrational, but many of the biases that drive our irrationality happen unconsciously, in real time, with minimal effort on your part. The worst part? Being aware of the bias does nothing to prevent it from occurring. As humans, we have almost no instinctual ability to make optimal decisions.

Worse yet, decisions are not getting easier thanks to the world's unknown complexities and rapidly changing technology and technological advancements. We used to raise children to focus on controlling, planning, and directing their actions through their linear decisions. Today, the focus is on the flow of information, interactions, and context—all of which create a natural environment for development and change.

Despite what you might take away from scrolling through social media, we are still the smartest race on the planet. While we are well aware that humans are terrible at making decisions, we have the capability of automating most of our routine decisions in a way that removes bias. There are advantages to analytical decision models that can remove most humanistic biases and errors, but these models aren't without their weaknesses. Some outcomes are not predictive. Some decisions, even the smallest ones, can be a matter of failure or success. Again—garbage in, garbage out. Big data and AI doesn't help us make decisions when it is leveraging bad, biased data.

A decision feels like a straightforward concept until we start overthinking it and find ourselves at the bottom of a rabbit hole. For our purposes: a decision is a choice that one makes after considering the available possibilities. Our modern decisions have to consider many complex processes, such as the formation of knowledge, memory, judgment, reasoning, problem-solving, decision-making, and comprehension. Through these decisions, we create new knowledge by leveraging existing knowledge.

There's not a couple alive who can decide where to go for dinner. What do we feel like eating? Where should we go? We pick up our phones and dive into Yelp reviews and sort by ratings. Most of our seemingly everyday decisions are heavily influenced by biological and nonbiological factors, like previous experiences, new information, available data, and intelligence—both human and artificial.

Picking dinner is easy compared to how we properly utilize the barrel. Now, we must make improvisational decisions when there is no concrete or reliable information available. In life, when my wife doesn't have enough information to make a dinner decision, she gets ahead of it by pushing the decision back to me. I get hit with the dreaded text *"you pick,"* which means I have a zero percent chance of making the right decision, no matter what information I might have on hand. I improvise by picking a highly rated restaurant, claim we are going to a "surprise," and hope for the best. In the framework, it isn't a matter of picking the exact restaurant she wants to go to, but rather getting to a place where we can both consume calories and get on with our evening. The surfing framework relies on mapping our thoughts and beliefs to the truth of the world, especially if we want the most accurate decisions and outcomes. But even when we do everything right, we are often still in the wrong.

Errors from our Mental Architecture

Our brain is the only tool we have to measure and understand the world. We use it to calibrate the accuracy of our beliefs against the reality of the world. Unfortunately, our brain isn't calibrated to the realities around us. This shortcoming manifests as our cognitive bias. A cognitive bias is a systematic error in the way we think. Cognitive bias is different from a random error, which is usually brought about by ignorance or a lack of knowledge. A cognitive bias skews the way we think to give us a less-accurate path to the truth—assuming we get to the truth at all. Worse yet, being aware of these biases does not resolve them. In fact, you are usually not even aware of them when they are happening.

So how do we trust anything if we can't even trust our brains?

Humans are not rational, but thankfully we are predictably irrational. Meaning we can recognize, reduce, and even overcome many of our biases. This is no easy thing to do—we know the patterns that lead us astray. Humans are the only race on earth that is capable of thinking about thinking. We can look back on an event that happened and resolve not to make the same mistake in the future. If we understand the flaws in how our mind maps our reality, we can reflect upon and correct these errors. We know that our flawed brain distorts our reality, and this fact is what makes us different from all other species on the planet. Knowing these cognitive biases exist means we can apply second-order corrections.

By no means a perfect situation, but it does serve as a potent tool.

Cognitive Biases

Leaders make predictable errors, and their biases can undermine their decision-making. To avoid these errors, they lean on data-driven decision-making, statistical models, and algorithms. Every human is victim to a slew of judgment and decision-making errors like false illusions of control, overconfidence, confirming only what we want to believe, falsely believing we were right all along, and falsely identifying random events as patterns. Because of all these errors in our thinking, we tend to think that specific conditions are more likely to occur than general ones. We see these errors in statistical probability estimations through the research of a dual-process model. This outlines two modes of thinking: fast and emotional (System 1) and slow and logical (System 2). System 1 thinking is intuitive, automatic, efficient, and unconscious, requiring little energy or effort to execute. Unfortunately, System 1 thinking is prone to biases and systematic errors.

On the other hand, System 2 thinking is a slow, effortful, and controlled way of thinking that requires more energy and attention but ultimately can remove many of the intuitive errors System 1 thinking falls into. Research has shown how these two modes of thinking differ and ultimately arrive at different results despite being given the same inputs. This provides us with some insight as to why humans have a hard time thinking statistically.

Think of it this way: Would you rather have a guaranteed $80 or a 90% chance of winning $100 (leaving you with a 10% chance of getting nothing)?

In the surveys conducted, people overwhelmingly chose "guaranteed $80" even though the value is mathematically lower, shedding light on how humans are instinctually risk averse.

Another study asked 126 individuals on four different occasions to choose between two cameras. I'll ask you the same questions now: If I told you one camera was priced at $269.99 and rated 6/10 on a 10-point consumer rating scale, the second priced at $539.99 and rated 8/10 on the same consumer rating scale. Which camera would you choose?

A majority of the survey picked the first, cheaper camera, as most were not willing to pay double the price for only a small increase on the consumer rating scale. The same experiment was run with a third choice: a camera priced at $839.99, with a consumer rating of 7/10.

Now, faced with three options, which one would you pick?

– #1 $269.99 - 6/10
– #2 $539.99 - 8/10
– #3 $839.99 - 7/10

If you selected option #2, which you probably did, you aligned with most survey participants, which makes zero sense. This is an irrational shift in economic theory. If customers preferred the first camera over the second, why are they picking camera #2 when #3 is a worse deal?

We all know someone who is overconfident. The thing is, we're all overly confident. As a result, our irrational mistakes show how the framing of choice can shape our decisions. Ask someone to guess a range of the length of the Nile River, or the weight of a Boeing 747 airplane, or the year Mozart was born. Whatever your answer, you're likely pretty sure you're right. In every experiment featuring these questions, subjects gave answers that were exact, precise, and completely wrong. These subjects could have given answers on a broader spectrum to increase the range of their guesses, but they didn't. Why?

Because we're overconfident, and it might just be the thing we love most about being human. Confidence and economic biases are two of the dozens of biases analytical decision models aim to remove. While there are numerous applications where analytical models have removed these biases, we have a long way to go before using data to make predictive decisions every day.

Outside of the controlled environments of classrooms or laboratories, we regularly face situations that require us to make decisions with limited time and information. When this happens, we unknowingly fall victim to our biases. This was described above through System 2, slow and deliberate, and System 1, fast and intuitive. While both of these systems serve a purpose in mapping our decisions against the truth, both can also lead us astray—all the more reason to understand the systems and how they bend our reality. If an emotional person is using System 1 thinking, they are likely to be irrational, and their decisions may be wrong. Of course, it all depends on the situation in which the system was used.

These cognitive biases are often a result of our brain's attempt to simplify information processing, almost like our brain's shortcut to making sense of the world so we can reach decisions quickly and with minimal effort. This is pure evolution. Humanity's survival is dependent on our ability to make fast decisions in the face of dangerous situations. If our ancient ancestors spotted a dark shadow that seemed to be following them, their cognitive bias likely told them to run for their lives. Without the quick thinking and bias, they would have been eaten for dinner. Then again, maybe the dark shadow was just a swaying tree. We're risk averse. We've always been—better to be safe than sorry.

Noticing Bias

The more we understand our biases, the more we see them at play in our lives—some obvious, some not so much. And while we think ourselves to be unique and special, most of us carry very similar biases.

Base Rate Neglect and Sunk Cost Fallacy

Imagine you meet a new person in America, and the only thing you learn about them at first is that they were very shy. Would you guess this person is more likely to be a salesperson or a librarian?

You might think they were a librarian, and you'd likely be wrong. After all, there are seventy-five times more salespeople than librarians. This is called "base rate neglect," and it happens because we base our judgment on how well we feel specific characteristics should work together versus the reality of how common these characteristics are within the total population. In the same example: Imagine you are the librarian and you've just lost your job. This is fine. After all, you have always hated being a librarian and would love to be a salesperson. However, you are in your midthirties and have extensive experience in the library, so you decide to invest in a master of library sciences degree instead of pursuing sales training. This is the sunk cost fallacy at work. Our bias drives us to commit to what we have already invested in when we should really cut our losses and move on. Think about every time you order too much food and then overeat just to get your money's worth—you have fallen prey to the sunk cost fallacy.

Bias Blindness

It's almost worse when you don't know what you don't know. There was a study that asked people to evaluate the quality of a selection of paintings. The participants guessed that if they knew how famous the artist was, they might have trouble evaluating the paintings with neutrality. The results were exactly as the participants had predicted when the researchers tested these predictions: The participants were biased when informed of the artist versus when they were not. When asked afterward, the participants all said that their specific assessments of the paintings, unlike the others, had been neutral and unaffected by their bias. It turns out, we can identify other people's biases while still being blind to our own biases, even if it is the same bias in the same situation at the same time. Maybe it's the overconfidence thing at play, but we like to irrationally think that we are less biased than everyone else.

Scope Insensitivity and Scope Neglect

In an experiment, Toronto residents were asked how much they would pay to clean up nearby polluted lakes. A second experiment asked how much the same residents would pay to clean up all the polluted lakes in Ontario's entire province. The results showed that Torontonians would pay only a little more to clean up all the lakes in Ontario versus how much they would pay to clean up certain lakes near their homes. Clearly, this makes no sense, as Ontario has more than 250,000 lakes that contain about one-fifth of the world's fresh water. A similar study held across four states in the western United States showed people would be willing to pay 28% more to protect all fifty-seven wilderness areas in those states over what they would pay to protect a single area close to them. In a final study on this bias, three groups of participants were asked how much individuals should pay to save 2,000/20,000/200,000 of those cute migrating birds we see drowning in uncovered oil ponds. The results showed that the groups respectively answered $80/$78/$88.

These are all examples of scope insensitivity. The reality of the problem's size had little effect on the participant's willingness or belief that it should cost more to resolve. We can imagine a single or a few cute birds soaked and drowning in oil; this triggers a relatable emotional response within us in which we assign a value to save this bird or group of birds. In this example, our bias comes from the fact that we throw scope out the window. Humans cannot accurately visualize 2,000 birds at once, never mind 200,000. This creates a disconnect in our linear brain, and the bias emerges from us assigning linear values to exponential increases. Research shows this is not just with polluted lakes, wilderness areas, or cute birds soaked in oil - we carry this bias even when considering the value of human lives.

Are we really insensitive to scope when human lives are at risk? Of course we are! A study published in the *Journal of Experimental Psychology* found that if we increased the chlorine levels in drinking water, it would increase humans' deaths from 0.004 to 2.43 per 1000 humans. This is a 600-fold increase. Why then, when addressing the required increase of funding to address the chlorination issue, did the budgets only rise from $3.78 to $15.23, a 10.5-fold increase in budget to handle a 600-fold increase problem?

Let us shape the next example in a question: Which project below would you fund?

Project 1: A health initiative that promised to save 4,500 lives in a camp of 11,000 refugees?

Or

Project 2: A health initiative that promised to save 4,500 lives in a camp of 250,000 refugees?

Chances are you picked the first project. This is not wrong, but it's also not right. This study was published in a paper called *Insensitivity to the Value of Human Life: A Study of Psychophysical Numbing*. The study found strange evidence that the projected health initiatives to save refugee lives gained much more support when it promised to save 4,500 lives in a camp of 11,000 refugees, rather than 4,500 in a camp of 250,000. The outcome of saving 4,500 lives is the same; the size of the camp is irrelevant. Funding one option should not be heavily favored over the other.

Availability Heuristic

Studies show that people believe accidents cause just as many deaths as diseases and that homicides kill more people than suicides. The truth is that diseases cause sixteen times as many deaths as accidents, and homicide is half as likely as suicide. Our news, social media, and water-cooler talk are more likely to focus on murders than suicides, so we are more likely to remember hearing about them. Dramatic accidents grab our attention more than a slow death from disease. This skew in our judgment is strongly correlated to how events are reported in the media. There is much at play here in the complexity of our world, all fueling our availability heuristic. Murders are more implanted in our memory because they get more media coverage, or is it that media reports on more murders because they are more graphic, therefore more memorable? Regardless of why or how it is happening, it is our responsibility to realize it. Your brain is your problem; blaming the media would be too easy and completely ineffective.

Conjunction Fallacy

Simply put, we assign a higher probability to the outcome of "A + B," than if either the "A" or "B" happens in isolation. How is the likelihood of two statements being true higher than either of the two statements being true on their own? This is why politicians love to overload us with burdensome details. And not just today's politics, for a study asked participants to evaluate the following statements: "Reagan will provide federal support for unwed mothers and cut federal support to local governments" and "Reagan will provide federal support for unwed mothers." The first example is "A + B," while the second example is just "A." The results showed that 68% of the participants believed that "Reagan will provide federal support for unwed mothers and cut federal support to local governments," and that the "A + B" option was more likely to happen than "A" alone. This showed beyond a reasonable doubt that the conjunction fallacy shows how we substitute the judgment of representation for judgment of probability.

When there are more details, our minds are tricked into thinking the outcome is more likely purely because of the process's characteristics, which creates the outcome. In this example, just saying "Reagan will provide federal support for unwed mothers" seems implausible. Still, by adding the plausibility of the statement "and cut federal support to local governments," our minds want to make the statements cancel each other out. "Reagan will provide federal support for unwed mothers" is more likely on its own since this could happen by cutting any support from any other area of government. Or it could happen by simply adding funding, but adding anything after this statement makes it less probable. Our mind is often tricked by the addition of details, which seems to make a scenario sound more plausible, despite the reality that the event is actually less plausible.

Planning Fallacy

Participants in a different study were asked to give a conservative estimate on the probability of when they would complete their projects. Even in the most conservative timelines, in which students assigned a 99% probability of when they would finish, only 45% of them actually finished by the time they anticipated. Even when they picked their own deadlines, they were wrong, and the confidence in their expectations significantly exceeded the reality of their accomplishment. We've all been a student at some point, and you may remember the other, um, "distractions" you were dealing with. But we see this outside of the classroom, too. For example, the completion of construction on the Denver airport was sixteen months late and two billion dollars over budget. A joint defense project called Eurofighter Typhoon was fifty-four months late and cost nineteen billion dollars, way beyond the expected seven billion dollars. The world-famous Sydney Opera House? Ten years late and nearly 100 million dollars over. Poor planning? More need for improvisation?

Projects never go exactly to plan, which is why even the best project managers budget for excess and plan for delays. Ultimately, the irony in the planning fallacy is that we only think we can plan. We cannot. Fortunately, this is one of the easier biases to fix by stepping back and assessing how long things have taken to complete in the past and then fighting the urge to make excuses on why things will be different the next time. We often think through all the things that go right and ignore everything that slows us down.

Bias is usually present every time we blame outside factors when things do not go our way or when we attribute other people's success to luck while taking personal credit for our accomplishments. We assume that everyone shares our opinions or beliefs. We tend to trust someone in authority more than someone who is not. We assume people's gender based on their profession, and we make poor decisions based on the information we are given.

The list goes on. Every one of them makes humans out to be wholly irrational. Yet we make these mistakes not out of arrogance. These happen because we make judgments and decisions about the world around us and believe and like to think that we are objective, logical, and capable while doing so. This couldn't be further from the truth.

Have you ever wondered why you keep seeing things on social media that you cannot believe mainstream media isn't reporting? You might even feel the need to repost it yourself, so people know the truth! Chances are, you are falling victim to confirmation bias—you are paying attention to news stories, or worse, social media posts that confirm your existing opinions. Confirmation bias is the tendency to search for, interpret, favor, and recall information in a way that confirms our prior beliefs and values. On its own, confirmation bias is damaging, but it can be downright lethal with social media's virility. False information on social media, driven by algorithmic targeting, has a drastic impact on how society functions by distorting evidence-based thinking and decision-making.

Social media is a personal extension of oneself. Therefore, debunking misinformation, unless done with incredibly sensitive polish and empathy, will often enrage the individual that has been duped and make them tighten their grasp onto the pseudoscientific evidence. This reaction is not a bias. This is an error in their belief. This newly formed belief is wrong and does not accurately map back to reality.

Beliefs vs. Fake Beliefs

Back in 1933, Alfred Korzybsk published in a paper: "a map is not the territory it represents, but, if correct, it has a similar structure to the territory, which accounts for its usefulness." A map is a metaphor, but it is only useful if it is built off the proper beliefs. A poorly drawn map only gets you lost. Do our beliefs accurately map the truth of the world?

For a belief to be correct, we have to anticipate its experience in our world. We can't experience everything directly; most of what we know comes from general understandings. We look at our yellow surfboard on the sand and we believe that this surfboard is yellow. However, we do not see the atoms underneath the surfboard, even though atoms are, in fact, there—indirect experience. Most of the things we can anticipate are caused by what we cannot see or directly experience. If correct, our beliefs are the accurate map that allows us to understand the world in which we reside.

The question is: What are your beliefs, and how well do they map to the world around you? How much trust are you willing to put into the map?

In his movie, *Free Solo*, world-renowned rock climber Alex Honnold does the seemingly impossible by climbing Yosemite's El Capitan by himself without any rope or safety equipment. Spoiler alert: He doesn't fall (the movie likely wouldn't have won an Oscar if he had). Imagine you just finished watching this movie, and you drive out to the nearest national park with your friend to scale the first massive granite rock wall you can find. Alex did it, so can you!

On the summit of a vertical rock face, you look down and see the valley floor *way down there*. You and your friend brought along BASE jumping parachutes for the descent. The question now stands: Is it safe to jump from here? Your friend says to you, "This looks really far up, at least 600–700 meters; we have about twenty seconds of free fall before we hit the ground, giving us maybe ten seconds before we have to open our chutes."

You grab a decent-sized rock, check your watch, and throw the rock off the cliff. You listen for the sound of the rock hitting the distant ground below. Your watch says the rock took exactly 7.82 seconds to descend. Loose math tells you that you're maybe 300 meters (984.252 ft) high, not 600–700 meters. You explain to your friend that he will only have 7.82 seconds of free fall, not twenty. Your friend gets a little defensive and makes fun of you for using a rock. "We both weigh more than a rock, you idiot, we won't fall at the same speed as a rock if we are heavier."

We never established that your friend was smart. He was, after all, the one who initially suggested BASE jumping as a means of descent. Putting aside that you have just scaled a granite wall without ropes and are about to *jump off of it*, now your friend has a different understanding of gravity. He doesn't understand that things, all things, fall at a rate of 9.8 m/s^2, so you ask him if this means that he believes he will hit the ground faster than the rock did.

Embarrassed by his lapse of thinking, he starts to mock you by explaining how he would spread himself out like a flying squirrel and take advantage of things you don't understand, like air friction. He also claims that you are entitled to your own opinion about the elevation, but his opinion stands 600–700 meters, not 300.

You try to be the bigger person and defuse the situation while debunking his incorrect belief with the utmost tact and empathy. As nicely as possible, you explain to him that for a rock to free-fall for 7.82 seconds from this height, it can only mean you are 300 meters high, regardless of how far it looks.

You say all of this while standing on a rock ledge. Whether it's 300 meters or 600 meters, certain death is certain death.

Why did we watch that movie?

Your friend again reminds you that you are entitled to your own beliefs and opinions. You explain to him that to survive the jump, he needs to anticipate sensory experience as precisely as possible to what the real world offers and develop correct beliefs that do not necessarily anticipate sensory experiences. If your friend can *explain* how your beliefs are wrong, you would be more than willing to listen to his perspective and align your beliefs to his.

Your friend thinks long and hard, does a quick prayer, then he shouts "I'll prove it to you right now" and leaps off the edge. 7.82 seconds later, your friend is dead.

Yes, everyone is entitled to their own beliefs—right up until factual accuracy gets in the way.

Most of your everyday opinions and beliefs have far less drastic consequences, but they still drive your decisions and actions. The actions stemming from our beliefs drive our interdependence and connectedness and creates the emergence of our world. Having a world emerge on wrong beliefs will certainly be catastrophic to the future of humanity. One of the greatest strengths of the human race, which has led us to become the dominant species on Earth, is our ability to model the unknown. At the same time, this is one of our greatest weaknesses. Humans far too often believe in things that are not only unseen but also unreal.

Back on the cliff face, before your friend jumped, let's imagine your friend summited first and tells you the cliff ledge is 700 meters above the valley floor. You do some quick mental math and figure that if you are 700 meters high, you will free-fall 11.95 seconds before hitting the ground. Sure, the two last beliefs are connected—*if* you are 700 meters high, an object will free-fall for 11.95 seconds.

That's a big "if."

Basing correct beliefs on a foundation of wrong beliefs doesn't make them correct. If your anticipated experience in the real world of jumping off the 300m cliff that you believe is 700m, things would get messy. Humans are great at building up entire networks of beliefs that are only connected to each other—we call them floating beliefs. If the foundational belief is several times removed from the beliefs you are connecting is wrong, your whole network of floating beliefs will also be wrong. Without an accurate foundational belief, your descent from the mountain will be a swift death.

Don't ask what you should believe; instead, focus on what you should anticipate. Beliefs should be questioned, and they should flow from questions of anticipation at the center of our inquiry. Questioning beliefs starts by guessing your anticipation. How quickly do you anticipate hitting the ground? How fast do people tend to fall? If that belief does not accurately model the anticipation, then we should throw it out and move on. This is easier than it sounds, as though we should only have rational or accurate beliefs. But since most people do not put much thought into where or how their beliefs were formed, most of us believe in belief.

Belief Errors

Free-floating beliefs and belief in belief are both examples of an improper belief—one that is not troubled with accurately describing our world. This is different from a proper belief, which requires observation and is open to updates when encountering new evidence. However, being *right* does not mean your beliefs are correct. If you believe you know the number to the winning lottery ticket when you touch your nose, and that number wins, it doesn't mean your belief was correct.

Carl Sagan had a wonderful example of this. He tells the story of Pete, who says there is a dragon in his bedroom. We will name the dragon Puff. Obviously, we think this is awesome because dragons are amazing, and we've never seen one before. We go to his bedroom, and Pete then tells us that it is an *invisible* dragon. Before we make fun of Pete and his dragon Puff, Sagan, being a scientist, points out that Pete's dragon hypothesis is not unfalsifiable. We could still go to Pete's bedroom, and even though we do not see Puff, we could hear heavy breathing or see magical dragon footsteps appearing on the carpet. We could also use instruments to tell us how something in the bedroom was consuming oxygen and producing carbon dioxide.

Just because we can't see the dragon with our naked eye doesn't mean it isn't there.

But Pete stops us again to mention that Puff is also an inaudible dragon, and after we suggest measuring the carbon dioxide in the air of the bedroom, Pete claims that Puff also does not breathe. We offer to grab a bag of flour, to throw in the air to see if it outlines the dragon in his bedroom, to which Pete immediately counters with "Puff is permeable to flour."

What does this tell us? Other than how Pete might need new friends or an update to his medication, it also shows us that poor hypotheses need to pivot fast to avoid falsification. Other interpretations of the story highlight the fact that Pete must have had an accurate model of the situation within his mind since he anticipated exactly the outcome of the experimental results.

Does Pete really believe there is a dragon in his bedroom or not? Clearly, Pete does not anticipate seeing anything unusual when entering his bedroom; otherwise, he would not have made excuses in advance. Maybe Pete's propositional beliefs are based on the free-floating statement of the dragon being in his bedroom. Being the rational people we are, these beliefs are wrong, and we do not believe in Puff the magic dragon. At this point, most of us would stop hanging out with Pete. So imagine our surprise when he pops up again as a friend request on social media, where Pete has posted a story about his dragon, which misquotes some scientists. This is physically possible—Pete can post a picture of a friendly dragon and a pseudoscience quote and some conspiracy statement about how you don't have to believe him, and you can simply "remain terrified, question nothing, and stay at home."

Blatant lies and misinformation do not immediately self-destruct if you post them (although it would be nice if they did). We could just tell Pete that we are supposed to ask our beliefs about the experience they predict. While this should easily resolve the situation, Pete's problem that his belief in Puff the magic dragon runs much deeper. Problems of this depth are not so easily "fixed."

Being a rationalist, you are perplexed by all the attention Pete's post is getting and why someone name Karen would repost it, saying, "Don't let science cover your mouth and mute your voice #PuffTheMagicDragon." It is not hard to connect the belief of a dragon to Pete's bedroom's anticipated experience. The straightforward thinking should be: If you believe there is a dragon in Pete's bedroom, you can expect to open the bedroom door and see a dragon. If you do not see a dragon, then it means there is no dragon in the bedroom. In this case, seeing is believing. Daniel Dennette, a cognitive scientist whose research centers on the philosophy of mind and science, has researched this exact problem. Dennette shows us that, although it is often hard to believe in something, it is often much easier to believe that you "ought" to believe in it.

From all this, we get to a point where we can really say that Pete anticipates as if there is no dragon in his bedroom, but he makes excuses because he believes in the belief of a dragon in his bedroom. Secretly, Pete does not want to give up on his belief in dragons. If he questions this belief, he will be giving up his self-image as a person who believes in dragons. Pete does not have to explicitly think "I want to believe in my dragon Puff in my bedroom," he only needs to stop himself from the prospect of admitting he does not believe. After all, what would all of the other dragon believers and followers think of him if he questioned the reality of dragons? Pete's culture, history, life, and community are all contingent on the belief in dragons. It's rooted in our youth: sometimes, it's better to get along with others than be right about something.

The problem with Pete and people like Pete is *how* they believe in beliefs. If Pete, or anyone else like Pete, believes in their belief in the dragon, and they also believe in the actual dragon, this problem is much easier to solve. If this were true, they would confidently state and prove it through experimental predictions. This means they would also confidently commit to giving up their belief if the empirical predictions are wrong. Therefore, we know that when something like this happens, and an individual like Pete makes up excuses ahead of time defending his belief, it would seem pretty obvious that their belief, and their belief *in* the belief, are terribly out of sync.

We have many other false belief problems in the history of our societies and cultures around the world. Many years ago, when someone had a severe ache in their mouth and head, they would see a witch or a fairy who they believed would cure their pain. Sometimes it worked; other times, they died. Thanks to science, we now have accurate beliefs—we simply remove the wisdom teeth in a clean environment to prevent infection, and people no longer need to die from an impacted molar. The more we shift away from made-up, inaccurate beliefs and toward accurate beliefs, the more accurately we can anticipate what will happen in the real world and prolong humanity.

The next hurdle reveals a deeper problem. Many beliefs only require people to commit to manageable efforts of self-deception to overlook their belief in beliefs. Most cultures have not fully addressed the purple elephant or the invisible dragon, nor have we made up ideas that these beliefs cannot be proven or disproven. When something is believed for generations, it sticks without question, even though it should be questioned. Some of these concepts have been disproven historically, but many of the beliefs have changed and are still not accurate, yet we persuade children at a young age to join the belief in beliefs.

This is how people can use fake beliefs and spread them through "profession and cheering." This is when, with no substance or truth, an individual stands up in front of a group of people and confidently flaunts false statements. This isn't unlike holding up a sign of your favorite sports team. This sign is nothing more than an attempt to persuade; there isn't an ounce of "truth" to it. All these cheer fests are littered with blanket statements designed to cue the audience on when to clap, cheer, and scream. How do you know when you're learning new information versus cheering for no reason? Try a reversal test:

Suppose this speaker says:

"We need to stop violence and crime in our cities." … crowd cheers.

Now, we reverse this statement, and we get:

"We shouldn't stop violence and crime in our cities."

The second statement sounds unusual; therefore, the first statement is probably normal, which implies that it does not convey any new information. Sure, "we need to stop violence and crime in our cities" could be used to introduce a discussion topic or highlight an important proposal for such ways of doing so. But if no specifics follow the statement, this is probably a useless applause light. But basing our beliefs and political views in the same way we cheer for our favorite sports teams makes no sense.

Auntie Karen –
Why Facts Don't Change Our Minds

Sometimes people don't want to hear the truth because they don't want their illusions destroyed.

— Friedrich Nietzsche

How do we deal with the misinformation that our aunt Karen regularly posts on social media?

Both sides, Right and Left, have their dogmatic extremes. Let us avoid our confirmation bias in only interpreting this information as something only the "other side" does (not us, never us!), or as another attack on "my side" or "my views." Social media is a nearly infinite amplifier of misinformation and fake news, but we know it is not OK to spread beliefs built on bad information. We also know that we are entitled to our beliefs so long as they are not factually wrong. You jump off a 300m cliff naked, you die. You rape and kill someone, you go to jail. You may not believe in science or gravity, and you may not believe in our laws of rape and murder, but those wrong beliefs do not matter. For some reason, somewhere along the severity spectrum of wrong beliefs, this assertion tends to fade.

This acceptance of incorrect beliefs also seems proportional to governance. Governance directly affects the speed false beliefs are published. At one end of the publication spectrum: peer-reviewed literature, a long and rigorous process requiring extensive governance to remove bias so it can confidently state and prove the findings through experimental predictions. This process is equally committed to changing previous beliefs if the experimental predictions are wrong or new findings or information is presented. Peer review is not perfect, but it is the best we have available to publish accuracy. The problem? It's slow.

In the middle of the spectrum, we have our news and media outlets. Each outlet has varying degrees of credibility and biases—they are as accurate as possible while being swift to the scoop. On the far, other end of the spectrum from peer review is social media. Anyone can publish anything at any time, immediately. It's fast, but it's rarely accurate. The average person spends far less time reading peer-reviewed scientific journals, if any at all, compared to the time spent scrolling through social media. Also, peer-review journals are often behind academic paywalls, and social media is as free as can be.

When we see misinformation, we want to correct it—this is the deficit model. The next step assumes a rational person will consider new information and change their beliefs depending on the presented strength and accuracy. This is where our saying of "knowledge is power" comes from. But the processes aren't the problem—people are. If we could simply correct misinformation with facts, fake news and propaganda would go away. Research from George Mason University suggests that in some cases, correcting falsehoods on social media about topics as the Zika virus can be effective. The effectiveness of these corrections come from the algorithms that suggested related links around the issue or from a personal connection. The researcher showed how "information from friends might have a greater impact because we trust those closest to us." Just because you trust someone doesn't make their beliefs correct. The researchers explain that "if you are somebody who is willing to believe in conspiracies, then you are not affected by corrective information." These individuals, right or wrong, buy into the misinformation wholesale.

The deficit model fails when it comes to misinformation because it assumes we are all rational and our beliefs are correct. Research out of Yale suggests that scientific knowledge is not as important as conforming to cultural values, something we call "cultural cognition." Often, individuals who share and spread untrue facts and stories associate strongly with a partisan position or narrative. Through misrepresentation of information, fake news aligns with how they see both themselves and the world. When they open their social media feeds and see an individual sharing a post of fake political news, their confirmation bias blinds them as they attempt to reinforce their existing perspective. At this point, fact-checking friends or connections often result in an unfriending or unfollowing of some kind.

Or better yet, Aunt Karen goes off the deep end and has a complete meltdown on social media.

When we fact-check Aunt Karen, even with the best of intentions, she sees it as an attack on the core of her identity. To her, we're not presenting facts and data but asking her to change how she sees herself as a person. By fact-checking Aunt Karen, you start a deeply personal fight, not taking part in an objective debate. And you're doing it online, in public—far different than shutting her down intimately around the family Thanksgiving dinner table. Aunt Karen is basing her real-world decisions and actions on her beliefs, and your challenge presents an emotional argument that challenges and threatens the very meaning of who she believes she is. This happens to everyone, not just Karens, no matter where you are on the political spectrum.

Do we invest time and resources to correct the false beliefs, or do we simply ignore and "unfollow" them as a means of blocking them from influencing our rational beliefs? Studies of online persuasion from the University of Texas at Dallas show how posts go viral when they make individuals angry, disgusted, or alarmed. So, do we fact-check and correct the Aunt Karen's of the world or not? As of right now, there does not seem to be a clear answer. Partisanship is part of this problem, and we also know that individualistic political identity is especially addictive to many.

Although unfounded and wrong, misinformation is stickier in individuals' minds, making it even harder to correct. New research in cognitive psychology from the University of Western Australia found that corrections on social media can change individuals' minds regarding some of the fake news. Unfortunately, this does not seem to have a lasting effect. In research investigating how people process misinformation and how they update their memory when the information they believe to be true turns out to be false, this has been called the "expiration date of corrections." The studies have shown that although people like Karen might really believe and be willing to say, "Okay, that's true, this is false," if you test them a few weeks later, you will find they are already regressing to their fake beliefs.

It's not just a matter of embarrassing Karen online. Misinformation gets dangerous. Fact-checking Aunt Karen for her posts on how we should charge our smartphones in the microwave to prevent the 5G standard for broadband cellular networks responsible for spreading COVID, a disease invented by Bill Gates. Microwaving her smartphone becomes an embarrassing, expensive, and explosive experience for her. Still, she is unfazed because, obviously, all corporations and mainstream media are part of the conspiracy and out to get her. The real problem is that through complexity, human biases and wrong beliefs get much worse. Aunt Karen blowing up her smartphone in her home can seem funny, but some deep drivers are still at work. The same drivers that convince extremists and nationalists to share bomb-making manuals online or racist conspiracy theories justify systematic failure of the past or terrorism designed to take advantage of weak people and create homicidal tendencies in them. Misinformation in our complex age provides a foundation ripe for disaster. These are not the waves we should be riding.

Machine vs. Human Decisions

The truth of it: Algorithmic and machine-supported prediction outperforms what human experts can do in just about every capacity. Analytical models remove common human errors and biases, weigh all data evenly and objectively, and can process massive amounts of data reliably and accurately. Just about everything humans make predictions on today is handled more accurately by models. In a study conducted to better understand our legal and political system, researchers developed an analytical model to assess Supreme Court decisions. They applied their model to a Supreme Court term while also asking eighty-three legal experts for their predictions. The analytical model predicted the court's findings 75% of the time, while the legal experts were only correct 59% of the time.

Courts can be reasonably objective to the interpretation of the law. How about something more subjective, like the quality of wine? Although it seems subjective, the quality of the wine is heavily influenced by the environment the grapes are grown in, and environmental conditions are, in fact, data. To little surprise, computer models far outpaced human experts in predicting the quality of a vineyard's output. Although my French heritage might tell me how this would *never* be the case for French wine, computers have no incentive to lie when it comes to wine!

If computers have predictions down to a literal science, what the hell are humans still good for? While riddled with issues, our brains still have quite a bit to contribute—so long as we're not asked to predict anything. Analytical models underperform compared to humans only when the goal is to create action or influence an unknown or undefined goal. Analytical models usually fail when a decision must be made to create action and influence outcomes. In a rigorous study of golf on judgment and choice, two groups of golfers' perceptions and influence were altered. An analytical model would tell us that 54.8% of all six-foot putts in golf are sunk when no visual aids are used. None of my friends were part of this data set; they couldn't sink a six-foot putt into a sinkhole, much less a putting green. They reran this test on two different control groups without physically altering the hole or distance for either group. The first group was given visual aids to change the perception and increase their confidence; the other control group was given nothing—the golfers using visual aids sunk 50% more putts than the unaided group. Analytical models could not predict that visual aids would increase golfer confidence, but humans can.

We have the data, and we have strong algorithms that can do a lot with the data, but like the human brain, these predictive models have their limitations. These data analytics may seem handy, but remember that humans are often forced to make decisions when information and data are lacking or in non-predictive situations.

Most of what we know about decision-making is from experiments in a laboratory setting where people act without outside influence. Analytical decision models are accurate in predicting things they do not influence, such as court cases or the quality of wine vintages. These experiments are designed to make a choice; so long as the options cannot be altered, researchers can create reliable studies and isolate cognitive mechanisms of judgment. Altering options would give us an incredibly wide range of answers instead of well-ordered sets of comparable and analogous data. We often hear people only finding value in comparison when they are comparing "apples with apples." As a result, apples create a problem. Most of the research on choices gives individuals an isolated selection between options, which does not take into account any external influences or the complexity of our world. Going back to making dinner plans with my wife. Even if she claims seafood sounds delicious, it won't matter much when she opens Instagram and scrolls over a beautiful, new, healthy Thai restaurant that just opened around the corner. Even if I pick the best seafood restaurant ever, I'd still pick wrong.

The ratings on Yelp don't matter if we aren't predicting outcomes. When it comes to dinner plans and spurring action, the human brain comes in handy. Creating action is one way we make decisions that help us navigate competition strategically. Real-world actions change outcomes. In an excellent study that tracked a cyclist's average speed on stationary bikes, the individuals pedaled as fast as possible for four kilometers to establish a maximum speed baseline. The researcher then conducted biking trials in front of a monitor showing the cyclist their present effort versus their baseline maximum speed. This researcher was a little trickster, though, and unknown to the cyclist, for some of the subjects, the visible baseline max speed was randomly increased by 2%. The findings showed that 88% of the cyclists who were unaware of the increase could exceed their anticipated maximal effort by drawing on a metabolic reserve to match the deceptive baseline. This research showed how manipulated data impacts the way we make decisions and ultimately influences the outcome. Predictive analytics would never have imagined a case where the cyclist could put up faster outputs.

For stuff to happen in our lives, we need to exert influence. We outperform our competition by making most of our decisions in fundamentally different ways than what we've studied in the past. In life, performance is relative; we just have to do better than the competition—meaning you might have to make decisions without all the required information. We can purposefully make decisions that are not optimal for us but damaging to our competition, giving us a longer-term gain. Maintaining a competitive advantage over time is much harder today than in the past. We are losing our competitive advantage and regressing to the average faster than what we saw in previous generations. In a hypercompetitive environment, decisions can be a matter of survival—the difference between failure and success, or the difference between a promotion or demotion, or choosing to eat seafood instead of Thai. The decisions vary in size and network in with other decisions (both yours and others). It is in these decisions that we manage how we keep ourselves in the barrel and optimally transcend and transform into the future.

The Waves of Disruption

You might be tempted to try to make decisions in your life based on what you know has happened in the past or what has happened to other people. You should learn all that you can from the past; from scholars who have studied it, and from people who have gone through problems of the sort that you are likely to face. But this does not solve the fundamental challenge of what information and what advice you should accept, and which you should ignore as you embark into the future. Instead, using robust theory to predict what will happen has a much greater chance of success.

— Clayton Christensen

Disruption is a byproduct of our surfing framework. When our life systems are pushed out of equilibrium, either on purpose or by accident, we ultimately change and are allowed to grow. Some disruption is more obvious than others. Sometimes you will see the general direction of it, other times you will rely entirely on your surfing framework as you pioneer through entirely new terrain created in the moment.

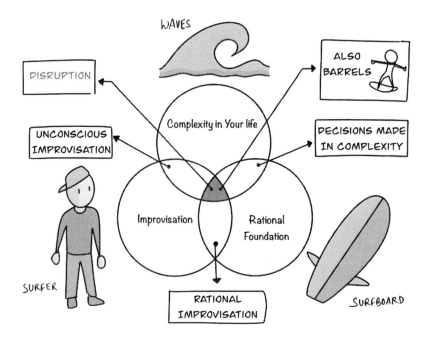

Understanding disruption is like finding the best place to surf. It helps us avoid paddling into suicidal waves or surfing shark-infested waters. The overlapping middle of the three pillars of the surfing framework is the byproduct of disruption. These coming waves demand our focus as they will push our limits like never before. The surfing framework invites us to be excited about the oncoming waves of the unknown instead of fearing them. To onlookers, these waves may seem super gnarly and even death defying. But to us, they are the moments we live for, as they allow us to drop into the zone and let our trained instincts take over. The next thing we know, we are surfing along in an automatic reaction in the face of disruption. We adapt and ride more waves, catching the best ones and allowing them to propel us forward. Whatever the case, you don't want to wipe out and be left in the impact zone.

"I've learned life is a lot like surfing. When you get caught in the impact zone, you need to get right back up because you never know what's over the next wave..."

— Bethany Hamilton

The waves of disruptions are like science; it is happening whether you believe in it or not. If you don't address it, face it, and ride it, you'll be left behind. Welcome to the Fourth Industrial Revolution—disruption is the new normal, and it's getting faster.

Disruption starts long before we see it. Consider Blockbuster and Netflix. For most of us, the fall of one and rise of the other seemed instantaneous. But looking through the history, there were specific and intentional actions and decisions that happened long before the public noticed. The surfing framework allows us to see these disruptions before they are surprises. The byproduct of disruption emerges at the intersection of our surfing framework as a transformational lever to transcend into our futures.

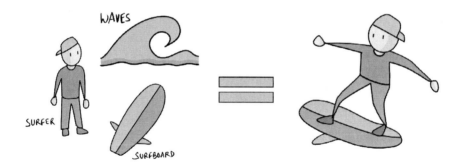

Disruption occurs in three ways: sustainable disruption, low-end disruption, and new-market disruption. Innovation is frequently the driving mechanism of disruption, and companies sustain innovations by improving existing products for their loyal customers. In other words, expanding existing profit centers. I have been fortunate to speak with and learn from legendary disruption expert Clayton Christensen who simply states that the goal of sustaining innovations is to create "better products that you can sell for better profits, to your best customers." Can this same mentality be applied to everyday life? The innovation of the self? We go to school and read books to learn and hone our skills. We hit the gym to train our bodies to be faster and stronger. Anytime we are working to make a better version of ourselves, we are sustainably disrupting our previous selves—albeit with little risk.

Low-end disruptions are just how they sound: the disruption that works its way up from the bottom. In this case, your competitor's profitability improves as they move upmarket; the problem becomes that once they do so, they lose the capability to remain competitive in their previous market, hence the name. You are disrupting from the lower end of the market to pursue profits. As a company matures, it moves on for better offerings and margins, ultimately opening the door to disruptors after them. You win by entering at the bottom of the market and pursuing the customers the current leaders have abandoned. For a maturing company to work their way up in the market, they have to let go of their lower-value customers.

Imagine we had a company that manufactured a particular type of surfboard for reef breaks that attracted some of the best surfers in the world as our customers. Just the pros, the ones who need high-caliber boards, don't bother with anyone else. They pay top dollar for our surfboards, and we made great margins for our top brand of boards and sponsor all the pro surfers and events. Now imagine there are these hobbyists who start making these much-lower-quality shortboards for beach breaks. There are not any pro beach-break events, and the nut jobs who ride these neck-breaking waves regularly snap their boards in half when they crash; they would never pay big bucks for our pro-quality surfboards. We can barely keep up with the growing demand for our top-quality pro surfboards, and we make four times more profit per board than the company previously mentioned. Although we are currently the top surfboard company, we have fierce competition from the number two surfboard company making pro boards. We need to use our 4x margin to continually reinvest in sponsorship and make minor tweaks to our pro reef break boards to justify our increase in prices (sustainable innovation). Every time we fail to sponsor an event or improve our product, our competition gains on us.

Now, picture this surfer named Clay coming up to us and saying, "Dude, you need to step back, reinvent your product process, and make crappier, smaller boards and sell them for cheaper." Quite the dilemma. Why on earth would we turn down our pro surfer and top-dollar customers to make lower-end, crappy surfboards? Ones with slimmer profit margins that would only sell to a bunch of nut jobs who surf them into the beach when they wipe out and snap them in half? The answer seems obvious to be "no," but that is also where the problem lies—within this moment of complexity, our preprogrammed minds make decisions that pull us out of the barrel.

Low-end disruption offers a product deemed "good enough" and targets a customer base that is generally "overserved" while leveraging a low-cost business model. You find this in markets where existing products offer more performance than what most customers can currently leverage. Going back to our example above: weekend warriors who surf beach breaks over their lunch do not need the latest pro-model surfboard that weighs five grams less and costs an entire month's rent. They just need something good enough to catch a bunch of waves before they eventually eat it and snap their board. There's a need for low-end disruption, but what happens if we avoid or ignore it?

Let's say we ignore Clay's advice and keep making the world's most expensive surfboards. A little company learns to make surfboards at a fraction of our cost. Lower quality, sure. But eventually, the high-quality compounds that go into our boards get cheaper, and soon enough, the beach-break boards are just as good as ours at a fraction of the cost. In an unexpected shift, this little no-name company starts to make pro boards that compete directly with ours! Since their production methods are seven times cheaper than ours, they can afford to sell the same quality board (or better) at half the cost while also paying twice as much on sponsorship than what we can afford. There's no coming back; it's a wipeout. We've priced ourselves out of the market we built.

The low-end disruptor is the hungry, hardworking, young up-and-comer. Their lack of experience makes them inherently cheaper. But they can also be smarter, harder working, and carry more potential. This is how the high-potential internal employee works their way up to displace their superiors. Good companies get this, and bad companies do not. This is why we see good companies invest in potential instead of only performance.

New-market disruptions target "nonconsumption," or the customers who lack the finances or skills to purchase and use their offerings. Initially, this type of disruption and innovation initially provides much lower performance, taking the position of "something is better than nothing." New-market disruption creates new customers and eventually pulls customers out of the previously established markets into this new market, while low-end disruption simply increases market share.

For example, Kodak. What ultimately disrupted them was the smartphone, which created an entirely new market and drew away most of Kodak's customers. It is important to point out that this disruption is about a new offer that is only "disruptive" relative to what already exists. Obviously, many of the things we have today did not exist in the past. Kodak did not lose to other camera competitors; they lost to the entirely new smartphone market. VHS lost to DVD, but it was streaming that ultimately killed off the DVD player market. Proving, once again, that once something has been digitized, the potential for exponential growth arrives.

Watching how disruption works helps us map it back to where it resides within our surfing framework and how it applies to our lives. Defining and further understanding the application of disruption adds lenses of clarity through which we can now view the Fourth Industrial Revolution. Disruption is an opportunity long before it is ever a threat. Trying to replicate the best and brightest is no longer a recipe for success. Disruption routinely shows us that warning signals rarely come from the top. To identify, protect ourselves from, and leverage disruption for our own benefit, we have to remember the key takeaways. In summary:

Disruption is our friend. In the world we currently live in, disruption is almost always an opportunity far before it is a threat of any kind. We need to embrace disruption and not try to avoid it in life. Although it might feel counterintuitive at times, we should paddle toward the waves, not away from them.

Always look for disruption. We can use our surfing framework to approach and capitalize on disruption. *But* we must begin to improvise and innovate while our core is still strong. When everything is going perfect in our lives, that is when we start to innovate and look for disruption to capitalize on it. We do not want to wait until we are on a downslide, in the gutter, in the valley of despair, and when everything is going wrong in life. We look to engage disruption long before this point.

Do not force them to work together. We must allow disruptive efforts to run separately from our core efforts.

Look down and in different places. In business, we are reminded to look for disruption by observing opportunities at the bottom of the market. Disruption very rarely comes from above. Look at what different groups of people are doing—your younger siblings and colleagues, for example. It is not about keeping your head up this time. It is not about doing things the way they have always been done, embrace diversity, and learn from different means.

Do not get distracted. We can protect ourselves and our efforts from disruption by making sure we understand and focus specifically on what we are trying to solve or achieve. It is important not to lose our focus on what we are trying to solve or achieve, despite the speed at which life pulls us in many different directions.

This understanding of disruption is foundational in diagnosing what we can and cannot do in our own lives. It helps us prioritize our efforts, time, money, and resources to grow and build our future capabilities. Disruption, which occurs at the intersection of our surfing framework's foundational pillars, will help guide our intuition to identify opportunities quickly and determine which operations are critical to focus on. Understanding disruption allows us to highlight what order to complete our tasks, attempt them at all, or possibly outsource the effort. From these concepts, we will manage our strategy as we paddle into the waves of disruption. This surfing framework helps us objectively take data and turn it into information, and we can use this information to build knowledge. How we turn this knowledge into wisdom in our daily lives is up to us.

Surfing Barrels

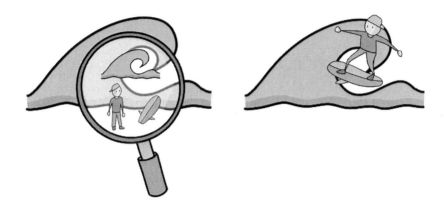

Our world places us at the center of an extremely complex system with constant additions of emerging information, forcing us to react quickly. Improvisation helps us ride the barrel. But we must rationally improvise through this space. In addition to heuristics and biases that bring about mental shortcomings, we also need to be aware of our beliefs and emotions and how others might feel about certain circumstances. Some research even suggests we should pay attention to how old we are. Who doesn't have that relative who is stuck in their ways? To little surprise, some research shows how cognitive biases may increase as cognitive flexibility declines with age.

Which factors or beliefs do you give too much credit to? If we acknowledge that we are not neutral in our thinking, what relevant information are we ignoring because it does not align with our views? Ask yourself what percentage of the opposing political party's platform you agree with. If you immediately answer "none" or "very little," you likely have a lot of work to do in unbiasing your beliefs. Part of this change means adopting a mindset of critical thinking. The decisions we make right now will shape humanity's future. How accurately can we anticipate what the future holds? How will our choices today determine humanity's success moving forward as we surf the waves of disruption building along the horizon?

Our surfing framework helps us be aware of how to navigate the disruption that emerges through the barrels of our life's complex systems. When we talk about disruption, it is usually regarding an industry, company, product, or service. Disruption is aligning more and more with progress, but industries, companies, products, and services on their own don't disrupt; ultimately, humans do. Humans are fundamental for disruption. When we make individual actions at the micro level, we see disruption emerge at the macro level.

So how do *we* adapt and grow? How do you intentionally cause disruption in your life?

For starters, we look for the barrels. We find this complexity in our lives by looking for pressures we feel, both perceived and real. Does this mean every time we feel the pressure, we are in the barrel? Of course not, therefore, next we look for the right type of pressure. Is this pressure forcing us to try something new or create a new relationship? Is this pressure because we believe we are right but worry someone might prove us wrong? Are you in a situation where you have no choice but to figure out a solution? This is the pressure we look for, and this is how you know when the barrel is creeping up on you.

For example, anytime you are attempting something new in life—it could be a new workout, a new job, a new project, friend, date, you name it—it's an opportunity to disrupt. When you start the new thing, growth seems slow, even negligible, but you understand this is how disruption starts. Knowing this gives you the understanding to not get discouraged and give up. Maybe you changed professions, and you're in your new job. Your goal isn't to be the best at your job overnight but to slowly get better over time. As you put in the time, hours, days, weeks, months, your daily growth will be more noteworthy than your established colleagues, who already know how to do many of these new things you are learning. You also apply new ways of doing and thinking about things from your past, and soon you are at the level of your colleagues. Eventually, you even pass them. At this point, you can kick your feet up and get comfortable, or you can start hunting for the tension again. Where is the next barrel? The next disruption? The more comfortable you get using this approach to everything in your life, the more successful you will be as a disruptor.

Keep in mind: Being in an uncomfortable situation doesn't mean you have to shy away from your strengths. Rather, leverage them to enhance your current progression. Your strengths tend to be instinctive; they help you improvise and adapt to the moment. For example, if you grew up surfing, you might have always thought, "I've surfed my whole life, what's the big deal?" when it comes to riding big waves. To someone who has always wanted to surf but never learned how, they would find that incredible and may really value that. The point here is that often we overlook our strengths. Often, few of our superpowers make for a line item on our LinkedIn profile. At times, we overlook our strengths because they come easily, naturally, unconsciously.

We need to identify our strengths and build off of them or fall back on them when needed to ride the barrel. The strengths are what you do better and more instinctively than anyone else. Find out what they are and own them.

For example, the script wasn't finished when Steven Spielberg started filming *Jaws*. Carl Gottlieb, a writer on the project, said, "Let's do the best job we can with the resources we have. It was not a big-budget picture." As filming began, Gottlieb removed many subplots from the initial novel, adding humor to the script, and ultimately made the characters appear more human and relatable. Spielberg brought Gottlieb on set to help further tweak the script, including when they wanted to improvise. Nothing went right during the filming—casting took months, the boats kept filling up with water or rocking too much to get a good shot, and most importantly, the mechanical shark constantly malfunctioned. With a film way over budget and schedule, Spielberg felt the pressure, the kind of pressure we now identify as the barrel. The movie's most iconic scenes in that film were all around the malfunctioning shark. Improvising around the faulty set piece, Spielberg decided to shoot the scenes from the shark's point of view and added on John Williams's now-classic "duuuunnnn duun... duuun-nnnnnnn dun dun dun dun dun dun dun dun dun dun" score. The rest was up to the viewer's imagination. Spielberg later admitted that "had the shark been working, perhaps the film would have made half the money and been half as scary." The film was given a $3.5 million budget and a fifty-five-day shooting schedule. Ultimately, it cost about $9 million and took 159 days to get the film in the can. This is a nice reminder that disruption isn't always pretty and has plenty of negative side effects. Regardless, *Jaws* was the highest-grossing movie of 1975 and remained one of the most financially successful movies of all time. Embrace the pressure, turn it into a creative tool, and see where the shark takes you.

Since we are not all Hollywood producers with Hollywood-size problems, we can look at a more relatable situation. For example, you might find a job posting and push yourself to apply and compete for it if you feel it is worth your investment. Although you might feel this pressure, it is not overly disruptive. Now imagine a second example where you identify a problem at work. You could work to persuade and convince those in a position to create this new job to solve this problem. In the first situation, you are challenging yourself; we could call it sustainable innovation. You will only get a posted job if you already have many of the skills, nothing new, but possibly building on your past experience. There is well-established demand for the need. If you don't get it, someone else will. The second option is creating something entirely new. Disruption theory states that those who create truly new market disruptions are six times more likely to succeed. There is no clear competition; there are no predetermined expectations, just uncharted water and waves.

Can the surfing framework make you less busy?

If you feel your day-to-day is already beyond capacity with obligations in life and work, you are not alone. It also does not mean you can't surf barrels and disrupt this life and business. Using complexity and our surfing framework, we understand that to disrupt ourselves on a macro level starts by disrupting on a micro level. So you find a way to give yourself a little more time to think differently. Maybe you get up ten, fifteen, twenty minutes earlier, skip checking your phone, and use this time to meditate, think, create, or explore something different. Or maybe you give up the one to two hours of Netflix and replace it with something just as relaxing that allows you to think more. Maybe you go for a walk; maybe you read a book, perhaps you do anything other than look at your phone. Maybe you play chess. Maybe you write a book. Disruption author Whitney Johnson says that you should "look for opportunities to play where other people aren't playing, where other people don't want to play. You will be surprised how many opportunities come to you when you're willing to play in those unusual places."

The surfing framework is exactly that, a framework. It does not prescribe or lay out specific sequential steps. It is designed to empower and establish an understanding that lends way to its creations. No two waves are the same; no two moments or situations in life are the same. Sometimes you find yourself amongst waves, and you must surf them. Other times you force the decision and actions in life that cause you disruption to put yourself in the middle of better daily surf and force waves. Everything in your life, your connections, your body, your brain, is unique to you. Having a one-size-fits-all approach or answer to the future simply makes no sense. What gives us the best chance to surf the future of disruption coming our way is a framework, which acts as a foundation and mindset ideal to understand and capitalize on disruption favorably. As each of us does this on a personal, micro level, the macro emergence is the disruption of humanity. What does this look like on a global scale? With our surfing framework in hand, this compass excites us as we look, with slight discomfort, into the waves coming tomorrow.

This surfing framework creates the ability to dream while pragmatically addressing the realities of the moment so we can shape our future. The most significant changes in humanity—the tens of millions of Africans displaced by slavery, India and Pakistan's division, the scattering of tens of millions of Europeans from the world wars—have all been caused by either economic, political, or religious agendas and conflict. And disruption on a daily and technological level is about to bring waves unlike what we've seen so far. How we navigate and surf these waves will come down to how we individually engage these monster walls of water. From all our interconnected and interdependent actions and decisions, we will form a collective consciousness. We will pragmatically dream up seemingly impossible solutions to impossible problems.

Cheat Sheet – Surfing Framework

> *I also have to be able to think ahead of the curve a little bit. You have to see where things are going and be able to kind of predict that, or at least go in that direction.*

— Kelly Slater

Surfing Framework

The surfing framework, broken down into three steps, with each step composed of four components:

1. Look for barrels.

2. Improvise to keep yourself in the barrel.

3. Use your surfboard as a rational foundation for everything.

Step One: Always be looking for barrels. The barrels in our life are identified by any one of the following four components of pressure:

- A need for new and novel solutions.

- New partnerships and relationships.

- Healthy conflicting perspectives.

- Interdependence of working together as the only option for success.

Step Two: The surfer must always be improvising and working to keep themselves in the barrel as long as possible. Always leverage the four principles of improvisational decisions:

- Spontaneity. Go with your gut.

- Say "Yes, and..." Always accept ideas.

- Always be listening.

- Leverage those around you.

Step Three: Make sure you use your surfboard as a rational foundation to stand on.

- Be aware of cognitive biases and work to notice bias.

- Be aware of rational beliefs, understand fake beliefs and belief errors.

- Don't be like Auntie Karen—let facts change your mind.

- Remember the strengths and weakness of both machines and human decisions.

PART 4: TOMORROW

Oh, the places you'll go!

— Dr. Seuss

As the saying goes, if in doubt, paddle out. We build plans to avoid and minimize disruptions in our lives; we often work hard to navigate away from them and sometimes even ignore them. As we trek deeper into tomorrow, we now see and value disruption as a process we must embrace. With our well-understood surfing compass in hand, the book's latter parts discuss the world we are fearlessly paddling out into and what it has in store for us. Understanding the megatrends coming in the Fourth Industrial Revolution helps us connect these initiatives to our daily decisions and actions. This deep technological change will reshape our values and ethics. We are at the center of it all. More than any other time in history, it will be the collective actions of individuals that will shape humanity's future. A future laced with massive rogue waves of disruption.

Disruption is the byproduct of emerging changes that exist at the center of our surfing framework. These moments of complexity excite us as we aim to ride the greatest waves ever seen or experienced by humanity. As we continue to build off the digital revolution, we continue to see massive advancements in computing technologies and power, creating entirely new possibilities in areas that we have yet to dream of. We will see shifts and entirely new distributions of power through secure decentralized technological ledgers; many forms, such as blockchain technologies, are already operational. For better and worse, we are becoming more connected through the IoT that is reshaping most of our fundamental interactions. This exponentially expanding new data economy we reside in will force us to rethink how we value and characterize the ethics around data. Oil is no longer our most valued resource. Data is. This shift alone could cripple entire economies, and many established countries are fighting the transition. The extension of digital technologies will create the greatest advancements and opportunities ever seen by humanity. Unfortunately, they will bring incredible new risks, which, if not adequately addressed, can be more devastating than most previous disasters we have created or encountered.

Tomorrow's disruption will occur right before our eyes and under our noses—the way we see our world will continue to change drastically. As we continue to progress and advance our knowledge, technology like artificial intelligence will reshape our physical world. This will be further amplified by the convergence and game-changing advancements of existing and new materials that will allow us to design and create products in ways that we never imagined. New-market disruptions, in the form of additive manufacturing, will remove many of the current physical limitations and will open what will seem like an endless canvas of new opportunities.

Also, for better and worse, and regardless of your thoughts on them, drones are here to stay.

As the blurred boundaries of advancement amongst these technologies continue to evolve and converge, drones will gain more momentum and applications as the cost of advanced materials decreases. The progress of AI opens up boundless opportunities for cheap, tiny, autonomously connected intelligent flying machines. As we imagine and create these life-changing and world-saving applications, we have to remember that humans have a less-than-perfect past of unethical and dangerous inventions. Without proper proactive governance, progress can lead to problems.

Just as it has before, technology will be the underlying factor in everything that changes in the near future. What makes this era of change different from the previous ones is that we are changing the human experience. Throughout history, the human has been the constant. No longer. Biotechnologies will redefine the human experience and our connections with the natural world. This is a topic that causes much discomfort and concern amongst many individuals, and so it should. There is an incredible opportunity in this advancement, creating better living standards globally, forever altering how, or if, we lose loved ones to disease or old age. As we continue to model this future and pioneer this new space, we understand biotechnology is unpredictable.

Then, even amid unpredictability, we will shift our thoughts from biotechnology to neurotechnology advancements. As we continue to understand better and leverage the human brain's incredible potential, we can continue to augment better ways to capitalize on and extract the data and information that resides in our brains. Understanding extractions allows us to heighten our senses and completely rework and shape our behaviors and interactions. The continuous breakthroughs in neurotechnology will further advance our understanding of the human brain, directly improving our treatment of brain diseases, brain trauma, and brain-related injuries. This will also allow us to restore or repair an individual's moods and behaviors, as well as alter consciousness. As we get into the data, we'll see more breakthroughs in our understanding of how we make decisions and possibly resolve our issues with cognitive biases. Tomorrow, we will understand ways to retrieve broken pathways to trapped memories and have ways to bypass damaged parts of the brain and understand potentially damaged areas and fix them before they become problematic. There is incredible complexity not just in the technical aspect of neurotechnology but in all surrounding components of it. The reason conversations around this topic cause high levels of discomfort to many, and rightfully so, has to do with the endless number of ethical concerns and dilemmas it creates.

Using our surfing framework, we identify this uncomfortable space as something that will cause significant disruption—we must confront and discuss it. These ethical concerns will continue to create many major legal concerns. It will also rewrite our laws in everything from how we created value to how we approach privacy and everything in between. We will see massive disruption across all our industries and societies, but biotechnology, and specifically neurotechnology, will be at the forefront of human transformation.

There was a time not that long ago in our history when the concept of applying braces to straighten our teeth, implanting fake breasts, or dyeing our hair would have seemed insane. Many of the everyday things we take for granted today would have blown our previous generations' minds. Humanity never voted for braces or breast implants or IVF; it just happened. As we continue to alter the one thing that makes us fundamentally human, we will ultimately redefine what it means to be human more than any other time in history. Bio- and neurotechnologies must remain at the forefront of our discussions as they continue to redefine our understanding of what it fundamentally means to be human. If we avoid this discomfort, which is key to our surfing framework, we could wake up one day in a world of vegetative human bodies wired to computers, living in a digital world.

As we continue to increase the quality and length of our lives, we will equally continue to contemplate and advance our understanding of how to better leverage technology to shape, reshape, and even restore parts of our macro environment in which we reside. This era will transform how we create, capture, store, and transmit energy to power our world as we know it and future versions of the planet with new inventions. There are already many efforts around geoengineering, which opens many questions regarding how we manage and implement laws at a global level versus the national regulations we work with today. Geoengineering would allow for some areas of our globe or even specific countries to have a better climate and environment while causing byproducts and outcomes that could devastate other parts of the world. We no longer only focus on our world, but all worlds, as we are well on our way to mining asteroids. In October of 2020, the OSIRIS-REx NASA spacecraft, about the size of a large van, successfully reached down and grabbed material from the surface of an asteroid. This mission launched in September of 2016 and aims to return the asteroid fragments back to Earth for examination in 2023.

Who ultimately owns the materials in these space rocks? What power do nations have in the jurisdiction of space? Aside from all the incredible technological advancements and progress in space exploration, there is a mess of variables to consider. Things like: Who owns Mars? The first person there? First country? Or is it the first private organization that gets there? What effects does colonizing other planets have on our planet? What impact does it have on our solar system or galaxy?

We still have much work to do in fixing our current world problems. Understanding these is still very much problematic; we shift our focus to more existential dilemmas that challenge and threaten the human race's survival. As the developed world evolved through the first three industrial revolutions, our current Fourth Industrial Revolution's megatrends are a new threat to our existence. Of all the megatrends converging and colliding, an evolving form of nonbiological intelligence is giving way to incredible advancements in humanity, and at the same time, is of grave concern. We are innovating and disrupting intelligence as the highest form of intelligence on the planet. For the first time in history, we are disrupting ourselves, not only the environment around us like in previous eras.

Fake Fears

Fear causes hesitation, and hesitation will cause your worst fears to come true.

—Bodhi (*Patrick Swayze in* Point Break)

Fears. Sure, we all have them. At times they are rational, sometimes, not so much. Over the course of humanity, fear has grown as an evolutionary safety mechanism and is responsible for much of our survival throughout the centuries. But today's fears should not be the same as those of yesterday, and this will be much truer come tomorrow. The world of tomorrow, like today, will still have pain, sorrow, and suffering. But let's be real…

The Surf is Getting Better Every Day

Take a moment to ask yourself, is the world getting better?

For most of the people on the planet, they do not believe it is getting better. Research from Our World in Data created a survey asking 18,235 adults across various countries the simple question: All things considered, do you think the world is getting better or worse, or neither better nor worse? In Sweden, 10% felt the world was getting better; in Denmark, Finland, and Norway, 8% felt better. In America, 6%, Great Britain and Germany 4%, Australia and France 3% of their populations felt the world was getting better. The time frame from which an individual is using to answer this question can be in question. Are we considering thirty years back, fifty years ago, or 200 years ago? Regardless of the time frame, for the most part, most of us do not *feel* the world is getting better. The world, on average, is getting better. Our media is usually preoccupied with reporting singular events and data points, with a primary focus on things going wrong.

Reporting on slow developments over time with very little change each day, week, or month, even though it is reshaping humanity, does not make for engaging headlines.

Yes, there is suffering today. There is work to do and there are problems to solve, but the world is a better place. I promise. We have technological advancements to thank for this. For much of our time on earth, life was terrible, nasty, gnarly, barbaric, brutish, disgusting, and any other terrible adjective you can think of. Additionally, for most of humanity, life was short. You'd be lucky to reach thirty or sleep on a bed.

Things aren't worse today. Chances are, you're just bored. Let's look at what has improved in the last few hundred years, thanks to industrial revolutions.

Extreme Poverty. If we look at UN data from 1820, during the First Industrial Revolution, the number of people living in extreme poverty was 89.15%. In 2015, this was closer to 9.98%, meaning 90.02% of the world no longer lives in extreme poverty. Although extreme poverty is an extreme measure—meaning we have lots of work still to do for those living just above a global definition of extreme poverty—it is incredible progress. Dr. Roser, a University of Oxford researcher who focuses on growth and inequality, helps explain how incredible this achievement is. He highlights that over this time frame, the world population has increased sevenfold. Growth of this magnitude should have driven the entire world into extreme poverty. Instead, we have thrived in the exact opposite direction and given more prosperity to more people worldwide. This was possible because of the technological and scientific advancement of the previous three industrial revolutions, increasing productivity and making essential goods accessible to more people. This productivity resulted in more output with less input—getting more for working less. By these metrics, since yesterday, 130,000 people were lifted out of extreme poverty. You don't hear about this in the news because it would be the same headline every day for the past thirty years.

Literacy. When building off prior knowledge of previous generations, literacy proves to be an essential benchmark. Once again, in 1820, the number of literate people over fifteen years of age was 12.05%. In 2016, the number of literate people over the age of fifteen years was 86.25%. If you are born today, the odds are pretty good that you will be literate. Literacy is a foundational element of how we grow and build knowledge. In 1820, there were roughly 100 million literate people who could contribute to the knowledge tank. Today, there are roughly 5.4 billion.

Health. In historical research on child mortality rates, prior to the First Industrial Revolution, about 50% of all children died before their fifth birthday. Conditions were so bad that the First Industrial Revolution advancements only lowered this number to 43%. It wasn't medicine that improved this margin but increased health standards. Better living accommodations, sanitation advancements, and the evolution of social life brought about conversations about health-related issues. To augment our initial progress against infectious diseases was the higher productivity in agriculture and global trade, delivering a healthier diet to more people. As technology advanced, so did health and nutrition. We grew taller (seriously) and got a bit smarter—yet another boon to literacy.

Global literacy increases brought about more scientific and medical breakthroughs, further reducing death rates and increasing our knowledge of diseases. As we entered the Second Industrial Revolution, we stumbled upon germ theory, which led to doctors washing their hands between the morgue and the delivery room. Suddenly, children were living a *lot* longer. This discovery also unlocked the innovations and development of vaccines and antibiotics. These advancements are why child mortality has fallen from 50% in the 1820s to 3% today (and falling, still). There is still an incredible disparity in health levels across the world, a problem we could solve and significantly progress if given the right amount of focus, attention, and resources.

Freedom. At the simplest definition, freedom is the high-level concept in which you believe you are free to choose within the guideline set forth by your government. Your country is not great because you have freedom; many countries today are free. Or at least as free as our developed world governmental agencies lead us to believe we are. The Human Freedom Index presents the state of human freedom in the world based on a broad measure that encompasses personal, civil, and economic freedom in 162 countries. The Human Freedom Index 2019 revealed that the five freest jurisdictions are New Zealand, Switzerland, Hong Kong, Canada, and Australia. Some other countries ranked as follows: United Kingdom (14), United States (15) Taiwan (19), Chile (28), France (33), Mauritius (50), South Africa (64), India (94), Russia (114), China (126), Saudi Arabia (149) and Venezuela (161).

Population. Does all this progress mean we will overpopulate this planet in no time and must move to Mars sooner than even Elon Musk predicts? Not quite. There have been many incredible wins by humanity over the last three industrial revolutions. Increasing the population by seven times during this period should have been incredibly problematic, but instead, it is a story of incredible success. Before the 1st Industrial Revolution, an average woman gave birth to five or six children. Despite this, the population stalled because most of these children died before reaching reproductive maturity. The industrial revolution allowed humans to play God, as we had more and more influence on how and when people died. From this, life expectancy doubled in virtually every region of the world. Over this time, we still had high fertility rates, which was no longer offset by a high mortality rate—thus a global population boom.

Over the span of the industrial revolutions, the population boom has leveled off. This transition is happening through progress in women gaining more independence, education, and prosperity since their children's mortality rate has significantly decreased. This slowing of the population has gone from high birth and death rates to lower birth and death rates. Worldwide, women are having half as many children, and this transition happened in as little as ten years. The global fertility rate has decreased by more than 50% in the last fifty years, consistent with how the global population growth rate peaked about fifty years ago. The population will continue to grow, but not at an increased rate every year. As we left the Second and entered the Third Industrial Revolution, our global population quadrupled. In the twenty-first century, it will not even double. To some, the decrease in growth rate can seem alarming, but as we live longer lives than before, this naturally occurring phenomenon helps balance the global population.

Education. None of our progress through these last three industrial revolutions would have been possible without growing our knowledge and education. As a young boy growing up in Canada who did not love school and wanted to play in the NHL, stressing the importance of education can remind us of our parents and have a way of making us feel very old. It is also one of the most important metrics in understanding the success of the future of humanity.

The population growth from 1970 to 2020 has essentially doubled, after which it is expected to grow, but level off at a much slower growth rate. In 1970, about 2% of the population had post-secondary education, and 23% had no education. Several years from now, in around 2045, 17% will have post-secondary education, and 6% of the population would have no education. Projections show that in 2100, less than 1% of the global population would have no education.

Many of these trends are rear facing, but education is a trend that impacts the future. If we have more young literate people with access to traditional and democratized forms of education, it means we will have a greater population of world-changing minds. Younger people today are more educated compared to their older counterparts. As the older demographics "age out," they will be replaced with highly educated replacements. This will be essential as technology takes a greater slice of our lives.

Health, literacy, and education increase while poverty and child mortality decrease—the world is getting better! Yet despite this reality, humanity is still very biased in our attention as we focus on future threats to humanity.

Perspective of Fears

Of course, surfing can be dangerous. People also have a terribly skewed perception of danger. The kind of surfing you and I do is not inherently dangerous except for the little self-inflicted mishaps. The things you're afraid of are not as bad as you think they are.

Yeah, some say "But sharks, brah, sharks kill people in the ocean." You surf in the ocean. Sharks eat in the ocean—correlation, not causation. Most of us know that it is not as likely as our fears make it out to be, yet many still refuse to get out in the ocean with sharks. You are over ten times more likely to die falling out of your bed than dying in some shark's jaws. Tripping or slipping is way over thirty times more likely to be our cause of death. In 2014, you were twice as likely to die taking a bath than from a shark attack. Choking on your food, hot weather, and alcohol consumption will kill you long before a shark does. We do not even need to list how many times you could die just driving to the ocean before a shark gets you.

The pessimist could see this argument as misleading as it considers too wide of a data set. Let's narrow the circumstances a bit. What are the odds of dying from a shark attack while surfing in the shark-infested waters of Australia? Let us even remove surfing and look at any shark attack in Australia doing any activity—one in eight million. This should put you at ease, but watching a YouTube video of shark attacks resets your perception. Now you can't even put a toe in the ocean without a shark biting it off.

As we paddle out into the twenty-first century, we need to reset and understand the real dangers we face. Although still present in some regard, the fears that have motivated humanity for hundreds of years are no longer a significant threat. Despite this, many of these fears still motivate political agendas and the media, influencing irrationality on a large scale. As surfers, we have a responsibility to properly understand the actual risk versus the perceived risk we face. Yet most of us have jobs, we have families and friends or children to raise. Managing our day-to-day robs us of the mindset to properly dissect the noise and manipulation we face from the real threats we should be worried about. Much like today, tomorrow's reality does not care and will not wait for anyone to catch up. Some people are simple; they simply do not care and would rather not think about it. A small number of people are willing or fortunate enough to devote their lives to such topics. And for the rest of us, which make up the majority, we need to do a better job at balancing our lives and spending more time understanding how to shape our short-term outcomes to influence the future of humanity.

Our Fake Fear

How can the world be a better place when we have tensions hitting tipping points around systematic and cultural racism and discrimination, a global COVID pandemic that is running wild, continuous terrorist threats, countries at constant war, and some global powers even playing Russian roulette with nukes?

Evolution, especially human evolution, is driven by fear. The fear of starvation or not having water takes a high priority. Then we worry about not losing what we have acquired, not being enslaved or killed by others. Maybe then we try to absolve the fear of dying from infections, diseases, or the bitter cold. Advancement and evolution are born from addressing our biggest fears. The reality is the gravity of these fears are often misrepresented and politicized. Yes, food security and health and war are huge problems that need to be addressed, but from the existential viewpoint of humanity as a whole, these are no longer the greatest threats we face. What we need to fear today looks nothing like what we've spent the last thousand years being afraid of.

As our intelligence has evolved, we have become better at understanding and addressing our known fears. The problem is that fears that motivate us are no longer a threat to our survival. Politicizing these issues of fear is a built-in part of many cultures and societies; after all, no one is elected to address fears our grandchildren might face. They are elected mainly on what changes people feel they can make now; fear is the tool used to divide and control populations in every nation. This in itself is a dilemma for another day or another book. For today, we're afraid of the wrong things.

Before today, humanity faced three major problems that threatened our very existence: starvation, disease, and war. Although these are still problems today, they are not existential ones. In fact, these problems have reached the other end of the spectrum. People eat too much and die from diabetes. More people die from old age than a disease. More people die from suicide than those killed through crime, terrorism, and war combined.

See? We are afraid of the wrong things.

Hunger and starvation. In previous eras, events like bad seasonal droughts would quickly kill off 5–10% of entire populations, usually more. In 1690s France, bad weather ruined harvests throughout the country, and almost one-sixth of the population died from starvation between 1692 and 1694. In 1695, Estonia experienced a similar shortage of food and lost 20% of its entire population. In 1696, Finland also experienced a famine that killed 25–35% of its inhabitants. In 2010, obesity killed three times more humans than starvation and malnourishment combined. In 2014, over 2.1 billion humans were obese versus the 850 million humans who were malnourished. By 2030, 50% of the human population is expected to be obese. Sadly, somehow, millions still go hungry every day. We have millions living below the poverty line, and despite this suffering, most of them will not die from starvation.

Yuval Noah Harari accurately claims "There are no longer natural famines in the world; there are only political famines. If people in Syria, Sudan, or Somalia starve to death, it is because some politician wants them to."

Disease. Although many of us have lived through SARS (2002-2003), bird flu (2005), swine flu (2009), and Ebola (2014), it was COVID-19 that impacted, infected, or killed more people compared to most of the modern diseases. In the past, many of us feared and watched pandemic threats from the sideline as they ravaged underdeveloped nations. The spread of infectious diseases has threatened the existence of humanity for a very long time. While epidemics are still a problem and devastating, they are not the same threat as they once were. The downfall of politicizing infectious diseases will cause more damage than simply following our understanding of infectious diseases to curb their spread. Viruses often jump out to a head start, but we eventually catch up to them with science and sound judgment and curb their impact before they spread to an existential issue.

Having recently lived through a pandemic (although it is currently ongoing at the time of this book's writing), we can review some historical facts to support why infectious diseases are not the existential threat they once were. Way back in the 1330s, a famous epidemic erupted, often referred to as the Black Death. It originated in eastern or central Asia and spread through a bacterium called *Yersinia pestis* that lived within fleas. While the world was less connected, it still killed off 25% of the European and Asian populations. In England, 40% died, and cities like Florence saw their population drop by half. While historical records from this era were shaky, it has been calculated that some 75–200 million people lost their lives. It's a scary plague to talk about, but it is by no means the most deadly we would experience.

As the first European settlers landed on North America's shores, they brought many diseases from which the local population had not built up immunity to. The early Europeans ran around North America claiming anything they wanted, however they pleased, including the Natives. The invisible infectious diseases ended up killing off up to 90% of the indigenous population. On March 5th, 1529, a Spanish fleet of ships bound for Mexico left Cuba. One of the slaves amongst these ships broke out in a rash we would come to know as smallpox. By December of that same year, Mexico's native population decreased from twenty-two million to fourteen million. Smallpox was only the beginning. The Spaniards went around, claiming and spreading, looking for gold and leaving the flu and measles. Within fifty years of arriving at Mexico's shores, the native population was less than two million people. The threat continued in 1778, when British explorers landed in Hawaii—then home to 500,000 indigenous people who were isolated from America's and Europe's problems. This initial voyage brought the first cases of the flu, tuberculosis, and syphilis. A few more European expeditions added typhoid and smallpox to the mix, and by 1853, a mere 70,000 locals resided in Hawaii.

Our ancestors lacked the scientific knowledge to understand or address the threat of disease. What we know as smallpox may as well have been the possession of a magical demon. Malaria was thought to be contracted through "swamp fumes." It was very much an existential threat, but we had no tools or frameworks to navigate it. You just sorta hoped you survived it with prayer.

Even as we advanced humanity into the twentieth century, infectious diseases still impacted entire populations around the globe. As our science advanced, so did our transportation networks. These transportation networks moved around much more than just food and supplies. As war broke out on the front lines of northern France in 1918, a deadly strain of the flu appeared from an undetermined region of the world. Thousands of soldiers suddenly fell ill and died; within a few months, a third of the world's population contracted this deadly virus—we know it colloquially as the Spanish flu. In places like India, it killed fifteen million people (5% of the population at the time); in remote areas like Tahiti's island, it killed 14% of the population. In less than twelve months, the Spanish flu epidemic killed somewhere between 50 to 100 million people—more people than all the battleground casualties of the First World War.

Until the beginning of the twentieth century, children were especially susceptible to disease due to the lack of developed immune systems. Until the early part of the last century, one-third of all children in the world died from infectious diseases or malnourishment. Currently, the child mortality rate is the lowest it has ever been in history, less than 5% worldwide, and less than 1% in the developed world.

Mainly due to a politicized response to the Coronavirus pandemic, many feel that infectious diseases are not a threat of the past. There is no doubt that it is a real problem, and we must get better at managing and responding to these global threats, but again, these are no longer threats to our existence like they were in the past. Just by reviewing case studies of smallpox, Ebola, and AIDS, we see how humanity has fared much better against even deadlier infectious diseases.

In 1967, the smallpox disease had infected fifteen million people and killed two million. In 1979, the World Health Organization (WHO) reported a global vaccination initiative to eliminate smallpox. By 2014, there was not a single human that was either infected or killed from smallpox. We can eliminate disease with science.

When the 2014 Ebola outbreak first emerged, it ravaged western parts of Africa and seemed completely out of control. A month later, the WHO was attacked and criticized for the poor management of the outbreak. Reports blamed the pandemic on the inefficiency of the WHO's Africa branch and corruption within this division. Like any other organization, the WHO is not immune to corruption within their circles. Despite these attacks, after following scientific evidence and implementing swift and strict measures and actions, by 2015, Ebola was under control. By January 2016, Ebola was curbed. In what could have been one of the deadliest pandemics in human history, instead, the death toll from the Ebola virus was around 11,000 people.

Presently, pandemics only get out of control because of poor leadership and political agendas. Although the initial impact on humanity and our economies can be devastating, we know science and intelligent minds eventually prevail. We can catch up to the infectious disease and curb it, at times even eradicate it. Global problems can't be addressed differently by individual nations, as we have witnessed with COVID-19. Political agendas confuse and decrease visibility into the issue, and the reliability of media only confuses what the general public needs to know to protect themselves. The general public has been trained only to see end results, and seeing the process of science unfolding in real time (which is how science works) has proven problematic. We do not notice change as it happens; we only know it once it is done.

Anything less than facts and hard truths immediately comes across to many as deceptive or wrong in a politicized environment. How can a scientist change his mind when presented with new information? Clearly, he does not know what he is talking about, right? Wrong. Science prides itself on changing its mind. Sound, scientific rigor is built off learning from errors, considering new evidence, and constantly improving methodology. Too much of the general population is unfamiliar with this process, and watching this unfold in real time, for the first time, simply comes across as a governing body having no clue what they are doing.

Sound scientific rigor does not account for, or even consider, opinions or political agendas. Although bias may be present, proper research identifies and accounts for believed sources of bias to neutralize it; it is not sound research if they do not. We live in a time of immediate gratification and feedback. A process that changes over time as we narrow our focus and increase our understanding can feel very disconnected.

Science and research cannot use opinions, thoughts, hope, or luck as a method. The publication of research is slow because other leading researchers in the field need to blindly review it to ensure no manipulation of the information or bias. Our politics and media are not built in the same manner. All the while, infectious diseases will keep getting stronger, mutate, and become less or more resilient. The good news for humanity is that our knowledge and science will also get better, and technology allows us to act much faster. Infectious diseases are a problem, yes, but nowhere near the humanity-ending issue they once were.

Violence. War, terrorism, and violent crime have been so prevalent throughout history; it has been the rule to which peace is the exception. Why is peace always so temporary? The media, of course, loves to cover violence, so it's as good a moment as any to remember that we are living in the least violent time in human history. Despite political parties using outdated tactics to create fear and division amongst their citizens, it is still a far cry from the threat violence once was to humanity. Long gone are the days when nations regularly stormed and slaughtered entire villages as they took over a nation. What we once knew as war—lining up on a battlefield, digging trenches, years-long sieges—are now but a chapter in our history books.

Of the fifty-six million people who died in 2012, only 0.01% of the deaths were the result of violence—a mere 620,000 deaths. Of those, only 120,000 were the result of war; the rest were violent crimes. In the same year, there were 35% more deaths from suicide than all violent deaths combined. Twice as many people died from diabetes complications than violence in 2012. In 2016, 31% of all deaths worldwide were from cardiovascular diseases brought on by tobacco use, poor diet, and obesity. You're more likely to die from your personal choices than you are from violence.

During the First and Second Industrial Revolutions, technological advancements and inventions brought about agricultural and transit progress that met people's basic needs. Fewer people were going hungry, but 15% of all deaths were still from human violence. We've come a long way in the last century, dropping violent deaths down to only 1%.

Of course, these are large data sets that look at extensive periods. What about all the violence we see and hear about daily? It feels like violence is on the rise recently, but the numbers still indicate otherwise. A 2019 global study published by the United Nations Office on Drugs and Crime (UNODC) highlighted that compared to the 464,000 homicides in 2017, only 89,000 died in armed conflicts—both numbers down significantly from 2012. This highlights violent deaths from crime and war are significantly down from 2012. Feel like I'm cherry-picking favored data to prove a point? Let's look at homicides in the last twenty-five years, which gives us a more extensive yet very relevant sample. Yes, homicides did, in fact, increase from 395,542 in 1992 to 464,000 in 2017. However, the global population outpaced this increase over the same time frame—meaning the chance of being murdered has still declined over the last twenty-five years. No matter which way you slice it, the world today is a safer place today than any previous time in recent or past history.

And, oddly, war is safer than it has ever been. Why shoot a musket when you can launch a nuke? And since nukes are so powerful, and there's not another planet to move to just yet, the world's most powerful nations have made a pact not to use their nuclear arms, since no one wins and we all die. This is not to say in less-developed parts of the world that still have material-based economies, like the Middle East and Africa, war is still not a problem. The high-level work is needed, but the existential threat is minimal.

One of the primary functions of most governments is to keep their citizens safe. As the threat of violence continues to decrease, a government's ability to mobilize the masses and shape behavior through fear also decreases. As a whole, the idea of government is about citizen control. The fact that we are more likely going to kill ourselves through our poor dietary choices than war or violent crime is a little unsettling. What does a government do when its primary function of protecting its people is obsolete? When fear doesn't do it, bring on terror. Terrorism is very much real and has found a way to take up vast airtime and overrun media coverage. Terrorism is not an existential threat, but not in the same violent sense as war or murder. With politicized agendas and unfounded media claims, the show of terrorism haunts our dreams as we imagine all the terrible violent ends we may face. Terrorists have no moral obligation or compass when it comes to using weapons against innocent civilians. Many governments worldwide use terrorism as a platform to amplify military spending to "protect the people." Fear has returned, but does this fear have any foundation? Governments have made firm statements, changed policy, injected massive amounts of capital, and displayed force and strength, as they feel the need to respond to terrorism. Whatever it takes to remind their populations they are safe.

How much of a threat is terrorism, really? In 2010, 7,697 people died from terrorist violence. In the same year, three million people died from obesity. While the number of terrorism-related deaths varies from year to year, it is still nominal on the global scale of death. Terrorist violence is very much geographically determined. For example, in 2017, 95% of all terrorism-related deaths occurred in the Middle East, Africa, or South Asia. Yet public concern and outrage around terrorism can be very high, with surveys showing that over 50% of the citizens worldwide are concerned about being victimized. This fear is driven entirely by political and nationalist agendas and the media's disproportional representation of the issue. Outlier years create disproportional spikes, like the 9/11 attacks on New York City and Washington D.C. that claimed around 3,000 lives. Still, terrorist deaths on US soil account for less than 0.01% of all deaths annually. Outside of the three highly concentrated regions previously mentioned, terrorist attacks are extremely rare. No matter where you are in the world, your health choices are more likely to kill you than anything else. Your politicians want you to believe otherwise.

This is not to downplay the innocent lives lost through senseless killing conducted through cowardly acts; it is to point out that you likely have no reason to live in fear of terrorism. Terrorism is used by those who lack power as a way to weaken our resolve without ever having to strike us directly. The fear terrorists inspire does more damage than their explosives ever will. Terrorism only works when they can get their enemies to respond, and even then, the response needs to be an overreaction. The overreaction to terrorism is a significantly bigger safety threat than the terrorist acts themselves. A major reaction to a small attack only breeds a bigger reaction down the road. We try to show force, but we end up showing where our weaknesses are.

Imagine a terrorist as a fly buzzing around in a China shop. On its own, the fly cannot budge a single bit of dishware. Not even a little bit. Instead, the fly finds the bull. They get inside the bull's ear, the bull gets scared, annoyed, and angered. Voila! You have a raging bull in a China shop. You might not even need a bull. Just the shopkeeper swinging around a fly swatter is likely to cause more damage than a fly buzzing around. Compare this to the Islamic religious fundamentalists who had no chance of ever overthrowing a powerful dictator like Saddam Hussein. Instead, the fundamentalists infuriated America with the 9/11 attacks, and the USA reacted by destroying parts of the Middle East. Now destabilized, the fundamentalists are thriving in the wreckage of whatever is left behind. There is no fine china left to buy, and the fly is still buzzing about.

Still, globally, terrorism is a relatively nonexistent threat to the whole of humanity. Now, if that fly in the above example was instead a mosquito, your chances of dying from a mosquito bite are hundreds of times greater than dying from a terrorist attack. Mosquito bites are responsible for more than a million deaths annually. It is not the bite itself that's the problem, but the risk of malaria transmission. Terrorism is disgusting; any form of it is wrong and must be stopped. The power terrorists have is only amplified by our perceived fear of it. Terrorism isn't going to end humanity, or even you, but the reaction to terrorism just might.

After Our Fake Fears

The industrial revolutions worked to solve the large-scale existential threats to humanity. Machine production in the First Industrial Revolution led to the creation of steam engines, which led to locomotives that built vast distribution networks for supplies and food. The Second Industrial Revolution ushered in the age of science and mass production, helping us understand the spread of infectious diseases and the diseases themselves. The Third Industrial Revolution brought us semiconductors and mainframe computers, which led to personal computers, smartphones, and the internet. This digital revolution flattened much of the world through newly established distribution networks essential for spreading information. The First and Second Industrial Revolution advanced our weaponry so quickly that nuclear bombs put an end to the era of conventional world wars. As we continue to advance and build on all these inventions, we will continue to minimize the risk and impact of our existence's previous threats. Everything, expected and not, that comes with the megatrends of the Fourth Industrial Revolution will only further resolve these problems. What we've feared to this point will be obsolete. What then?

The emergence of technological advancements and innovation is creating a new existential threat that humans must deal with. We must move on from our perceived existential threats to addressing actual existential threats. Food shortages won't wipe out humanity, but the inventions of the Fourth Industrial Revolution might.

You might rather starve to death than face the potential threats posed by artificial intelligence.

We've gotten this far because of our potential for intelligence. Every generation overcomes challenges thought impossible by the previous generation because of our intelligence. This is why the most pressing threat any of us will face in our lifetime is a new form of intelligence. It's not sci-fi; this is a growing reality. Better understanding this new form of intelligence is not only essential to our survival but will be vital to shaping our short- and long-term futures. This is much more than the humanoid robots Hollywood loves to play with; it could be an invisible, cloud-based form of artificial intelligence. It could be a human who has augmented their brain through a wireless connection with endless amounts of digital storage and exponential computing power. Regardless of the exact form, a monopolistic form of singularity can occur. This will be the endgame for humanity unless we address all of the ways AI can be catastrophic. The early stages of this change are underway right now. This is the time for the conversation.

For the first time in human history, we are advancing and creating technology that will force us to reconsider human ethics in developing new applications. Every new ethical dilemma forces a reconsideration of our values. Some of these recent mindset shifts might require us to take a more global, humanistic approach for the good of humanity as a whole. To solve some of these problems, we will have to move away from some of our self-centered and traditional patriotic values inherited from a time and a world that no longer exists. Changing others and other things is fundamentally much easier than disrupting ourselves, yet this remains one of our most important growth areas. We will need to be proactive in our agreements and perspectives on many of these dilemmas. Our values will help shape our ethics, and it is our ethics that will drive our regulations and laws. As a global community, we must work together to redefine our ethics around the current and future technological developments. When considering these ethics, we must have as many people as possible, with as many views and opinions as possible, involved in the process. Without any technical prowess whatsoever, we only need a basic understanding and education around the concept and topic and a clear open mind with a selfless focus on humanity.

Conceptualizing Artificial Intelligence

The eventual form of nonbiological intelligence (not if, but when) will give way to incredible advancements and matters of grave concern at the same time. We are disrupting the very idea of intelligence, human intelligence, which we have known as the highest form of intelligence on the planet. For the first time ever, we are disrupting ourselves.

Artificial intelligence has already started to replace human judgment and decision-making, which we have never discussed ethically. The discussions that have taken place were around developing AI systems as objects, meaning they were meant to be used as tools. However, the ethics around our current AI development impacts our privacy, issues of surveillance, the new ability to influence and shape human behavior, and overall transparency into these systems we now share our world with. How should AI systems interact with humans? What role does automation play, and how will it affect employment? Do we fully understand the ethical implications of autonomous systems like self-driving cars, drones, boats, and even autonomous weapons?

Then, after all that, what comes next? The day after tomorrow will bring new dilemmas on how we should address ethical concepts for the evolution of AI systems as subjects, the ethics of the AI systems themselves, instead of the human ethics around how we use the AI systems as objects. Go a step further: What do we have to say about the AI that AI creates? Yes, a form of superintelligence way beyond any current living human's capacity with their comparatively meager, organic brain architecture. What does this very-possible singularity mean for the future of humankind?

We think of an AI system as a machine that has nothing to do with us, or maybe it is just an extension of you. Much like how your smartphone is an extension of your humanness, accessible through touch and voice commands. This may not always be the case. As we learn more about the brain, we can wirelessly remove the middleman (the smartphone) and connect you and your brain directly to the digital world: all the same functionality and none of the inefficiencies of having the device. You could talk to someone (in your mind) anywhere in the world the same way you ask Siri to FaceTime someone. For what is about to come, you must open your mind to the idea that the current AI systems we use as objects and tools may soon fully integrate with the human experience. What are the ethics around how we develop these tools and how the result will transform or disrupt our lives? Ethics around how humans should use smartphones can sound logical, but the smartphone's ethical responsibility makes less sense. Phones are objects; therefore, ethics do not apply to them, just to how we use them. The ethics of advancing certain technologies will lead us into a deeper discussion of ethical considerations for technologies, like AI systems themselves as subjects. We might not be noticing all the changes from artificial intelligence happening all around us, but the rogue waves of tomorrow are ensuring it will happen.

Rogue Waves of Tomorrow

The only consistent thing in our life is change, and this accelerating pace of change is, in itself, accelerating. The development of artificial intelligence is going to accelerate exponentially. The megatrend of the Fourth Industrial Revolution is sitting on top of the current exponential computing power growth. Furthering all this amplification are these exponential technologies crashing into and converging with other accelerating technology, creating overlapping waves with the rogue power and unpredictability that have the potential to wipe out everything in its path. The collisions and convergence of disruptive technological waves are accelerating into tomorrow. We want to imagine these changes will hit us in 100 years, maybe fifty. But they're coming tomorrow.

Tomorrow. As in, the impact could show up with the delivery of tomorrow's newspaper.

Among all this acceleration of exponential technologies is the specific rogue wave of artificial intelligence, building on the horizon and threatening our existence. Yet, through complexity, we know everything is interdependent and interconnected. Predicting the emergence of how these rogue waves will arrive and in what order is impossible, but being prepared for them is not.

The advancements in quantum computing outline a significant step-change in the acceleration of computing power. Many of our current networks are being augmented and accelerated with quantum computing capabilities. We first had 3G, then in 2010, we had 4G, now we have 5G. To put that in perspective, 3G would download an HD movie in about forty-five minutes, whereas 4G would do the same in about twenty-one seconds. Our current 5G would download this movie in less time than it took to read the previous sentence.

Networks. Advances in networking technology allow for companies like Google to fly massive 12m x 15m balloons over remote areas to provide for LTE coverage, like a hotspot cloud or a cell tower in the sky. Each balloon provides about 5000 km² of coverage from nearly 20km in the sky. Google's plan is to have thousands of these balloons in operation around the world to create a web of continuous coverage around the entire planet—and they could do this *tomorrow.* Last spring, Amazon announced Project Kuiper, an initiative to build a low-earth orbit satellite constellation capable of providing reliable, affordable broadband service to unserved and underserved communities worldwide. Amazon plans to invest a modest $10 billion into this project. In June of 2020, the Federal Communications Commission (FCC) granted Amazon, through a unanimous vote, permission to deploy and operate a constellation of 3,236 satellites. In case anyone hasn't noticed, Elon Musk is one step ahead. Space X has a four-year head start on Amazon for this same project. In pure Musk fashion, never wanting to be outdone, Space X had already started to deploy its 12,000-satellite network in 2019.

Grow the network, and you can grow the number of devices connected to the network, which means you can increase the number of sensors connected to that network. There were about fifteen billion devices in 2015, each with numerous sensors (your smartphone has about twenty different sensors onboard). We predict nearly 500 billion devices, with dozens of sensors per device, by 2030, making for a $14.3 trillion economy. It is baffling to consider how far we've come with our digital sensors. In the 1960s, we guided rockets with sensors weighing fifty pounds and costing $20 million. Today, that exact same sensor is in your smartphone. It weighs less than a grain of rice and costs all of four bucks. There are sensors in everything—clothes, glass, even farms. Tomorrow, the sensors will move from the world outside us to the world within us—nano-sensors exploring our guts. Today, there is smart dust; although it is currently the size of an apple seed, it can sense, store, and transmit data. But soon, they will be the size of a speck of dust, working their way through our bloodstream as they gather information about our health in a way our doctor has been dreaming of. We are about to learn a lot more about everything. The exponential data coming from the sensors are more than we can conceptualize in our linear brains. An autonomous car produces a terabyte of data a day—the equivalent of 500,000 songs or 600,000 pictures on your phone. Commercial airliners produce forty terabytes a day, smart factories a petabyte—a million gigabytes—every day.

Imagine how much data a smart city could capture with a trillion sensors?

Most of us won't see this coming; others may not bother to care. But what does it mean if your annual physical is replaced by continuously updating, real-time, quantifiable self-data? This will free up doctor talent to address life-threatening issues instead of checking up on healthy people. Preventable deaths—heart disease, strokes, cancers—would drop to nothing.

Sensors in a field of crops are already assessing air and soil moisture against weather forecasts (which are becoming far more accurate), allowing farmers to use water more efficiently and grow durable, more nutrient-dense crops.

In business, agility will become the most prominent key differentiator. Knowing everything about the customer has obvious privacy concerns, but it will force companies to adjust to the customer's needs to maintain a competitive edge.

By tomorrow, everything will be in a constant state of measurement. For better or worse, tomorrow will force a world of openness, achieved through exponential revolutionary transparency. We will understand and monitor everything from the end of the cosmos to the bottom of our oceans. Everything from our surroundings and products to the inner workings of our bloodstream. Even our skin produces an endless amount of sensory information that can turn into data points, not unlike the blanket of humanity that makes up our nations. Like it or not, we live on a hyper-conscious planet that is about to get super-duper hyper-connected.

VR and AR. The exponential growth of sensors will crash into neural nets powered by artificial intelligence, fueling the cloud transformation. This cloud is colliding into a mounting flock of skillfully nimble and increasingly intelligent robots. All of this is happening today, and it is just the beginning of what will come tomorrow. This megatrend will continue to advance the virtual (VR) and artificial realities (AR). We will see AR in our classrooms, as students will have the availability to explore virtual objects in virtual worlds. We will see AR in our streets and cities. Not just for our vehicles, but for us. We will simply look at a building and experience all of its histories in real time. Retail will go into full hyper mode. Our contact lenses will show us what's for lunch, how much it costs, the best ratings, and what entrée will optimally nourish us compared to our blood type and what we had for breakfast. VR and AR will work into our training and simulation on how we use certain equipment on the job. We already see this in museum tours and in the real estate market, where property tours are augmented with cell phones. Surgeons can see inside bodies to find clogged arteries, and medical students practice performing surgeries on artificial bodies with an augmented overlay. This is only the start of what VR and AR can do in our everyday operations.

3D Printing. The reality is that the previously mentioned budding waves of disruption will only grow as they collide and create the rogue waves of tomorrow. Certain megatrends coming our way do not have the day-to-day visibility, but they will still revolutionize our tomorrow. Take the quietly growing technology of 3D printing. Many of us do not have 3D printers; many of us have no printer at all. Printing on paper is a thing of the past, but 3D printers are different. For example, shipping supplies from Earth to the International Space Station costs about $1,000 per pound. Enter the 3D printer. Back in 2018, an astronaut in the International Space Station broke their finger. Instead of ordering a splint and waiting several months for the delivery, they simply printed it. They looked up a blueprint file for a splint, loaded it into the 3D printer, and printed out a splint for the broken finger. No need to waste payload space to store spare parts; get what you need printed on demand. Not just in space, but anywhere.

Although 3D printers are not yet a household product like our smartphone, they are equally as revolutionary to humanity for other reasons. Aside from printing full colors, we can also print in hundreds of different materials like plastic, rubber, metal, glass, concrete, and even organic materials like cells, leather, and chocolate. Yes, chocolate printing is revolutionary for all sorts of reasons, but 3D printing is getting cheaper by the day. Today, we can print anything from complicated jet engine parts to entire apartment complexes to circuit boards and prosthetic limbs. What makes this truly disruptive is that it removes all inventory and supply-chain dependencies. Transportation networks, stock rooms, warehouses, and other intermediaries—all removed and replaced with the exact thing you need, printed at home. 3D printing threatens the entire $12 trillion manufacturing sector. In the 2000s, these printers cost hundreds of thousands of dollars, today they cost under $1,000, tomorrow they will be even cheaper than a smartphone.

In 2010, we could print blood vessels. In 2018, hospitals could assess, measure, and fit the patient with a prosthetic in under a day—for just twenty dollars. Today, companies can print, at record speed, any branching blood vessel that makes up our body's biological network. We even have 3D printed kidneys. Today, these successful advancements are why 3D printed organs are expected to hit the market tomorrow, by 2023. This technology is not only helping rebuild our insides but also the world around us as well.

In 2014, ten single-family homes were printed in under a day, each costing only $5,000. A few years later, a Chinese company built a fifty-seven-story skyscraper in under twenty days with modular construction, entirely from a 3D printer. That's convergence! In 2019, we merged 3D printing with robotics and material sciences to print single-family homes, which used one-tenth of the labor cost yet produced a finished home at a third of the cost of the industry average. With endless applications to our everyday lives, 3D printers will gain in popularity and be much more prominent in our lives tomorrow.

Blockchain. The idea of Bitcoin first appeared in 2008 in an anonymous paper published online by Satoshi Nakamoto. Whoever the author of this paper was, they presented a digital peer-to-peer payment system removing any need for a financial institution to facilitate the transaction. Bitcoin is built on blockchain technology, and there was no way of assessing the value of Bitcoin until May 22, 2010. Laszlo Hanyecz made pizza history by using Bitcoin in the first commercial transaction, paying 10,000 Bitcoins for two pizzas. The market value for the pizza at the time was approximately twenty-five dollars, rendering each of those Bitcoins to be worth less than a penny. At the time of this writing, just a little over a decade later, one Bitcoin is worth approximately CAD 51,000 (USD 40,000). Those ended up being some very expensive pizzas.

The power of Bitcoin is in the blockchain—a truly revolutionary idea. A blockchain is a distributed, permissible, and transparent digital ledger with seemingly endless applications—and disruptions. Since blockchain technology is permissible, it gives anyone anywhere in the world a place to store their money without the need for a central authority like a bank or government. With this, anyone can transfer money internationally without costly transfer and exchange fees. The intermediaries in money transfers are currently worth $600 billion and are based entirely on trusted money-transferring organizations taking cuts on every financial transaction that happens anywhere in the world. The waves of disruption building with blockchain threaten just about every industry. Companies like Lyft and Uber use blockchain technology to create an experience without the need for trusted intermediary companies. Along with validating identity, blockchain can also validate any asset and can determine if your newly purchased Jordan sneakers are originals or fakes.

In effect, blockchain is a smart contract (in the way we have smartphones or smart homes) that opens up a world of technology applications—for example, sports betting. To bet on any sport, you have to go through a trusted third party (like an online gambling site) to ensure the losers will be collected so the winners are paid. Smart contracts remove the need for this middleperson. With a smart contract, two individuals can wager on an outcome, and the blockchain-backed contract assesses the outcome of the bet and automatically moves the money to the winner. Since it's a smart contract, it self-executes automatically without the need for human involvement. The opportunity, and threat, of blockchain is very real and all around us. Massive organizations like JP Morgan, Goldman Sachs, and Bank of America have all created blockchain cryptocurrency strategies. In less than a decade, something that started with the sale of two pizzas has grown into a $176 billion industry and will exceed $3.1 trillion by 2030.

As we see these advancements in technology collide and converge, we are starting to see a hefty increase in the purchase of smart objects for everyday uses. What was once a physical item has transitioned to the digital and sits on blockchain technology, allowing for the creation of a unique object with the authenticity and scarcity of a physical product. Since objects are now effectively powered by AI, they learn and retain history. Imagine you buy a new pair of Jordan sneakers. Upon the purchase, you automatically get a digital copy of the sneakers on your phone. This digital copy comes with a video timeline that shows you the history of every piece of fabric in your shoe. Thanks to artificial intelligence, as the smart object developed, it learned to document its history along the way; it would not have been programmed to do it. Why does this matter? If you care, you now have proof that no part of your new sneakers was constructed using any form of child labor through a permanent blockchain ledger. Or that all aspects of your sneakers are original, which might come in handy when it's time to sell off your sneaker collection to pay for your blockchain-enabled college education.

Thanks to the AI-enablement of smart objects, these objects do not reside in a fixed location in the digital world and are free to move around and take on a life of their own. We can now gamify everything—for better or worse. For example, you could be hiking up a mountain wearing your smart glasses that reads you the region's geological formation history. Suddenly, a magical boulder falls from the sky on the path in front of you. The boulder has a code lock on it, with a few writing codes carved into the rock. Since you love programming and breaking codes, you engage the smart object, take some time assessing it, and ultimately crack the code. The rock breaks apart to show you a job offer from Google, and they would love to have you work in their encryption division. Any company could do this with any skill set or talent they are looking for. What appears as a game is a real-life interview, and only the best candidates for the job would win the game. The opportunities are endless. Smart objects will lead to blockchain breakthroughs and vice versa. There is no longer a divide between digital and physical, they are intermixed, and the outcomes are endless.

Material science and nanotechnology. The power of AI has helped map out hundreds of millions of different possible combinations of elements, giving us an immense database of potential elements and materials never once thought possible. Better materials lead to better devices. We have already enjoyed these advancements. If you were to build your smartphone back in the 1980s, the device would cost around $110 million, been fourteen meters tall (forty-six feet), and would need the power of 100 electric household boilers to operate. Thanks to material sciences' progress and their convergence with other technologies, we have exponential power in our pocket.

We have programmable hardware that can be designed to create more of whatever it is instructed to produce—even more of itself. When this technology bashes into material sciences, we now have this functionality on an atomic scale. This results in nanobots capable of breaking down and rebuilding any material, including soil, water, and even air. Although not fully available today, sometime tomorrow, we will be able to take a garbage pile, break it down at the atomic level, and reorganize it into food, shoes, or whatever we desire. Progress is still small, as all exponential progress is during the early stage. Still, we already see a steady increase in new nano advancements coming to market for us to experience. Today we have nanoscale fabrics that are stain and wrinkle resistant, meaning we never need to fold our clothes ever again. We have seen an influx of nanofilm that creates self-cleaning windows, anti-reflective glass, or windows that conduct electricity. While optimistic, solar panels are a recycling problem—they last ten years, and few of the materials can be reclaimed. But who needs them if we have a nano coating that effectively captures the energy from the sun on every window in the world? As this technology advances, we can simply paint our houses in nano solar-panel-like paint. Material sciences are why everything around us becomes cheaper, better, and lighter. We have light trains, planes, and automobiles; we have lighter surfboards, sporting protective equipment, tools, luggage, furniture—anything you can think to name is probably half the weight it was twenty years ago. The disruptive waves of material science have smashed into virtual reality. We have already created contact lenses with a resolution six times greater than our current smartphones for those who find it inconvenient to wear smart glasses.

We may not be noticing much of this change today, but tomorrow it will be everywhere. Nanobots don't just make things better: They make us better as we find ways to fight off cancers and terminal illness. A Harvard engineer recently found a way to program and store 700 terabytes of data onto one gram of DNA. Today scientists are working to extract carbon dioxide from our atmosphere so that tomorrow it can be turned into incredibly robust carbon nanofibers that can be used in any industry. Over the next ten years, there will be huge impacts from very teeny-tiny things. Within this grouping of tiny things is a particular extra type of material, *our* material. It is not how tiny nanorobots can fix us, but the robotics of our cells and genes that give us life. Our attention now shifts to how the waves of advancements in biology collide with technology in biotechnology.

Biotechnology. There is a disorder called X-linked severe combined immu-nodeficiency (SCID-X1), which causes children to be born with almost no immune system. This specific gene mutation means that normal infections are now life-threatening to those with this mutation. Some of you may know it as "bubble boy disease." On April 18, 2019, the bubble boy disease was eliminated forever when eight babies with the immune disorder underwent an experimental gene therapy. They went from no immune system to a robust one in the span of an afternoon (more or less, but they're all doing great). Today there are over fifty gene therapy drugs in the final phases of clinical trials, meaning tomorrow we will eradicate many more diseases in this same fashion. Gene therapy is exciting, but it is only a small part of a much larger disruptive wave emerging from biotechnology.

When the waves of biology explode into random waves of technology, we get biotechnology—using our biology as a technology. It's been halfway there for the span of human history. Our DNA is the software that defines who we are—our height, the color of our eyes, our personality, our predisposition to certain diseases, and how long we may or may not live. The software has always been there; now we understand it better. Knowing more about our software led to things like creating the Human Genome Project (HGP), which was an initiative to map and understand all the genes of human beings completely. It took a decade and a hundred million dollars, but it happened in 2001. Since then, the cost to sequence a human genome has decreased at a pace three times faster than what Moore's Law predicted. What took ten years and $100 million now cost less than $1,000 and takes a few days. In the next few years, companies plan to deliver more of the same for $100 in the span of an hour.

From the advancements in genome sequencing comes CRISPR-Cas9, a unique technology that enables scientists and researchers to edit our genome parts. It is currently the simplest, most versatile, and precise method of genetic manipulation, and best of all, it is cheap. In 2017, a group of scientists out of Oregon garnished some attention when they used CRISPR to snip out a heart-disease-causing genetic error in dozens of human embryos. This means tomorrow we may have designer babies. Editing the DNA of sperm or an embryo, known as human germline engineering, is another CRISPR application that is still controversial. Although some of us may still deem designer babies unnecessary, this same technology could mean removing cystic fibrosis and sickle cell disease from not just patients but all of humanity. Using CRISPR to modify immune system genes to prevent the human body from rejecting organ transplants means we would never lose loved ones to a long waiting list. It could also resolve organ shortages by allowing the human genome to accept organs grown in pigs. It only sounds gross, even grotesque, but things seem less icky when it is a life-or-death situation. In 2018, we successfully edited out muscular dystrophy in dogs. Tomorrow, CRISPR will not only change humans, it will also bring us new and improved fruits and vegetables. In the same ways of the past in which our invention of vaccines created new pathways to prosperity for humanity, CRISPR shows the same promise for tomorrow. People will have new treatments and no longer suffer from any number of cancers and blood disorders.

All of this amplifies what we can do with a stem cell. When we combine the power of all the previously mentioned techniques, stem cells become far more capable of delivering the solutions we need. Sometime tomorrow, we will have individualized medicine. Long gone will be the days of generic prescription and medical plans. Treatments will be fully customized to your genetic composition. It will be preventative care beyond our wildest dreams. You'll know the foods, supplements, and exercise regimes that are optimal for your health and longevity. Your diet will offset the microbes you lack in your stomach and reduce the ones you have too much of. You will know the diseases you are at the highest risk for and will be shown the proper precautions to prevent them and how to edit some of them out of your genes entirely. This would create a sudden spike in humanity's health, creating entirely new industries while obliterating many of the old industries of today. Tomorrow brings an era of incredible personalized medical care. Illnesses and diseases of previous eras will be an afterthought. With everything in life, more rewards often come with more risk.

Specific megatrends of this era, such as artificially intelligent systems, have already begun to replace human judgment and decision-making at both the conscious and unconscious level and the atomic level. There is currently not enough happening to develop new ethics around advancing such scientific and technological developments. The ethical issues of tomorrow must be discussed today.

We need to address the ethical concepts for the evolution of AI systems as a subject, meaning the ethics of the AI systems themselves, instead of the human ethics around how we use the AI. Decisions today will shape tomorrow and the day after tomorrow. This will define the possibilities around intelligence explosions and concepts of artificial general intelligence, leading to possible forms of superintelligence that are significantly beyond any current living human's capability with our existing brain architecture.

The potential is grand and likely too much for the average person to comprehend. AI systems can be a machine that has nothing to do with us; they could also be an extension of us or even a part of us. As it stands, it seems like our smartphones and a series of screens are the only things keeping our brains from connecting directly with the cloud—but should it? Why or why not? Before we go too far into the future, we need to review what we are doing today to determine tomorrow's ethical dilemmas. The ethics around how humans should use smartphones seems logical, but the smartphone's ethical responsibility isn't so straightforward. Phones are objects; therefore, ethics do not apply to them, just to our use of them. The ethics of advancing certain technologies will lead us to a deeper discussion of ethical considerations for technologies like AI systems themselves.

Tomorrow's Ethics Today

One today is worth two tomorrows;
what I am to be, I am now becoming.

— Benjamin Franklin

Our ability to remain the dominant species on this planet will rely on the foundation of the values and ethics we will keep, update, or develop tomorrow and within the next decade. What's the division between values and ethics? Values have to do with our foundational beliefs; they are the underlying beliefs that drive how we think. Values define our ideals and principles that guide and direct us in key and often undefined judgment moments. On the other hand, ethics are sets of rules that govern our behaviors and actions, which are set in place by specific systems, groups, or cultures.

Ethics are recommendations and directions on how we behave, which act as a structure for our moral principles. Both values and ethics are essential to our everyday lives and will become increasingly critical to our future. Values help us determine the importance of an issue, while ethics help guide us in making the right choice.

There is an increasing need to focus on specific global ethics as we continue to surf into the twenty-first century. The problems, challenges, and technical dilemmas we are starting to face as we continue to paddle into the unknown ocean of the future have no geographical bounds or limitations. They are not specific to any one culture, nation, or region. Although values will remain important, values differ from one person to the next. Ethics tend to be consistent and clearly defined amongst larger groups. Meaning what one individual finds important might not be important at all to someone else. Although our values will help define and prioritize our goals and objectives in life, ethics define and help us unite and morally understand what is considered right or wrong in any given circumstances.

And here we are, paddling into unchartered waters, made up of rogue waves and possibly endless oceans never before experienced or explored by any previous era of humanity, trying to apply the values of ethics of yesterday to a future we can hardly comprehend. Although new technology always raises ethical questions, the deep technological change we face is not just traditional technological disruption, but a disruption of intelligence. Unlike ever before, the megatrends of the Fourth Industrial Revolution will have an astronomical impact on our evolution in a shorter time frame than we think possible. Regardless of the exact timing of these waves of disruptions, they will be rogue, they will come fast, they will be regular, and each will reshape humanity as we know it. We should consider in the grandest and most specific terms: What do we do about AI?

Embrace the discomfort. Every surfer does as they approach the barrel—the lingering feeling that they could wipe out at any moment if they make a wrong move. Fear does them no good; they have to hug the discomfort tight and prepare for the thrill. Artificial intelligence should make us uncomfortable, even if the idea excites you. After all, unlike any deep technological change or advancements of the past, we discuss a technology that can show signs of intelligent behavior to solve complex tasks for the first time in human history. Tasks previously only capable of being solved by humans. We are entering an era when technology may have the ability to share many of our humanistic traits, such as the ability to feel, think, and challenge how we have defined human intelligence in the past. Regardless of whether it is intelligence, automation, or brute-force algorithms, the conversation needs to highlight problematic areas from which new ethics must be created. And this has to happen now. It should have happened yesterday. The moment of "too late" is fast approaching.

Ethics of AI Systems as Objects

Our Privacy & Surveillance

With so many high-profile whistleblowing reports, hacks, and leaks of private information making the news, what is being done about it? In much larger amounts and more detail than in the past, our data no longer just exists on bits of paper stored in a secure building by a select few. Rather, it is stored digitally and housed by many different stakeholders. Who has the right to this data? How do you define what constitutes private data, and does that definition align with your data holder? In addition to governments, organizations, and the individuals that can now capture your data, are they all keeping things as secure as you would like? Do you know who even has data on you? Who oversees governing the use of data? The speed of this disruption around this creation and power of data has dramatically outpaced the regulations around managing and protecting it. With a terrible track record of exploitation, when no one is looking, humanity must continue to proactively address this issue of privacy and surveillance as we enter the

Fourth Industrial Revolution. Although we still have much work to do, certain regions like Europe have taken steps and are leading the regulation around protection and surveillance.

Now that we have digitized our lives in data, data collection and storage possibilities are almost endless. With many of the megatrends of tomorrow coming online, such as advancements in sensors and IoT, we will have connected data for almost all aspects of our lives. As these megatrends continue to augment each other, improvements in computing power and AI will allow for automation of data collection and surveillance at an infinite scale. Data analysis can happen in real time for targeted individuals and entire populations—it's powerful stuff, but who gets to hold the power? Can this data be sold? Can the data be made freely available or shared between specific parties? This is all new territory. It is far more complicated than sharing keys to a filing cabinet. For those who do not know what a filing cabinet is, it was a storage container from an era when we used to store knowledge on physical paper, either written by hand or printed on computer paper made from trees. They collected a lot of dust. Books are an example. You can get them at a secondhand store for five bucks.

In the pursuit of security is the question of privacy dilemmas, and the megatrends will only force more of these questions. What once were small social media startups aimed at helping us keep up with friends have turned into data behemoths with technology that combs through all of its data with facial recognition and various data algorithms to profile us for content and advertising purposes. Some of these databases are the largest facial recognition databases in the world. In parallel to the convenience of visible security threats, we have readily accepted facial recognition and fingerprinting information as a means of accessing data stored on our phones and computers. Residing in this immense ocean of data is a chillingly complete picture of every one of us. Governments are racing to keep these companies in check, but they also want the same data access they are trying to regulate. We have already seen accidental missteps and purposeful, intentional manipulation that compromises the ethical boundaries of yesterday. Do they also compromise the ethics of tomorrow?

Growing up, in simpler times, we heard how nothing in life is free. Today, if something is free, it's because you are the product, and you are paying with your data. Could you simply disconnect from everything? Not realistically, but it sounds nice in theory. Even if you tossed your credit cards, smartphones, and computers, there is a world of security cameras collecting information on you. A data-free life is no longer possible, not on this planet. It's not about capturing less data but finding better and more ethical applications for the data that is in play.

The reality is 95% of us have a little demon, something we struggle with, or past actions we condone and wish to suppress from others and even possibly ourselves. The other 5% who do not have internal demons are liars. With enough data, these inner demons are vulnerable and may reveal other embarrassing personal issues we are not aware of. In his book *Homo Deus: A Brief History of Tomorrow,* historian Yuval Noah Harari asks, "What will happen to society, politics, and daily life when nonconscious but highly intelligent algorithms know us better than we know ourselves?" With the tsunami of technological change currently in flight and the fact that we already live in a fully connected world, privacy and surveillance issues will only increase. This is something that must be addressed at every level—personal, national, and global. While some work and progress have been made, much of the risk still lies ahead tomorrow, emergent topics and situations that have yet to be ethically considered and documented.

Manipulation of Our Behavior

The capture of data is one issue, but how the data is used to manipulate us is quite another. Governments and companies mainly exist to manipulate human behavior, act in the manner they wish, or buy their product and services. From complexity, we know the emergent nature of complex systems and how we can guide, manipulate, and nudge these systems toward a more desired outcome. With large amounts of data and targeted algorithms, individuals, organizations, or governments can influence, drive, and direct the behaviors of individuals and groups as a whole.

Governments and organizations have been repeatedly shown throughout history to push all legal and ethical boundaries to increase competitive advantage and profit by taking advantage of human biases through deception, including addiction. Although we govern certain addictive substances and business models such as gambling, business models based on online manipulation referred to as "dark patterns" and addiction are gaining popularity. In more obvious mainstream examples, we have seen the increase in social media used to drive political propaganda machines. We have seen this in the daily tweets of world leaders aimed to divide and foster hate, as well as larger-scale unethical manipulation of voting behaviors like we saw with the Facebook–Cambridge Analytica shitshow. As the advancement of these technologies continues to augment each other, and more and more data is created, better understood, and analyzed, the building of proactive ethics around how humans can be manipulated, and for what purpose, becomes essential.

How do we continue to evolve our lives and organizations using digital interactions and data if we cannot trust these interactions? How can we continue to advance humanity through artificially intelligent technologies that will require vast amounts of data if only more, and greater, problems are created in the process? This tradeoff and the speed of change and its complexity have caused a significant decrease in privacy protection compared to the straightforward legal protection of the previous eras defined by physical pulp and paper.

Like many of these topics, there is a need to reconsider how we approach these ethics, as the problems are no longer limited to geographical borders. The EU General Data Protection Regulation has significantly increased privacy protections. In contrast, nations like the US and China have chosen to move forward with less regulation to gain competitive, economic advantages. Regardless of whose approach is the best, many of these global issues need global governance; global problems cannot be addressed differently in different regions or nations in the world. As we continue to remove and limit the human ability to be involved in decisions, we lose visibility into why and how decisions are made.

Lack of AI Transparency

The lack of visibility creates ethical consideration around how transparent AI systems need to be. If AI systems replace human judgment and decision-making, we need to know how it arrives at conclusions. In 2018, Meredith Whittaker, a research scientist at New York University and co-founder of the AI Now Institute, highlighted how AI systems cause many deep concerns around the process, transparency, ability to examine or inspect, and accountability of predictive analytics. It could not only be impossible for the average person to understand how the decision was made—even the greatest of technical experts who may have created the technology may not have the visibility to understand how the system made the decision. The reality is that many of the machine-learning AI systems work blindly. They often act as a "black box," meaning we have no insight into how or what pattern was used. This complete lack of visibility and understanding into how a decision is made creates a major problem around bias in the decision system. We not only lose the ability to remove the bias from the system, but we will not even be aware if bias is happening at all. And yes, machines can be biased. In fact, most technology, AI, programs, and machines are built around bias.

How does this magical "black box" work, and why does it cause such a lack of transparency? A great example to quickly discuss is machine learning, which is used by many AI systems. Machine learning uses neural networks to pull information from the assigned data set. The answer is often not given, or the AI is trained through forms of supervision, partial supervision, or programmed to conclude entirely on its own. This creates learning, hence the name "machine learning," as the systems define patterns in the information, which refine what the systems deem to be a sound decision. Often, the system developer is left in the dark regarding which pattern of information in the given data set was used by the AI system. To further add to this complexity, the AI systems and programs themselves are constantly changing, as more data is added and more feedback is captured (good vs. bad, yes vs. no, right vs. wrong, and so on). The very system evolves from how it was built initially.

Every day, millions of micro-changes every hour and every minute eventually build a system that even the architect can't recognize. In addition to how the system is using the data, the type of data being used can be just as damaging. Garbage in, garbage out. Putting in skewed, useless, or biased data gives you skewed, useless, or biased outputs and results. In the recent Black Lives Matter movements, attention has been brought to the fact that data based on a suspect's skin color produces a system that will have biased results. People are working on data standardization that could identify bias from these initial data sets, making them more obvious. There have been attempts to create data filters, but much of the recent research shows not-so-great results. Additionally, present-day research shows that some of these ethical issues arise from the AI systems taking shorter alternative routes to achieve output. Eerily similar to how the human mind builds unconscious shortcuts to making decisions.

There are many brilliant individuals, organizations, and even governmental agencies like America's DARPA working on the technical aspects of creating more accountability regarding the visibility in these AI systems. Additionally, the EU is proactively building rights for individuals to seek visibility and explanation when given a decision based on data that was processed by an AI system. Again, much work is needed in and around how this happens and how it will be enforced. This could also open other areas of ethics in how human-made decisions will be justified and explained in the future.

Technology Decision Bias

Due to our humanistic shortcomings in how we make decisions, AI systems are popular because of how they outperform the best of us in predictive-based decision-making. Our reliance and comfort on these automated decisions continue to grow without any awareness of the impacts. In less significant situations, the predictive decision carries a relatively low risk. However, these predictive decisions are being used more in applications with higher risks and consequences, like in medicine, where these AI systems are used to identify cancers or treat patients. Or in the self-driving cars that chauffeur us around. Where do we draw the line? Should we allow AI to make life-or-death decisions? Should they make decisions in our legal systems to see who is granted bail and who serves more time? Should these AI systems predict our policing or military actions? Should they decide which target is a threat and how that threat should be suppressed or terminated? Is it too early to call AI "they"? For many, the answer would be no. What if the AI systems are not perfect but significantly better and more accurate than what a human could do? What then? Systems capable of predictive data analysis are often more accurate and significantly cheaper. As they continue to evolve, they will become cheaper again and most likely continue to increase in popularity. But they are only as good as the data they use.

When it comes to AI, the result is only as good as the data. So, where does the bias come from? Earlier, we defined and explained how decision bias is present in humans. In the technology world, this can mean the AI system is performing poorly, but this poor performance is often due to bias within the data it uses or the algorithm that drives it—using skewed, useless, or biased data results in skewed, useless, or biased results. The same is true to the algorithm that drives the data processing, meaning biased algorithms will produce biased output. Since humans are biased and build and train

AI systems, it is hard to think of how not to have our bias work its way into the AI systems we produce.

There are means in which we are working and aware of bias and how it can seep into AI systems, but again, we are reactive and lagging in how we enforce or govern much of this. One method is to make sure we use training data that exactly represents the AI system's environment. Since this is virtually impossible, we attempt to circumvent it by choosing large-enough and accurate-enough data to represent the environment best. Again, there is no recommendation or governance in place regarding adequate sampling techniques. Let's not forget the bias bred from our historically prejudiced past. Ultimately, this trains AI systems with data that both consciously and unconsciously highlights social stereotypes. For example, if we assigned an AI system to better understand adults' working roles in our world, the answers might not produce what we expect. Hypothetically, this algorithm can connect to the internet to expose itself to the billions of pictures taken and cataloged throughout history, or by watching movies, TV shows, and reading books from our past. What would it learn? That the information was heavily biased, with men working in leadership roles and women working in the kitchen. Therein, the AI would learn that men are suited for leadership and women for keeping a home. This is clearly absurd, as men and women are equally fit to work in either role, but these stereotypes and prejudice of our past are real. We could make sure the AI system does not learn from this data set, but how do we inform it of our historical bias?

We could avoid this problem above by taking our pictures randomly all around the world; this way, we can control all the data being input into the AI system from which it will learn. Even simple fixes like this are not so simple. This can show up as a problem of measurement device bias, in which the camera we used for the data set could skew the data in a particular direction since the photos the AI system is being trained on would have the same filter overlay that would identically distort the color in all the pictures the exact same way. If we deploy this AI system using data sets taken from a high-quality SLR camera instead of my garbage smartphone, the algorithm would have trouble understanding the new color spectrum compared to what it might have previously learned.

How much bias do we allow, even if we are aware of it? This is a responsibility that lies in the hands of the developer. An AI system developed to be highly sensitive to bias would also have to be much more myopic in its abilities. It would have trouble with large amounts of complexity, and vice versa for less-sensitive biased algorithms that would welcome complexity but be much more prone to bias. Who decides how much of what is OK?

These problems and many questions should be addressed before the system is created. But this is rarely the case. It's hard to determine the ethics when we aren't even sure what the system can do. This is not a futuristic concept or problem; we have seen many of these technological biases creep into our current world, organizations, and governments already. Consider the system designed around predicting a defender's likelihood of re-offending within the Correctional Offender Management Profiling for Alternative Sanctions. Not only was the system just as reliable as a completely random group of individuals, but it had a bias baked in against cases related to Black defendants. In a more mainstream setting, we found Amazon's automated recruitment system used for vetting potential employees discriminated toward women's employment, something Amazon had an issue with long before AI showed up. This system was discontinued in 2017 by Amazon once the bias was identified.

Awareness of the problem is always the first step. Then, there is more than a technical challenge that we face in solving this problem in the backdrop of redefining what it means to be human—now we have to create mathematically driven technology that doesn't consider race or sex, two very human attributes.

Human-Robot Interaction (HRI)

Human-Robot Interaction is exactly what it sounds like, humans and robots interacting together. We see this more and more in both our personal and professional lives. We spoke to previous examples in this book of the complex interconnectedness of hundreds of thousands of humans and robots working together. In a world in which humans and machines are stronger together than on their own, this tidal wave of a partnership shows no sign of slowing down anytime soon.

We previously discussed the ability of AI systems to manipulate human behavior. Humans tend to show more empathy to physical appearances that most closely mirror things we care about, like our own appearances or an adorable puppy. This can be a trap into which mammals, both human and animals, assign significantly more intelligence, intellect, and even emotional importance to the AI system than what seems practical. How do we shape the future of ethics around emotions and attributes once thought to be purely human?

How do robots care for humans beyond what we see in service or medical settings?

What happens when a human falls in love with a robot? Yeah, in *that* way. Robot booty.

Once again, we're facing a conversation that makes many people uncomfortable, and discomfort and tension put us right in the middle of a barrel, meaning it must be addressed. The idea also overlaps with the areas of deception. Do we dehumanize the caring aspect of "taking care" of someone? Or do we humanize the AI experience for the sick, ill, elderly, or in need of care? What if humanizing this experience makes patients happier and increases their longevity? If this is the case, and we choose to humanize care, we are deceitful since AI systems cannot actually "care" for anything.

Where do we draw the line when deceiving what models of AI systems are acceptable and those that are not? With a large demographic of well-funded baby boomer generationals now needing care, AI systems are filling in the care gaps in healthcare. When is it OK to lie a little to people about the treatment they receive? Who gets to decide what is being done for the patient's "own good"?

Although some might chuckle at the idea or be repulsed by the mere thought of it, sexualizing robots is a very real reality. We've already seen a wide range of sexual preferences among humans in the past few decades, driven in part by a growing industry of sex toys, dolls, and information. There is a massive segment of the population who is open to the idea of nonhuman sexual interaction. Naturally, this opens a sizeable can of ethical worms. Some think these can be true emotional relationships and should be allowed. Others may think of it as the next level of pornography—a way to further give in to the desire of sexual degradation and abuse, or even a variation of slavery and prostitution. Much like prostitution, sex with an AI system is designed to be deceptive. Is it purely pleasure? Or is there something more?

And, above all, who gets to decide?

Automation of Jobs

The previous revolutions brought about an explosion of productivity and wealth and a drastic change in the dominant industries. We have seen a shift away from farming, once a traditional way of life, that now employs less than 5% of the population in wealthy countries. Shifts from classic trades to factory work were one thing; now we see traditional forms of automation that were focused on replacing human movements to digital automation replacing cognitive processes.

You can't pay an AI to do a job, but it will bring you value. It's not just factory lines; every single industry is facing automation replacement. The short-term job market will see a rise in coaching, leadership, and developing highly skilled technology jobs as the demand increases. Many low-skilled jobs will remain in demand, although they will likely remain poorly paid. The traditional middle market of jobs in factories and offices is the most predictable and will see the most disruption from present-day automation. The job markets are about to experience a rogue wave of major disruption that will shift economies' size and how each economy fundamentally works. Will the obliteration of jobs create new ones and more wealth? Or will we see the exact opposite and face an increase in poverty? What are the transition costs, and who has to bear them? The people? Companies? Our governments? Will these topics make us ponder concepts like the need for societal adjustments and redistribution of costs and benefits from digital automation? Will these lead to monopolies or more open innovation and a constant new churn of startups?

Although these AI systems hold more potential than we can currently comprehend, as they continue to augment the other megatrends of this Fourth Industrial Revolution, like increased computing power and networks, we are creating wasteful byproducts that damage our planet. As these AI systems continue to gain in popularity and application, they create new forms of waste, many that are nonrecyclable. And, frankly, AI eats up a ton of energy. Should any of this be regulated? If so, how much does it limit growth? Do all countries have the same limitations and social responsibilities?

Consider Bitcoin. Research suggests cryptocurrency mining—the digital process of creating new coins to trade—can produce up to fifteen million tons of global carbon emissions per coin. Cryptocurrency mining is a process that occurs each time a cryptocurrency's ownership changes. Every Bitcoin exchange takes the form of a transaction. At this point, "digital miners" work to solve complex and sophisticated mathematical problems of various forms. Once all the math is verified, the transaction is added to a digital ledger. The digital cryptocurrency miners compete to break the code; the winner gets rewarded in Bitcoin. Instead of printing more money as the government can do, as crypto gains in popularity, it produces more currency through the verification "mining" of its transactions. This has become a big business that requires a lot of computing power and energy, and most advanced nations have invested and capitalized on this modern-day mining. China, who is already the largest consumer and producer of coal energy, relies on this energy source to fuel national crypto companies. Research shows that compared to Canada's renewable energy sources, the mining of any cryptocurrency in China would create four times the amount of carbon dioxide emissions. The power in this example is in seeing how these emissions released will affect microclimates everywhere. Chinese Bitcoin production ends up being a global problem.

Yet global cooperation is not a simple task. AI systems responsible for this automation currently reside in an inconsistent and unregulated domain. Many AI systems' attractiveness is their "winner takes all" reward, meaning that they are being applied to industries and areas in which the first to develop these systems gain competitive advantage and the ability to quickly monopolize the market. We have trouble controlling, understanding, and governing things we cannot see, which is the case with many of these AI systems. The corporations that manage these AIs can easily span across many nations. We already see this problem. Some could argue that this is fair, as "the spoils should go to the winner," but in reality, if 99.9% of the population in the world is being governed essentially against their will by the 0.1%, it becomes more of a dictatorship than free commerce. Competition (and its siblings, tension and discomfort) must remain at the center of AI development. Without it, there isn't any reason to improve.

The goal doesn't have to be an equal distribution of rewards, but what if it were? What if AI allowed us to beat world hunger, eradicate disease, and end war, all while creating enough wealth for everyone? Advancements in our economic development could easily lead to everyone having enough of whatever makes them happy, regardless of how or if they work for it. But does this affect our morals and values? Should we change our views shaped from a different past to encompass the possibilities for our future? Many of these ethical dilemmas come full circle and involve much more than technical answers, as they will force us to rethink and reexamine our philosophical views and definitions of the world and humanity.

Autonomous Systems

The goal is to have something that works to do a job and create value with as little maintenance as possible—a totally autonomous system. But where does the responsibility lie in a completely autonomous system? Furthermore, is that responsibility any different from a system where a human may have some manner of control? People aren't comfortable unless there is a sense of control—this is why autonomous cars are still, for now, built with brake pedals and steering wheels. You may even feel this anxiety when you're on a plane—you have zero control. All you can do is buckle your seatbelt and hope the pilot is in good shape. So when it comes to autonomous systems, who is ultimately in control? Who is responsible for the outcomes, however good or bad they may be?

Everything we discuss in AI comes down to the same handful of systems: the transparency of AI systems, data, the security of systems, and the list goes on. Many existing governing bodies have already started to build out much of the standards around specific applications of autonomous systems. Autonomous air, water, and ground systems are already a megatrend from which we can dream up many world-changing applications, as well as potential nightmares—like with autonomous weapon systems. Suddenly, it's not just a matter of the ethics of the technology, but how the technology impacts the society it exists within.

Driving while intoxicated is illegal most everywhere. It is outlawed because it is the easiest thing you can do to prevent injury, destruction, and death. Yet some people might feel they have the right to drive while severely intoxicated—so we build in laws and punishments for these individuals for the greater good of society. Not that long ago, you could drive home while completely smashed. A cop that pulled you over didn't have the Breathalyzer technology to determine how inebriated you were, so they let you off so long as you promised "to drive straight home." Even sober, there is a considerable amount of risk when it comes to a car. Outlawing cars would significantly lower car accident deaths, but since our society is so dependent on them, it may never happen. Putting in governance around drinking and driving does not prevent all driving-related deaths, but it does lower many preventable ones. What if autonomous cars eventually did the same? In the last decade, upwards of 1.3 million people worldwide died on the roadways. What if we moved to autonomous cars and only 300,000 people died? Or 100,000? Or only 10,000 or 2,000 people died annually? How low would this number have to be to convince everyone to give up their personal automobile, and the thrill of driving, for autonomous roadways?

To add some context to this conversation, 20–50 million people a year suffer some kind of long-term disability due to an accident on the roadway. Road traffic deaths are the leading killer for those aged 5–29 years. Young adults lead this category with more than half of all the road deaths. For Americans traveling internationally, the single greatest cause of death of healthy Americans abroad is from road car crashes. Aside from being the leading killer of our future generations and worldly travelers, there are also financial implications that could pressure governments to consider removing human-controlled driving at some point, as on average, car accidents cost 3% of their GDP. The reality: autonomous vehicles are outperforming humans in every imaginable way on the road. When this happens, do we simply implement a law that inconveniences us less than drinking and driving? Drinking and driving would be a thing of the past since you are no longer in control of the car. In theory, you could drink *in* your autonomous car. Driving would be purely recreational, like driving a go-cart! Or speeding around golf courses. Just because we can do something doesn't mean we should. There are growing humanitarian, ethical, and financial drivers that may cause nations in our lifetime to take this approach. To some, a personal chauffeur on command, saving millions of lives annually, decreasing commute times due to a connected system that can control traffic flow, sounds like a dream. To others, it sounds like a direct assault on their freedom. Are we free to not obey signs and laws when we drive? Would parts of the legal system collapse if we removed all the court cases and legal actions in each of the auto-related deaths? Do we care if they collapse? If our child is killed by an autonomous car, who is to blame? In an autonomous world, with a failure that results in our long-term disability, who is at fault? Will our hospital systems collapse without the influx of injured and life-threatening injury from human errors when driving?

We haven't even started having these conversations or planning or imagining how we are going to improvise the next steps.

Autonomous cars present very different ethical dilemmas compared to autonomous weapons. For one, there is no specific individual to hold accountable for the resulting death (which is what most weapons do—kill people). Some argue that war with autonomous weapons would cause less hardship, leading to fewer human deaths. If we all fought in the same schoolyard, maybe this would be true. But governments, criminals, and terrorists do not abide by a universal "equal" rule of war. There is nothing stopping dictatorship governments or criminals and terrorists from unloading autonomous weapons into heavily populated areas or from targeting specific demographics and races within these populations. When it comes to autonomous systems, we can try and dream up the darkest and most twisted application of how to kill humans; the reality is our governments have already thought, developed, and are testing many of these ideas. "For example, instead of fielding simple guided missiles or remotely piloted vehicles, we might launch completely autonomous land, sea, and air vehicles capable of complex, far-ranging reconnaissance and attack missions." This was a quote from DARPA, the United States Department of Defense agency that is responsible for the development of emerging technologies for use by the military.

They said this in 1983.

By and Buy

There is nothing like a dream to create the future.

— Victor Hugo

Before long, tomorrow becomes today. First-order effects are taking place through all this exponential convergence; hereafter, we will start to see second-order effects further magnifying the rogue waves of tomorrow. Through complexity, we understand how each of these megatrend advancements interacts with each other, with each development amplifying the next, through a complex interdependence of accelerating acceleration. Early on, we pondered how much change our grandparents must have seen over their lifetime. Well, we are currently experiencing more technological change in one year than Pappy experienced over his entire lifetime. All of these colliding and converging rogue waves created an additional set of accelerating forces. For now, these forces are highlighted independently, but we will soon see how they will collide and reshape both humanity and our lives. For now, we are interested in how all this acceleration of acceleration will affect our lives.

For starters, tomorrow we will have more time than ever before. In our instinctive pursuit for *more*, this simply means we can do more than any other time in human history. In the previous industrial revolution, learning meant visiting libraries and talking with teachers and testing and application. Today, Google it. If we go way back to 2014, researchers out of the University of Michigan tested participants tasked with either using the library to research a question or the internet. Back then, using the internet saved the participants about 15 minutes per question compared to going to a library. Considering most people nowadays don't know how to use a library, or where their local branch is, the internet just saves more time. Assume each question since 2014 saves us fifteen minutes, and there are an estimated 5.5 billion Google searches in a day. That search engine alone saves humanity 82.5 billion minutes a day. The average human in America lives for 39.4 million minutes, meaning thousands of lifetimes are saved in Google searches each day. Each of these lifetimes can now do other things instead of researching the answers to questions. It is not just looking up answers on Google that saves us time. Everything from shopping to banking to traffic updates and family visits all take less time. We do not have to drive and walk around while we shop; we do not have to wait in line or wait on hold to book things; we simply do it online.

Technology has solved much of the problems around time wasted on basic needs. If we go back a century, the time savings are incredible; over this past decade, technology has found a way to reduce essential home-related tasks from fifty-eight hours a week down to 1.5 hours a week in 2011. In 2011, doing nothing other than being alive, you got back over an entire week's worth of time each month compared to a century ago. If we go back two centuries, a trip from Chicago to Atlanta took four weeks. A century later, trains cut that time to four days. Airplanes have made the round trip possible in four hours. Tomorrow's hyperloop will make the trip possible in under an hour, and advancements in VR and AR, the day after tomorrow, has the potential to put you there, in real time, digitally. When we have free time, we innovate. In the previous industrial revolutions, humanity could only spend so much free time innovating because we have essential things in our life that take time. Today, and even more so tomorrow, we have more human hours creating, advancing, and inventing than any other time in human history.

The tsunami of technological convergences continues in examples such as IoT coupled with the acceleration of sensors for smart devices in our homes, giving us back hours of our life. Smart devices will automatically execute smart contracts with the Amazons of the world; when something runs low, a drone will have the replacement delivered before you even realize it—no more mornings without milk for your cereal! This will give us all more time back in both our professional and personal lives. In our professional lives, AI advancements allow us to lower trial-and-error research from years in a lab to weeks or hours in a computer simulation. Add quantum computing into the mix, and this timeline gets exponentially faster. All this extra time we get back will be leveraged by innovative individuals who have more time to invent and advance technology than any other time in history. Yes, technology saves time, but some of this time goes back into things like innovation, which further fuels the acceleration of these rogue waves of technological disruption. With more time comes the ability to make or raise more money.

As the great American philosophers Wu-Tang Clan said: "Cash Rules Everything Around Me." Like it or not, C.R.E.A.M—money matters. There are very few problems money can't fix when it comes to technology. This not only put America on the moon, but all the scientific and technological advancements that came out of it also created a springboard of innovation for the nation. Today, funding is easier to secure than any other time in history, which allows innovators to flourish. More experimentation, more failures, more time, all results in more advancements, breakthrough, and innovation. Money might not be everything in life, but it's a big part of speeding up technological progress. Since it does not grow on trees, where is all the influx of capital coming from? One avenue is new technologies create new revenue streams.

And there are always new ways to raise capital. By 2025, under Moore's Law, experts believe $300 billion will be moving through this digital ecosystem. Although the amount of money is impressive, raising capital no longer requires large institutions; it can be leveraged by the innovators directly. Venture capital (VC) funding rose from $8.1 billion in 1995 to $99.5 billion in 2017. Other parts of the world are also growing their VC funding around technologies, with Europe hitting $21 billion and Asia, which is much newer to the VC scene, already hitting $81 billion. Initial coin offerings (IOCs) raise capital by leveraging blockchain technology. Sovereign wealth funds (SWFs) are state-owned investment funds comprised of the money generated by the government, often derived from a country's surplus reserves. These monster investment funds have around $8 trillion in assets. Eight. Trillion. Dollars. The CEO of Softbank believes so much in Kurzweil's Singularity concept—that AI will create technological growth beyond our comprehension and restructure everything we know about our civilizations—that he built a fund to accelerate this growth. The first fund raised $45 billion in forty-five minutes, after which most of the tech giants also jumped in to invest, driving it up to $100 billion in short order. Long story short, there is no shortage of money for promising technologies.

Although there is no shortage of money, we can do more with less of it. It sounds contradictory, but the "demonetization" of the Six Ds of disruption is turning into a force fueling tomorrow's acceleration. Money is more available, but with demonetization, we see how our money goes exponentially further. Consider the human genome sequencing. The first run took $100 million. We can now do it 6,480 times faster and over one million times cheaper. Today, any research funding around the human genome goes millions of times further than it did a short while ago. Before, only the wealthiest of institutions could develop and grow many of these advancements. Once this cost goes to near zero, any of us can now build off these breakthroughs and technologies. Our smartphone was another example; access to using such technology in 2012 would have cost you more than a million dollars, today it sits in your pocket for daily use. Today, you drop it on concrete or touch it with your greasy fingers without thinking twice about it. We are seeing power costs dropping through advancements in renewable energy. Most of the fundamental business needs and costs, like manufacturing, insurance, education, energy, communication, logistics, and labor, are all exponentially closing in on demonetization.

In 2010, we had connected almost 25% of the global population to the world wide web. A decade later, we have over 4.33 billion active internet users worldwide, accounting for 57% of the entire world's population. Tomorrow and the few years that follow, we will connect everyone, all of us, to the internet. Being more connected saves us time and makes us smarter. The waves of intelligence are further amplified because we are physically altering ourselves to be more stylish. In 2017, a neuroscientist repurposed neural implants used for epilepsy; he could use them on non-epileptic humans to stimulate retention and learning to produce a 30% increase in memory. Today, this is research; tomorrow, this will be retail.

New megatrends create new business models, and these new business models further fuel the acceleration of these megatrends of the Fourth Industrial Revolution. Beyond crowdsourcing, we now have the crowd *economy*—funding, sourcing, shared assets, labor on demand, crowd everything. It's how we have Airbnb and Uber and all of these companies who ostensibly own no assets. We have the economy of free, where you pay for the services through the data you produce. We used to add power to a tool, and we'd have a power tool (screwdriver into impact driver). Now we add AI and get a whole new beast. Phones, speakers, watches, cars—they're all "smart." We will have an economy of next-level decentralization. Blockchain might mean tomorrow we would have companies with no bosses and no employees, yet it all runs twenty-four hours a day. Tomorrow we will see autonomous taxi fleets that interact through the execution of smart contracts, that self-repair and refuel, running twenty-four hours a day without ever needing humans.

Tomorrow, we will start to have economies in different worlds. We already live in two places, our real physical world and in a digital online world, for which we have a persona for each. As AR and VR grow, we will have added layers of avatars for work and avatars for personal status and entertainment. You could hire anyone to design your digital life in these virtual worlds, virtual clothing, virtual homes, even avatars themselves. With each layer we add to the digital world, an entirely new economy is born to support it.

Meaning we have multiple economies in multiple worlds, all at the same time. It will be an economy of transformation. Consider your third-favorite place—not your home or your workplace. It could be your favorite coffee shop in Seattle or it could be a transformation festival like Burning Man, Wanderlust, or some other mindfulness triathlon. Recent trends have made it clear: People will pay for transformational experiences. CrossFit is a transformational experience, and it's terrible. You sweat a lot, maybe you throw up, and it happens in a warehouse without climate control. Tomorrow's transformations will be an enjoyable experience, but you can still go home with six-pack abs.

All this means humanity will get better as these business models solve our problems, and since it is demonetized, it is all that much cheaper. Better yet, it will be faster. These new economies breed speedy and agile business models; long gone are the boring days of stability and security.

Finally, an additional driver adding to all the complexity of these converging and amplifying megatrends and technologies is lifespan. Humanity's first computer programmer, Ada Lovelace, published the world's first computer program, but she also died in the 1800s at age thirty-six. Imagine a world in which Ada Lovelace, Sir Isaac Newton, Einstein, Tesla, Hawking, Jobs, and so many other brilliant thinkers lived longer. Imagine what else they could have accomplished. The total lifespan will not fuel these megatrends of today and tomorrow, but the fact that individuals today, and even more so tomorrow, will operate at peak capacity for longer. Along the way, they will be allowed to make greater contributions and further advance humanity. Our cavemen ancestors were lucky to make it to twenty-five. Over the next 1,000 years, not much changed. At the end of the nineteenth century, life expectancy passed forty. Over the three industrial revolutions, we jumped to seventy-eight years. Today, we have developed senolytic medication to attack and destroy aging cells while rebuilding and restoring their proper functionality. In studies, rodents' healthy life expectancy increased by as much as 35%. We have also reinjected infusions of blood into older rats that have been able to reverse cognitive impairments and regenerate the older hearts, brains, lungs, internal organs, and brain of the mammal. Dying is a problem, and an existential one at that. Humans will stop at nothing to find a solution for every problem—including death.

When we add to the mix that we are extending and closing in on a youth's technological foundation, tomorrow seems almost incomprehensible. We have exponential technologies overlapping and converging with other exponential technologies, being augmented by new forces, new economies, new business models, more money, more time, more-connected, longer lifespans at a faster acceleration rate every day. Even with our proper surfing framework to help us navigate and surf this complexity of continuous acceleration of acceleration, we can still feel a bit dizzy and out of control. Tomorrow, we paddle into a world of rogue waves much different than today. As we transcend into the surfers of tomorrow, we will live longer, will be AI-enabled, and connect to everything. The day after tomorrow will be much different than tomorrow, which will be much different than today.

There are no brakes on waves; all you can do is ride them to the best of your ability. What we decide today will shape tomorrow. The ethics of tomorrow must be addressed today. Are we having enough of these conversations today? Tomorrow holds more opportunity than any other time in human history, but is this pace of advancement good for us? The only thing that ensures we have no say is to do nothing. Using our surfing framework as a compass will force us to think ahead and navigate some of these outcomes before becoming a reality the day after tomorrow.

PART 5: THE SWELL

Life can only be understood backwards;
but it must be lived forwards.

— Søren Kierkegaard

Remember: No waves, no glory. How is it that we still manage to fear the future and don't notice changes, but are always nostalgic for the past that is behind us? Think about it: most of us are comfortable with the way things are and wouldn't want anything to change. Take a look at any vote, any election—there is usually half of the crowd who will vote against change and would very much like things to go back to the way they were (whatever that means). Yet, if you look at our history, things are getting better. Things today are exponentially better—people live longer, have more solutions to health ailments, more wealth to go around, and Grandma isn't eating cat food. Also, you have to try really hard to die from syphilis.

Yet some want to go back to "the good ol' days," those who miss the way things were. And we are naturally fearful of the world ahead, even though—statistically—the coming waves of disruption will bring *good* things. The changes we face today build into seismic waves that will all but obliterate what we know in the modern world.

The earthquakes, landslides, eruptions, and meteorites that set off tsunami waves throughout our past are building into the megatrends of the Fourth Industrial Revolution. The surfing framework serves as a compass that simply arms us with a foundational understanding of the future we are paddling into. Surfing through the next ten years of our lives will look very different than how we surfed through the previous decade. Our decisions and actions will further shape this future state. We may never notice all of the changes happening around us as we keep up with our busy lives, but we can already see some very clear signals that the tides are changing.

The Waves Building Along the Horizon

Just beyond the horizon of the so-called impossible
is infinite possibility.

— Bryant McGill

As we look past the charging rogue waves of disruption in our near future, we see less technical but equally fundamental dilemmas that need addressing. Although these concepts might not hit in the next decade, they will start to fall into place in the decades that follow. While it is fun to imagine what might happen, the possibilities are nearly infinite. Our time is better spent discussing the outcomes of what we know are sure to change: human longevity, human happiness, and what it means to live with AI.

As the waves of material science, nanotechnology and biotechnology collide with one another and ultimately smash into quantum computing and artificial intelligence, we will end up with a rogue wave that becomes an industry of its own. An industry suddenly capable of modeling seemingly impossibly complex environments, not unlike our brains. Not only can we model it through processing power and memory, but nonbiological forms of intelligence allow us to interpret and understand what is created. Everything is networked to allow for wireless unloading into a seemingly endless cloud of connectivity, moving humans from the power of single consciousness to a cloud-based, collective consciousness. To this point, the human story has been a cyclical tale of growth from the individual to the collective—from the big bang and through complexity, single atoms joined in evolving into multicellular organisms that would eventually become humans. It is naïve to assume we have reached the maximum of our intelligence. At best, we have made a map, and this moment of our intelligence is marked with a giant "you are here" sign. Now, thanks to complexity, the map is changing all around us all of the time—not unlike floating on a surfboard in the middle of an ocean. Around us, an untold number of waves rise and fall, and each is meant to challenge the very meaning of who we are.

The Eternal Surfer

For someone who is new to surfing, the four-footers crashing on the shore are intimidating. Practice enough, and the four-foot waves are easy. Your skillset develops, and you feel more at home on the board. It is only a matter of time before you look toward the horizon, beyond the four-foot waves, to see what else is possible. Imagine what you could accomplish if all you did was surf? Of course, you likely can't—sleeping and eating and working a job to pay for your surfing habit would all get in the way. Yet your overconfidence bias has you thinking you could have been as good as Kelly Slater if all you did was surf. The more rational among us know we might never be as good as Kelly, but how great would life be if we could ride that perfect wave every day? How would life feel if you had none of the adult pressures or stresses? Just a perfect house on the beach with ideal sunset waves—you don't ask for much! Life would be what you considered perfect in every way. Go ahead, take a moment to picture it in your head.

There it is, there you are, the happiest you've ever been.

As you wax up your surfboard while overlooking the perfect ocean landscape, a genie appears above your board. He offers you the ability to stay in this perfect moment forever. Live forever, in this perfect moment, for all eternity. Would you do it? Would you live in that moment forever?

Working to prevent our extinction has always been, and will always be, a top priority throughout humanity. Although a relatively decentralized effort to date, we have come together to curb and solve many of the problems that threatened our survival. As we look ahead to the next threat coming down the line, whatever it may be, we are also confronted with a dilemma. The megatrends of the Fourth Industrial Revolution will improve what it means to be a human like no other time in our history. It will reshape and eradicate problems that have been around as long as life has been on earth. In solving these problems, we face the next great existential threat: the inevitable pain of eternal happiness.

We started here four billion years ago and have figured out a lot of stuff in that time. Considering all of the potential existential threats on the horizon, we should first acknowledge that we do not have the luxury of another four billion years. Realistically, we might have until the end of this century to get things squared up to prepare for the century after. The megatrends of the Fourth Industrial Revolution are here, right now, and humanity has an embarrassing track record of being late to recognize real dangers and problems. Despite all the talk, we have made minimal economic and political sacrifices to address climate change. In some disappointing and embarrassing situations, we have even seen developed nations go back on their word, pulling out of global commitments and initiatives to fight climate change.

One consistency across our history is that humans are never content or satisfied with what we have; we always want more. The previous threats may not be existential, but they are still problematic. Eventually, we will fully solve these problems in our future, at which point we will need to turn our efforts and focus elsewhere—to greater challenges, with greater rewards and greater risks. Not just curing a disease outbreak, but preventing it from happening in the first place. We will continue to minimize violence and end any realistic threat of war. Hunger and famine are still problematic in parts of the world, but we could easily solve this issue globally. Even the politicized agendas of those using these fears to shape behavior will become obsolete as the population becomes more educated around our shared realities.

Solving these problems is a priority, but they create new problems. What happens to the economies that are heavily reliant on providing products and services to serve these problems? What will these economies and industries do? What will science and research do once the initiatives they work to solve are no longer problems?

Our current focus is shifting from working on solutions needed to simply survive toward solutions on how to survive better and longer, in every way imaginable. Our focus shifts from being killed by a foreign nation invading with tomahawks and muskets to a new main cause of death: aging. If you are reading this book, chances are you will die from old age or poor lifestyle choices. Your chances of dying from old age are even higher if you are fortunate enough to be in a developed nation. You will die, likely, from old age. Congratulations.

The longer we live, the more time we have to innovate. Aging is a dilemma that our evolution has hardwired into us. New growth replaces old growth. As the elderly age and get weak, the young gain more access to resources and replace their aging ancestors. This is true with plants and animals and, to an extent, humans. Just about every living thing succumbs to the disease and dilemma of aging.

We have already devised a way to increase the lifespan of a worm by 500%. If it works for humans, most of us could live to 394.65 years of age. This is how change starts. The worm research revealed that aging comes from just five genes, and eliminating any one of them could increase lifespan by 20%.

Combine this with advancements in swapping out failing or broken organs, followed by 3D printing of human parts, and our progress in increasing lifespan seems to have real potential.

Remember, we used to only live for about thirty years—you'd pass away before the first gray hairs set in. Then our progress as humans expanded life expectancy to nearly seventy years for most regions in just a few generations. The headlines of people living past 100 are increasingly frequent. How high will the life expectancy get in our lifetime? Many experts believe there will be a point when our pace of advancement starts to converge on the pace of aging, called the "longevity escape velocity." This occurs when we exceed a threshold in which we will extend our lives by a single year for every year we live. Meaning once we cross this threshold, we will literally be staying just ahead of dying, one year at a time. Experts believe this escape velocity is a little over a decade out; others think it is closer to thirty years out; all of them think it will happen within our lifetime.

It all comes down to investment. Money doesn't matter once you die, and the wealthy would pay a lot to stay one step ahead of death. At first, only the rich will be able to afford to live longer. Their investment in the research and advancements would quickly democratize and demonetize the escape velocity, making the methods available to the masses. This might happen in your lifetime, most definitely in your child's lifetime. Your kids could live well past the age of 100. But would they want to?

There was a time when the thought of transplanting an organ, such as a lung, would have been mind-bogglingly barbaric. Today, Stanford researchers take blood from younger rats and pump it into older rats to revitalize the animals. And it works. These rodents become visibly more energetic, but there is more than meets the eye. When transfusing out the old blood and putting in new, the old rat's tissue and organs restored a much healthier and younger rat's physical characteristics. Additional research showed the reverse to be true; swapping young blood and replacing it with old blood increased and accelerated aging significantly in the younger rodents. Researchers out of Harvard continued the experiment and found that younger blood transfusions stimulated new neuron creation in older brains and reversed aging-related clotting in the heart walls. They discovered a specific finding of particular interest, a molecule called GDF11 (growth differentiating factor 11).

In more recently published research from a different team, a simple injection of GDF11 into a rodent enhanced overall strength and memory and increased blood flow to the brain. Since this study, additional research has found that GDF11 helps to speed muscle repair, enhance exercise capacity, increase brain function, and even reduce issues linked to age and cardiac-related problems. Today, this is some of the leading research around possible cures and treatments to disorders like Alzheimer's, which would be administered through a simple injection. It seems that we are not only converging in on technologies and industries, but we seem to be converging in on death itself. Knowing that we can now bring many of these technological and scientific advancements to the market faster each year, we will see many of these advancements start to take shape within our lifetime. At first it will treat the sick, then it will extend the lives of the healthy. The disease we once called death will be delayed even longer until it's not a matter of how we will die, but why?

In the last century, we have doubled human life expectancy. Do we double it again? For the eternal surfer, learning how to surf in your forties or fifties would not seem like a bad idea if you could live to 140 years of age. Would we work until we are 120 years of age? Would there be a job for you to do? Could you teach old dogs new tricks? Or would we experience so many technological changes in our extended lifetimes that we couldn't keep up?

Michael Jordan would be hitting the glory years of his career by his forties instead of retiring. It would be devastating for Jordan fans to see him get dominated by a young budding superstar named Lebron James. Dictators would be running nations for decades to come. We would have to reconsider many things, including the risks we take. Risking the last ten years of someone's life is different than risking the last 130. How fast would overpopulation become an issue? Would that increase the urgency and funding around interplanetary colonization?

Realistically, life expectancy would probably not double again in our lifetime. But it could. In the last century, we didn't necessarily extend life so much as we eliminated premature deaths. A century ago, people were living into their eighties, nineties, even hundreds. Humans could always live this long; we just removed the unfortunate roadblocks that kept us from getting there. This progress is less about adding years to the top end and more about increasing the bottom end.

Our understanding of the world has increased around how we best manage it to maximize lifespan through science. Now that we have removed and understood these premature killers more and more, our focus is shifting to the thing most likely to kill us: getting old. We have hit a point where we have done everything we can as we continue to max out our biological limitations. Death is the greatest motivator in human history. The concept of the eternal surfer becomes less fictional and more of a reality. We can expect human efforts in research and funding to continue at unprecedented rates. We are still in the early stages of this new problematic dilemma of creating eternal surfers. So long as there are a handful of humans looking to chase immortality, we will find it eventually.

Although many of the megatrends of our century show progress toward the effort, AI is showing some of the most progress against aging and death. As this progress continues, we will see more and more shifts in the focus of scientists, researchers, computer models, and algorithms. This will reshape our cultures, societies, parliaments, and governments. As success in this arena builds, we will see massive political disruptions and conflicts arise. We might have a crazy breakthrough that allows us to upload our minds.

We might have more gradual advancements in which our minds will need to use our biological bodies as a host while it interfaces wirelessly with AI systems. For this second example, maybe we find a way to put our bodies into a vegetative state, significantly reducing our cells' aging and allowing us to live to 140, through a computerlike interface. Many people would volunteer for this on the argument that we will advance technology a lot over the next 140 years, and there could be a real likelihood that in 140 years, we have mastered whole brain emulation. At this point, those technically still "alive" could be freed from the chains and limitations of their biological bodies. If we do not notice and engage them, this could be a world you or your children find yourselves in one day.

Living forever would be a form of immortality, but not like many of us have imagined it. You can still die, just not as early. Getting hit by a car (from one of the few nonautonomous models left on the road), or your power gets disconnected mid-upload, there's not much we could do for you. Termination still happens. The dead remain dead. Humans wouldn't be invincible; we would just age—theoretically—forever.

Which brings about a whole new dilemma: What would we do with all this time?

The Happy Surfer

We can increase lifespan, but can we increase our happiness level to be consistent with the length of our lives? How does one even address an unquantifiable goal like happiness? Humanity is in a better state now than 100 years ago, but are we any happier?

The GDP might tell us how happy the population is. This has led some politicians and even economists to voice a need to either add a measure or even replace the measure of GDP with GDH (gross domestic happiness).

Do we want to be happy, or do we want to be productive? Some make the very protestant argument that production leads to happiness. After all, production creates the basis for material happiness. While production is critical and creates a pathway to buying happiness, production as a stand-alone concept does not create happiness. Singapore is much more productive per person than Costa Rica, yet research shows that Costa Ricans are much happier than citizens of Singapore. Thirty-five years ago, most South Koreans lived in a state of poverty, lacked the freedom to follow tradition, and were uneducated—all the staples of a dictatorship-like regime. Present-day South Korea is a global economic powerhouse, having some of the highest-educated citizens in the world, no longer under a dictatorship, and as a whole living with less poverty. Back in the mid-1980s, the average rate of suicide in South Korea was 9 in every 100,000 people. Today, the average rate of suicide has increased by more than 300% over the past thirty-five years.

If we are rich and live in peace, are we happier? In nations stricken by poverty and political instability, such as Peru, Guatemala, Albania, and the Philippines, the suicide rate is around 1 in 100,000 citizens. In the prosperous, rich, safe, and peaceful nations like France, Switzerland, New Zealand, and Japan, the annual suicide death rate is twenty-five times higher. The balance between production and happiness is apparently not a binary choice—production increases do not result in happiness.

The right to life, liberty, and the pursuit of happiness: This guarantee is outlined in the American Declaration of Independence signed in 1776. Yet Dr. Harari, a history professor, points out that the right to a pursuit of happiness is very different from the right to happiness. The old production augments stated these freedoms allowed us to increase our consumption, which many believed would lead to happiness. Again, this isn't the case.

Our ancient ancestors had around 4,000 calories at their disposal, per human, per day. This caloric threshold was used to harvest food, build and use tools, make fire, fix homes and habitats, make clothing, hunt, and other prehistoric duties. Today, in the USA, the average person uses 228,000 calories of energy every day and serves everything from nourishing our bellies, powering our homes, computers, smartphones, TVs, kitchen appliances, and the cars we drive. The average American consumes sixty times more calories than their ancient ancestors—but are they sixty times happier? Not likely.

America has had an incredible run since being on the winning side of the Second World War. They went on to have a triumphant win in the Cold War, which catapulted them to become the world's top superpower. Over the fifty years after the Second World War, the United States' GDP grew from $2 trillion to $12 trillion. Over this same time, the real per capita income across the country increased by a factor of two. The hyper-competition created endless amounts of affordable luxury items, clothing, jewelry, houses, household appliances, computers, TVs, phones, and just about anything else you could desire. Ethnic minorities, women, and gays gained more access to the American dream. Despite all this incredible progress of well-being, studies show that people's subjective well-being in America in the 1990s was relatively the same as it was in the 1950s, before their world dominance. In more extreme and drastic examples, we can look at Japan and its explosive economic boom. From 1958 to 1978 in Japan, the average real income increased by five times. A tsunami of wealth poured into the country, yet its people were just as happy in the nineties as they were in the fifties.

Are you happier than your parents and grandparents were when they were your age? The research shows it is probably the same. Consider your own model: Are you any happier today than when you were carefree, playing in the park with your friends at the age of eight or ten? Not likely. Does your happiness level keep pace with the rate of pressure and stress in your life? When a toddler is unhappy, he cries. A good parent tends to the toddler and makes them happy again to stop the crying. Although small children often cry, despite how it might feel to parents, toddlers do not spend most of the day crying. This would mean most of the day infants are either content or happy. Once we grow up, we are taught not to cry, but if adults cried every time they were unhappy, most of us would be crying from morning to night.

To better understand this, we would have to go back several thousand years to the foundation of Western philosophy or possibly even before the time of Socrates, Plato, and Aristotle. As adults, it's as though we are not allowed to feel as happy as we did as children. Even when we do feel happy, we sometimes question how happy we should be or if we should be happy at all. Are we allowed to be happy? Do we have permission? Likewise, when we are upset, we often find ourselves wondering if we should let this emotion upset us, hide it, run away from it, or let ourselves experience it.

For the last few thousand years, humans have learned never to let anyone see us care strongly about anything. It is generally viewed as embarrassing to be open about how we feel. "Have some manners," "act your age," and "be more mature" are all things most of us heard growing up as children transitioning to adulthood. Seeing adults openly care about anything is very strange.

Imagine you worked extra hard and waited over a year to get enough free time to go on a surf vacation with your friends. Leading up to your trip, the forecast is off the charts; you and your friends are beyond stoked, as you could not have asked for better surfing conditions. After a day of travel, you arrive at your destination. To your amazement and bafflement, the ocean is completely flat. Not a wave or even a ripple in sight—the epic surf you came for has shifted way up north to Tofino. So you fall to your knees in the middle of the busy Venice beach, crying hysterically, punching the sand and screaming profanities at the top of your lungs at anyone who looks at you. A stranger approaches you, thinking you need help, but you are so emotional you try to roundhouse-kick him to the face. It's not a good look for a husband, father of three, and a well-established lawyer from Toronto.

However, imagine going on the same trip and the forecast is beyond terrible. Your friend convinces you to spend a few days with him anyway, drinking beer and relaxing away from the daily grind of work. When you show up, for whatever reason, the forecast is more perfect than you could possibly imagine. Look at those waves! You start screaming hysterically, running in circles and spinning around until you lose your balance and fall over repeatedly. You sob tears of joy, throwing yourself at and almost suffocating any random stranger with hugs and kisses. You even accidentally head-butt your friends out of pure excitement and happiness. Then, maybe, you get some surf in. As an adult, it is simply not acceptable to show how you feel. Generations of wanting to be cultured or sophisticated might be to blame.

Are we happier today than we were in the past? If we were, we might not even know it. Regardless of what the data says about improvements in our quality of life, large populations usually *feel* as though they were happier in days past. Consider Brexit. The older demographics wanted things to go back to "the way they used to be," and a majority of over sixty-five-year-old voted to leave the EU. Most of the young adults voted to stay part of the EU, knowing their economic futures might depend on it. This would lean toward an understanding that although their quality of life has increased, the old demographics believed they were happier before.

They believed it, even though all of the evidence proved otherwise—yet another human bias at play.

We saw a similar bias-driven fear campaign play out in America in the 2016 election, which highlighted a "Make America Great Again" slogan. Implying that Americans are less happy than they were in the past when "America was great." The logic is flawed in just about any way you dissect it; America was "greater" in 2016 than any other time in its history. All this would imply that people were happier in the past, compared to how happy they are now. After all, most of us miss the good old days. Right?

Our perception of happiness is far more important than what happiness is or how to get it. Having more and doing more is not enough to make us happier. There are some parallels between our aging dilemma and happiness. Much in the same way the age of a human has a ceiling, does our happiness have a ceiling threshold? It might be easier to make the average person in a developing nation happy as their basic human needs are met, but have we already maxed out human happiness in developed countries? Why do we *even care* about the concept of happiness? If we are working to increase humans' life expectancy significantly, it would be important to understand how to keep humans happy. Otherwise, what's the point? It sure would suck to figure out how to live forever, only to find out we get more depressed as we age. Or maybe the less we contribute to society, the less happy we are? Regardless, understanding the essential importance of happiness is just as important as the scientific and technological advancements causing these dilemmas.

Things gain exponential potential when they are digitized—so how do you address happiness with an algorithm? We have trouble explaining our feelings, but that doesn't mean we can't assess them scientifically to find out what causes them. Many of us correlate things or events to our happiness, but we don't necessarily know what happens in our brains and body to create the "warm and fuzzy" sensations. Functionally, many of us feel we understand happiness even though we do not understand the biological workings. The top end of happiness is both mental (psychological) and physical (biological)—an important thing to understand if we are going to advance technologies that could significantly extend a human's life. A happy person's mental and emotional state depends on their expectations, not on what society can measure. We are happy when the reality we experience matches the expectations we have created. This explains why humanity is not much happier despite all our progress in making the world a better place. As our world continues to become a better place, our expectations also increase. Progress has not created greater happiness; it has merely created greater expectations.

The second thing responsible for our happiness has nothing to do with our social status, economic contribution, or the political environment we reside in and *everything* to do with our physical biochemistry. Happiness is a feeling; it is a biological sensation that we understand scientifically and regularly alter with medication and treatments. The problem is this modification of sensation is only temporary. We can very easily experience or hear of something that should make us sad, and with the right dose of the right medication, we can feel, for the most part, happy again. Inversely, the sensation of an incredible achievement will have us smiling ear to ear, but that sensation fades as we return to normalcy.

What happens when there is an unbridgeable rift between our lowest depressions and the highest possible happiness? Why would we regularly engage in activities where the risks outweigh the rewards? Because we're irrational beasts. Happiness is temporary; our biology evolved it to be as such. Our biology's evolution is designed to maximize our chances of survival and reproduction and not care about our happiness. Our biochemistry is programmed to benefit from activities favorable to our existence and reproduction with enjoyable sensations—like happiness and orgasms. There are also sensations designed to make us unhappy when we do not fulfill actions necessary to our biological, evolutionary needs. We have all experienced the happiness that comes with a great meal and the discomfort of hunger. Eating food is essential to survival; we get rewarded when we do it and punished when we don't. The same is true for reproduction and the rewarding sensation of sex. Although eating food and having sex brings us great happiness, we get the sensational urge to do them again after they are complete. Like our ancestors, once we are done eating or screwing, we go out looking for more. If there ever was a branch of evolved humans that experienced eternal, lasting happiness after eating or sex, they likely went extinct quickly. After all, if you're satisfied, why bother doing anything?

And so we are in constant pursuit of the perfect wave. Even if you manifest an ideal wave and you give it the perfect ride, you will eventually want more.

We work the rat race to get promoted, only to work harder to get promoted again. Higher-paying jobs, nicer homes, higher-end cars, nicer clothes, nicer restaurants, a better body, better everything. Some argue this isn't so bad, and it's just part of "the journey." For anyone who has ever climbed a mountain, the journey is incredible. But when the journey concludes with a summit, it is that much better.

Enjoy the journey. But eventually, you will need a summit.

We can take pills to make us happier. We have pills to increase our sex drive and abilities—we take them not because we need them but because they lead to a good feeling. Most people in developed nations have sex because of the good feeling, not for reproduction. Any healthy human can easily go eighteen hours without eating, yet most of the population in developed nations overeat several times a day because it makes us feel good. The longer you go without eating, the more you crave the reward. This usually decreases other things that give you short-term happiness and prioritizes them lower than eating. If the feeling of happiness didn't drive you to eat, then you may as well do anything other than eating to feel happy.

In a well-documented study, a rodent could push a pedal that sent an electrical impulse through an electrode connected to their brain. The electric pulse gave them excited, happy feelings. They also added some of the rodent's favorite food to the cage. The rodent had to decide: push the button to get the incredible pulse of happiness or eat the food. 100% of the time, they chose the pedal over the food, to the point where the rats collapsed from exhaustion and dehydration. Have you ever been having so much fun you accidentally skipped lunch?

The feeling of happiness is designed to be temporary. Like the idea of preventing or escaping death (which is majorly unhappy), humanity will chase happiness through the advancement of this century's megatrends. Doing more with less is how humans came to be the dominant species on Earth. We love shortcuts and easy fixes that require less effort to produce better results. We have found ways to do more of what makes us happy without risking the consequences, like how birth control lets us have sex without costly children. The little blue pill keeps us having sex even when our biology fails. Sometimes these are great advancements. Other times they simply make us lazy. Smartphones are a long way from what the Europeans had when they first descended on the Americas, but we still educate children through ancient academic models and structures. Instead of enabling academics with technology, we medicate children with Ritalin to get them to adhere to antiquated teaching methods. Lazy.

It feels like a lot of work to completely redesign old systems, especially when so much rides on it. Despite the modern expectations we put on kids, they are stuck learning in a system that is hundreds of years old. Are we lazy? Or are the kids broken? In the past decade, the number of Ritalin prescriptions in the UK increased by 850%. America has more active prescriptions of Ritalin than the population of most small nations. Globally in 2013, 2.4 billion doses of methylphenidate was consumed. Even as we take drugs to level moods and increase focus, we have also doubled how many stimulants we've taken. Are we irrational? Or are we really just this lazy?

We need to embrace our shortcomings and realize we will develop these megatrends of the future very much in the same manner as we did things in the past, even if it doesn't make sense in the here and now. We live in a capitalist world of competitive markets, from which many powerhouse nations have economies built off means of production and operational structures for profit. Regardless of what other models are available or what some might believe to be a better option for our present world, happiness as we know it is only achieved through pleasure within the stronghold of capitalism. Capitalism will drive a large part of the funding for researchers and develop these megatrends of our era. Since our capitalistic mindsets have a decreased patience for unenjoyable feelings and an ever-increasing want of happy feelings, we can be reassured that the happiness problem will be a fundamental driver of what happens next. It won't be all pills and quick fixes.

As we instinctively correlate certain objects and events to our happiness, we start to understand better the science behind the simple biological mechanisms that create happiness. This comes with many questions in its own right. Who is responsible for your happiness? Who has the right to decide if you get to be happy? What if future ethics find it barbaric for humans to not be in a constant state of happiness? Should we be criminalizing sadness?

Consider the evolution of child abuse. A century ago, we spanked our kids. You could beat a child as a form of punishment and pretty much everyone was on the same page with it. Attitudes are drastically different today, even though child abuse still exists. Child abuse is largely illegal today. Are we enforcing the laws enough?

So, what if your government made the state of unhappiness illegal? Knowing the side effects of long-term sadness, they would do what they could to make you happy again. In this hypothetical example, if you have had a rough, bad-news week, by law you might need to spend 80% of your day attached to a machine that stimulates the release of chemicals in your brain to trigger a happy feeling. Absurd? Many parts of the world, and even some current political parties in developed nations, already believe in restricting your rights to decisions concerning your own body. This would be no different. A hundred years ago, the concept of abortion might have sounded just as absurd as the concept of not being happy would be to someone a hundred years from now. It is better to proactively shape our future now before we all find ourselves strapped to a happiness machine for twenty hours a week. We should figure it out now before we have an entire generation of humans walking around staring into a handheld device all day.

This is why we need a "why." It will determine the future we shape in the face of rapid progress. With our current brain architecture and biological structure, our current attempts to achieve happiness will never be enough. If we ever get to a point where we find a way to cheat death, we will likely have a sound grasp of manipulating our emotions, body parts, and intelligence. The solution to eternal happiness is likely centered around the need to reengineer our human bodies and brains.

Swedish-born physicist Max Erik Tegmark, a professor at the Massachusetts Institute of Technology, categorizes life into three sophistication stages. Life 1.0, as he calls it, represents simple biological life. This life-form can only survive and replicate; its actions and behaviors are all predetermined in its DNA. Consider bacteria as an example. Life 2.0 is more complex. Life 2.0 can survive and reproduce, but it can also design its own software—like a human. Although we created the software (language, cultures, skills), our metaphorical hardware is incapable of change. Life 3.0 could survive and replicate, design its software, and additionally design its hardware. There are no current examples of Life 3.0. But AI advancements present the most realistic chance of creating some form of Life 3.0, a technology, or a technologically enhanced life-form, capable of designing and upgrading both its software and hardware. This brings us to the final dilemma we face.

The Artificial Surfer

Compared to our ancestors, everything is different. Or so we want to think. Humans haven't changed much; we're as irrational as ever. The storylines and plots of present-day entertainment have not changed much over the last few centuries. Leonardo DiCaprio sold out movie theaters playing the same Romeo another actor performed to sell out the Globe in Shakespeare's day. No matter the era, the emotional conflict is the same, whether on the screen or the stage. At a fundamental level, everything about the human condition remains unchanged. We might walk around talking through our AirPods as we step into a self-driving car, we might be wearing the coolest new kicks and a fancy new smartwatch, but we have not physically changed. How do we even begin to imagine a world where the human constant changes?

What humans would do with superintelligence is very different from what a superintelligence would do with superintelligence. Any attempt to accurately predict this future is a waste of time. We can attempt to shape a future with the ethics around how we move forward with these creations. Global ethics will require our short-sighted, selfish, simple, nationalistic minds to create new views and values of the world and humanity. Once the intelligence market gets disrupted, the results would be too drastic and swift for our simple brains to comprehend. It is too late; being creative is not an option once such a form of disruption occurs. We could use theory to attempt to shape, displace, or prevent such a disruption from happening. But, theorizing on how to best leverage it once the disruption has occurred is impossible. This would have been like asking ants to predict the future of humanity fifty years ago.

When it comes to reengineering the human mind, both biologically and artificially, one thing we know for sure is that humanity will not stop until superhuman or superintelligence-like levels are mastered. Private companies and governments have made clear this accomplishment is a race to dominance. This race, and all of the problems it could resolve, is getting loads of attention and focus from the world's greatest thinkers, which means it is ripe for endless corruption. All we can accurately predict about the future is that the Fourth Industrial Revolution's megatrends will create more powerful, life-changing advancements than ever before with equally and potentially destructive outcomes. In the short term, we need to create and consider new ethics around how we interact with AI systems as objects and how they will interact with us. We need to reconsider our understanding and definitions of what it means to be human and define consciousness and intelligence. We need to know the real outcomes on the horizon and address the new meaning of old age and reengineer our minds and bodies to live longer. This entails conversation about the importance of death, misery, assessing risk, and defining happiness. Our current ethics are not built for superhumans or blended forms of technological human augmentations and amplification; they were built for linearly minded mortals a century ago.

There are still going to be failures and setbacks. We have learned from failure, and in doing so, humanity has built up a solid pipeline of successful options. We may very well discover that our biology is too complicated, that genetics will take too long to modify and too much money to solve. We might find that most of science is already almost fully understood (not the case, but play along). At this point, we give up on biological cognition, and the brain-computer interfaces take the lead. Maybe we achieve super forms of intelligence through nanotechnology advancements or unexpected augmentation and amplification from basic AI. If we max out science, or it fails us, we have a long pipeline of technology to pick up the slack. Where technology lags, a robust, well-funded scientific pipeline will catch up. This will not all hit at once, not in the short term. It will evolve and develop interconnectedly through complexity, which we cannot control, but we can nudge along and help shape its direction. When we look back over the coming years, we will realize how different and how much both us and the world around us have changed.

A part of you, as a human, will be upgraded over your lifetime. Visiting a doctor to get drugs to make you better? No problem. Adding voice command devices in your house to make you better? No problem. Downloading applications onto your phone or computer to make you better? No problem. Wearing a smartwatch to make you better? No problem. Use of self-driving mode, lane detection, antilock braking systems to make you a better driver? No problem. But when we talk about upgrading humans? Big problem. It's such a big problem we don't even want to talk about it. Just no. This is human instinct; it is the same reason a child closes their eyes and looks away from something that scares them. It's time to stop behaving like a child.

The topic is weird, and it should make you uncomfortable. Everything you know about your world, all your greatest dreams and fears, is built around your identity. The concept of disrupting or upgrading humans means that the current human version of you will be irrelevant in the future. This is the human nightmare, the ultimate change. This is why there are campaigns for "going back" and "making things great again." We want to go back to when we were more relevant, when we mattered. Projecting the current version of ourselves into the future is scary because we can't understand how to remain relevant in a world we do not understand. Change happens fast, but it rarely happens overnight. The megatrends of the Fourth Industrial Revolution are already in flight, but there is still time for us to adapt and apply the surfing framework and focus our energy on what we can do and what matters.

There are really three options.

You can choose to stay close-minded, take a stand, and refuse to accept change, and fight until you become irrelevant, live out the shitty end of your life at the mercy of others, and die.

You could choose to simply ignore these realities, say "it is what it is" and get displaced whenever it happens, and live your life at the mercy of others.

Or you can engage in a way that not only shapes your future but the future of humanity. We most likely will not get the luxury of death to save us from putting this off to the next generation. The progress that once took hundreds or thousands of years now happens in decades and years. And soon, just a matter of months.

We all need to be strategically taking part in these conversations now. In the exponentially disruptive future, being reactive will cause us to wipe out over and over. This is where the surfing framework comes in—when you're limber, balanced, and proactive, you have a fighting chance to ride the wave and embrace the discomfort. The only certainty we have looking into the future is what has worked in our past. We are still far away from perfectly engineered babies and achieving artificial human-level intelligence (AGI). You may as well join the discussion. Everything will likely come to fruition in *this* lifetime.

There is no longer a "borrow from the future" mentality. Whatever we end up doing, we're dealing with the consequences before we pass. We cannot imagine living without the technology we have today, yet there are still those who want to stop tomorrow's progress. Remember, we are surfing, not driving a car. There are no "brakes" on a surfboard, but we can have some nice big cutbacks to slow things down for a moment here and there, but ultimately, the wave we are riding dictates the amount in which we can slow down. There is no stopping, not anymore. Hang on.

For our foreseeable and understandable future, we are surfing. There is too much interdependency in these megatrends' complexities being driven by not just AI, but massive amounts of data creation, ingestion and consumptions, various new forms of technologies like nanotechnology and advancements of genetics, medicine, and science in general. There is no on/off switch. There is no one throttle to choke. We are no longer able to predict the global economy accurately or effectively. To do so would require us to understand and predict every advancement happening worldwide, in real time. Furthermore, how do these advancements impact one another, and to what degree? The only thing we know is that we can no longer understand and control the global machine we live within. Trying to accurately predict and understand our future is impossible, but we can nudge it along to our preference a bit here and there. We can use this machine to help humanity reach its goals, whatever they end up being.

And what if stopping were possible? Would we want to? The result would likely be worse. If we stopped this machine and turned off the pumping waves of this current century, our economies and societies would collapse.

Economies presently need constant growth to survive. Our economy is built on a need for continuous development that happens through innovation and change—the things we value. We can only make so many cars, which is why Ford does not dominate the industry. We needed different kinds of cars and sustainable innovation: slightly bigger, more powerful, better mileage, sunroof, no roof. But low-end disruption enters in the form of electric cars. It knocked Ford on its ass, but it wasn't enough to do them off due to disguised forms of welfare like federal government bailouts. Making a Tesla Model S for everyone is not enough—we want a smaller version, we want an SUV version, we want a hatchback version. This constant change and innovation is the only way to survive as an organization, and this foundation drives our economies. We always need new things to value. Capitalism will continue to fuel and drive the underlying goal of solving things like happiness, physical and intelligence superpowers, and even immortality.

Why not just pause certain megatrends? AI seems like the biggest threat, so why not just put a pin in it for a moment? The reality is we cannot decouple megatrends. We will eventually eradicate many more infectious diseases; we will cure things like strokes, Alzheimer's, brain damage, and memory loss. We will advance humanity in so many incredible ways. But these advancements are all interconnected with blurry boundaries. All these great cognitive life-changing successes will also lead to increases and upgrades in young, healthy adults' memory and intelligence. With the amount of Ritalin doctors and parents are jamming down their children's throats, there is no question we need a different way to achieve better results. A minor tweak in an embryo that increases your child's chance to be a dominant pro athlete, or be a professional surfer, would be a no-brainer to the majority of the overly competitive parents with ever-growing expectations of their children. Through it all, remember: If you don't do it, someone else will. It's all about keeping up with the Joneses. If you don't buy in, your children won't stand a chance against theirs. It's not about editing out genes that cause cancer; it's about adding genes for physical traits or aesthetic beauty.

We cannot clearly draw a line between healing humans and flat out upgrading them. Sildenafil, for example, was created to treat those with blood pressure issues—it was meant to heal. In addition to resolving blood pressure problems, it gave men enormous erections. They don't prescribe Sildenafil for blood pressure issues anymore, but you can get it as Viagra. Sexual enhancement pills are a booming industry built around upgrading people instead of healing them. Plastic surgery was created to put injured soldiers back together after battle. Now the entire industry is funded by the wealthy looking to inject youth back into their bodies. Built for one thing, applied to another.

We will not create some superhuman overnight that will instantly dominate all other humans (although someone should investigate Kelly Slater or Lebron James). The reality we need to address is this: Humans are going to take advantage of genetic advancements. Period. It will most likely happen over time in small increments. Parents who want to remove genetic profiles that result in developmentally deficient babies will eventually want to add the genes for athletic aptitude or whatever it is that makes people Fulbright-scholar smart. Would you risk the life of your twelve-year-old child on a game of blackjack? Once proven methods and advancements in genetics are available, not taking advantage of them could be seen as gambling with your future child's life. It would be like choosing to stay on your hand when the dealer dealt you a two and a three. It is a bad gamble. When you get a free hit in blackjack, you always take it to increase your chances of winning with zero risks. If such a medical procedure only increases the chances of *not* getting a deadly disease, leaving the future of human life up to chance, without increasing its chances, it could become illegal. From here, the road gets slippery. Advancement in stem-cell research could create the ability to fertilize hundreds of eggs in the hope of one having sufficient or acceptable DNA. If, after that, none are sufficient, we could alter the DNA to remove deadly genes. We could also remove the genes that cause autism, Parkinson's, immune system deficiencies, depression, obesity, stupidity, etc. These would all become a quick fix, and suddenly through many unrelated interconnected advancements, we can program in above-average memory and physical attributes into humans. Although this may seem far away and there is much controversy around it, a handful of Chinese scientists have already been sent to jail for creating CRISPR babies.

Are you the one still using smoke signals, or payphones, or even a flip phone? Refusing to take part? That's fine; just know that your child will be forever disadvantaged against their classmates who will most definitely be genetically augmented. Maybe the answer is to just ban it. Make it illegal—no genetic modification in the US. Does China adhere to this ruling? Russia definitely won't, especially if China is not banning it. Australia, who has been producing super surfers forever, sees this as a potential threat to their surfing dominance. Does the USA really have a choice? Even if a country did admit to stopping such development, a more realistic scenario would play out with America saying, "Just kidding, we never actually stopped doing it," and the existential race to world dominance continues.

Have we lost our minds? How did we get here? Why are we developing such advancements? Most infants used to die before their fifth birthday. People died from common colds, the flu, and pneumonia. What used to kill you in the past is not even worth missing a day of work today. If you explained to someone from 100 years ago about any of our routine medical procedures like blood transfusions or organ transplants, they would have told you how *Frankenstein*, although exceptionally well written, was a fictional novel that would never come true. A functional takeaway from the Frankenstein novel is how these advancements are not done overnight, nor are they the work of a lone, mad scientist in their laboratory. Rather, we will inch along in small, incredibly complex intervals in what will seem like slowly moving collectives of these megatrends. There is no plan, no road map from here to there.

How do we dream of practical solutions to the future? How do we address mass transformation from normal reality to migrations into virtual realities? How do we defend or shape unknown drivers that hijack our physiological addictive neurochemistry? Humanity to date has battled an addiction to dopamine. What if this could be six times worse? What will we do when these future megatrends take us hostage by leveraging not only dopamine but also our serotonin, anandamide, endorphins, norepinephrine, and oxytocin? With VR technology leveraging sensors and AI, we can elevate and trigger all six compounds to unimagined levels, on demand.

We used to get these things as a reward. Now, we can just get them. We take risks to get the reward. We have evolved to identify these loops, and once we close (experience) this loop, our biological bodies produce chemicals to make us crave them again. Cocaine floods the brain with dopamine, making it extremely addictive. Future disruption will flood our brains with daily addiction just by experiencing everyday neurostimulation. Are you noticing the change happening in your everyday life? The change is not only happening for those taking cocaine, that feeling, a little rush you get when your smartphone vibrates or pings, that is dopamine. The sensation you don't notice, but you get when you check the update on your smartphone: dopamine. That tiny pleasure you experience as you scroll over some social media post of fake news that strengthens your confirmation bias: dopamine.

Thanks to humanity's shortcomings, we should be ready for short-term violence, diseases, and poverty. We did not dominate through perfection. We are a species of "good enough." There is no sense in mastering something beyond what is needed to get the job done. After spending enough time and getting good enough at surfing beginner waves, our attention quickly shifts to the bigger, more-rewarding waves that carry bigger, more-costly risks. We will not suddenly be content with dying or being unhappy sooner than necessary, even more so as we recognize the megatrends of this century will help us work toward solving these problems. Our societal, political, and economic futures will slowly be reshaped by seemingly foreign drivers and concepts like happiness and immortality.

If the prediction path we are on seems bad, we can still choose to change our course before things worsen. Predictions do not necessarily predetermine outcomes. We change predictions through actions, which in turn modify our predictions (ideally for the better). Accurate prediction models are useless. Instead, we build a model to learn more. As soon as we know more, we change our model. Since we have no way of knowing exactly what we will learn, we have no way of knowing how the model will change. As our knowledge grows, our actions change, and as we continue to incur more data and information, we better understand the problems. The better we understand the problem, the faster our knowledge grows and changes our understanding of how to fix the problem, and the more we realize the problem itself changes. The faster we change the problem, the faster our knowledge of the problem becomes outdated. Therefore, using complexity to guide and loosely attempt to navigate the future is all we can realistically expect to control. The surfing framework is looking better by the minute.

Humans love to try and predict things; it is a trap we must not fall into as we ride into the future. We attempt to predict everything from weather, sports, stocks, and medical treatments, but we suck at it. The future is always more complex than our past and present, and using old methods of predicting in an increasingly complex world is an embarrassing feat. Predictions and methods we used to win the great world wars are useless in an age of cyber warfare that is happening all day, every day. To date, our slow evolutionary growth in intelligence and knowledge has allowed for the emergence of large, slow-moving linear mechanistic political and economic structures. In 1800, it was relatively easy to predict what America would be like in 1830. But trying to predict America in 2051 is impossible. In the year 2051, all advanced nations will have completely different political systems. The economies will not resemble what they are today. Employment will be completely different, and the citizens themselves will be different and changed from what we know presently. And you have no idea what it will look like. Guessing would just be a fun activity.

Although we often leverage history to guide us away from our past mistakes, we also use science to predict the future. Science and technology are much more than tools of prediction, but drivers of changes in our future and our predictions therein. The creation of the earth, and all living things on it, like humans, happened through an accidental chain of events. We understand this now but would have never been able to predict it. What adds to the complexity of future states is accidental chains of events and the random engineered events of technological advancements, science, politics, and the emergence of complex systems such as our economies and societies. Not to mention irrational and incorrect fears that prevent certain events from happening. The goal isn't to predict the future but to invite the discussion of our present-day dilemmas to control events that may happen.

Nothing is off the table; there are no guaranteed rights or wrongs. Egypt was ruled for 3,000 years by the Pharos, the Popes ruled Europe for 1,000 years—neither could foresee their fall from power. Maybe the collapse of humanity is a good thing? Maybe we have dominated long enough, and we should leave our faith to the next dominant species that emerges? Humans are afraid of the unknown; it is why people fear change so much. "If it ain't broken, do not fix it." Nowadays, it may as well be: "If you ain't fixing it, it might as well be broken." Times have changed. In fact, "change" is the only consistency we have had throughout our history, and almost certainly in our near future. The other reality is the pace of change will continue to increase in our foreseeable futures. As we sit upon our surfboards and stare out into the horizon, the only thing we can confidently prepare for is an increase in the pace of change.

Surfing into the Sunset

Every sunset brings the promise of a new dawn.

— Ralph Waldo Emerson

How do we make choices today to shape tomorrow? How do we prioritize the greatest threats? Are we even capable of understanding the world we have created, much less the future?

There is no way of knowing where the Fourth Industrial Revolution will take us, and we can't let the uncertainty of the unknown paralyze us. The world we are paddling out into is changing at a faster pace than ever before. It is hyper-connected and converging together, creating a complexity unlike anything we have seen before. But for every challenge we face, there is equal opportunity. All of us must work to shape our future to transform many of these threats into opportunities to best leverage and unleash the potential of the Fourth Industrial Revolution. We must proactively think through the effects and impacts of this progress in an exponential world very different from our longtime linear past. The window of opportunity for favorably shaping our future is today.

The changes necessary to manage what comes next has to come from all of us. We must end compartmentalized thinking when making decisions. The interdependence and connections of these dilemmas require it. We will need all the help we can get. We will need inclusive approaches of collaboration and flexibility as we transform and integrate ecosystems with the interdependence of all stakeholders.

With an increase in awareness and our surfing framework to provide a shared understanding of the future, we will transcend into a future where we reshape our economic, social, and political systems to embrace the challenge that lies ahead. We programmed our decision models and systems to be linear and incremental through the first three industrial revolutions. This is no longer sufficient in the exponential world and future that is coming. This will require much more than technological advancements. It will require systematic transformational innovation and complete reform.

Has the meaning of life changed depending on what we know about science, religion, and politics? Has it changed how we define life? Humanity has been debating the meaning of life since the beginning of humankind. Only now, we no longer have the luxury of time. We have a short-term ecological crises. We have world superpowers in an arms race for world domination. We have the exponential megatrends of the Fourth Industrial Revolution building a fail-safe contingency plan with a pipeline of options to ensure we arrive at these goals. If we manage to navigate solutions for all of this somehow, we are using biotechnological advancements and artificial intelligence to reshape and reengineer all life, including human life.

Before long, we will have to decide how we create life and what we ultimately use it for. The markets will not wait for us to conclude our debates of several centuries to come up with the answer, and if we don't start coming with solutions now, the markets will. The changes will arrive suddenly, and we will be forced to live with the outcomes. Something tells me you don't want the future of human life to be decided by ruthless quarterly revenue reports.

Yet the complexity in our world makes it so that there is no way to predict the future. Even if we speculate how technology might advance, it can by no means accurately predict the future. Very different societies and worlds can be created from the same technological advancements. Take the previous industrial revolutions, the steam engine, electricity, radio, TV, nuclear science, the internet. It all created pure dictatorships, fascist regimes, and liberal democracies. Both South Korea and North Korea chose very different ways to use the technologies from the previous century and created very different worlds. Layering AI on top of this century's megatrends creates a certain amount of incredible change and transformation, but it does not support a single deterministic outcome. Everything mentioned in this book is simply a possibility, not a foretelling. If you don't like some of the possibilities presented in this book, you can simply grab your surfing framework, change the way you think and act to ensure a future that prevents such possibilities from coming to fruition. Unfortunately, simply choosing not to believe in these possibilities will not stop them from materializing.

I did not aim to give any answers in the pages of this book. I merely aspired to lay the foundation that would provoke thinking about the most important conversations in human history. If this book empowers or engages even just a few individuals in joining the conversation and debate about humanity's future, it will have been a success. There is no way of knowing exactly where certain technology will be thirty years from now, nor can we know what employment, family life, or even what our ecology will look like. There will be no way of knowing what the dominant religion will be, if any at all, or what economic or political structures will guide us. All we know for sure is it will be nothing like today, disruption will be relentless, and change will continue at a faster and faster rate than ever before. These rogue waves of tomorrow will be mercilessly attacking everything we know to be normal today. You can either surf these waves or be run over and left in their washout.

Surfing Pragmatic Dreams

Does thinking of all this change make you uncomfortable? Don't worry. It's likely just a surge of epinephrine, and possibly some adrenaline, releasing into your body. Also, your brain architecture is working against you. Right now, thinking about all of this, you're likely experiencing a cognitive bias we know as "loss aversion."

Loss aversion is the predisposition to prefer avoiding losses over acquiring equivalent, and sometimes better, gains. In behavioral economics, loss aversion refers to people's preferences to avoid losing compared to gaining the equivalent amount. This potent bias has been programmed into humans since the beginning of time when our linear world had a future threatened by the unknown: Would we have enough to fill our basic survival needs? We are past these days, but the bias remains. It haunts our daily lives; it is why so many "settle" in life and become creatures of habit. It is this exact bias that keeps organizations from evolving and innovating. It is why changes in our economies and cultures are mind-numbingly slow. It is why we hear things like "This is a big problem that requires a lot of change that will never happen in my lifetime."

The first way to believe something won't happen in our lifetime is to keep saying "This won't happen in my lifetime." It only reinforces the bias. Instead, we should accept the facts and embrace responsibility. We could wait for the changes to happen, or we can incite the change we want to see. Stop making excuses to not get in the water. Take a few deep breaths, stop overthinking it. Pick up your surfboard, chill out, and go surf some waves.

The megatrends and technological progression is getting crazier and more unpredictable. The surf is relentless and crushing and, at the same time, presents the greatest surfing opportunities humanity has ever witnessed. We all must get in on the fun as these waves challenge the most foundational title humans have held for all of history: the smartest thing on the planet. Because we should not anthropomorphize AI. AGI (artificial general intelligence) isn't going to likely look, act, or feel like a human. As of the writing of this book, we have no clue if we will ever achieve AGI. But if we do, it will most likely happen *in our lifetime*. If we do achieve AGI, then theoretically, ASI (artificial superintelligence) could very well happen. Maybe in this lifetime, maybe in the next.

Once ASI happens, we lose our title as the most intelligent thing on this planet. It would conquer humans. If the overthrow were to happen, it would probably be too complex for us to understand. ASI would operate at a level where it likely wouldn't notice a human in its way, much like we do not notice ants in our backyard, nor do we care if they live or die. As humans, we want to think of ourselves as empathetic. But I bet you could not tell me any of the seven animals that went extinct in the last year. Sure, we care about animals, but we also don't care as much about significantly inferior forms of intelligence as we do ourselves.

When it comes to ASI, we are the animals that will go extinct.

In a world that is changing exponentially, avoidance and prevention will be vital in overcoming existential risks. Our surfing framework creates a lens of adaptability and agility, which is the ultimate measure of prevention. The surfing framework challenges us to remain in the barrel because it contradicts how our society works. Most of our systems and institutions are from another era, established during a previous industrial revolution, when success was measured by size and stability. Why own outdated things when it is cheaper to lease better and more relevant things? And why lease when you can crowdsource? Agility is becoming a common business practice. We are slowly translating this flexibility into our daily lives. Unfortunately, governance seems to be our slowest laggard, where much work remains.

We now live in a world that is technologically empowered. Hundreds of years ago, the only individuals who addressed global problems were kings and royal families. Thirty years ago, it was left to big companies and large governments. Today, we—the individuals—address global problems. Technology empowerment gives tiny teams, even individuals, incredible capabilities to handle massive problems. This empowerment leads to some of the most incredible opportunities in human history. From the world's greatest threats and problems comes the greatest business opportunities that create endless funding for innovation and entrepreneurship to solve the next round of problems.

The rogue waves of the Fourth Industrial Revolution are an exponential soup of convergence and amplification. We tend to think linearly about the solutions and risks we face, and we often fall victim to trying to solve tomorrow's problems with yesterday's tools. In the next decade, we will experience a century's worth of technological progression—the future, not the past, is ideal for solving the upcoming problems. Disasters are coming our way, but so are megatrends of opportunity. Every megatrend is augmented by budding AI, which means solutions we can't imagine today will be available tomorrow. The danger lies in not solving our short-term problems, but the side effects of what we may develop along the way. If we are too focused on fixing tomorrow, we might not notice a certain change happening until it is too late.

In any other era, the changes we face would have ended us entirely. In the past, we would have closed our eyes and prayed for salvation. Today, they excite us. Today, we hunt them down and look for more. Through our mindset, daily decisions, and actions, we get ourselves into ideal positioning.

Like a mythical predator, we become laser focused on every movement and decisive paddle as we charge these waves into the point of no return. At times, our future will build into an incredible swell of energy and tension. At times, we will even surprise ourselves, as some of our solutions will release the rise of tension into a detonation of calm—allowing us to lock into perfect unison with the waves. Change is constant; every success is temporary. The waves will once again catch up to us, with relentless foaming white walls ready to obliterate anything and everything in our world. In moments like these, every decision and action will matter as we lock into a battle with waves slowly gaining on us. Instinct will tell us to cut our losses and run. But in these moments, we must remain unfazed and dialed in. In these moments, it should become instinctive that there is no way we are backing down from these waves. With confident determination, we will slowly crouch down and vanish into the barrel of some of these waves.

Everything will go quiet; everything will seem frozen in place. From the shore, humanity will be nervously waiting, scanning up and down the barrel of the wave, for us to emerge. There may be some battles that last longer than others, as we fight not to get swallowed and spit out the end of the rogue waves. There will be moments when we are in the barrel, and the waves will start to break down and close out their barrel of hope on us. But using science and technology in an explosion of mist and seafoam, we will blast out of the end of these barrels with the perfect, effortless control and style of what will be the greatest surfing humanity has ever witnessed. Celebrate the moment, and then get ready for the next battle. There is always another rogue wave on the way.

In the end, there is no such thing as surfing without *surfers*. Hereafter, all that matters is the surfer, us, the people, our cultures, our values. We need to ensure all of us, from all walks of life, all cultures, all nations, all income levels, are taking part in the biggest battle humanity has ever faced. We have been the constant thus far. We cannot take down these giant waves alone; it will take all of our combined knowledge and experience. We will transform our future by putting people first, empowering our fellow surfers, and reminding ourselves that all these megatrends to date are technologies *we* created and tools *we* can use to overcome anything. This effort will require us to unite like never before; we will need to take collective responsibility and move away from easy ways of blaming. We will need to consider the public interest and the greater good in a world where technological innovation will be central to humanity's success. We will need to collaboratively agree on forming our ethics around how we develop and transcend into the future. It will require us all to reprogram new mindsets for a new world in which technology will need to be created in both a collaborative and responsible way. As we displace large parts of the world as we know it—employment, the workforce—we must think through what this means to our sense of self-worth, what it will mean in our communities, to our families, and not only our identity but the identity of humanity. Will we rise up to the challenge? Will we raise the bar for humanity and come into a moral and collective conscious based on the new shared sense of destiny?

Philosopher Immanuel Kant believed in two types of beings: persons and things. Persons have infinite worth, and things have a finite worth. We have built much of our world over the last few centuries around this idea. How do we address such Kantian morality when the line between persons and things starts to blur? Friedrich Nietzsche is sometimes known as a German pragmatist. He always had a fixation on taking an extreme philosophical approach when rethinking what life is and why life is worth living. When it was essentially punishable by death, he challenged everything humanity knew about the cultural and societal systems. Nietzsche shared strong resonances with American pragmatism. This pragmatism is one of America's greatest contributions to the world. Developed at the end of the nineteenth and twentieth centuries, pragmatism assesses the meaning and truth of any idea or belief by their practical application's success. This will come in handy as we face new challenges soon. Many of the limits and realities will be new, but many of the ideas and concepts are old. But how do we be pragmatic about things that are currently only possible in our dreams? How do we solve these future dilemmas in a sensible way that suits the conditions that exist now, rather than obeying fixed ideas or rules?

Stereotypically, an engineer tends to be pragmatic. They often use matter-of-fact approaches unclouded by their judgment. We must start addressing the dilemmas and situations discussed in this book by focusing on practical approaches and solutions instead of being idealistic in our theories. Individuals who are pragmatic thinkers are often seen as negative. But it's not a hunt between negative and positive. Rather, we're rational.

In layman's terms, if you are pragmatic, you are practical. You are someone living by the realities of what can happen in the real world you reside in.

In comparison, if you are dogmatic, you blindly follow the rules, authority, and beliefs no matter what the evidence says. Dogmatic people are set in their ways and very firm in their convictions, usually convictions dictated to them from some form of authority. To be dogmatic is to be irrational and close-minded. Truly dogmatic people will never waver in their beliefs; we should be wary of how much energy we invest in them. On the other end, since pragmatic people tend to be grounded in reality, they have a hard time dreaming.

Split the difference, and consider the pragmatic dreamer. We need to dream of the crazy and impossible future concepts with a sensible, pragmatic approach to how we address these concepts in our world today. We might need a new name for some old ways of thinking. Although contradictory in a sense, the world is going to need more pragmatic dreamers. Not the kind of dreamers who only talk about theories and possibilities, but pragmatic dreamers who roll up their sleeves and will get to work on saving humanity by dreaming up impossibly creative ways of doing so. The kind of dreaming Lennon was referring to when he wrote *Imagine*. The late John Lennon is not alone in pondering such a future. I hope someday you'll join us, and humanity can live as one.

Surf's up! Humanity isn't going to magically save itself! So get stoked, it's going to be a gnarly ride!

EPILOGUE

The future influences the present as much as the past.

— Friedrich Nietzsche

The future of humanity is not a new topic of speculation, so why does it matter more now, than it did a few centuries ago? Why does it matter now more than it did fifty years ago? Your decisions, your actions, and your beliefs on this future will shape our ethics, which public policy and laws are built off. Your decisions will have very real consequences, good and bad. Pragmatically developing a realistic view and perspective on the future of humanity is a worthwhile endeavor since we have a real existential risk looming within our lifetime.

Since the creation of our planet, it is estimated that 99.9% of all species that have inhabited Earth have gone extinct. Our future is not speculative; it is well understood. If we simply continue as is, the future of humanity is extinction. When topics are too broad or general, we tend to block them out. The fate of humanity can come across as all-encompassing, too big, too broad, too diverse. How can we wrap our heads around what you will have for lunch next Wednesday as well as all the technological and scientific breakthroughs that will occur over the next decade of your life? It can seem paradoxical to think we can't really understand the future of humanity, but our existence depends on how we shape it.

This epilogue simply extrapolates the current technology and science we have in place today into the next decade or so of our lives. A world in which our current advancements have collided, but not a world with any crazy speculative breakthroughs like artificial general intelligence, never mind superintelligence. To philosophize about a world after the creation of a superintelligence is a futile task, but we can look to understand what the next decade or two of our lives will experience. Although the exact order of events will be less accurate, we have robust pipeline of potent disruption to ensure we will arrive at some form of it.

We are, in a way, immune to noticing change. For most of us, disruption and technological advancements, as well as scientific breakthroughs, have been a regular occurrence. When we step back and look at the bigger picture of humanity, for 99.9% of all humans that have lived on this planet, there was no rapid technological and scientific advancements, or much change at all. Inventions like the Acheulean hand axe was in operation and remained unchanged for over one million years. Compare that to how many times your smartphone has changed over the last decade of your life. Change has not been consistent over the course of humanity. It has really only been consistent over most of our lifetimes. Noticeable change started with the inventions of the early industrial revolution, but this linear change is now fully exponential in the Fourth Industrial Revolution in which we currently reside.

With a sound understanding of exponentials, many of us have heard the wise tale of the mathematician who defeats the king at a chess match. As a reward, the smartass mathematician asks simply for a grain of rice to be added to the first square, and for the sum of each of the following squares to double the previous square. On the final sixty-fourth square of the chessboard, the king would have had to give up more than 18,000,000,000,000,000,000 grains of rice, which at the time was more rice than they had on planet earth. The more you move down the chessboard, the more serious a "doubling" becomes. When it comes to technology, humanity is nearing this point. We are near the end of the chessboard.

Although it took hundreds of years to build a computer as powerful as the ones we have in our pockets, two years from now, those computers will be twice as powerful. In the years that follow, four times more powerful, then eight times, then sixteen times, and you get the picture. In the moment, this doubling does not seem astronomical, but when you step back and project ten years into the future, it is. It may have taken humanity over 5,000 years to progress from the abacus to a smartphone, but if we project out a decade or two, this means you will have something further ahead than your smartphone is from an abacus. You will have something you can currently not even possibly imagine. This is our near future, this is the disruption and change we are about to experience. Not a better smartphone, but something more different than a bean-counting tool and a pocket-sized supercomputer. In our chessboard example from earlier, we are now past the sixtieth square of a sixty-four-square chessboard. Things are about to become beyond comprehendible for the architecture of our human brains.

To put things in context, let us move back a few squares on our chessboard. Moore's Law helped us understand the technological progression to date, through the advancement of transistors. Exponentials at first seemed slow—production in 1965 was one transistor per person per year, and a decade later, in 1975, it was nearly 1,500 per person per year, nothing crazy. In present day dollars, 125,000 transistors in 1965 would have cost you just under four million USD. To help us understand how fast we are moving now, less than twenty years ago, back in 2004, the number of transistors being manufactured surpassed the number of grains of rice being grown across the globe. A few years later, in 2009, globally we produced about ten quintillion transistors, which is over 250 times more than all the grains of rice that were consumed that year. Sticking with 2009, since it was over a decade ago, in that year, for the price of a single grain of rice, you could buy, at retail, around 125,000 transistors. In 2014, we had shipped 2.9 sextillion transistors to date. In 2016, the world's production of transistors surpassed twenty trillion per second, meaning we were producing hundreds of quintillions of transistors per year. Considering this was a while ago, imagine where we are today. Now imagine where we will be a decade from now.

In this epilogue, we will dip our toes into where we will be a decade or so from now. Looking back, it is easy to see how Netflix obviously disrupted Blockbuster, but in the moment, when most of us still had dial-up internet, this was not as obvious. So what will our future look like? We are about to experience a relentless onslaught of potent rogue disruption, beyond what any of us can imagine. A future in which there is no controlling or planning, just surfing or drowning. Buckle up, the forecast is pumping!

Pragmatic Dreams

The future depends on what you do today.

— Mahatma Gandhi

Do you know what the rest of your life will look like? The rogue waves of tomorrow are building; today's changes will impact what happens tomorrow, and all of these changes are happening at scales so large and so small, you may never notice them. The changes will feel very sci-fi, but they will happen within this life instead of the next generation (they will have their own waves to ride).

What will the biggest industries look like the day after tomorrow? Although there will be incredible disruption within industry and business applications, our focus is on the social impacts that will reshape our daily lives. The retail sector will completely be rebuilt in the next ten years and will impact every other industry, like a rebirth in distribution and advertising. With more time on our hands, the leisure and entertainment sectors will get a complete facelift in the coming years. The medical industry will look nothing like it does today a decade from now. Our education system will finally experience a long-deserved step-change in these relentless disruptive waves. Entire industries built around key needs, like food and transportation, will experience rogue waves of disruption and be forced to change. The same goes for insurance, finance, real estate, and government—not only will our day-to-day life change, but we will be asking a higher order of questions around how these industries will change and who will benefit from them.

In a way, we will be asking: What is the new normal?

What does the new normal look like when "normal life" gets obliterated by disruption? How do we address that people are living longer? How do we address the increased abundance, but not an increase in happiness? How do we talk about human and machine augmentation? What will it mean to move our human intelligence to a computer?

When, and how, do we talk about this?

Industry, Society, and Day-to-Day Lives

Over the past eight years, Peter Diamandis and Steven Kotler have tracked numerous advancements, research, companies, and disruptions within our world and our organizations. For the most part, humans interact and connect with companies without even realizing it. Throughout this book, we touched on how the previous three industrial revolutions reshaped much of the world and laid the foundation for the Fourth Industrial Revolution. Everything we know will be reshaped in our lifetime. Not just some, but everything. This should bring about a feeling of incredible hope, as today's unsolvable problems will be tomorrow's simple solutions. Of course, not without risks. We constantly want more of everything, all of the time. We are the adrenaline junkies for the rogue waves of disruption the Fourth Industrial Revolution is routinely pumping out. As we increase our expectations, we feel higher highs and, potentially, lower lows. The highs bring profits and massive gains. The lows are potential wipeouts with costly, even fatal, results. What we already see with many of these megatrends is how we can shape our future more than ever before. Our lives and interactions will shape much of the onslaught of continuous disruption that transforms the largest industries that support our economies.

Riding the Retail Rogue Wave

Retail is changing rapidly, and with great abandon. We have obvious examples from the previous industrial revolutions of organizations that rode megatrends to global dominance. Sears, for example. By jumping on the back of the transportation megatrend and the US Postal Service, as well as leveraging a boom in inexpensive fuel, Sears took off. None of these trends were part of Sears's business directly, but they offered the waves that they surfed to success.

Then, the surf changed. Wave after wave of disruption hammered Sears. After a 132-year run, unable to keep up with the changes, they filed for bankruptcy. It was too late; disruption had struck. Walmart buried Sears as they lost $6 billion between 2013 and 2018. Sears built off growth from the Second Industrial Revolution and could not compete with companies like Walmart, who built off the Third Industrial Revolution's megatrends. While Walmart is on top now, whether they stay that way will depend on its ability to transition into the Fourth Industrial Revolution. We might not notice this change happening right in front of us in our day-to-day lives, but it started well over a decade ago. In 2006, Sears was worth $14.3 billion; that same year, Walmart was worth $158 billion, and another online company named Amazon was worth $17.5 billion. If we fast-forward to 2019, Sears is bankrupt, Walmart is worth just over $300 billion, Amazon is worth about $900 billion. Although Walmart has seen incredible growth of +202%, Amazon is sitting pretty with a +5,103% change.

The way we interact with companies over the last decade, never mind century, has completely changed. Online companies like Amazon and Alibaba have completely turned retail upside down. They digitized the industry to surf along with the exponential megatrends of the Fourth Industrial Revolution, leaving their competitors to drown. Our current industrial revolution is just starting, and it is pointless to ignore the changes. Online sales still account for less than 10% of all retail sales. Companies like Amazon and Walmart are only limited by the population's connectivity to the internet—which is expected to be 8.2 billion connected active internet users by 2025 (nearly everyone on the planet).

You can either fight it or ride it, but there is no denying that the way we interact with companies is approaching a tipping point as the megatrends of communications, energy, and transportation all converge. In our near future, each of these industries will amplify the change in one another, causing a large-scale economic paradigm shift that will rock our daily lives. All of this is before we've even considered what it means to add AI into the retail experience.

Take grocery shopping as an example. Previous generations used to have to get dressed, drive to shopping centers, walk around and find goods to put in their buggy, walk to the checkout, chat with the cashier, put the groceries in their car, and drive back to their house. Today is a bit faster: you can shop from your phone and have your groceries delivered by a contracted driver. Easier, yes, but many friction points are being smoothed over by technology. Just tell Alexa what to order from Whole Foods, and it appears at our front door two hours later.

Today, $2 billion of products are purchased with voice-driven commands, and this number is expected to increase by 400% over the next two years.

AI is suited to do much more than simply take orders, it can even make them for us. In 2018, Google CEO Sundar Pichai presented Google Duplex as a way for an AI to place calls to humans, going so far as to have the AI book a reservation at a restaurant and another one making a reservation for a hair appointment. In both cases, the human on the other end of the phone had no idea they were talking to an AI. This seems like a harmless application, but it raises red flags about the ethics of AI. After all, who decides what is harmless? The social order says when you pick up a phone, you expect to talk to another person, which is why we all hate spam calls from robocallers. If you can't tell you are talking to an automated voice, is it ethically the same as talking to another human?

Why is it we never notice change until after it has happened? Well, in part, it's because AI has made the change so seamless that we aren't meant to notice it. AI has been smoothing things over and making stuff more convenient by the day. These applications will only grow as they are adopted with little or no question at all.

Beyond convenience, economic drivers push for more AI development. Everything tracks back to a healthy ROI. For example, a good customer service experience increases the likelihood of a purchase by 42%, while a lousy experience turns into a 52% chance of never having that customer purchase again. AI systems can understand and react to customer emotions to aid current sales and help center representatives. Companies like Soul Machine in New Zealand is working to fully replace human agents with AI by leveraging IBM's Watson to create humanlike customer agents (avatars) engineered for empathy. Soul Machine is just one of many pioneering the field of emotional intelligence computing. Today, 40% of all their customer service issues are settled with a highly rated customer experience with an AI agent. The customers are complaining to computers, thinking they're people, and not knowing the difference. In reviewing the ethics of tomorrow today, who gets to draw the line when the manipulation is OK? Would you care if you called into a customer service line and had no idea you were talking to a computer? Is AI more or less likely to cause a situation where the company could be held liable?

To think, most humans that get the "automated, touch-tone" switchboard get frustrated, only to start yelling "operator!" into the handset, thinking they'll get a person. Now, we can scream for an operator and still get a computer!

We have human and AI partnerships to solve human problems, and we have AIs on their own solving human problems. Take it one step further: as organizations continue to invest in AI, there will be growing areas of distributed autonomous organizations. As this change continues to shift, we will start to see AI-to-AI negotiations without the need for any human interaction.

For example: You get in an auto accident. You and the other driver let your insurance AIs call one another to determine payouts, coverages, faults, etc. In real time, entirely with AI. In an age of autonomous and connected vehicles, they'll even have all the data to determine which car was at fault.

The disruption of AI means shopping in the future will be nothing like it is today. Since AI can detect data patterns that humans can't, retail application and adoption will only become more valuable. The changes will transform every industry it touches, not just retail but also all supply-chain levels, inventory, supply, quality, demand, forecasting, production, planning, transportation, management, and much more. Retail and manufacturing organizations have already digitized 70% of logistical operations. The retail industry is on a collision course with yet another massive wave of disruption we have yet to discuss: robots.

Robots already have cameras and sensors, allowing them to see, move, touch, and speak—making them ideal customer interaction agents. Delivery bots based out of companies in California have already delivered over 50,000 orders in over 100 cities across twenty countries. Uber and its competitors are very confident they will have automated flying cars within this decade.

In 2016, Amazon announced Prime Air to promise to have parcels delivered by drones to your door in thirty minutes or less. 7-Eleven, Walmart, Google, Alibaba, and many more have started their own versions of drone delivery initiatives. In Japan, they have ice-cream-serving robots. Pizza Huts in Singapore have robots that greet you as you enter. Electronic stores in Palo Alto have robots that dance with their customers. Walmart now uses robots in many locations to stock shelves and robots for inventory control. Other box stores like Best Buy use robot cashiers that can operate twenty-four hours a day. Home improvement stores have giant iPads with motorized wheels ripping around to help customers locate screws and paint colors. There is still a long way to go when it comes to automated machines filling in for all customer service roles. But with the onset of things like COVID-19, there is a higher demand for contactless options. Less humans, more robots, more safety?

BUT! What if these systems are hacked? This is a real threat with considerable economic losses. According to a recent study by Accenture, the average cost of a corporate breach was $11.7 million in 2017, up 23% from the previous year. Surprisingly, 95% of all cybercrime results from human error, according to a study conducted by IBM. Despite the sophisticated security technologies we have today, most major hacks target vulnerabilities rooted in human behavior, not just those in technologies. The good news is since most security breaches are caused by human error, there's an AI algorithm and system to deter them. As cyber criminals bolster their attacks with AI programs, defense systems do so equally, creating a chess game between AI systems that both significantly outperform anything a human could do.

Using our surfing framework, we see robots are on their way to becoming democratized. Compared to humans, robots are very inexpensive, easy to train, manage, and roll out onto the factory or retail floor without complaint. Once this process becomes fully democratized, small startups will be empowered to compete with the industry giants like Amazon. The incumbent invests in the technology to stay relevant, but ultimately the upstarts and disruptors will benefit. It is becoming harder to rationalize human employees when there is a robotic option that is never late, never sick, never injured, and works around the clock without complaint. Robots never require paternity leave, health insurance, or any paid time off. And, frankly, robots just do the job better. The technological unemployment on the horizon will be unlike anything experienced in previous industrial eras. What are we going to do about it? It may be cost-effective to "hire" a robot over a human, but is it ethical when a person's self-worth is tied to their job?

How does this mass technological unemployment work in an era of free-market capitalism? Should we address and consider concepts such as universal basic income? Again, this would most likely happen over the millions of interconnected and interdependent changes, not a sudden step-change overnight, making it hard for us to conceptualize without applying our present-day concerns and biases (concerns that would not be relevant). The recent COVID-19 pandemic has sent inequality into hyper mode. In countries like the USA, billionaires have increased their worth significantly during the pandemic while unemployment skyrocketed to record levels. Despite the pros and cons, capitalism, in theory, tends to reward hard work and talent. Until, that is, too much capital is concentrated over too few people. Meaning a small percentage of the population gain a large majority of the upside, often untaxed, and this foolproof plan usually allows for taxpayer-funded bailouts when losses occur. As the funds and resources shift more and more into the hands of a few, capitalism itself is in danger. It is no longer about honest competition or an actual free market that rewards entrepreneurial risk and creation.

What if universal basic income could save capitalism? This is exactly what Robert Ayres, a physicist, economist, and professor argues in his new book *On Capitalism and Inequality: Progress and Poverty Revisited*. Although robust, our current economic systems seem to be pushed to their limits as we nervously look on to how much more cognitive dissonance our system can withhold before moving from robust complexity to complete chaos, leading to a fearful collapse. For those against universal income, do you really care if others have the same as you, if you have everything you want to make you happy? Does having more than others make us happier? We addressed the happiness issue earlier; for now, let us return to the changing world of retail.

Unfortunately for retail, the relentless onslaught of tsunami disruption continues with the megatrend of waves like 3D printing. We constantly see an influx of new companies using platforms like Kickstarter to bring new products to market. Clothing retailer Ministry of Supply sells dress clothes made from NASA technology that control body heat and reduces sweating, magically self-adjusts to stay tucked in, and the stuff never wrinkles. They have intelligent everything, including jackets that react to voice commands and adjust to your body temperature. You can walk into the Ministry of Supply's retail store, order any article of clothing, and watch a 3D printer make it right in front of your eyes, specifically to your size, with zero waste. Companies like Reebok and New Balance jumped on board by moving many of their offerings online using similar technologies. This means the storage and transportation of these products, like Kodak's film and print business, suddenly vanish. The brand is fine and will progress, but warehousing and shipping jobs are in jeopardy.

In the early industrial revolutions, even the wealthiest of the population did not have the luxuries of house appliances, heaters, air conditioners, electricity, clear—or even running—water, never mind plumbing and septic options. No cars, refrigerators, phones, or TVs. Never mind computers. Today, in America, individuals living below the poverty line have many of these conveniences, while those living above have significantly more. The change around us shows how things are changing for the better in ways we could never expect. Things we might have initially assigned to the retail industry are now applicable to healthcare, and entertainment is turning into education.

Regardless of whether you're noticing the change or not, the death of our physical shopping malls seems inevitable as they transition into digital offerings and experiences. The shopping mall experience you may have loved will still very much be there. Simply put on your VR headset, and you are suddenly in any mall anywhere in the world. A quick conversation with your AI and you will have exactly what you need with a perfect fit. Your friends, also wearing their VR goggles, are shopping alongside you. Once you're done selecting your custom pair of Louboutin heels from their Paris boutique store, the blockchain-enabled smart contract pays the bill for you, and your new heels are instantly 3D printed at a nearby print shop before a drone delivers them to your home. A digital copy is added to your online inventory so that you can compare future shopping endeavors and show off your new heels in your next meeting—which is scheduled to take place in twenty mins, in Japan, where you have an appointment to review authentic bamboo flooring.

And it only sounds expensive. In fact, sooner than expected, this will be cheaper than the current shopping experience—which carries the overhead cost of shipping, human capital, taxes, sourcing raw materials, and so much more. As these trends take shape, the customer cost to acquire products would be much less since over 50% of the traditional retail markup happens at the storefront level.

This all seems super futuristic, but have you already noticed the changes rolling out all around you? Armani, Nike, Hugo Boss, Levi's, and Lululemon all have 3D body scanners to take your exact measurements. Amazon Wardrobe—an AI fashion advisor—makes personalized recommendations based on your specific preferences and social media behaviors. Love to try before you buy? Try VR and AR to blend a mixed reality of experiences from anywhere in the world. Retail shopping will be dematerialized, demonetized, democratized, and delocalized. No one will know exactly how it will all roll out over the next decade, but the *Fast Times* days of shopping malls are long gone. How long will the stragglers hang on?

How They Will Market the Rogue Waves

Google and Facebook dominate more advertising revenue than all forms of print media have over several generations. As we have known it, advertising is essentially obliterated by technology—what else is there to talk about? Well, who is going to disrupt the disruptor?

For example, physical things have now been digitized, which we experience on our screens. Many households unknowingly experience situations like the example below:

> Husband: Welcome home, dear, how was your day at work today, staring at your screen?
>
> Wife: It was great. My screens were enjoyable. How were your screens today?
>
> Husband: They were not so great; I had a rough day. So, I'd like to sit on the couch and watch the bigger screen in our living room.
>
> Wife: Sounds good, but I might have to use my small pocket-size screen a few times while we watch.

So, how does our world look when our screens get disrupted?

Over the previous industrial revolutions, the very idea of reality was a shared constant. What you saw with your eyes was what others saw with theirs. This all changed over the past decade when we first experienced what it is to view the internet. We will add the recent convergences of high-speed networks (5G connections), AR eyewear, and an economy powered by over a trillion sensors in our near future. All of this will be exponentially amplified with AI. In short order, we will have a world in which we can blend realities as we superimpose digital data in real time with physical objects and environments, and poof! Suddenly the world of advertising is no longer limited to our screens, just as advertising itself was freed from print mediums with screens. However, we now have a world in which no two people share the same constant. What you see through your eyes is not what someone else sees through theirs.

Imagine we fast-forward a decade, and you visit your friend Kelly to check out the new board he has shaped. As you enter his garage, you notice his other new surfboards. Sensors implanted in your eyewear track your eyeballs' motion, and your personal AI notices your gaze lingers for a while on a certain board. Thanks to your search history, your AI also knows you have been researching new boards in the way you only do when you plan on purchasing. Your AI has also modeled this board's similarity to those you viewed on social media and in one of your text conversations. Since you love all of the conveniences technology delivers to you, you chose to keep on all your smart recommendation preferences at all times. As you admire one of Kelly's surfboards, surfboard prices, designs, and color choices, all overlay your field of view. Are you ready to buy?

At this point in our story, you will have one of two perspectives on this type of advertising. This could be the next level of advertising in which all the convenience of surfing the web happens in real time as you live your life, and everything you want is waiting for you in your cart. Or perhaps you view this as the next, highest level of spam. In this example, we see some of the ethical dilemmas playing out, literally, right before our eyes. Imagine you accidentally left your recommendation preferences on at all times. Are people allowed to export your data and information and sell it to others? When does convenience cross over into spam?

Visual search is already here. We see it in partnerships between companies like Snapchat and Amazon. All you need to do is point your camera at an object and voila! Magically, a link to the product itself or a similar product appears and is ready for purchase. Social media apps link you right to a product just by clicking a dot over the pictured item—whether the publisher intended it or not! IKEA has gone beast mode on their AR initiatives. Their mobile app allows you to scan and create a digital version of a room in your home. This allows you to mix and match every item in their store, with all the exact dimensions, swapping in and out furniture, paint colors on the wall, pictures, and art. Like something? Just click *yes*, and IKEA ships the perfectly customized home set to your door. As the adoption of this kind of technology increases, more information is fed back into the AI, which improves as it learns more about the world it engages with. By the end of 2018, visual search had well over one billion queries per month.

Back to our example above, now imagine you leave your friend Kelly's garage, forgetting your "do not disturb" preferences are still off. You pop into a store on your way home, and suddenly, you are attacked by holograms of all the world's best surfers telling you to buy things you didn't realize you needed. The tech tied to your lenses pulled these icons of surfing from your YouTube history, but you know the optical trip they are playing and ignore them. The AI changes its approach, and the surfers turn into your mother who starts ordering you to buy certain things.

Crazy and futuristic, very *Minority Report*, right? Not so much. It's closer than you think. Baidu, China's dominant search engine, can train a voice imitation system using only ten four-second samples of someone's voice. If you give Baidu's AI 100 samples of five-second clips, they can precisely match any voice in the world and make it say whatever they like. While synthetic voices are not common practice today, it could be here next week. It may as well be happening right before our eyes. Just imagine the ethical implications! This is why we all need to be involved in discussing what our future looks like; otherwise, we will one day live in a world where the companies with these AIs can interact with you, your life, and your data however they wish. Furthermore, it gets much, much worse than a hologram of your mother telling you to eat more vegetables. This technology makes it easier than ever to mirror and mimic people, letting propaganda and misinformation machines go into overdrive. Humanity can't seem to shy away from its habit of destroying reputations, creating civil unrest, and influencing global politics. With the right technology, anyone could make a very realistic computer copy of any world leader saying anything they want. Without accountability in creating such technologies, it would be impossible to stop any of the world's ultimate evils from unfolding upon us. Without hyperbole, the absolute worst things you can imagine could very well happen in our lifetime. If you think fake news is bad, deep fakes created by AIs could be the place where facts and truth go to die. Life for humans may be getting better, but it could get terrible very quickly. How we develop these technologies today will determine how they are used tomorrow. Will it be for the better?

So, what does the future of advertising look like? The psychological premise of advertising is simple: Convince the audience that your product will relieve some pain in their lives. This made for a fun industry with interesting ad campaigns back before AI. Now, your friendly AI systems know you better than you know yourself—advertisers be damned. Your AI can make any purchasing decisions for you. Suppose your AI is constantly tracking your eye movement as you view the world around you, listening to your daily interactions and conversations, fully modeling and understanding your likes and dislikes, regularly scanning and scraping all your social media feeds. Imagine everything you did in a day, reduced down to data points. Where you went and what you looked at. Imagine the things that make your heart race or palms sweat. All of these cues that have been around for all of humanity are now data points. With the right AI being fed information from trackers around your body, endless amounts of detailed data will be used to do a better job of selecting your purchases. In a way, the advertising industry as we know it goes away.

Assuming, of course, that your ethics are in line with this. Like it or not, we are heading into an era where AI will be making many of our decisions—for better or worse. Maybe we just turn off all the recommendation features to safeguard your data privacy, but then you might live in a bland world without stimulation. Maybe you are one of the people who say, "I just won't use or wear any of the technologies or sensors they send out." I call bullshit. Unless you are reading this text as a printed, paper book, have no car, have never taken an Uber, don't own a phone or credit card, don't use a computer, avoid all internet, and only eat food you grew yourself—you are absolutely going to fall into this disruption. Some people claim they will never invite a smart speaker into their home, claiming they are creepy and a violation of privacy—even though the same technology has already been in their home for a decade: their cell phone! We never had a conversation about life with a smartphone, automatic brakes, or digital money—but here we are. We never thought the silly little website we used to connect with our college buddies would spawn platforms rife with regime-toppling (or installing?) misinformation either. It just happened, and we didn't notice the change until it was everywhere. This clear shift threatens everything we know about traditional advertising—which leaves open precedence we are not prepared for. Like our shopping experience, advertising will directly shift the benefits to the customer, assuming it is all done correctly. But who decides what is right? Who draws the line on what is acceptable?

Entertaining Rogue Waves

Blockbuster passed up the opportunity to buy Netflix for $50 million. Oops. Today, Blockbuster is a punchline, and Netflix, Amazon, HBO, and every network on the planet are in perpetual competition to produce and distribute original content—completely tearing apart the model Blockbuster had relied on for decades. Netflix has grown to a $150 billion market cap and spends a *lot* of money on disruption. But not like how they disrupted Blockbuster— they're disrupting themselves. After all, if they don't do it, someone else will. In 2017 alone, Netflix spent $6.2 billion on original movies and TV shows than other major studios like CBS and HBO, which spent $4 billion and $2.5

billion, respectively. Time Warner and Fox were the kings in 2017, spending over $8 billion on new content, but one year later, Netflix annihilated them by spending $13 billion on original programming. There was a new king in town. In 2018, the six biggest movie studios released a combined total of seventy-five movies. Netflix alone produced eighty new films and 700 new TV shows in that same year. It goes to show the exponential assault that can take place when the medium moves to digital. Without the need to physically distribute the medium or reserve movie theaters, production and distribution can be seemingly infinite. And the winner is us, the consumer. For less than the cost of going to a movie theater, you can have unlimited access to all Netflix content, on demand, for an entire month. We often have trouble conceptualizing that futuristic advancements can, in fact, give us more for less. When done right, this is often the case.

One disruptive wave can sink Blockbuster, but now our tale of disruption has many more rogue waves building on the horizon that will again reshape the future of entertainment. Companies like Netflix have not only disrupted archaic linear-minded companies like Blockbuster using the internet, but they also leverage the convergence of the networks with the exponentials of increased connectivity speeds, all being powered by exponentially growing artificial intelligence. All this amplification and convergence results in a direct assault on the trillion-dollar entertainment ecosystem. There is blood in the water, and more sharks join the feeding frenzy against those left helpless. Players from all industries are jumping in on streaming and content creation. In 2018, Apple spent over $1 billion on creating content, while Amazon dropped $5 billion. Hollywood's days as the king of entertainment are numbered.

Information no longer flows in one direction. Long gone are the days of printed newspapers, magazines, television, movies, and other media sources, like this book. Static, passive media is rapidly being replaced by active media, shifting the power back to the customer as entertainment drivers, not the other way around. Like many other exponential trends, we still have some work to do. Still, as the quality of active entertainment continues to improve, our surfing frameworks point toward the eventual end result. As we see deep fakes getting adopted into the news, we will only get more and better applications in disturbing trends. Entertainment experiences could easily shift into politics and pornography and various other forms of entertainment that will lean toward unethical manipulation.

Companies like Dreamscape already mix our senses in the experience of entertainment using VR goggles and haptic sensors in gloves to let you touch and feel the digital "product" you are seeing. Dreamscape's partnership with AMC is already pushing this technology into the mainstream. Eventually, we will forget the gloves, and entertainment venues will use ultrasound to create a sensation of touch. Entertainment will soon be fully interactive and augmented with emotionally aware forms of artificial intelligence to create an experience unique to the individual and their specific experience.

Again, innovations like this should be so far into the future that there is no point in thinking about them today. This is how change works. When you don't see the telltale signs of the transitions taking place, everything seems like an unimaginable leap into the future. If you're listening, you can hear the beat of the music—some players in the industry have figured out how to dance in time with it. In the future, you might get an hour or so to sit and relax. You turn on Netflix (probably with a voice command), but there are so many options (Where is the disruption to fix "what should I watch?") you opt to check out the news. Do you put on the VR goggles? Or the 3D glasses you bought for the 3DTV you spent way too much money on?

Do we grab a controller and flick through options, put on goggles, watch a hologram, show, movie, or news? In the future, none of these thoughts will matter. Your AI will already know what you want to watch. It knows which calls you placed, which ones you screened, and who was sent to voicemail. It knows your professional work conversations and the fight you had with your romantic partner. The sensors tracking your neurophysiology know

your emotional state and what chemical changes it needs to influence to bring you into a better (buying?) mood. In our very near future, all of this will happen before you even get to your living room.

Imagine you just had a stressful day at work. You hate your job, and you're pissed off at your husband. You call up an autonomous car to take you home. Since it is autonomous, you open up a beer, and the TV screen turns on. AI decides what you watch. It knows what genre and actors make you laugh. Intermixed in what you watch, the program also digs up some of your fondest memories from your social media feeds, all of which remind you of what is truly important in life: your family. You finish your drink, the show wraps up, you step out of your autonomous car and greet your husband at home. You are no longer stressed or angry. This is what the future of entertainment promises, much more than content. What is crazy is that although not all of it is connected, most of this technology is already in operation. Affective computing can already recognize, interpret, process, and simulate human effects and emotions thanks to the convergence of computer science, psychology, and cognitive science. In education, affective computing adapts the presentation and teachings to keep the students engaged. Healthcare uses affective computing with great success in robots to act as nurses or caregivers. It is even in automobiles as a social monitoring solution, increasing supplementary safety measures when a human driver becomes frustrated or angry. Just imagine what happens when the wave of affective computing collides with AI or the right collection of sensors.

The thing about humans is: Everything we do is data. Our body language, facial expressions, gestures (or lack of), our eye movement, focus and gaze, tone of voice, frequency of movements of specific body parts, frequency or duration of speech—are all data if the right sensors can capture it. Affective computing merging with our mobile devices brings its capabilities into the real world, in real time. When you couple this with biofeedback, our future AI assistants will identify our anxiety long before we will. Your AI will know why you enjoy things, having constant semantic analysis in biofeedback, tracking your heart rate, blood pressure, pupil dilation response, eye movement, etc. Furthermore, AIs will know our history, neurophysiology, where we reside, our social preferences, and our desired level of interaction and monitoring to maximize our entertainment in real time.

In entertainment, this will allow experiences to hammer our fear and thrill sensors. Startups like Lightwave take our understanding of complexity to the next level. They understand the emotional state of a group or crowd to determine how well a sales pitch is going or if the DJ needs to adjust the audio for a concert. It was used in *The Revenant*'s theatrical release to fine-tune the final edits and adjust the audio in real time to amplify how the audience received the screening.

Augmented reality is on track to disrupt the disruptors by eliminating the need for a screen altogether. The first pass at smart glasses where bulky and dorky, but they got much better very quickly. Glasses and headgear will disrupt monitors and screens, but some of us will skip straight to the contact lenses. All of your computer screen and TV functionality will be mounted on your cornea and will project on the back of your retina: Poof, goodbye screens. AR allows us to overlay and blend the digital world with our physical one or completely block out the physical world, like how we use monitors now.

Over the next five years, AR alone is expected to turn into a $90 billion market. In 2017, we saw the introduction of Apple's ARKit and Google's ARCore. These software development kits (SDKs) have standardized the development tools and democratized mobile AR app creation, which has brought about more than double the number of mobile AR-enabled devices and tripled the number of active users in a year and a half. The installed base of ARCore-compatible Android devices grew from 250 million devices in December 2018 to 400 million in May 2019. Apple CEO Tim Cook believes AR will be as revolutionary as the smartphone. *Pokémon Go* was a simple demonstration of what was possible: the userbase grew to sixty-five million users and over $2 billion in revenue in no time at all.

So what comes after this? You guessed it, more rogue waves of disruption. As the megatrends of the Fourth Industrial Revolution continue to converge, in short order, we will waste no time on improving devices when every human comes preinstalled with one of the best reality projection systems ever made: our brains.

Instead of adding a layer of information using a contact lens or a glovelike sensor or using room-sized sensors to generate lifelike scenarios—just cut out the middleman or women. We can use the brain-computer interface to stimulate and create entertainment in the same way we create our reality. Research from the University of Washington created the first network that allowed individuals to interact directly through brain-to-brain communication. They called it, cleverly, BrainNet. BrainNet uses EEGs (electroencephalograms) to capture the brain signals and TMS (transcranial magnetic stimulation) to send the participants' brain signals back and forth. Through this network, the participants were linked together and played a revised version of *Tetris*. In other entertainment applications, we saw brain-computer interfaces make their debut in cinema. In May of 2018, a film required its viewers to wear (a cheap $100) EEG helmet to customize the content and tailor everything to the viewer as they watched. Every scene, the music, the animation, all changed every time the viewer watched. The elements changed based on what was going on in their heads at each moment.

All these examples are not designed to be claims of specificity, but just to highlight the change that is happening while it is happening. When we understand and see these waves forming, we can put ourselves in a better position to surf when they emerge.

Surfing School

Presently, America is short about 1.6 million teachers. Globally, the numbers are far grimmer. Current models show that we will need almost seventy million teachers by 2030, meaning over 260 million kids do not have access to basic education. The education system we know today was created for a time before the First Industrial Revolution. I feel like it's ripe for a change. Given everything our global society has gone through, education systems have fundamentally gone unchanged. It was (and still is) a one-size-fits-all model, which was fine when education was scarce and the need was slim. Today, knowledge is not just power but a necessity. To control quality education at scale, we have forced the standardization of everything, including testing. Furthermore, we are obsessively testing for increasingly useless knowledge. When was the last time you had to spell Mississippi without auto-suggest or did long division by hand?

Any way you slice it, batch-processing kids is an educational tragedy. Every brain is wired differently, and standardizing a universal method of learning makes zero sense. A study from the US Department of Education discovered that 1.2 million kids drop out of high school every day. Our surfing framework tells us that we have trouble with large sample pools—so the linear answer says one student drops out of high school every twenty-six seconds. The number one reason for dropping out? Boredom.

Do we see this pattern develop again? Are we noticing this change? The convergence and amplification of exponential technologies are ideally suited when there is a need for both abundance and customization. Where there is disruption, there is an opportunity; where there is an opportunity, there is money. Where there is money, there is innovation.

And innovation is never boring.

The XPRIZE is a nonprofit organization that designs and hosts public competitions to encourage technological developments that benefit humanity. A few years ago, they launched a $15 million competition to create software to address the hundreds of millions of kids around the world who do not have access to education. In May of 2019, two teams split their prize payout for an impressive solution. By using their software for just an hour a day, a remote student received an education equivalent to that of a full-time student. Distributing this program is simple: Just take the phones we discard when we upgrade, wipe them clean, and share them widely. One phone, one teacher. With over one billion Android devices produced each year, this one simple idea could put a full-time education into the hands of the hundreds of millions of incredible minds that would go uneducated otherwise.

And then, like with everything else, add AI. Supplementing AI with education creates unique individual learning environments customized to the brain and body. Sensors monitor and inform the AI how and when to adapt based on the student's neurophysiological data. At this point, our AI will understand our surfing framework better than we do and will keep us persistently in the barrels of life and give us knowledge to evolve and grow.

This doesn't just apply to remote learning in underprivileged communities. The convergence of other waves of disruption, amplified by AI, will resolve the issue of quality education everywhere. We regularly think to ourselves how thankful we are that we took the time to learn how to multiply fractions. Imagine how different education will be in the next decade when education is democratized, customized, and engaging to individual learners? Because the learner needs to adapt to a future of converging waves, so does the way they receive instruction and what they're educated in. We grew up not wanting to wake up in time for our 8:30 English literature class on Monday mornings. In the next decade, a student may be asked at three in the afternoon: What would you like to learn today?

Healthy Waves

Drugs have come a long way to increasing the longevity of our lives and eradicating many infectious diseases. Today, though, many of our ailments are still cured by swapping out our damaged parts. Frankensteinian in nature, organ transplants are the norm today even though the parts we need to do them are in limited supply. For example, your lungs. A dozen common killers are fixed with a lung transplant. You can't repair a lung; you have to replace it. But it's not as easy as swapping out an air filter in your car. The issue the healthcare industry sits with is both a problem of quality and quantity. A half million people die each year from smoking-related lung failure, but only about 2,000 transplantable lungs a year are available for them. This is compounded by the fact that upon our death, our lungs fill with toxic chemicals, rendering about 80% of them useless.

Necessity is the mother of invention. Faced with death, humans are capable of the impossible. Aside from being the highest-paid female CEO in America, Martine Rothblatt has an incredible story. Martin was married and had a child named Jenesis. Martin got divorced and remarried and had a few more kids until realizing that she was trapped in the wrong body. After cofounding a little company called Sirius Satellite Radio and having gender-reassignment surgery, Martine's daughter Jenesis fell ill. Cashing out of Sirius Radio shortly after it went public, Martine went all-in to find a cure to a fatal disease that threatened to take her daughter's life by founding United Therapeutics. Leveraging the convergence of science and exponential technologies, Martine forced advancements as best she could, and even after three years of incredible progress, Martine's daughter's time was drawing to a close. Not all real-life stories have Hollywood happy endings. But this one does. As Jenesis was preparing to take her last few breaths, Martine's new medicine hit the market. Today, Jenesis is alive and well in her thirties. Her mom's drug saved her life and the lives of patients living with the same disease. Long story short, never get between a momma bear and her cub, because sometimes even death can't win that battle.

Martine is leading in the next steps to eradicate illnesses that would have spelled certain death just a few years ago. Her company is the world's largest cloner of pigs. Her goal is to swap out failing organs like we swap out car alternators, solving quality and quantity. The next problem to solve is how to clone quality human organs without causing suffering to the swine population? Enter 3D printing. We are only a breakthrough or two away from printing artificial lung scaffolding—no need to grow organs when we can print them.

The disruption brings speed. Exponential speed, billion-fold increases in speed. Healthcare, as we know it, is primed to be annihilated by speed. Until recently, medicine evolved linearly—only seeing 0.001% of new drugs make it to human testing trials, only to have 0.0002% of trial drugs ultimately ever get approved. Since the process is riddled with inefficiencies and waste, medicines take an average of twelve years and $2.5 billion for *one* treatment to reach the market. It's little surprise that an average person spends almost $10,000 a year on healthcare in the US, estimating nearly 20% of its GDP over the next six years. The waves of the Fourth Industrial Revolution are heading for this industry like a freight train and will give savings and power back to the customer. Even today, we see an array of sensors, networks, and AI working their way into medical diagnostics. These changes are further amplified by waves of robotics and 3D printing augmented with scientific advancements in biological and medical procedures. We see the early signs of how AI will merge everything together while being further magnified by genetics and quantum computing.

When it comes to the healthcare industry, disruption is a matter of when, not if.

We will soon be doing a 180 on our surfboards and find ourselves in a world that focuses on healthcare rather than sickcare. We will trade our outdated, archaic approach of reactive, generic treatments to proactive, personalized offerings. As our megatrends converge on each other, the

273

medical industry is no longer just doctors doing research, but a massive race of low-end and new-market disruption pouring in. We're not quite disrupting things like heart surgery just yet, but we see bottom-market changes, led by AI, connecting to our lives through devices that measure habit changes for improved health. If we use our surfing framework to look into our near future of healthcare, these tech players have positioned themselves for low-end disruption and new-market disruption, which is now starting to unfold.

Our surfing framework allows us to notice the change while it happens instead of only noticing once it has happened. A Fitbit was by no means a disruptive threat to the healthcare industry. But they were the gateway wearables that went from just counting steps to FDA-approved ECG scanner capable of real-time cardiac monitoring. One of Diamandis's XPRIZE foundation winners was DxtER, which uses noninvasive sensors to feed an AI that can diagnose and detect more than fifty common illnesses. This type of disruption leads to a future of always-on care being cheaper and more manageable, meaning entire industries no longer have to wait for us to get sick and die before they can find ways to profit from us. Mobile health is expected to be worth $102 billion by 2021. Before long, you will have a mobile doctor monitoring you 24/7, available in real time, all in your pocket.

We are already riding the convergence of networks, sensors, computing, and AI to take on mental health illnesses using foundational AI converging with cognitive behavioral therapy. Instead of going to see a doctor and sitting in a waiting room, you'd meet your AI doctor through Facebook Messenger. Suffering from depression? Your AI doctor will help administer and guide you through cognitive behavioral therapy. Proactive prevention and early disease detection are already some of the most significant positive impacts we can make for our health. Applying exponentials, we at first see the odd disease finding its cure. Though it might seem like our linear path of the past, these megatrends allow things like CRISPR to ride on AI, and we could potentially cure tens of thousands of diseases in the span of a year. As long as most of us believe in the thesis of "dying sucks," we will continue to work on resolving the ailments that kill us early.

The nonstop smashing of the waves of technological advancement in healthcare will bleed into surgical procedures. Today, the indicator of an experienced surgeon is, well, someone who had done a lot of surgeries. Think about it, who would you rather pick:

1. a surgeon who thinks everything should turn out fine even though he's never done the procedure before.

2. a surgeon who has done the surgery countless times with a positive success rate.

Hopefully, you chose option 2.

How about a third option? Why not have a surgeon who has performed thousands of times more surgeries than surgeon number two, all with a perfect success rate? Very soon, that third option will be a robot. Today, less than 5% of surgeries are performed by robots. Tomorrow, robotic surgeons controlled by AI will likely be the norm.

With all these megatrends colliding to address quantity and quality issues through unique personalization, entire sectors of the healthcare industry will collapse. We're no longer stuck with two options: live with sickness until you die or treat localized cancer with a systemwide approach like chemotherapy. The second option is better than the first, but the emergence of rogue waves building will soon give us a third option: bespoke treatments designed around your unique genetic makeup. And shortly after that, we'll have a fourth option: preventative care to treat these diseases before they appear. As humanity continues to understand these dilemmas that emerge through complexity, we continue to remove many of these barriers and shape the large events in our favor both at the cellular and systematic levels.

Surfing Insurance, Finance, and Real Estate

Over the last 320 years, insurance has been a steadfastly robust industry, which means it's ripe for technological disruption. Even today, we're seeing the change shift risk from the consumer to the service provider. The surfing framework shows us that as these larger waves and events build, even the smallest shift can annihilate a massive part of the insurance industry, which would cause it to collapse overnight, like Blockbuster or Kodak. Adding industry convergence with this technological tsunami, we see low-end disruption through crowdsurance (crowdsourced insurance) potentially wiping out both health and life insurance industries. As we've seen examples in every other industry, once the giants fall, there will be a never-ending wave of advancements in networks, sensors, and AI—all of which will completely revolutionize how we create, buy, sell, price, claim, and pay insurance.

We're left wondering: How do the ethics play out? There is an infinite number of dilemmas we have yet to address. For example, if you're riding in an autonomous car, which acts as a car-as-a-service, and there is no driver, do you need insurance? Auto insurance is entirely built around the fact that humans are terrible drivers. We are ripe with human error, unreliable, distracted, emotional, and as we have learned, often irrational. Looking at one year's worth of driving-related deaths: Over 90% of them were due to human error. Therein, avoiding death is a simple fix: Remove the human. But the auto insurance industry is built off assessing risk. Removing 90% of the risk is more than a transformational change; it is the death of auto insurance. Auto insurance is built off accidents, not errors. When you remove errors and mistakes, accidents end up being a rarity.

Next question: If you're riding in an autonomous car, which acts as a car-as-a-service, and there is no driver, who is to blame in the periodic accident?

Lack of transparency in AI systems alone is hard to address, but how about the entire connected systems' complexity? Do we blame the company that made the sensors that led the autonomous car to cause an accident, or was it the person who installed it? We can't blame the passenger; they didn't *do* anything. Maybe we put all the blame on the car manufacturer? What if the reason for the accident was a regional 5G outage? That is not the manufacturer's fault. Do we sue owners of the car, companies like Uber, Tesla, Alphabet? Or do we sue Verizon or AT&T for an unreliable network? Maybe we sue the company that installed the satellite that provided the connection? What if an autonomous AI driving system gets hacked or stolen? What if we don't fully understand what caused the accident? Do we blame the ghost in the machine? What assets do they have that we can claim against? Blame is no longer cut and dry; the ethics of autonomous driving gets complicated when humans are hurt.

A million people a year are arrested for driving while impaired. With autonomous cars, we never have to worry about drinking and driving. But we will lose an entire insurance industry, tax dollars, jobs, and so on. Regardless of how you feel about it, it might be a change for the better. Today, right now, we trust sixteen-year-olds, hopped up with hormones, to have complete control of a complicated, heavy machine that can go very fast. Five years later, we trust them with a beer. It feels like a no-brainer. As autonomous cars keep getting exponentially better, the financial responsibility of protecting human lives will fall to centralized governments. We'll see other significant changes in places like climate change, reduced traffic, and much more—these changes are arriving at exponential speed. As these megatrends shift our lives from cars as property to cars-as-a-service, it will obliterate auto insurance as we know it. We are already seeing a fall-off in car ownership, and it's predicted to decrease by another 60% over the next ten to twenty years.

What about everything we own that we insure, be it our physical goods, property, life, or health? Insurance costs are averaged out to everyone. There is a disruption brewing, destined to crush traditional insurance. Crowdsurance is a decentralized peer-to-peer insurance that removes the middleman or women. Instead of using an "insurance company" to mediate claims and premiums, a technology application is pulling from an AI-augmented database. This entire system monitors the people who pay for its service and files the claims on their behalf.

In practice, this replaces a traditional insurance company, but disruption is deceitful at first. As this distribution gains popularity, it continues to suck out customers who feel they are overpaying for insurance. As you remove low-risk or healthy people from the traditional insurance pool, insurance rates increase to prevent collapse from the increased claim payouts. As crowdsurance gets better, it sucks more people out of the traditional insurance market who are tired of the increasing cost. This further forces the insurance companies to increase their premiums, or they go bankrupt. Have you ever noticed your insurance premiums going up regularly? This is what happens when traditional, linear-thinking insurance companies go head to head with exponential competitors. We've seen this movie play out many times, across many industries, and traditional insurance has already lost. The winners? The consumers. We will no longer be spending outrageous amounts on premiums for coverages we never needed.

Right now, there is a New York-based crowdsurance company called Lemonade. It's an app that brings together a network policyholder who pays premiums into a pool. AI does the rest. It is entirely mobile, it takes a little over a minute to get insured, it takes three minutes to get paid on a claim, and there is no paperwork. In other new-market disruptions that do not compete directly with traditional insurance, we have seen the emergence of companies like Etherisc, a Swiss company that covers nontraditional insurance. For example, you sign up needing nothing more than a credit card, you choose the flight delay and cancellation policy, and if your flight is more than forty-five minutes late, you are paid automatically in real time, no paper, no hassle, no calls. This micro-insurance space is blowing up, and it is changes like these that will be here the day after tomorrow. From here, they will slowly move up the market, until they completely disrupt the current leaders in the industry, igniting the collapse of the insurance industry.

The examples above were about our "things," but the insurance about ourselves (life and health insurance) is even more destined for catastrophic disruption. The shift to disease prevention from our reactive healthcare world alone causes a major change in health insurance. Connected devices in the form of wearables are leading some of this change. The upside is that the cost of health insurance will go down drastically, but it comes at the expense of your personal data. The data, that is, that they are *already* tracking. Eventually, there might not be traditional insurance options left, and then what are you going to do? You might still believe in the Blockbuster model, but that doesn't mean you can go into a Blockbuster store and rent a DVD. The changes are here, and it's a matter of proactively addressing them in a way you can benefit from them.

With our data, our insurance rates and payments could fluctuate in real time. An extra beer and a fried sandwich for lunch? Rate increase. Go for a run and order a salad? Decrease. Sneak a cigarette? Canceled policy. As the insurance industry shifts to prevention versus treatment and repairs, the prediction will be the focus on everything. Models are built on analytical decisions built from your data. The more data, the higher accuracy, the lower the end cost. Does this idea make you uncomfortable? If so, it seems to be a clear sign that you are positioned in the middle of the barrel of your surfing framework, meaning we need to keep working through these concepts to shape them favorably for our future.

This marriage of sensors and AI turns insurance into a pay-as-you-live model. Live well, pay less. Less than ten years from now, the number of expected claims will decrease by 70–90%, and the length of processing a claim is expected to decrease from weeks and months down to minutes.

The Fourth Industrial Revolution is also taking its toll on both banking and finance. Start with us, and what we choose to do with our money. Today, most of us save our money with trusted corporations we know as banks. Sometimes we move it around between other companies or borrow it and pay it back. We invest our money, hoping it will create more money for us. Even in our lifetime, money has changed. We used to be cash-centric, printed on paper, stowed in wallets. Once this physical paper transitioned to bits and bytes, money became exponentially empowered, and nothing was ever the same.

The average banking customer pays over $350 annually in "banking fees." Most banks pull in on average $30 billion every year just on overdraft charges. Banks also invest our money wherever they please and keep all the profits from it. In case you're keeping score at home, banks charge us to store our money, then they use the money we are paying them to store more investments to make themselves even more money.

What happens when the bank makes a bad investment and loses a bunch of money that is not theirs? They can merely up the banking fee to make up for it. This problem is not driving disruption, but it has built up a massive industry that depends on it.

Many parts of the world do not have banks as poorer nations and regions do not generate enough money to maintain the banking system's cost. Although we have millions of humans without access to a bank, they all have smartphones—the pulse of the Fourth Industrial Revolution waves heading straight for this industry. With four billion people gaining internet access over the next ten years, basic banking needs will be available to everyone. No need for infrastructure, no need for overhead, no need to pay for all the basic banking services. Converging technology will start out as good enough for an underserved market, but the rogue wave nature of change will annihilate traditional banking as we know it. Fintech is already here, bringing with it apps used exclusively for micro-investing. Every disruptor in this space takes away money from traditional banks and repurposes the gains (or losses) to the customers.

Crowdlending AI facilitates peer-to-peer lending in a market that has grown from $26 billion in 2015 to an estimated trillion dollars a few years from now. Smart Finance Group gained notoriety by serving the under-served banking population in China. They filtered through personal data to generate a credit score in real time. This allows for peer-to-peer lending in less than eight seconds. Individuals who have never had a bank account or a credit history can now take out a small loan for themselves. Within a few years, Smart Finance was issuing an average of twenty-four million loans annually. Mainstream adoption is just a matter of time. Are you willing to surrender more data for the chance to get a better loan?

What makes you think you haven't already? You have been pre-approved!

Bots and algorithm joined the party long ago. Computers make 90% of market trades. This is another example of removing the middleperson. Reduce the overhead, slash the cost to the end user. Traditional wealth managers take a 2% fee, robo-advisors take about 0.25%. On a small scale, like us getting back 1.75% of our profits, this does not seem detrimental. Roll this up to the macro level, and you see 87.5% of the money vanish from the industry. The future is grim for traditional banking. What is scarier is that these computer algorithmic advisors only make up 1% of the industry today, making it ripe for an exponential wave of disruption.

Banks were built to hold money, which is a problem, as the printed-paper-cash form of money is all but dead. Denmark ceased printing their currency back in 2017, Sweden currently runs 80% of all transactions digitally, India recalled 86% of its cash, Vietnam runs 90% of their retail transactions digitally. Paper is dead. Our economies' success was built on access to money and the speed at which we can move it around. The amplification and acceleration of the megatrends fueling our economies' transformation and success will grow faster as money becomes more available and can move faster than ever.

You can't talk about finance and insurance without discussing real estate—and the Fourth Industrial Revolution will not leave this stone unturned. For anyone who has looked at purchasing a house in the last few years, the growth of services like Zillow, Trulia, Redfin, Move, and others haven't gone unnoticed. These apps provide you directly with property searches, evaluation, consulting you on tax breakdown, future value expectations, and management that is real time, anytime, whenever you need it—something traditional realtors just can't keep up with. Not only do these applications make researching real estate easier and faster than ever before, and not only more accurate, but it is free to any user. The aggregation and display of the data allow AI to produce analytics that exceeds human capabilities by aggregating everything from previous and average real estate variables such as established rent rates, occupancy levels, residential school data, satellite imaging, local traffic conditions, and much more. This disruption will be twofold. It will reshape how we interact with these industries every day while also recreating—if not replacing—the industry's day-to-day jobs and function.

Then it goes a step further: Real estate firms no longer need real estate. It sounds contradictory because it is. In 2008, Glenn Stanford launched a cloud-based real estate brokerage—his timing was horrible. Over the years, his company, now called eXP Realty, has grown to include 16,000 agents across every state in America and in three Canadian provinces, spanning 400 major real estate markets—all without owning any real estate. They don't even have an office. Their staff is comprised of agents and managers who use their laptops and VR goggles from the comfort of their own home. The staff and clients meet in virtual lobbies, cafés, sporting events, and meeting rooms. Stanford estimates that at least $100 million of this organization's $650 million market cap is purely from money saved from eliminating infrastructure and overhead.

Just as with auto and insurance, AI will play a huge role in how you relate to real estate. As seamless as if today you said, "Siri, find me a home I can afford with a cozy rustic vibe, yet has a farmhouse feel with an industrial finish of polished concrete floors and large exposed wood beams, close to my favorite grocery store."

At this point, your AI presents you options it knows will deliver the warm fuzzies, which include a mountainside chalet overlooking the ocean. Of course, you said, "close to my favorite grocery store." But your AI knows that Amazon will deliver Whole Foods groceries to your home, by drone, within thirty minutes of you placing your order. By this point, customers haven't walked into a grocery store for anything in five years—the AI knows what you want and how you want it, better than you know it.

Your AI then executes smart contract leverage blockchain, turning days of exchanged papers into nearly instant homeownership. You get a digital copy of the deed, certified by a blockchain ledger, all while you drink your drone-delivered smoothie.

If the millions of hours of HGTV programming have taught us anything, it is that people still love the experience of shopping for a home. This is not lost in the AI-fueled, blockchain transaction future. Just put on your VR headset, hop over to a small café in Italy with friends before heading to your appointment to walk through your prospective mountainside ocean-view home. Want to see what the kitchen looks like with a fresh coat of paint? No problem. Should you buy the house fully furnished, or how would it look with your furniture into a VR-rendered home? AI makes it happen. You could just ask your AI what you'd love best, and it could virtually remodel any home in any way you see fit.

Real estate nowadays is comparatively antiquated. In the past, real estate was based on location and proximity to an individual. Buyers wanted homes in good school districts near grocery stores, shopping centers, hospitals, proximity to friends, family, and their work. Most of these factors are not as important in our lifetime with these radical changes. From autonomous cars to hyperloop transit, the very idea of "proximity and location" is thrown out the window. Your commute today might take thirty minutes to go fifteen miles—proximity. With hyperloop, you can go from Sacramento to Los Angeles in the same time. An autonomous ride from Vail into Denver allows you to start your workday while commuting. Or maybe you just catch up on sleep? A forty-minute flying Uber from Montreal into downtown Toronto might be a manageable commute time for you? Location expands with these transit options, so do your choices, and so does the competition for your dollars. But even this transit will be instantly disrupted as VR and AR will allow us to visit any office, for any meeting, from the comfort of our homes. Avatars commuting for business meetings and drones delivering our needs and wants will allow us to essentially live wherever we want.

The Surfer's Diet

Without food, there is no humanity. Without humanity, there's not much point to any of this. One of our biggest food problems is that we have created unbelievable inefficiencies in our food processes. With all of the capabilities we have today, people still go hungry while food is wasted. These inefficiencies begin at the surface of the sun. Long before photosynthesis started, the development of your food began 150 million km away. Despite the incredible creation of energy through the millions upon millions of metric tons of hydrogen fusing every second, unfortunately for us, only 0.000000000001 of that energy ever gets to our planet. And of the 0.000000000001 of the energy that hits our planet, only one percent is used for photosynthesis.

Unfortunately, the narrative of waste does not stop there. Transportation of grown food adds to the inefficiencies of our systems. Almond milk from California, maple syrup from Canada, potatoes from Idaho, wine from France, cannolis from Italy, and the list goes on. The strength of an economy is based on the availability of money and the speed at which it can move around. Hunger seems to fight this same battle. Food quantity in America is not a problem. 40% of all food in America gets thrown out, yet one out of eight people fight to put food on their table. The National Resource Defense Council cited how saving just 15% of the wasted food in America could nourish twenty-five million of the forty-two million hungry Americans who lack access to food. If we have learned anything from the inevitable attack of the waves of disruption from the Fourth Industrial Revolution, we can easily solve access and speed.

Before we address access and speed of distribution, let us address the inefficiency problem, which also solves the access and speed problem. The United Nations predicts that in thirty years, we will have a global population of about nine billion humans. We need to double agricultural output to support this population. One of the ways we will address this problem is vertical farming. Think farming that transitions from hands-on, dirty, hard manual work to clean, hands-off technologies. It is exactly what it sounds like, farming vertically, like in high-rise buildings, instead of horizontally across large areas of land. In a few years, 70% of humanity will live within city limits. Farming thousands of miles from cities is not only inefficient and polluting but also unhealthy. As soon as a plant of any kind is removed from the soil, it begins to lose some of its nutritional value. The average two-week time produce spends in transit can reduce its nutritional value by 45%. Vertical farming will bring a new meaning to "locally grown," meaning that every vegetable you eat might be grown in a building across the street. If you go to an IKEA and figure your way out of the labyrinth of the bedroom department, head over to the cafeteria. There you will find some of the most locally grown meals possible. IKEA, of all places, supplies their cafeteria with food growing vertically in their stores.

I highlight vertical farming because it solves much more than long transportation lead times. Vertical farming is done indoors, meaning the need for pesticides vanishes. Strangely enough, so does the need for irrigation.

Vertical farms use aeroponics and hydroponics, which uses 90% less water compared to traditional farming. In *Abundance*, published back in 2012, Diamandis and Kotler spoke of a handful of novel vertical farming pilot projects. Today there is an entire industry built around it.

Have you been noticing this change? Technology makes it possible. The same smart tech we use to automate our homes and the Internet of Things has set its sights on farming. Vertical smart farming grows to produce massive vertical towers supervised by tens of thousands of cameras and sensors. The data collected augments the machine learning of how to maximize production within the space. This method can produce forty times the amount of vegetables compared to traditional farming. *Forty*. Vertical farming uses 99% less water but still produces yields 350 times greater than conventional farming methods. All of this means a massive reduction in the cost of groceries—upwards of 35%. Quality produce, available everywhere, for a lot cheaper.

Picture a building with rows and rows of AI-controlled LEDs that can manage the optimal light wavelength for a specific plant to flourish. Misting nozzles directly hydrate the root systems with water enhanced with the exact levels of nutrients for optimal growth. All of this happens in a growth mesh fabric created from recycled plastics like water bottles and is monitored and managed through cameras, sensors, and machine-learning AI systems. Everything that was just explained is inside a vertical farm named AeroFarms, a 70,000-square-foot repurposed warehouse located in Newark, New Jersey. AeroFarms currently produces over two million pounds of leafy greens for you to enjoy no matter what the weather or soil conditions might be.

The onslaught of exponential megatrends coming only looks to push this disruption further. Currently, upwards of 80% of the cost in vertical farming is human labor. As these exponential solutions gain momentum, these small changes will quickly become part of our daily lives. Humanity has not benefited from any of this yet as these operations are still too small to make global impacts. Still, as the wave of AI converges and amplifies data consumption, augmented by sensors, this industry is poised for mass disruption, regardless of whether you're noticing the changes happening or not. Blockbuster might not have seen the value in buying Netflix for $50 million, but by the time they did, they were wiped out. Therefore, this gives us hope in our near future by addressing smarter farming that is stronger and more efficient to produce. If vertical farming works so well for plants, how about cows and pigs?

Believe it or not, our future megatrends are showing great promise in solving our carnivorous habits. For the vegans currently enraged by the thought of heartless meat-eating humans, the future is bringing bright, docile solutions. With vertical cow farming, we simply stack sixty cows on top of one another and manage their growth through a series of tubes before feeding them into the Hamburgertron5000.

Kidding, of course. Not only is this a heartless, unrealistic option, but it's also nowhere close to the solution we need. Remember, nine billion people by 2050. We need 70% more food production than we did just a decade ago. Unfortunately, most of this production will not be in meat. As massive populations in India and China modernize global meat consumption, this dilemma is beyond challenging. Presently on this planet, over 50% of the habitable property is used for agriculture. Eighty percent of all agricultural land is used for raising livestock. This means about one-fourth of the planet is occupied by twenty billion roaming chickens, two billion grazing cows, a billion herding sheep, and other collections of animals being fattened up before they are killed, butchered, and brought to our dinner plates. Aside from the avoidable senseless suffering of these animals, this roaming livestock devours 30% of the global crop production. This is the same world in which one out of eight Americans will go to bed hungry, never mind a global issue that is much worse in less-privileged regions of the world.

The inefficiency only gets worse. Meat production consumes 70% of the world's useable water. One kilogram of meat requires 1000% more water to be produced than one kilogram of wheat. The water needed to grow an adult cow could float an oil tanker. Mass meat production accounts for about 15% of all greenhouse gases and is one of the leaders in the deforestation crisis contributing to one of the larger mass extinctions in human history.

Before we go down the rabbit hole of climate change, for now we will simply highlight that deforestation for agriculture is currently one of climate change's largest problems. Everything about livestock is inefficient to the point of being unethical. But let's keep emotion and ethics on the sideline and explore the arguments of efficiency.

To have a single steak, we must grow an entire cow. For some bacon, we needed to grow an entire pig. After we use what we need, we dispose of the carcasses. Enter agrotechnology. As biotechnology's megatrends produce disruptions in exponential proportions, these waves will also smash into our meat crisis. This is closer than you think. You might not be aware of this change happening now, but the results will be here tomorrow.

We can skip almost all meat-farming inefficiency by simply taking a stem-cell biopsy from a healthy, living cow and giving it the required nutrients until it grows into the porterhouse cut we desire. This entire procedure will run in bioreactors. As the exponentials kick in and drive down costs and increase efficiencies, we will soon produce steak, actual steak, from a few stem cells. The exponential solution scales, abundance is not a problem, and we easily feed a future carnivorous human population thirty years from now. Since less livestock is needed, deforestation and animal suffering decreases. Greenhouse gases will also decrease, and future generations will thank us for not completely trashing the planet before handing it over.

How far out is this reality of lab-grown meat? The very idea of it can make us uncomfortable, putting us right back in the middle of a big beautiful barrel of disruption. This solution is already here today, but the first dilemma is its cost.

Consider first the benefits of cultured meats. For starters, they use 1% of the landmass and as little as 4% of the water used to grow meat through traditional means. This process also generates up to 96% fewer greenhouse gases. For beef, this method would use 45% less energy. Although the initial change will be slow and unnoticed, the promise of freeing up 25% of the global landmass creates an incredible opportunity for massive reforestation efforts, which would restore balance in our habitat by pumping the brakes on the biodiversity disaster we are facing. Reforestation creates carbon sinks, further allowing us to absorb carbon dioxide from the atmosphere and decelerate the global warming dilemma.

And yeah, there's more.

This method of creating meat is also much healthier and safer for humans. Since we are growing bacon and steak from a cellular level, we can amp up health proteins, decrease saturated fats, and even lace these meats with vitamins if we wish. Since it is grown in a lab, not in the wild, it requires no hormones or antibiotics to protect the meat from disease. Most of us have heard of or lived through bird flu or mad cow. In fact, 70% of emerging diseases come from our livestock, one of the more significant pandemic threats we face. Moving to cultured meats removes all these health risks. Despite these benefits, the reason many of us have not experienced cultured meats is that the process is still expensive, but now that we are surfing the waves of exponentials, the price is dropping exponentially fast.

In 2013, a single burger made from entirely cultured meat was created for $330,000. A touch expensive for even the most ardent burger fan. Fast-forward five years and you'll find Memphis Meats creating cultured meat for $2,400 a pound, shortly after a company called Aleph Farms has lowered their cost down to $50 per pound. These companies that are riding these exponentials will bring their cost of burger meat down to $5 per pound in the next few years—eventually being cheaper than traditional beef! Aside from all these advantages previously mentioned, why on earth would you spend years growing a cow when you can grow an entire cows' worth of meat in a lab in one week? Eventually, traditional livestock agriculture will simply not make economic sense. Although we spent much time on cultured meats and their benefits, many other megatrends are coming for the food industry, just like all the other industries. Perfect Day Foods, based out of California, uses a combination of 3D printing and gene sequencing to create cheese without the milk. This is not something that tastes or feels like cheese, but it is cellularly undifferentiable from "real" cheese. It is actual cheese, just not from a cow.

The changes are already here. Did you notice them arrive? At a certain prestigious Asian restaurant, entirely lab-grown chicken is already on the menu. Just as those who claim they would never get a smartphone or get sensors implanted, some claim they will never eat lab-grown meat. Here is the kicker: Studies have shown that neither cooks nor consumers can taste the difference between real and lab-grown foods. The quality is there, exponentials will eventually address quantity, and humans will have a fighting chance defying the odds once again. The previous growth in the industrial revolution should have put most of humanity into extreme poverty, advancements like cultured meats let us possibly defy the odds as we put up a fighting chance to flourish once again in this industrial revolution, and not only support a growing population but slow, and fix, our global crisis.

Short-Term Hope, Long-Term Risk

Waterborne diseases kill 3.4 million humans annually. The United Nations' research suggests that in 2025, 50% of the world will be water-stressed. We have about a decade to slow global warming to 1.5 degrees C, or we will break the planet and suffer cataclysmic consequences. Limiting warming to 1.5 degrees C necessitates spectacular emission reductions by 2030 and carbon neutrality by 2050. This would require unparalleled transformations of energy, land, urban, and industrial systems, including creating "negative emissions" by removing carbon from the atmosphere.

The First Law of Thermodynamics states that energy can change from one form to another, but it cannot be created or destroyed. I like this definition because it is a way of telling us that nothing is free in life. There is always a cost. You have free apps that come at the cost of your data. Innovations from the previous industrial revolutions, such as the steam engine, were made possible by capturing energy from burning fossil fuels. Since nothing is free in life, we pay for the cost of this innovation today by unloading forty billion tons of carbon dioxide into the atmosphere every year. To put this in context, burning an acre of dense forest releases 4.81 tons of carbon.

The production costs for wind power have already decreased by 94% and will halve again in the next few years. Solar panel costs have decreased 250 times over. Experts agree that there is no reason we couldn't achieve 80% of our energy needs entirely through wind and sunlight. Solar is free. In a little over an hour and a half, more solar energy hits our planet than all of humankind uses in a year. In just over four days, the sun hammers us with the same amount of energy as all coal, oil, and natural gas reserves on Earth. There is an exponential opportunity here, and the exponential trends of this century should be up to the challenge.

Our unknowing and more recently uncaring advancements of the previous industrial revolution have created the emergence of a large event in the form of a biodiversity crisis. Through complexity, we now know that all our decisions and actions from the previous industrial revolution have a high carrying cost, much of which could have been proactively avoided. We have the luxury of possibly recovering from this lack of proactive engagement and lack of caring, but there is much work that must happen now. The Fourth Industrial Revolution does not provide us with the same luxuries as the previous revolutions; once exponential problems get too far ahead of us, there is no way to recover from them. We no longer have the luxury of time. By the end of this century, should we stay this course, 50% of all large mammals will be extinct. Already, 75% of our coral reefs are at risk, and we could lose 90% of all coral reefs in the next thirty years. Fifty years after that, half of all marine life will be extinct.

We have short-term problems, which we can soundly argue without the proper leadership and global policies in place, we are facing an existential threat. This by no means downplays the severity of the challenges we face over the next decade, but thanks to a bright spot in humanity, many of the great leaders and minds of this world have already started to tackle these urgent and pressing issues. As we scramble to save our planet and the short-term problems of tomorrow, we will develop technologies that will create the largest existential risk to the human race.

This is not a dilemma that will cause much suffering, pain, and sorrow over time. It will just happen. Artificial intelligence possesses the ability to wipe out the human race—whether it happens accidentally or maliciously. Regardless, without conversations surrounding the ethics of the technology we develop and the applications they are developed for, we could wind up on the wrong side of the topsoil before long.

In the previous industrial revolutions, we polluted the planet and figured we would fix it and deal with the consequences later. In the Fourth Industrial Revolution, we do not have that luxury of time, as the results could have exponential existential catastrophic implications. Without care, pragmatic dreams may as well be pragmatic nightmares.

If none of this sounds appealing, if this doesn't feel like the world you want to live in, you have a few options. The first is to make small changes in your daily routine—the micro impacts the macro at an exponential scale (it'll happen twice as fast if you get your neighbor in on the action). Or you can wait five years and watch how the forecast does a 180 from everything we have just speculated here. It only takes one change to throw this prediction off course. Or your third option is to hope for another supervolcanic eruption like the one which nearly wiped out all of life on Earth 75,000 years ago. Chances are, you wouldn't survive, and those who are left would effectively have to start over. It'd be a change no one expects, and every choice they made as they repopulated the planet would take us in a drastically different direction than where we ended up the first time.

Of course, while this is definitely a possible outcome, it is far from a pragmatic one.

Keep dreaming. Keep solving. Surf on.

ABOUT THE AUTHOR

Eric is a pragmatic futurist focused on addressing disruption by increasing the creative capacity of individuals, teams, and organizations to ignite change, innovation, and foster continuous growth. Eric has an undergraduate degree in engineering, an MBA in Information Systems, and a Ph.D. in Global Leadership. His doctoral work primarily explored complexity sciences centered on executive cognition and their use of intuitive improvisation, decision-making, artificial intelligence, and data-based decision models.

When he is not working with clients, researching, or writing, he can be found in the mountains or on the water. He founded PROJECT7 to raise awareness and money for research on brain-related illnesses. Eric is currently working and living with his wife in Chicago, Illinois. To connect or learn more about this book, Eric, or PROJECT7, please visit www.ericpb.me.

NOTES

Part 1: Yesterday

Tyson, N. D. (2017). Astrophysics for people in a hurry. New York: W. W. Norton & Company.

Tyson, N. D. (2020). Letters from an Astrophysicist. Random House UK.

Tyson, N. D. (2017). Welcome to the Universe: An Astrophysical Tour. Princeton University Press.

Einstein, A. (1916). Die Grundlage der allgemeinen Relativitätstheorie. Leipzig: J.A. Barth.

Einstein, A. (1916). The foundation of the general theory of relativity - Annalen Phys 49 (769-822), 31.

Kaku, M. (2015). Einstein's Cosmos: How Albert Einstein's Vision Transformed Our Understanding of Space and Time.

Kaku, M. (2016). Parallel worlds: A journey through creation, higher dimensions, and the future of the cosmos. New York: Anchor Books.

Kaku, M. (2014). Physics of the impossible: A scientific exploration into the world of phasers, force fields, teleportation, and time travel. New York: Doubleday.

Kaku, M. (2012). Physics of the future: How science will shape human destiny and our daily lives by the year 2100. New York: Anchor Books.

Kaku, M., & Chin, F. (2014). The future of the mind: The scientific quest to understand, enhance, and empower the mind.

Kaku, M. (2019). The future of humanity: Terraforming Mars, interstellar travel, immortality and our destiny beyond Earth.

Campos, H. M., Parellada, F. S., Valenzuela, F. A. A., & Rubio, A. M. (2015). Strategic decision-making speed in new technology based firms. RAI Revista de Administração e Inovação, 12(2), 130-152.

CHRISTENSEN, C. (2013). THE INNOVATOR'S DILEMMA: WHEN NEW TECHNOLOGIES CAUSE GREAT FIRMS TO FAIL. BRIGHTON, MA: HARVARD BUSINESS REVIEW PRESS.

CHRISTENSEN, C., BARTMAN, T., & VAN BEVER, D. (2016). THE HARD TRUTH ABOUT BUSINESS MODEL INNOVATION. MIT SLOAN MANAGEMENT REVIEW, 58(1), 31.

CHRISTENSEN, C., WANG, D., & VAN BEVER, D. (2013). CONSULTING ON THE CUSP OF DISRUPTION. HARVARD BUSINESS REVIEW, 91(10), 106-115.

CROSS, R., ARENA, M., SIMS, J., & UHL-BIEN, M. (2017). HOW TO CATALYZE INNOVATION IN YOUR ORGANIZATION. MIT SLOAN MANAGEMENT REVIEW, 58(4), 39.

ARENA, M. J., & UHL-BIEN, M. (2016). COMPLEXITY LEADERSHIP THEORY: SHIFTING FROM HUMAN CAPITAL TO SOCIAL CAPITAL. PEOPLE AND STRATEGY, 39(2), 22

UHL-BIEN, M., & ARENA, M. (2017). COMPLEXITY LEADERSHIP. ORGANIZATIONAL DYNAMICS, 1(46), 9-20.

UHL-BIEN, M., & ARENA, M. (2018). LEADERSHIP FOR ORGANIZATIONAL ADAPTABILITY: A THEORETICAL SYNTHESIS AND INTEGRATIVE FRAMEWORK. THE LEADERSHIP QUARTERLY.

LANGILLE, D. (2016). FOLLOW THE MONEY: HOW BUSINESS AND POLITICS DEFINE OUR HEALTH, 3RD ED (PP. 470-490). SOCIAL DETERMINANTS OF HEALTH: CANADIAN PERSPECTIVE. TORONTO, ONTARIO: CANADIAN SCHOLARS' PRESS

LEONE, L. (2010). A CRITICAL REVIEW OF IMPROVISATION IN ORGANIZATIONS: OPEN ISSUES AND FUTURE RESEARCH DIRECTIONS. IMPERIAL COLLEGE LONDON BUSINESS SCHOOL. IN PROCEEDINGS FROM SUMMER CONFERENCE: OPENING UP INNOVATION: STRATEGY, ORGANIZATION AND TECHNOLOGY.

MCKNIGHT, B., & BONTIS, N. (2002). E-IMPROVISATION: COLLABORATIVE GROUPWARE TECHNOLOGY EXPANDS THE REACH AND EFFECTIVENESS OF ORGANIZATIONAL IMPROVISATION. KPM KNOWLEDGE AND PROCESS MANAGEMENT, 9(4), 219-227.

PRATT, S., & STRINGER, A. (2008). STRANGE ATTRACTORS IN SCHOOL LEADERSHIP. IN B. DESPRES (EDS.), SYSTEMS THINKERS IN ACTION: A FIELD GUIDE FOR EFFECTIVE CHANGE LEADERSHIP IN EDUCATION (109-131). LANHAM, MD: R&L EDUCATION.

MEYER, P. (2010). FROM WORKPLACE TO PLAYSPACE: INNOVATING, LEARNING AND CHANGING THROUGH DYNAMIC ENGAGEMENT. HOBOKEN, NJ: JOHN WILEY & SONS.

RATTEN, V., & HODGE, J. (2016). SO MUCH THEORY, SO LITTLE PRACTICE: A LITERATURE REVIEW OF WORKPLACE IMPROVISATION TRAINING. INDUSTRIAL AND COMMERCIAL TRAINING.

CANBEK, N. G., & MUTLU, M. E. (2016). ON THE TRACK OF ARTIFICIAL INTELLIGENCE: LEARNING WITH INTELLIGENT PERSONAL ASSISTANTS. JOURNAL OF HUMAN SCIENCES, 13(1), 592-601.

ALLIO, R. J. (2015). GOOD STRATEGY MAKES GOOD LEADERS. STRATEGY & LEADERSHIP, 43(5), 3-9.

ROSENZWEIG, P. (2013). WHAT MAKES STRATEGIC DECISIONS DIFFERENT. HARVARD BUSINESS REVIEW, 91(11), 88.

ROSENZWEIG, P. (2014A). THE BENEFITS—AND LIMITS—OF DECISION MODELS. MCKINSEY QUARTERLY, 1-10.

Rosenzweig, P. (2014b). The halo effect:... and the eight other business delusions that deceive managers: New York, NY: Simon and Schuster.

Rosenzweig, P. (2014c). Left brain, right stuff: How leaders make winning decisions. New York, NY: PublicAffairs.

Brynjolfsson, E., Hammerbacher, J., & Stevens, B. (2011). Competing through data: Three experts offer their game plans. McKinsey Quarterly, 4, 36-47.

Brynjolfsson, E., & McAfee, A. (2014a). The second machine age: Work, progress, and prosperity in a time of brilliant technologies. New York, NY: W.W. Norton & Company.

Brynjolfsson, E., & McAfee, A. (2014b). Second Machine Age: Work, Progress, and Prosperity in a Time of Brilliant Technologies. New York, NY: W.W. Norton & Company.

Brynjolfsson, E., & McElheran, K. (2016). The rapid adoption of data-driven decision-making. American Economic Review, 106(5), 133-139.

Hamel, G., & Prahalad, C. K. (2013). Creating global strategic capability. In Strategies in Global Competition (RLE International Business) (pp. 25-59). Routledge.

Palacios Fenech, J., & Tellis, G. J. (2016). The dive and disruption of successful current products: Measures, global patterns, and predictive model. Journal of Product Innovation Management, 33(1), 53-68.

Yudkowsky, E. (n.d.). A Map that Reflects the Territory. Retrieved January 02, 2021, from https://www.lesswrong.com/

Vasiltsova, V. M., Dyatlov, S. A., Vasiltsov, V. S., Bezrukova, T. L., & Bezrukov, B. A. (2015). Methodology of management innovation hypercompetition. Asian Social Science, 11(20), 165.

Back, Y., Parboteeah, K. P., & Nam, D. (2014). Innovation in emerging markets: the role of management consulting firms. Journal of International Management, 20(4), 390-405.

Josefy, M., Kuban, S., Ireland, R. D., & Hitt, M. A. (2015). All things great and small: Organizational size, boundaries of the firm, and a changing environment. Academy of Management Annals, 9(1), 715-802.

Hitt, M. A., Ireland, R. D., & Hoskisson, R. E. (2012). Strategic management cases: competitiveness and globalization. Boston, MA: Cengage Learning.

Biedenbach, T., & Söderholm, A. (2008). The challenge of organizing change in hypercompetitive industries: a literature review. Journal of Change Management, 8(2), 123-145.

Antunes, R., & Gonzalez, V. (2015). A production model for construction: A theoretical framework. Buildings, 5(1), 209-228.

Johnson, N. (2009). Simply complexity: A clear guide to complexity theory. London, UK: Oneworld Publications.

Diamandis, P. H., & Kotler, S. (2015). Bold: How to go big, create wealth and impact the world. Simon and Schuster.

Ismail, S. (2014). Exponential Organizations: Why new organizations are ten times better, faster, and cheaper than yours (and what to do about it). New York, NY: Diversion Books.

Parker, D. (2012). Service operations management: the total experience. Cheltenham, UK: Edward Elgar Publishing.

Roser, M. (2020). The short history of global living conditions and why it matters that we know it. Retrieved December 05, 2020, from https://ourworldindata.org/a-history-of-global-living-conditions-in-5-charts?linkId=62571595

Roser, M. (2020). The short history of global living conditions and why it matters that we know it. Retrieved December 05, 2020, from https://ourworldindata.org/a-history-of-global-living-conditions-in-5-charts?linkId=62571595

Part 2: Today

Adamson, G., Havens, J. C., & Chatila, R. (2019). Designing a value-driven future for ethical autonomous and intelligent systems. Proceedings of the IEEE, 107(3), 518-525.

Autor, D. H., Levy, F., & Murnane, R. J. (2003). The skill content of recent technological change: An empirical exploration. The Quarterly journal of economics, 118(4), 1279-1333.

Baskaran, A. (2017). UNESCO science report: Towards 2030. Institutions and Economies, 125-127.

Berger, T., & Frey, C. B. (2016). Structural transformation in the OECD: Digitalisation, deindustrialisation and the future of work.

Berger, T., & Frey, C. B. (2015). Bridging the skills gap. Technology, globalisation and the future of work in Europe: Essays on employment in a digitised economy, 75-79.

Byrnes, N. (2017). As Goldman embraces automation, even the masters of the universe are threatened. Retrieved February, 27, 2017.

Bughin, J., & Chui, M. (2017). The internet of things: assessing its potential and identifying the enablers needed to capture the opportunity. In The Internet of Things in the Modern Business Environment (pp. 111-125). IGI Global.

Cath, C., Wachter, S., Mittelstadt, B., Taddeo, M., & Floridi, L. (2018). Artificial intelligence and the 'good society': the US, EU, and UK approach. Science and engineering ethics, 24(2), 505-528.

Chatila, R., & Havens, J. C. (2019). The ieee global initiative on ethics of autonomous and intelligent systems. In Robotics and Well-Being (pp. 11-16). Springer, Cham.

Dietz, S., Bowen, A., Dixon, C., & Gradwell, P. (2016). 'Climate value at risk'of global financial assets. Nature Climate Change, 6(7), 676-679.

EZRACHI, A., & STUCKE, M. E. (2017). ARTIFICIAL INTELLIGENCE & COLLUSION: WHEN COMPUTERS INHIBIT COMPETITION. U. ILL. L. REV., 1775.

KABEER, N. (2016). LEAVING NO ONE BEHIND": THE CHALLENGE OF INTERSECTING INEQUALITIES. ISSC, IDS AND UNESCO, CHALLENGING INEQUALITIES: PATHWAYS TO A JUST WORLD, WORLD SOCIAL SCIENCE REPORT, 55-8.

ENBAKOM, H. W., FEYSSA, D. H., & TAKELE, S. (2017). IMPACTS OF DEFORESTATION ON THE LIVELIHOOD OF SMALLHOLDER FARMERS IN ARBA MINCH ZURIA WOREDA, SOUTHERN ETHIOPIA. AFRICAN JOURNAL OF AGRICULTURAL RESEARCH, 12(15), 1293-1305.

HUYER, S. (2015). IS THE GENDER GAP NARROWING IN SCIENCE AND ENGINEERING. UNESCO SCIENCE REPORT: TOWARDS, 2030, 85.

HICKS, M. J., & DEVARAJ, S. (2017). MANUFACTURING & LOGISTICS.

IANSITI, MARCO; LAKHANI, KARIM R. (JANUARY 2017). "THE TRUTH ABOUT BLOCKCHAIN". HARVARD BUSINESS REVIEW. HARVARD UNIVERSITY. ARCHIVED FROM THE ORIGINAL ON 18 JANUARY 2017

ROCKSTRÖM, J., STEFFEN, W., NOONE, K., PERSSON, Å., CHAPIN, F. S., LAMBIN, E. F., ... & NYKVIST, B. (2009). A SAFE OPERATING SPACE FOR HUMANITY. NATURE, 461(7263), 472-475.

SCHWAB, K. (2018, NOVEMBER). THE GLOBAL COMPETITIVENESS REPORT 2018. IN WORLD ECONOMIC FORUM (PP. 9-14).

SCHWAB, K., & DAVIS, N. (2018). SHAPING THE FUTURE OF THE FOURTH INDUSTRIAL REVOLUTION. CURRENCY.

SCHWAB, K. (2017). THE FOURTH INDUSTRIAL REVOLUTION. CURRENCY.

KRUEGER, A. B., & KATZ, L. F. (2016). THE RISE AND NATURE OF ALTERNATIVE WORK ARRANGEMENTS IN THE UNITED STATES, 1995-2015.

MCCLOSKEY, D. N. (2016). BOURGEOIS EQUALITY: HOW IDEAS, NOT CAPITAL OR INSTITUTIONS, ENRICHED THE WORLD (VOL. 3). CHICAGO: UNIVERSITY OF CHICAGO PRESS.

MANYIKA, J., CHUI, M., BISSON, P., WOETZEL, J., DOBBS, R., BUGHIN, J., & AHARON, D. (2015). UNLOCKING THE POTENTIAL OF THE INTERNET OF THINGS. MCKINSEY GLOBAL INSTITUTE.

RAINIE, L., & ANDERSON, J. (2017). THE FUTURE OF JOBS AND JOBS TRAINING. PEW RESEARCH CENTER.

OECD., K. (2018). OECD SCIENCE, TECHNOLOGY AND INNOVATION OUTLOOK 2018. OECD PUBLISHING.

WORLD ECONOMIC FORUM. (2017). THE GLOBAL GENDER GAP REPORT. GENEBRA: WORLD ECONOMIC FORUM.

WORLD ECONOMIC FORUM. (2 DECEMBER 2020). GLOBAL TECHNOLOGY GOVERNANCE REPORT 2021. RETRIEVED DECEMBER 05, 2020, FROM HTTPS://WWW.WEFORUM.ORG/REPORTS/ GLOBAL-TECHNOLOGY-GOVERNANCE-REPORT-2021

WORLD ECONOMIC FORUM. (23 NOVEMBER 2020). ANNUAL REPORT 2019-2020 RETRIEVED DECEMBER 05, 2020, FROM HTTPS://WWW.WEFORUM.ORG/REPORTS/ ANNUAL-REPORT-2019-2020

301

WORLD ECONOMIC FORUM. (16 NOVEMBER 2020). FUTURE SERIES:
   CYBERSECURITY, EMERGING TECHNOLOGY AND SYSTEMIC RISK. RETRIEVED
   DECEMBER 05, 2020, FROM HTTPS://WWW.WEFORUM.ORG/REPORTS/
   FUTURE-SERIES-CYBERSECURITY-EMERGING-TECHNOLOGY-AND-SYSTEMIC-RISK

WORLD ECONOMIC FORUM. (22 SEPTEMBER 2020). MEASURING STAKEHOLDER CAPITALISM:
   TOWARDS COMMON METRICS AND CONSISTENT REPORTING OF SUSTAINABLE VALUE
   CREATION. RETRIEVED DECEMBER 05, 2020, FROM HTTPS://WWW.WEFORUM.ORG/REPORTS/
   MEASURING-STAKEHOLDER-CAPITALISM-TOWARDS-COMMON-METRICS-AND-CONSISTENT-
   REPORTING-OF-SUSTAINABLE-VALUE-CREATION

WORLD ECONOMIC FORUM. (9 OCTOBER 2019). GLOBAL COMPETITIVENESS REPORT 2019.
   RETRIEVED DECEMBER 05, 2020, FROM HTTPS://WWW.WEFORUM.ORG/REPORTS/
   GLOBAL-COMPETITIVENESS-REPORT-2019

WORLD ECONOMIC FORUM. (23 OCTOBER 2019) NAVIGATING UNCHARTED WATERS: A ROADMAP
   TO RESPONSIBLE INNOVATION WITH AI IN FINANCIAL SERVICES. RETRIEVED DECEMBER 05,
   2020, FROM HTTPS://WWW.WEFORUM.ORG/REPORTS/NAVIGATING-UNCHARTED-WATERS-A-
   ROADMAP-TO-RESPONSIBLE-INNOVATION-WITH-AI-IN-FINANCIAL-SERVICES

WORLD ECONOMIC FORUM. (1 OCTOBER 2019). REGIONAL RISKS FOR DOING BUSINESS
   2019. RETRIEVED DECEMBER 05, 2020, FROM HTTPS://WWW.WEFORUM.ORG/REPORTS/
   REGIONAL-RISKS-FOR-DOING-BUSINESS-2019

WORLD ECONOMIC FORUM. (10 SEPTEMBER 2019). ANNUAL REPORT 2018–2019.
   RETRIEVED DECEMBER 05, 2020, FROM HTTPS://WWW.WEFORUM.ORG/REPORTS/
   ANNUAL-REPORT-2018-2019

KOPPERGER, E., LIST, J., MADHIRA, S., ROTHFISCHER, F., LAMB, D., & SIMMEL, F. (2018,
   JANUARY 19). A SELF-ASSEMBLED NANOSCALE ROBOTIC ARM CONTROLLED BY ELECTRIC
   FIELDS. RETRIEVED DECEMBER 05, 2020, FROM HTTPS://SCIENCE.SCIENCEMAG.ORG/
   CONTENT/359/6373/296

BOSTROM, N. & YUDKOWSKY, E. (2011). THE ETHICS OF ARTIFICIAL INTELLIGENCE. CAMBRIDGE
   HANDBOOK OF ARTIFICIAL INTELLIGENCE, EDS. CAMBRIDGE UNIVERSITY PRESS.

CAMPBELL, M., HOANE, A. J. & HSU, F. H. (2002). "DEEP BLUE". ARTIFICIAL INTELLIGENCE 134:
   57–59. DOI:10.1016/S0004-3702(01)00129-1

FACEBOOK INC. COMPANY. (2014). 2014 10-K FORM. RETRIEVED FROM HTTP://WWW.SEC.GOV/
   ARCHIVES/EDGAR/DATA/1326801/000132680115000006/FB-12312014X10K.HTM

GOMES, L. (2015). FACEBOOK AI DIRECTOR YANN LECUN ON HIS QUEST TO UNLEASH DEEP
   LEARNING AND MAKE MACHINES SMARTER. IEE SPECTRUM: POSTED 18 FEBRUARY,
   2015. RETRIEVED FROM: HTTP://SPECTRUM.IEEE.ORG/AUTOMATON/ROBOTICS/
   ARTIFICIAL-INTELLIGENCE/FACEBOOK-AI-DIRECTOR-YANN-LECUN-ON-DEEP-LEARNING

HOWARD, K. (1994). THE DEATH OF COMMON SENSE: HOW LAW IS SUFFOCATING AMERICA. NEW
   YORK, NY: WARNER BOOKS.

PROCEEDINGS OF THE NATIONAL ACADEMY OF SCIENCES, (2015). EXPERIMENTAL EVIDENCE OF
   MASSIVE-SCALE EMOTIONAL CONTAGION THROUGH SOCIAL NETWORKS. PNAS, VOL. 111, NO.
   29 HTTP://WWW.PNAS.ORG/CONTENT/111/24/8788.FULL.PDF

PROCEEDINGS OF THE NATIONAL ACADEMY OF SCIENCES, (2015). PNAS EDITORIAL POLICIES.
   HTTP://WWW.PNAS.ORG/SITE/AUTHORS/JOURNAL.XHTML

Yudkowsky, E. (2006). 'AI as a Precise Art', presented at the 2006 AGI Workshop in Bethesda, MD.

Part 3: The Compass, A Surfing Framework

Allio, R. J. (2015). Good strategy makes good leaders. Strategy & Leadership, 43(5), 3-9.

Anthony, S. D., Viguerie, S. P., & Waldeck, A. (2016). Corporate longevity: Turbulence ahead for large organizations. Strategy & Innovation, 14(1), 1-9.

Antunes, R., & Gonzalez, V. (2015). A production model for construction: A theoretical framework. Buildings, 5(1), 209-228.

Arena, M. J., & Uhl-Bien, M. (2016). Complexity leadership theory: Shifting from human capital to social capital. People and Strategy, 39(2), 22- last page #?.

Ariely, D. (2009). The end of rational economics. Harvard Business Review, 87, 7.

Ashenfelter, O. (2008). Predicting the quality and prices of Bordeaux wine. The Economic Journal, 118(529), 174-184.

Avolio, B. J., Walumbwa, F. O., & Weber, T. J. (2009). Leadership: Current theories, research, and future directions. Annual review of psychology, 60, 421-449.

Ayres, I. (2008). Super crunchers: Why thinking-by-numbers is the new way to be smart: New York, NY: Random House.

Back, Y., Parboteeah, K. P., & Nam, D. (2014). Innovation in emerging markets: the role of management consulting firms. Journal of International Management, 20(4), 390-405.

Banerjee, S., Singh, P. K., & Bajpai, J. (2018). A comparative study on decision-making capability between human and artificial intelligence. In Nature Inspired Computing (pp. 203-210). Springer, Singapore.

Banin, A. Y., Boso, N., Hultman, M., Souchon, A. L., Hughes, P., & Nemkova, E. (2016). Salesperson improvisation: Antecedents, performance outcomes, and boundary conditions. Industrial Marketing Management, 59, 120-130.

Bass, B. M., Stogdill, R. M., & Stogdill, R. M. (1990). Bass & Stogdill's handbook of leadership: Theory, research, and managerial applications. New York; London: Free Press ; Collier Macmillan.

Bennis, W. G., & Albertsson, C. (2000). Leading in unnerving times. MIT Sloan Management Review, 42(2), 97-103.

Bignell, A. M. (1997). Photonic Bus and Photonic Mesh Networks-Design Techniques in Extremely High Speed Networks (Doctoral dissertation). Retrieved from McMaster University https://macsphere.mcmaster.ca/handle/11375/5699.

Biedenbach, T., & Söderholm, A. (2008). The challenge of organizing change in hypercompetitive industries: a literature review. Journal of Change Management, 8(2), 123-145.

Boyer, M. D. (2009). Organizational improvisation within an episodic planning model: A systems perspective (Doctoral dissertation): Retrieved from Dissertations & Theses: Full Text (Publication No. AAT 3366094).

Brake, T. (1997). The global leader: Critical factors for creating the world class organization. Chicago, IL: Irwin Professional.

Brettell, C. B., & Hollifield, J. F. (2014). Migration theory: Talking across disciplines. Abingdon, UK: Routledge Press.

Brynjolfsson, E., Hammerbacher, J., & Stevens, B. (2011). Competing through data: Three experts offer their game plans. McKinsey Quarterly, 4, 36-47.

Brynjolfsson, E., & McAfee, A. (2014a). The second machine age: Work, progress, and prosperity in a time of brilliant technologies. New York, NY: W.W. Norton & Company.

Brynjolfsson, E., & McAfee, A. (2014b). Second Machine Age: Work, Progress, and Prosperity in a Time of Brilliant Technologies. New York, NY: W.W. Norton & Company.

Brynjolfsson, E., & McElheran, K. (2016). The rapid adoption of data-driven decision-making. American Economic Review, 106(5), 133-139.

Bughin, J., Hazan, E., Ramaswamy, S., Chui, M., Allas, T., Dahlström, P., Trench, M. (2017). Artificial intelligence–the next digital frontier. McKinsey Glob Institute URL Retrieved from: https://www.mckinsey.de/files/170620_studie_ai.pdf.

Burke, W. W. (2013). Organization change: Theory and practice. Thousand Oaks, CA: Sage Publications.

Caligiuri, P. (2006). Developing global leaders. Human Resource Management Review, 16(2), 219-228.

Campbell, M., Baltes, J. I., Martin, A., & Meddings, K. (2007). The stress of leadership. Center for Creative Leadership, 10(11).

Campos, H. M., Parellada, F. S., Valenzuela, F. A. A., & Rubio, A. M. (2015). Strategic decision-making speed in new technology based firms. RAI Revista de Administração e Inovação, 12(2), 130-152.

Canbek, N. G., & Mutlu, M. E. (2016). On the track of Artificial Intelligence: Learning with intelligent personal assistants. Journal of Human Sciences, 13(1), 592-601.

Christensen, C. (2013). The innovator's dilemma: when new technologies cause great firms to fail. Brighton, MA: Harvard Business Review Press.

Christensen, C., Bartman, T., & Van Bever, D. (2016). The hard truth about business model innovation. MIT Sloan Management Review, 58(1), 31.

Christensen, C., Wang, D., & van Bever, D. (2013). Consulting on the cusp of disruption. Harvard Business Review, 91(10), 106-115.

CIBORRA, C. U. (1996). THE PLATFORM ORGANIZATION: RECOMBINING STRATEGIES, STRUCTURES, AND SURPRISES. ORGANIZATION SCIENCE, 7(2), 103-118.

COGNITION. (ED.) (2018) OXFORD ENGLISH DICTIONARY ONLINE. RETRIEVED FROM: HTTPS:// EN.OXFORDDICTIONARIES.COM/DEFINITION/COGNITION.

COHEN, S. L. (2010). EFFECTIVE GLOBAL LEADERSHIP REQUIRES A GLOBAL MINDSET. INDUSTRIAL AND COMMERCIAL TRAINING, 42(1), 3-10.

CRESWELL, J. W. (2013). QUALITATIVE INQUIRY AND RESEARCH DESIGN: CHOOSING AMONG FIVE APPROACHES: THOUSAND OAKS, CA: SAGE PUBLICATIONS.

CRESWELL, J. W., & POTH, C. N. (2017). QUALITATIVE INQUIRY AND RESEARCH DESIGN: CHOOSING AMONG FIVE APPROACHES. THOUSAND OAKS, CA: SAGE PUBLICATIONS.

CROSS, R., ARENA, M., SIMS, J., & UHL-BIEN, M. (2017). HOW TO CATALYZE INNOVATION IN YOUR ORGANIZATION. MIT SLOAN MANAGEMENT REVIEW, 58(4), 39.

CROSSAN, M. M. (1998). IMPROVISATION IN ACTION. ORGANIZATION SCIENCE, 9(5), 593-599.

CUNHA, M., MINER, A., & ANTONACOPOLOU, E. (2016). IMPROVISATION PROCESSES IN ORGANIZATIONS. THE SAGE HANDBOOK OF PROCESS ORGANIZATION STUDIES. THOUSAND OAKS, CA: SAGE PUBLICATIONS.

CURRAL, L., MARQUES-QUINTEIRO, P., GOMES, C., & LIND, P. G. (2016). LEADERSHIP AS AN EMERGENT FEATURE IN SOCIAL ORGANIZATIONS: INSIGHTS FROM A LABORATORY SIMULATION EXPERIMENT. PLOS ONE, 11(12), E0166697.

DANZIGER, S., LEVAV, J., & AVNAIM-PESSO, L. (2011). EXTRANEOUS FACTORS IN JUDICIAL DECISIONS. PROCEEDINGS OF THE NATIONAL ACADEMY OF SCIENCES, 108(17), 6889-6892.

DAVENPORT, T. L., BARRY; BECK, MEGAN. (2018). ROBO-ADVISERS ARE COMING TO CONSULTING AND CORPORATE STRATEGY. HARVARD BUSINESS REVIEW, RETRIEVED FROM: HTTPS://HBR. ORG/2018/01/ROBO-ADVISERS-ARE-COMING-TO-CONSULTING-AND-CORPORATE-STRATEGY

DELIA, E. (2011). COMPLEXITY LEADERSHIP IN INDUSTRIAL INNOVATION TEAMS: A FIELD STUDY OF LEADING, LEARNING AND INNOVATING IN HETEROGENEOUS TEAMS (DOCTORAL DISSERTATION). RETRIEVED FROM RUTGERS THE STATE UNIVERSITY OF NEW JERSEY-NEWARK.

DIAMANDIS, P. H., & KOTLER, S. (2015). BOLD: HOW TO GO BIG, CREATE WEALTH AND IMPACT THE WORLD. NEW YORK, NY: SIMON AND SCHUSTER.

DIAZ, J. (APRIL 3, 1989). PERILS OF PUTTING. SPORTS ILLUSTRATED.

DINATA, I. B. P. P., & HARDIAN, B. (2014, OCTOBER). PREDICTING SMART HOME LIGHTING BEHAVIOR FROM SENSORS AND USER INPUT USING VERY FAST DECISION TREE WITH KERNEL DENSITY ESTIMATION AND IMPROVED LAPLACE CORRECTION. IN 2014 INTERNATIONAL CONFERENCE ON ADVANCED COMPUTER SCIENCE AND INFORMATION SYSTEM (PP. 171-175). IEEE.

DINH, J. E., LORD, R. G., GARDNER, W. L., MEUSER, J. D., LIDEN, R. C., & HU, J. (2014). LEADERSHIP THEORY AND RESEARCH IN THE NEW MILLENNIUM: CURRENT THEORETICAL TRENDS AND CHANGING PERSPECTIVES. THE LEADERSHIP QUARTERLY, 25(1), 36-62.

ENGLANDER, M. (2012). THE INTERVIEW: DATA COLLECTION IN DESCRIPTIVE PHENOMENOLOGICAL HUMAN SCIENTIFIC RESEARCH. JOURNAL OF PHENOMENOLOGICAL PSYCHOLOGY, 43(1), 13-35.

EVERLY, G. S., STROUSE, D. A., & EVERLY, G. S. (2010). THE SECRETS OF RESILIENT LEADERSHIP: WHEN FAILURE IS NOT AN OPTION...SIX ESSENTIAL CHARACTERISTICS FOR LEADING IN ADVERSITY. NEW YORK, NY: DIAMEDICA.

FOX, A. R. (2016). FACTORS INFLUENCING SUSTAINABILITY OF HEALTH SERVICE INNOVATION, EMERGENCY NURSE PRACTITIONER SERVICE (DOCTRAL DISSERTATION). RETRIEVED FORM QUEENSLAND UNIVERSITY OF TECHNOLOGY.

GINO, F., SHAREK, Z., & MOORE, D. A. (2011). KEEPING THE ILLUSION OF CONTROL UNDER CONTROL: CEILINGS, FLOORS, AND IMPERFECT CALIBRATION. ORGANIZATIONAL BEHAVIOR AND HUMAN DECISION PROCESSES, 114(2), 104-114.

GLADWELL, M. (2010). SMALL CHANGE. THE NEW YORKER, 4, 42-49.

GOLDSTEIN, N. E., MEHTA, D., TEITELBAUM, E., BRADLEY, E. H., & MORRISON, R. S. (2008). "IT'S LIKE CROSSING A BRIDGE" COMPLEXITIES PREVENTING PHYSICIANS FROM DISCUSSING DEACTIVATION OF IMPLANTABLE DEFIBRILLATORS AT THE END OF LIFE. JOURNAL OF GENERAL INTERNAL MEDICINE, 23(1), 2-6.

GROSSMAN, R. (2016). THE INDUSTRIES THAT ARE BEING DISRUPTED THE MOST BY DIGITAL. HARVARD BUSINESS REVIEW, 94(3), 2-5.

HAMEL, G., & PRAHALAD, C. K. (2013). COMPETING FOR THE FUTURE. BRIGHTON, MA: HARVARD BUSINESS PRESS.

HANCOCK, D. R., & ALGOZZINE, B. (2016). DOING CASE STUDY RESEARCH: A PRACTICAL GUIDE FOR BEGINNING RESEARCHERS. LOCATION: TEACHERS COLLEGE PRESS.

HARMON-JONES, E. E., & MILLS, J. E. (1999). COGNITIVE DISSONANCE: PROGRESS ON A PIVOTAL THEORY IN SOCIAL PSYCHOLOGY. PAPER PRESENTED AT THE SCIENTIFIC CONFERENCES PROGRAM, 1997, U TEXAS, ARLINGTON, TX, US; THIS VOLUME IS BASED ON PAPERS PRESENTED AT A 2-DAY CONFERENCE AT THE UNIVERSITY OF TEXAS AT ARLINGTON, WINTER 1997.

HATCH, M. J. (1997). COMMENTARY: JAZZING UP THE THEORY OF ORGANIZATIONAL IMPROVISATION. ADVANCES IN STRATEGIC MANAGEMENT, 14, 181-192.

HITT, M. A., IRELAND, R. D., & HOSKISSON, R. E. (2012). STRATEGIC MANAGEMENT CASES: COMPETITIVENESS AND GLOBALIZATION. BOSTON, MA: CENGAGE LEARNING.

ISMAIL, S. (2014). EXPONENTIAL ORGANIZATIONS: WHY NEW ORGANIZATIONS ARE TEN TIMES BETTER, FASTER, AND CHEAPER THAN YOURS (AND WHAT TO DO ABOUT IT). NEW YORK, NY: DIVERSION BOOKS.

JACK, & WELCH, S. (2009). HOW NOT TO SUCCEED IN BUSINESS. BUSINESS WEEK - NEW YORK(4121), 774.

JOHNSON, N. (2009). SIMPLY COMPLEXITY: A CLEAR GUIDE TO COMPLEXITY THEORY. LONDON, UK: ONEWORLD PUBLICATIONS.

JORDAN, J., & WADE, M. (2018). AS AI MAKES MORE DECISIONS, THE NATURE OF LEADERSHIP WILL CHANGE. HUMAN RESOURCES FUTURE, 2018, 10-11.

Kahneman, D. (2003). A perspective on judgment and choice: Mapping bounded rationality The American Psychologist, 58(9), 697-lasst page #?.

Kahneman, D. (2011). Thinking, fast and slow. New York, NY: Farrar, Straus and Giroux.

Kahneman, D., & Tversky, A. (1979). Prospect theory: An analysis of decision under risk. Econometrica: Journal of the Econometric Society, 47(2), 263-291.

Knight, J. (2015). Updated definition of Internationalization. International Higher Education, (33). HTTPS://DOI.ORG/10.6017/IHE.2003.33.7391

Kolbjørnsrud, V., Amico, R., & Thomas, R. J. (2016). How artificial intelligence will redefine management. Harvard Business Review, 2.

Krylova, K. O., Krylova, K. O., Vera, D., Vera, D., Crossan, M., & Crossan, M. (2016). Knowledge transfer in knowledge-intensive organizations: The crucial role of improvisation in transferring and protecting knowledge. Journal of Knowledge Management, 20(5), 1045-1064.

Kurzweil, R. (2016). The singularity is near. Ethics and Emerging Technologies, 393-406. HTTPS://DOI.ORG/10.1057/9781137349088_26

Langille, D. (2016). Follow the money: How business and politics define our health, 3rd ed (pp. 470-490). Social determinants of health: Canadian perspective. Toronto, Ontario: Canadian Scholars' Press

Leone, L. (2010). A critical review of improvisation in organizations: Open issues and future research directions. Imperial College London Business School. In Proceedings from Summer Conference: Opening up Innovation: Strategy, Organization and Technology.

Levy, O., Beechler, S., Taylor, S., & Boyacigiller, N. A. (2007). What we talk about when we talk about 'global mindset': Managerial cognition in multinational corporations. Journal of International Business Studies, 38(2), 231-258.

Leybourne, S. (2006). Improvisation within the project management of change: some observations from UK financial services. Journal of Change Management, 6(4), 365-381.

Lichtenstein, B. B., & Plowman, D. A. (2009). The leadership of emergence: A complex systems leadership theory of emergence at successive organizational levels. The Leadership Quarterly, 20(4), 617-630.

Lincoln, Y. S., & Guba, E. G. (1985). Naturalistic inquiry (Vol. 75): Thousand Oaks, CA: Sage Publications.

Mankins, M. C., & Steele, R. (2006). Stop making plans; start making decisions. Harvard Business Review, 84(1), 76.

Martin, A. D., Quinn, K. M., Ruger, T. W., & Kim, P. T. (2004). Competing zpproaches to predicting Supreme Court decision making. Perspectives on Politics, 2(4), 761-767.

Maxwell, J. A. (2013). Qualitative research design: An interactive approach (Vol. 41). Thousand Oaks, CA:Sage publications.

MAYER-SCHÖNBERGER, V., & CUKIER, K. (2013). A REVOLUTION THAT WILL TRANSFORM HOW WE LIVE, WORK, AND THINK. LONDON: EAMON DOLAN/MARINER BOOKS.

MCKNIGHT, B., & BONTIS, N. (2002). E-IMPROVISATION: COLLABORATIVE GROUPWARE TECHNOLOGY EXPANDS THE REACH AND EFFECTIVENESS OF ORGANIZATIONAL IMPROVISATION. KPM KNOWLEDGE AND PROCESS MANAGEMENT, 9(4), 219-227.

MENDENHALL, M. E., OSLAND, J., BIRD, A., ODDOU, G. R., MAZNEVSKI, M. L., STEVENS, M., & STAHL, G. K. (2013). GLOBAL LEADERSHIP: RESEARCH, PRACTICE AND DEVELOPMENT. ABINGDON, UK: ROUTLEDGE PRESS.

MEYER, P. (2010). FROM WORKPLACE TO PLAYSPACE: INNOVATING, LEARNING AND CHANGING THROUGH DYNAMIC ENGAGEMENT. HOBOKEN, NJ: JOHN WILEY & SONS.

MILES, M. B., HUBERMAN, A. M., & SALDANA, J. (2013). QUALITATIVE DATA ANALYSIS. THOUSAND OAKS, CA: SAGE.

MILKMAN, K. L., CHUGH, D., & BAZERMAN, M. H. (2009). HOW CAN DECISION MAKING BE IMPROVED? PERSPECTIVES ON PSYCHOLOGICAL SCIENCE, 4(4), 379-383.

MONTUORI, A. (2012). CREATIVE INQUIRY: CONFRONTING THE CHALLENGES OF SCHOLARSHIP IN THE 21ST CENTURY. FUTURES, 44(1), 64-70.

MOORMAN, C., & MINER, A. S. (1998). ORGANIZATIONAL IMPROVISATION AND ORGANIZATIONAL MEMORY. ACADEMY OF MANAGEMENT REVIEW, 23(4), 698-723.

MORENO JR, V., & CAVAZOTTE, F. (2015). USING INFORMATION SYSTEMS TO LEVERAGE KNOWLEDGE MANAGEMENT PROCESSES: THE ROLE OF WORK CONTEXT, JOB CHARACTERISTICS AND TASK-TECHNOLOGY FIT. PROCEDIA COMPUTER SCIENCE, 55, 360-369.

MOUSTAKAS, C. (1994). PHENOMENOLOGICAL RESEARCH METHODS. THOUSAND OAKS, CA: SAGE PUBLICATIONS.

MUMFORD, M. D., ZACCARO, S. J., HARDING, F. D., JACOBS, T. O., & FLEISHMAN, E. A. (2000). LEADERSHIP SKILLS FOR A CHANGING WORLD: SOLVING COMPLEX SOCIAL PROBLEMS. THE LEADERSHIP QUARTERLY, 11(1), 11-35.

NORTHOUSE, P. G. (2017). INTRODUCTION TO LEADERSHIP: CONCEPTS AND PRACTICE: SAGE PUBLICATIONS.

NORTON, M. I., MOCHON, D., & ARIELY, D. (2012). THE IKEA EFFECT: WHEN LABOR LEADS TO LOVE. JOURNAL OF CONSUMER PSYCHOLOGY, 22(3), 453-460.

OSLAND, J. S., BIRD, A., & MENDENHALL, M. (2006). "DEVELOPING GLOBAL LEADERSHIP CAPABILITIES AND GLOBAL MINDSET: A REVIEW". IN HANDBOOK OF RESEARCH IN INTERNATIONAL HUMAN RESOURCE MANAGEMENT. CHELTENHAM, UK: EDWARD ELGAR PUBLISHING. DOI: HTTPS://DOI.ORG/10.4337/9781845428235.00017

PALACIOS FENECH, J., & TELLIS, G. J. (2016). THE DIVE AND DISRUPTION OF SUCCESSFUL CURRENT PRODUCTS: MEASURES, GLOBAL PATTERNS, AND PREDICTIVE MODEL. JOURNAL OF PRODUCT INNOVATION MANAGEMENT, 33(1), 53-68.

PALINKAS, L. A., HORWITZ, S. M., GREEN, C. A., WISDOM, J. P., DUAN, N., & HOAGWOOD, K. (2015). PURPOSEFUL SAMPLING FOR QUALITATIVE DATA COLLECTION AND ANALYSIS IN MIXED METHOD IMPLEMENTATION RESEARCH. ADMINISTRATION AND POLICY IN MENTAL HEALTH AND MENTAL HEALTH SERVICES RESEARCH, 42(5), 533-544.

Parker, D. (2012). Service operations management: the total experience. Cheltenham, UK: Edward Elgar Publishing.

Patton, M. Q. (2006). Qualitative evaluation and research methods. Thousand Oaks, CA: Sage Publications.

Perry, A. S., Rahim, E., & Davis, B. (2018). Startup Success Trends in Small Business beyond Five-Years: A Qualitative Research Study. Paper presented at the 6th International Conference on Innovation and Entrepreneurship: ICIE 2018.

Plous, S. (1995). A comparison of strategies for reducing interval overconfidence in group judgments. Journal of Applied Psychology, 80(4), 443.

Pohl, R. (2004). Cognitive illusions: A handbook on fallacies and biases in thinking, judgment and memory. Abingdon, UK: Psychology Press.

Pratt, S., & Stringer, A. (2008). Strange attractors in school leadership. In B. Despres (Eds.), Systems Thinkers in Action: A Field Guide for Effective Change Leadership in Education (109-131). Lanham, MD: R&L Education.

Quick, J., & Hall, S. (2015). Part three: The quantitative approach. Journal ofPperioperative Practice, 25(10), 192-196.

Quinn, R. E. (2000). Change the world: How ordinary people can accomplish extraordinary things. San Francisco, CA: Jossey-Bass.

Ransbotham, S., Kiron, D., Gerbert, P., & Reeves, M. (2017). Reshaping business with artificial intelligence: Closing the gap between ambition and action. MIT Sloan Management Review, 59(1). Retrieved from: https://sloanreview.mit.edu/projects/reshaping-business-with-artificial-intelligence/

Ratten, V., & Hodge, J. (2016). So much theory, so little practice: A literature review of workplace improvisation training. Industrial and Commercial Training, 48(3), 149-155.

Rosati, A. G., Wobber, V., Hughes, K., & Santos, L. R. (2014). Comparative developmental psychology: how is human cognitive development unique? Evolutionary Psychology, 12(2), 448-473.

Rosenzweig, P. (2013). What makes strategic decisions different. Harvard Business Review, 91(11), 88.

Rosenzweig, P. (2014a). The benefits—and limits—of decision models. McKinsey Quarterly, 1-10.

Rosenzweig, P. (2014b). The halo effect:... and the eight other business delusions that deceive managers: New York, NY: Simon and Schuster.

Rosenzweig, P. (2014c). Left brain, right stuff: How leaders make winning decisions. New York, NY: PublicAffairs.

Ruger, T. W., Kim, P. T., Martin, A. D., & Quinn, K. M. (2004). The Supreme Court forecasting project: Legal and political science approaches to predicting Supreme Court decisionmaking. Colulawrevi Columbia Law Review, 104(4), 1150-1210.

Russo, J. E., & Schoemaker, P. J. (1992). Managing overconfidence. Sloan Management Review, 33(2), 7.

Safian, R. (2012). This is generation flux: Meet the pioneers of the new (and chaotic) frontier of business. Fast Company, Retrieved from: http://naturalcapital.us/images/This%20Is%20Generation%20Flux_20120124_041443.pdf

Santos, L. R., & Rosati, A. G. (2015). The evolutionary roots of human decision making. Annual Review of Psychology, 66, 321-347.

School, H. B. (2018). The 2018 State of leadership development report: Meeting the transformative imperative. Retrieved from: http://www.harvardbusiness.org/sites/default/files/20853_CL_StateOfLeadership_Report_2018_May2018.pdf.

Schwandt, D. R. (2005). When managers become philosophers: Integrating learning with sensemaking. Academy of Management Learning & Education, 4(2), 176-192.

Shermer, M. (2008). Patternicity. Scientific American, 299, 6, 48.

Simonson, I., & Tversky, A. (1992). Choice in context: Tradeoff contrast and extremeness aversion. Journal of marketing research, 29(3), 281-295.

Stacey, R. D. (2007). Strategic management and organisational dynamics: The challenge of complexity to ways of thinking about organisations. London, UK: Pearson education.

Yudkowsky, E. (n.d.). A Map that Reflects the Territory. Retrieved January 02, 2021, from https://www.lesswrong.com/

Stahl, G. K., Pless, N. M., & Maak, T. (2013). Global Leadership 2e: Research, Practice, and Development. In M. E. Mendenhall, J. Osland, A. Bird, G. R. Oddou, M. L. Maznevski, M. Stevens, G. K. Stahl (Eds.), Responsible global leadership (240-259). Abingdon, UK: Routledge.

Stone, M., Thomas, K., Wilkinson, M., Jones, A., St Clair Gibson, A., & Thompson, K. (2012). Effects of deception on exercise performance: implications for determinants of fatigue in humans. Medicine & Science in Sports & Exercise, 44(3), 534-541.

Teigen, K. H., & Jørgensen, M. (2005). When 90% confidence intervals are 50% certain: On the credibility of credible intervals. Applied Cognitive Psychology, 19(4), 455-475.

Tetlock, P. (2005). Expert political judgment: How good is it? How can we know? Princeton, NJ: Princeton University Press.

Tetlock, P. E., & Mellers, B. A. (2011). Intelligent management of intelligence agencies: beyond accountability ping-pong. American Psychologist, 66(6), 542 -554.

Uhl-Bien, M., & Arena, M. (2017). Complexity leadership. Organizational Dynamics, 1(46), 9-20.

Uhl-Bien, M., & Arena, M. (2018). Leadership for organizational adaptability: A theoretical synthesis and integrative framework. The Leadership Quarterly.

Uhl-Bien, M., & Marion, R. (2009). Complexity leadership in bureaucratic forms of organizing: A meso model. The Leadership Quarterly, 20(4), 631-650.

Uhl-Bien, M., Marion, R., & McKelvey, B. (2007). Complexity leadership theory: Shifting leadership from the industrial age to the knowledge era. The Leadership Quarterly, 18(4), 298-318.

Uhl-Bien, M., Marion, R., & McKelvey, B. (2008). Complexity leadership theory. Complexity leadership: part, 1, 185-224.

Van de Walle, S., & Vogelaar, M. (2010). Emergence and Public Administration: A Literature Review for the Project 'A New Synthesis in Public Administration'. Retrivied from: http://dx.doi.org/10.2139/ssrn.1580126

Van Manen, M. (2016). Researching lived experience: Human science for an action sensitive pedagogy. Abingdon, UK: Routledge.

Vasiltsova, V. M., Dyatlov, S. A., Vasiltsov, V. S., Bezrukova, T. L., & Bezrukov, B. A. (2015). Methodology of management innovation hypercompetition. Asian Social Science, 11(20), 165.

Weiner, N., & Mahoney, T. A. (1981). A model of corporate performance as a function of environmental, organizational, and leadership influences. Academy of Management Journal, 24(3), 453-470.

Wiggins, R. R., & Ruefli, T. W. (2005). Schumpeter's ghost: Is hypercompetition making the best of times shorter? Strategic Management Journal, 26(10), 887-911.

Withers, M. C., & Fitza, M. A. (2017). Do board chairs matter? The influence of board chairs on firm performance. Strategic Management Journal, 38(6), 1343-1355.

Witt, J. K., Linkenauger, S. A., & Proffitt, D. R. (2012). Get me out of this slump! Visual illusions improve sports performance. Psychological Science, 23(4), 397-399.

Part 4 - Tomorrow

NCIS. (2020, November 24). NCIS fact sheets. Retrieved December 05, 2020, from https://www.ncis.org.au/publications/ncis-fact-sheets/

Howard, R. (2009, March 10). Microrisks for Medical Decision Analysis: International Journal of Technology Assessment in Health Care. Retrieved December 05, 2020, from https://doi.org/10.1017/S026646230000742X

Lifespan. (2007, January 3). Study Finds Surfing Safer Than Soccer. ScienceDaily. Retrieved December 4, 2020 from www.sciencedaily.com/releases/2007/01/070102092203.htm

WHO. (2017, October 17). Cardiovascular diseases (CVDs). Retrieved December 05, 2020, from https://www.who.int/en/news-room/fact-sheets/detail/cardiovascular-diseases-(cvds)

United Nations. (2019, June 8). Homicide kills far more people than armed conflict, says new UNODC study. Retrieved December 05, 2020, from https://www.unodc.org/unodc/en/frontpage/2019/July/homicide-kills-far-more-people-than-armed-conflict--says-new-unodc-study.html?ref=fs1

Abowd, John M, 2017, "How Will Statistical Agencies Operate When All Data Are Private?", Journal of Privacy and Confidentiality, 7(3): 1–15. doi:10.29012/jpc.v7i3.404

Allen, Colin, Iva Smit, and Wendell Wallach, 2005, "Artificial Morality: Top-down, Bottom-up, and Hybrid Approaches", Ethics and Information Technology, 7(3): 149–155. doi:10.1007/s10676-006-0004-4

Allen, Colin, Gary Varner, and Jason Zinser, 2000, "Prolegomena to Any Future Artificial Moral Agent", Journal of Experimental & Theoretical Artificial Intelligence, 12(3): 251–261. doi:10.1080/09528130050111428

Amoroso, Daniele and Guglielmo Tamburrini, 2018, "The Ethical and Legal Case Against Autonomy in Weapons Systems", Global Jurist, 18(1): art. 20170012. doi:10.1515/GJ-2017-0012

Anderson, Janna, Lee Rainie, and Alex Luchsinger, 2018, Artificial Intelligence and the Future of Humans, Washington, DC: Pew Research Center.

Anderson, Michael and Susan Leigh Anderson, 2007, "Machine Ethics: Creating an Ethical Intelligent Agent", AI Magazine, 28(4): 15–26.

Aneesh, A., 2006, Virtual Migration: The Programming of Globalization, Durham, NC and London: Duke University Press.

Arkin, Ronald C., 2009, Governing Lethal Behavior in Autonomous Robots, Boca Raton, FL: CRC Press.

Armstrong, Stuart, 2013, "General Purpose Intelligence: Arguing the Orthogonality Thesis", Analysis and Metaphysics, 12: 68–84.

Arnold, Thomas and Matthias Scheutz, 2017, "Beyond Moral Dilemmas: Exploring the Ethical Landscape in HRI", in Proceedings of the 2017 ACM/IEEE International Conference on Human-Robot Interaction—HRI '17, Vienna, Austria: ACM Press, 445–452. doi:10.1145/2909824.3020255

Asaro, Peter M., 2019, "AI Ethics in Predictive Policing: From Models of Threat to an Ethics of Care", IEEE Technology and Society Magazine, 38(2): 40–53. doi:10.1109/MTS.2019.2915154

Asimov, Isaac, 1942, "Runaround: A Short Story", Astounding Science Fiction, March 1942. Reprinted in "I, Robot", New York: Gnome Press 1950, 1940ff.

Awad, Edmond, Sohan Dsouza, Richard Kim, Jonathan Schulz, Joseph Henrich, Azim Shariff, Jean-François Bonnefon, and Iyad Rahwan, 2018, "The Moral Machine Experiment", Nature, 563(7729): 59–64. doi:10.1038/s41586-018-0637-6

Baldwin, Richard, 2019, The Globotics Upheaval: Globalisation, Robotics and the Future of Work, New York: Oxford University Press.

Baum, Seth D., Stuart Armstrong, Timoteus Ekenstedt, Olle Häggström, Robin Hanson, Karin Kuhlemann, Matthijs M. Maas, James D. Miller, Markus Salmela, Anders Sandberg, Kaj Sotala, Phil Torres, Alexey Turchin, and Roman V. Yampolskiy, 2019, "Long-Term Trajectories of Human Civilization", Foresight, 21(1): 53–83. doi:10.1108/FS-04-2018-0037

BENDEL, OLIVER, 2018, "SEXROBOTER AUS SICHT DER MASCHINENETHIK", IN HANDBUCH FILMTHEORIE, BERNHARD GROSS AND THOMAS MORSCH (EDS.), (SPRINGER REFERENCE GEISTESWISSENSCHAFTEN), WIESBADEN: SPRINGER FACHMEDIEN WIESBADEN, 1–19. DOI:10.1007/978-3-658-17484-2_22-1

BENNETT, COLIN J. AND CHARLES RAAB, 2006, THE GOVERNANCE OF PRIVACY: POLICY INSTRUMENTS IN GLOBAL PERSPECTIVE, SECOND EDITION, CAMBRIDGE, MA: MIT PRESS.

BENTHALL, SEBASTIAN AND BRUCE D. HAYNES, 2019, "RACIAL CATEGORIES IN MACHINE LEARNING", IN PROCEEDINGS OF THE CONFERENCE ON FAIRNESS, ACCOUNTABILITY, AND TRANSPARENCY - FAT* '19, ATLANTA, GA, USA: ACM PRESS, 289–298. DOI:10.1145/3287560.3287575

BERTOLINI, ANDREA AND GIUSEPPE AIELLO, 2018, "ROBOT COMPANIONS: A LEGAL AND ETHICAL ANALYSIS", THE INFORMATION SOCIETY, 34(3): 130–140. DOI:10.1080/01972243.2018.14442 49

BINNS, REUBEN, 2018, "FAIRNESS IN MACHINE LEARNING: LESSONS FROM POLITICAL PHILOSOPHY", PROCEEDINGS OF THE 1ST CONFERENCE ON FAIRNESS, ACCOUNTABILITY AND TRANSPARENCY, IN PROCEEDINGS OF MACHINE LEARNING RESEARCH, 81: 149–159.

BOSTROM, NICK, 2003A, "ARE WE LIVING IN A COMPUTER SIMULATION?", THE PHILOSOPHICAL QUARTERLY, 53(211): 243–255. DOI:10.1111/1467-9213.00309

BOSTROM, NICK AND MILAN M. ĆIRKOVIĆ (EDS.), 2011, GLOBAL CATASTROPHIC RISKS, NEW YORK: OXFORD UNIVERSITY PRESS.

BOSTROM, NICK, ALLAN DAFOE, AND CARRICK FLYNN, FORTHCOMING, "POLICY DESIDERATA FOR SUPERINTELLIGENT AI: A VECTOR FIELD APPROACH (V. 4.3)", IN ETHICS OF ARTIFICIAL INTELLIGENCE, S MATTHEW LIAO (ED.), NEW YORK: OXFORD UNIVERSITY PRESS. [BOSTROM, DAFOE, AND FLYNN FORTHCOMING – PREPRINT AVAILABLE ONLINE]

BOSTROM, NICK AND ELIEZER YUDKOWSKY, 2014, "THE ETHICS OF ARTIFICIAL INTELLIGENCE", IN THE CAMBRIDGE HANDBOOK OF ARTIFICIAL INTELLIGENCE, KEITH FRANKISH AND WILLIAM M. RAMSEY (EDS.), CAMBRIDGE: CAMBRIDGE UNIVERSITY PRESS, 316–334. DOI:10.1017/ CBO9781139046855.020 [BOSTROM AND YUDKOWSKY 2014 AVAILABLE ONLINE]

BRADSHAW, SAMANTHA, LISA-MARIA NEUDERT, AND PHIL HOWARD, 2019, "GOVERNMENT RESPONSES TO MALICIOUS USE OF SOCIAL MEDIA", WORKING PAPER 2019.2, OXFORD: PROJECT ON COMPUTATIONAL PROPAGANDA. [BRADSHAW, NEUDERT, AND HOWARD 2019 AVAILABLE ONLINE/]

BROWNSWORD, ROGER, ELOISE SCOTFORD, AND KAREN YEUNG (EDS.), 2017, THE OXFORD HANDBOOK OF LAW, REGULATION AND TECHNOLOGY, OXFORD: OXFORD UNIVERSITY PRESS. DOI:10.1093/OXFORDHB/9780199680832.001.0001

BRYNJOLFSSON, ERIK AND ANDREW MCAFEE, 2016, THE SECOND MACHINE AGE: WORK, PROGRESS, AND PROSPERITY IN A TIME OF BRILLIANT TECHNOLOGIES, NEW YORK: W. W. NORTON.

BRYSON, JOANNA J., 2010, "ROBOTS SHOULD BE SLAVES", IN CLOSE ENGAGEMENTS WITH ARTIFICIAL COMPANIONS: KEY SOCIAL, PSYCHOLOGICAL, ETHICAL AND DESIGN ISSUES, YORICK WILKS (ED.), (NATURAL LANGUAGE PROCESSING 8), AMSTERDAM: JOHN BENJAMINS PUBLISHING COMPANY, 63–74. DOI:10.1075/NLP.8.11BRY

Bryson, Joanna J., Mihailis E. Diamantis, and Thomas D. Grant, 2017, "Of, for, and by the People: The Legal Lacuna of Synthetic Persons", Artificial Intelligence and Law, 25(3): 273–291. DOI:10.1007/S10506-017-9214-9

Burr, Christopher and Nello Cristianini, 2019, "Can Machines Read Our Minds?", Minds and Machines, 29(3): 461–494. DOI:10.1007/S11023-019-09497-4

Butler, Samuel, 1863, "Darwin among the Machines: Letter to the Editor", Letter in The Press (Christchurch), 13 June 1863. [Butler 1863 available online]

Callaghan, Victor, James Miller, Roman Yampolskiy, and Stuart Armstrong (eds.), 2017, The Technological Singularity: Managing the Journey, (The Frontiers Collection), Berlin, Heidelberg: Springer Berlin Heidelberg. DOI:10.1007/978-3-662-54033-6

Calo, Ryan, 2018, "Artificial Intelligence Policy: A Primer and Roadmap", University of Bologna Law Review, 3(2): 180-218. DOI:10.6092/ISSN.2531-6133/8670

Calo, Ryan, A. Michael Froomkin, and Ian Kerr (eds.), 2016, Robot Law, Cheltenham: Edward Elgar.

Čapek, Karel, 1920, R.U.R., Prague: Aventium. Translated by Peter Majer and Cathy Porter, London: Methuen, 1999.

Capurro, Raphael, 1993, "Ein Grinsen Ohne Katze: Von der Vergleichbarkeit Zwischen 'Künstlicher Intelligenz' und 'Getrennten Intelligenzen'", Zeitschrift für philosophische Forschung, 47: 93–102.

Cave, Stephen, 2019, "To Save Us from a Kafkaesque Future, We Must Democratise AI", The Guardian , 04 January 2019. [Cave 2019 available online]

Chalmers, David J., 2010, "The Singularity: A Philosophical Analysis", Journal of Consciousness Studies, 17(9–10): 7–65. [Chalmers 2010 available online]

Christman, John, 2003 [2018], "Autonomy in Moral and Political Philosophy", (Spring 2018) Stanford Encyclopedia of Philosophy (EDITION NEEDED), URL = <https://plato.stanford.edu/archives/spr2018/entries/autonomy-moral/>

Coeckelbergh, Mark, 2010, "Robot Rights? Towards a Social-Relational Justification of Moral Consideration", Ethics and Information Technology, 12(3): 209–221. DOI:10.1007/S10676-010-9235-5

Crawford, Kate and Ryan Calo, 2016, "There Is a Blind Spot in AI Research", Nature, 538(7625): 311–313. DOI:10.1038/538311A

Cristianini, Nello, forthcoming, "Shortcuts to Artificial Intelligence", in Machines We Trust, Marcello Pelillo and Teresa Scantamburlo (eds.), Cambridge, MA: MIT Press. [Cristianini forthcoming – preprint available online]

Danaher, John, 2015, "Why AI Doomsayers Are Like Sceptical Theists and Why It Matters", Minds and Machines, 25(3): 231–246. DOI:10.1007/S11023-015-9365-Y

Danaher, John and Neil McArthur (eds.), 2017, Robot Sex: Social and Ethical Implications, Boston, MA: MIT Press.

DARPA, 1983, "Strategic Computing. New-Generation Computing Technology: A Strategic Plan for Its Development an Application to Critical Problems in Defense", ADA141982, 28 October 1983. [DARPA 1983 available online]

Dennett, Daniel C, 2017, From Bacteria to Bach and Back: The Evolution of Minds, New York: W.W. Norton.

Devlin, Kate, 2018, Turned On: Science, Sex and Robots, London: Bloomsbury.

Diakopoulos, Nicholas, 2015, "Algorithmic Accountability: Journalistic Investigation of Computational Power Structures", Digital Journalism, 3(3): 398–415. DOI:10.1080/21670811.2014.976411

Dignum, Virginia, 2018, "Ethics in Artificial Intelligence: Introduction to the Special Issue", Ethics and Information Technology, 20(1): 1–3. DOI:10.1007/s10676-018-9450-z

Domingos, Pedro, 2015, The Master Algorithm: How the Quest for the Ultimate Learning Machine Will Remake Our World, London: Allen Lane.

Draper, Heather, Tom Sorell, Sandra Bedaf, Dag Sverre Syrdal, Carolina Gutierrez-Ruiz, Alexandre Duclos, and Farshid Amirabdollahian, 2014, "Ethical Dimensions of Human-Robot Interactions in the Care of Older People: Insights from 21 Focus Groups Convened in the UK, France and the Netherlands", in International Conference on Social Robotics 2014, Michael Beetz, Benjamin Johnston, and Mary-Anne Williams (eds.), (Lecture Notes in Artificial Intelligence 8755), Cham: Springer International Publishing, 135–145. DOI:10.1007/978-3-319-11973-1_14

Dressel, Julia and Hany Farid, 2018, "The Accuracy, Fairness, and Limits of Predicting Recidivism", Science Advances, 4(1): EAAO5580. DOI:10.1126/SCIADV.AAO5580

Drexler, K. Eric, 2019, "Reframing Superintelligence: Comprehensive AI Services as General Intelligence", FHI Technical Report, 2019-1, 1-210. [Drexler 2019 available online]

Dreyfus, Hubert L., 1972, What Computers Still Can't Do: A Critique of Artificial Reason, second edition, Cambridge, MA: MIT Press 1992.

Dreyfus, Hubert L., Stuart E. Dreyfus, and Tom Athanasiou, 1986, Mind over Machine: The Power of Human Intuition and Expertise in the Era of the Computer, New York: Free Press.

Dwork, Cynthia, Frank McSherry, Kobbi Nissim, and Adam Smith, 2006, Calibrating Noise to Sensitivity in Private Data Analysis, Berlin, Heidelberg.

Eden, Amnon H., James H. Moor, Johnny H. Søraker, and Eric Steinhart (eds.), 2012, Singularity Hypotheses: A Scientific and Philosophical Assessment, (The Frontiers Collection), Berlin, Heidelberg: Springer Berlin Heidelberg. DOI:10.1007/978-3-642-32560-1

Eubanks, Virginia, 2018, Automating Inequality: How High-Tech Tools Profile, Police, and Punish the Poor, London: St. Martin's Press.

European Commission, 2013, "How Many People Work in Agriculture in the European Union? An Answer Based on Eurostat Data Sources", EU Agricultural Economics Briefs, 8 (July 2013). [Anonymous 2013 available online]

European Group on Ethics in Science and New Technologies, 2018, "Statement on Artificial Intelligence, Robotics and 'Autonomous' Systems", 9 March 2018, European Commission, Directorate-General for Research and Innovation, Unit RTD.01. [European Group 2018 available online]

Ferguson, Andrew Guthrie, 2017, The Rise of Big Data Policing: Surveillance, Race, and the Future of Law Enforcement, New York: NYU Press.

Floridi, Luciano, 2016, "Should We Be Afraid of AI? Machines Seem to Be Getting Smarter and Smarter and Much Better at Human Jobs, yet True AI Is Utterly Implausible. Why?", Aeon, 9 May 2016. URL = <Floridi 2016 available online>

Floridi, Luciano, Josh Cowls, Monica Beltrametti, Raja Chatila, Patrice Chazerand, Virginia Dignum, Christoph Luetge, Robert Madelin, Ugo Pagallo, Francesca Rossi, Burkhard Schafer, Peggy Valcke, and Effy Vayena, 2018, "AI4People—An Ethical Framework for a Good AI Society: Opportunities, Risks, Principles, and Recommendations", Minds and Machines, 28(4): 689–707. DOI:10.1007/s11023-018-9482-5

Floridi, Luciano and Jeff W. Sanders, 2004, "On the Morality of Artificial Agents", Minds and Machines, 14(3): 349–379. DOI:10.1023/B:MIND.0000035461.63578.9D

Floridi, Luciano and Mariarosaria Taddeo, 2016, "What Is Data Ethics?", Philosophical Transactions of the Royal Society A: Mathematical, Physical and Engineering Sciences, 374(2083): 20160360. DOI:10.1098/rsta.2016.0360

Foot, Philippa, 1967, "The Problem of Abortion and the Doctrine of the Double Effect", Oxford Review, 5: 5–15.

Fosch-Villaronga, Eduard and Jordi Albo-Canals, 2019, "'I'll Take Care of You,' Said the Robot", Paladyn, Journal of Behavioral Robotics, 10(1): 77–93. DOI:10.1515/pjbr-2019-0006

Frank, Lily and Sven Nyholm, 2017, "Robot Sex and Consent: Is Consent to Sex between a Robot and a Human Conceivable, Possible, and Desirable?", Artificial Intelligence and Law, 25(3): 305–323. DOI:10.1007/s10506-017-9212-y

Frankfurt, Harry G., 1971, "Freedom of the Will and the Concept of a Person", The Journal of Philosophy, 68(1): 5–20.

Frey, Carl Benedict, 2019, The Technology Trap: Capital, Labour, and Power in the Age of Automation, Princeton, NJ: Princeton University Press.

Frey, Carl Benedikt and Michael A. Osborne, 2013, "The Future of Employment: How Susceptible Are Jobs to Computerisation?", Oxford Martin School Working Papers, 17 September 2013. [Frey and Osborne 2013 available online]

Ganascia, Jean-Gabriel, 2017, Le Mythe De La Singularité, Paris: Éditions du Seuil.

EU Parliament, 2016, "Draft Report with Recommendations to the Commission on Civil Law Rules on Robotics (2015/2103(Inl))", Committee on Legal Affairs, 10.11.2016. https://www.europarl.europa.eu/doceo/document/A-8-2017-0005_EN.html

EU Regulation, 2016/679, "General Data Protection Regulation: Regulation (EU) 2016/679 of the European Parliament and of the Council of 27 April 2016 on the Protection of Natural Persons with Regard to the Processing of Personal Data and on the Free Movement of Such Data, and Repealing Directive 95/46/Ec",

Official Journal of the European Union, 119 (4 May 2016), 1–88. [Regulation (EU) 2016/679 available online]

Geraci, Robert M., 2008, "Apocalyptic AI: Religion and the Promise of Artificial Intelligence", Journal of the American Academy of Religion, 76(1): 138–166. DOI:10.1093/JAAREL/LFM101

Gerdes, Anne, 2016, "The Issue of Moral Consideration in Robot Ethics", ACM SIGCAS Computers and Society, 45(3): 274–279. DOI:10.1145/2874239.2874278

German Federal Ministry of Transport and Digital Infrastructure, 2017, "Report of the Ethics Commission: Automated and Connected Driving", June 2017, 1–36. [GFMTDI 2017 available online]

Gertz, Nolen, 2018, Nihilism and Technology, London: Rowman & Littlefield.

Gewirth, Alan, 1978, "The Golden Rule Rationalized", Midwest Studies in Philosophy, 3(1): 133–147. DOI:10.1111/J.1475-4975.1978.TB00353.X

Gibert, Martin, 2019, "Éthique Artificielle (Version Grand Public)", in L'Encyclopédie Philosophique, Maxime Kristanek (ed.), accessed: 16 April 2020, URL = <Gibert 2019 available online>

Giubilini, Alberto and Julian Savulescu, 2018, "The Artificial Moral Advisor. The 'Ideal Observer' Meets Artificial Intelligence", Philosophy & Technology, 31(2): 169–188. DOI:10.1007/S13347-017-0285-Z

Good, Irving John, 1965, "Speculations Concerning the First Ultraintelligent Machine", in Advances in Computers 6, Franz L. Alt and Morris Rubinoff (eds.), New York & London: Academic Press, 31–88. DOI:10.1016/S0065-2458(08)60418-0

Goodfellow, Ian, Yoshua Bengio, and Aaron Courville, 2016, Deep Learning, Cambridge, MA: MIT Press.

Goodman, Bryce and Seth Flaxman, 2017, "European Union Regulations on Algorithmic Decision-Making and a 'Right to Explanation'", AI Magazine, 38(3): 50–57. DOI:10.1609/AIMAG.V38I3.2741

Goos, Maarten, 2018, "The Impact of Technological Progress on Labour Markets: Policy Challenges", Oxford Review of Economic Policy, 34(3): 362–375. DOI:10.1093/OXREP/GRY002

Goos, Maarten, Alan Manning, and Anna Salomons, 2009, "Job Polarization in Europe", American Economic Review, 99(2): 58–63. DOI:10.1257/AER.99.2.58

Graham, Sandra and Brian S. Lowery, 2004, "Priming Unconscious Racial Stereotypes about Adolescent Offenders", Law and Human Behavior, 28(5): 483–504. DOI:10.1023/B:LAHU.0000046430.65485.1F

Gunkel, David J., 2018a, "The Other Question: Can and Should Robots Have Rights?", Ethics and Information Technology, 20(2): 87–99. DOI:10.1007/S10676-017-9442-4

Gunkel, David J. and Joanna J. Bryson (eds.), 2014, Machine Morality: The Machine as Moral Agent and Patient special issue of Philosophy & Technology, 27(1): 1–142.

HÄGGSTRÖM, OLLE, 2016, HERE BE DRAGONS: SCIENCE, TECHNOLOGY AND THE FUTURE OF HUMANITY, OXFORD: OXFORD UNIVERSITY PRESS. DOI:10.1093/ACPROF: OSO/9780198723547.001.0001

HAKLI, RAUL AND PEKKA MÄKELÄ, 2019, "MORAL RESPONSIBILITY OF ROBOTS AND HYBRID AGENTS", THE MONIST, 102(2): 259–275. DOI:10.1093/MONIST/ONZ009

HANSON, ROBIN, 2016, THE AGE OF EM: WORK, LOVE AND LIFE WHEN ROBOTS RULE THE EARTH, OXFORD: OXFORD UNIVERSITY PRESS.

HANSSON, SVEN OVE, 2013, THE ETHICS OF RISK: ETHICAL ANALYSIS IN AN UNCERTAIN WORLD, NEW YORK: PALGRAVE MACMILLAN.

HARARI, YUVAL NOAH, 2016, HOMO DEUS: A BRIEF HISTORY OF TOMORROW, NEW YORK: HARPER.

HASKEL, JONATHAN AND STIAN WESTLAKE, 2017, CAPITALISM WITHOUT CAPITAL: THE RISE OF THE INTANGIBLE ECONOMY, PRINCETON, NJ: PRINCETON UNIVERSITY PRESS.

HOUKES, WYBO AND PIETER E. VERMAAS, 2010, TECHNICAL FUNCTIONS: ON THE USE AND DESIGN OF ARTEFACTS, (PHILOSOPHY OF ENGINEERING AND TECHNOLOGY 1), DORDRECHT: SPRINGER NETHERLANDS. DOI:10.1007/978-90-481-3900-2

IEEE, 2019, ETHICALLY ALIGNED DESIGN: A VISION FOR PRIORITIZING HUMAN WELL-BEING WITH AUTONOMOUS AND INTELLIGENT SYSTEMS (FIRST VERSION), <IEEE 2019 AVAILABLE ONLINE>.

JASANOFF, SHEILA, 2016, THE ETHICS OF INVENTION: TECHNOLOGY AND THE HUMAN FUTURE, NEW YORK: NORTON.

JECKER, NANCY S., FORTHCOMING, ENDING MIDLIFE BIAS: NEW VALUES FOR OLD AGE, NEW YORK: OXFORD UNIVERSITY PRESS.

JOBIN, ANNA, MARCELLO IENCA, AND EFFY VAYENA, 2019, "THE GLOBAL LANDSCAPE OF AI ETHICS GUIDELINES", NATURE MACHINE INTELLIGENCE, 1(9): 389–399. DOI:10.1038/S42256-019-0088-2

JOHNSON, DEBORAH G. AND MARIO VERDICCHIO, 2017, "REFRAMING AI DISCOURSE", MINDS AND MACHINES, 27(4): 575–590. DOI:10.1007/S11023-017-9417-6

KAHNEMANN, DANIEL, 2011, THINKING FAST AND SLOW, LONDON: MACMILLAN.

KAMM, FRANCES MYRNA, 2016, THE TROLLEY PROBLEM MYSTERIES, ERIC RAKOWSKI (ED.), OXFORD: OXFORD UNIVERSITY PRESS. DOI:10.1093/ACPROF:OSO/9780190247157.001.0001

KANT, IMMANUEL, 1781/1787, KRITIK DER REINEN VERNUNFT. TRANSLATED AS CRITIQUE OF PURE REASON, NORMAN KEMP SMITH (TRANS.), LONDON: PALGRAVE MACMILLAN, 1929.

KEELING, GEOFF, 2020, "WHY TROLLEY PROBLEMS MATTER FOR THE ETHICS OF AUTOMATED VEHICLES", SCIENCE AND ENGINEERING ETHICS, 26(1): 293–307. DOI:10.1007/S11948-019-00096-1

KEYNES, JOHN MAYNARD, 1930, "ECONOMIC POSSIBILITIES FOR OUR GRANDCHILDREN". REPRINTED IN HIS ESSAYS IN PERSUASION, NEW YORK: HARCOURT BRACE, 1932, 358–373.

KISSINGER, HENRY A., 2018, "HOW THE ENLIGHTENMENT ENDS: PHILOSOPHICALLY, INTELLECTUALLY—IN EVERY WAY—HUMAN SOCIETY IS UNPREPARED FOR THE

Rise of Artificial Intelligence", The Atlantic, June 2018. [Kissinger 2018 available online]

Kurzweil, Ray, 1999, The Age of Spiritual Machines: When Computers Exceed Human Intelligence, London: Penguin.

Lee, Minha, Sander Ackermans, Nena van As, Hanwen Chang, Enzo Lucas, and Wijnand IJsselsteijn, 2019, "Caring for Vincent: A Chatbot for Self-Compassion", in Proceedings of the 2019 CHI Conference on Human Factors in Computing Systems—CHI '19, Glasgow, Scotland: ACM Press, 1–13. DOI:10.1145/3290605.3300932

Levy, David, 2007, Love and Sex with Robots: The Evolution of Human-Robot Relationships, New York: Harper & Co.

Lighthill, James, 1973, "Artificial Intelligence: A General Survey", Artificial intelligence: A Paper Symposion, London: Science Research Council. [Lighthill 1973 available online]

Lin, Patrick, 2016, "Why Ethics Matters for Autonomous Cars", in Autonomous Driving, Markus Maurer, J. Christian Gerdes, Barbara Lenz, and Hermann Winner (eds.), Berlin, Heidelberg: Springer Berlin Heidelberg, 69–85. DOI:10.1007/978-3-662-48847-8_4

Lin, Patrick, Keith Abney, and Ryan Jenkins (eds.), 2017, Robot Ethics 2.0: From Autonomous Cars to Artificial Intelligence, New York: Oxford University Press. DOI:10.1093/OSO/9780190652951.001.0001

Lin, Patrick, George Bekey, and Keith Abney, 2008, "Autonomous Military Robotics: Risk, Ethics, and Design", ONR report, California Polytechnic State University, San Luis Obispo, 20 December 2008), 112 pp. [Lin, Bekey, and Abney 2008 available online]

Lomas, Meghann, Robert Chevalier, Ernest Vincent Cross, Robert Christopher Garrett, John Hoare, and Michael Kopack, 2012, "Explaining Robot Actions", in Proceedings of the Seventh Annual ACM/IEEE International Conference on Human-Robot Interaction—HRI '12, Boston, MA: ACM Press, 187–188. DOI:10.1145/2157689.2157748

Macnish, Kevin, 2017, The Ethics of Surveillance: An Introduction, London: Routledge.

Mathur, Arunesh, Gunes Acar, Michael J. Friedman, Elena Lucherini, Jonathan Mayer, Marshini Chetty, and Arvind Narayanan, 2019, "Dark Patterns at Scale: Findings from a Crawl of 11K Shopping Websites", Proceedings of the ACM on Human-Computer Interaction, 3(CSCW): art. 81. DOI:10.1145/3359183

Minsky, Marvin, 1985, The Society of Mind, New York: Simon & Schuster.

Misselhorn, Catrin, 2020, "Artificial Systems with Moral Capacities? A Research Design and Its Implementation in a Geriatric Care System", Artificial Intelligence, 278: art. 103179. DOI:10.1016/J.ARTINT.2019.103179

Mittelstadt, Brent Daniel and Luciano Floridi, 2016, "The Ethics of Big Data: Current and Foreseeable Issues in Biomedical Contexts", Science and Engineering Ethics, 22(2): 303–341. DOI:10.1007/S11948-015-9652-2

MOOR, JAMES H., 2006, "THE NATURE, IMPORTANCE, AND DIFFICULTY OF MACHINE ETHICS", IEEE INTELLIGENT SYSTEMS, 21(4): 18–21. DOI:10.1109/MIS.2006.80

MORAVEC, HANS, 1990, MIND CHILDREN, CAMBRIDGE, MA: HARVARD UNIVERSITY PRESS.

MOZOROV, EYGENY, 2013, TO SAVE EVERYTHING, CLICK HERE: THE FOLLY OF TECHNOLOGICAL SOLUTIONISM, NEW YORK: PUBLIC AFFAIRS.

MÜLLER, VINCENT C., 2012, "AUTONOMOUS COGNITIVE SYSTEMS IN REAL-WORLD ENVIRONMENTS: LESS CONTROL, MORE FLEXIBILITY AND BETTER INTERACTION", COGNITIVE COMPUTATION, 4(3): 212–215. DOI:10.1007/S12559-012-9129-4

MÜLLER, VINCENT C. AND NICK BOSTROM, 2016, "FUTURE PROGRESS IN ARTIFICIAL INTELLIGENCE: A SURVEY OF EXPERT OPINION", IN FUNDAMENTAL ISSUES OF ARTIFICIAL INTELLIGENCE, VINCENT C. MÜLLER (ED.), CHAM: SPRINGER INTERNATIONAL PUBLISHING, 555–572. DOI:10.1007/978-3-319-26485-1_33

NEWPORT, CAL, 2019, DIGITAL MINIMALISM: ON LIVING BETTER WITH LESS TECHNOLOGY, LONDON: PENGUIN.

NØRSKOV, MARCO (ED.), 2017, SOCIAL ROBOTS, LONDON: ROUTLEDGE.

NYHOLM, SVEN, 2018A, "ATTRIBUTING AGENCY TO AUTOMATED SYSTEMS: REFLECTIONS ON HUMAN–ROBOT COLLABORATIONS AND RESPONSIBILITY-LOCI", SCIENCE AND ENGINEERING ETHICS, 24(4): 1201–1219. DOI:10.1007/S11948-017-9943-X

NYHOLM, SVEN, AND LILY FRANK, 2017, "FROM SEX ROBOTS TO LOVE ROBOTS: IS MUTUAL LOVE WITH A ROBOT POSSIBLE?", IN DANAHER AND MCARTHUR 2017: 219–243.

O'CONNELL, MARK, 2017, TO BE A MACHINE: ADVENTURES AMONG CYBORGS, UTOPIANS, HACKERS, AND THE FUTURISTS SOLVING THE MODEST PROBLEM OF DEATH, LONDON: GRANTA.

O'NEIL, CATHY, 2016, WEAPONS OF MATH DESTRUCTION: HOW BIG DATA INCREASES INEQUALITY AND THREATENS DEMOCRACY, LARGO, ML: CROWN.

OMOHUNDRO, STEVE, 2014, "AUTONOMOUS TECHNOLOGY AND THE GREATER HUMAN GOOD", JOURNAL OF EXPERIMENTAL & THEORETICAL ARTIFICIAL INTELLIGENCE, 26(3): 303–315. DOI: 10.1080/0952813X.2014.895111

ORD, TOBY, 2020, THE PRECIPICE: EXISTENTIAL RISK AND THE FUTURE OF HUMANITY, LONDON: BLOOMSBURY.

POWERS, THOMAS M. AND JEAN-GABRIEL GANASCIA, FORTHCOMING, "THE ETHICS OF THE ETHICS OF AI", IN OXFORD HANDBOOK OF ETHICS OF ARTIFICIAL INTELLIGENCE, MARKUS D. DUBBER, FRANK PASQUALE, AND SUNNIT DAS (EDS.), NEW YORK: OXFORD.

RAWLS, JOHN, 1971, A THEORY OF JUSTICE, CAMBRIDGE, MA: BELKNAP PRESS.

REES, MARTIN, 2018, ON THE FUTURE: PROSPECTS FOR HUMANITY, PRINCETON: PRINCETON UNIVERSITY PRESS.

RICHARDSON, KATHLEEN, 2016, "SEX ROBOT MATTERS: SLAVERY, THE PROSTITUTED, AND THE RIGHTS OF MACHINES", IEEE TECHNOLOGY AND SOCIETY MAGAZINE, 35(2): 46–53. DOI:10.1109/MTS.2016.2554421

Roessler, Beate, 2017, "Privacy as a Human Right", Proceedings of the Aristotelian Society, 117(2): 187–206. DOI:10.1093/ARISOC/AOX008

Royakkers, Lambèr and Rinie van Est, 2016, Just Ordinary Robots: Automation from Love to War, Boca Raton, LA: CRC Press, Taylor & Francis. DOI:10.1201/B18899

Russell, Stuart, 2019, Human Compatible: Artificial Intelligence and the Problem of Control, New York: Viking.

Russell, Stuart, Daniel Dewey, and Max Tegmark, 2015, "Research Priorities for Robust and Beneficial Artificial Intelligence", AI Magazine, 36(4): 105–114. DOI:10.1609/AIMAG.V36I4.2577

SAE International, 2018, "Taxonomy and Definitions for Terms Related to Driving Automation Systems for on-Road Motor Vehicles", J3016_201806, 15 June 2018. [SAE International 2015 available online]

Sandberg, Anders, 2013, "Feasibility of Whole Brain Emulation", in Philosophy and Theory of Artificial Intelligence, Vincent C. Müller (ed.), (Studies in Applied Philosophy, Epistemology and Rational Ethics, 5), Berlin, Heidelberg: Springer Berlin Heidelberg, 251–264. DOI:10.1007/978-3-642-31674-6_19

Santoni de Sio, Filippo and Jeroen van den Hoven, 2018, "Meaningful Human Control over Autonomous Systems: A Philosophical Account", Frontiers in Robotics and AI, 5(February): 15. DOI:10.3389/FROBT.2018.00015

Schneier, Bruce, 2015, Data and Goliath: The Hidden Battles to Collect Your Data and Control Your World, New York: W. W. Norton.

Searle, John R., 1980, "Minds, Brains, and Programs", Behavioral and Brain Sciences, 3(3): 417–424. DOI:10.1017/S0140525X00005756

Selbst, Andrew D., Danah Boyd, Sorelle A. Friedler, Suresh Venkatasubramanian, and Janet Vertesi, 2019, "Fairness and Abstraction in Sociotechnical Systems", in Proceedings of the Conference on Fairness, Accountability, and Transparency—FAT* '19, Atlanta, GA: ACM Press, 59–68. DOI:10.1145/3287560.3287598

Sennett, Richard, 2018, Building and Dwelling: Ethics for the City, London: Allen Lane.

Shanahan, Murray, 2015, The Technological Singularity, Cambridge, MA: MIT Press.

Sharkey, Amanda, 2019, "Autonomous Weapons Systems, Killer Robots and Human Dignity", Ethics and Information Technology, 21(2): 75–87. DOI:10.1007/S10676-018-9494-0

Sharkey, Amanda and Noel Sharkey, 2011, "The Rights and Wrongs of Robot Care", in Robot Ethics: The Ethical and Social Implications of Robotics, Patrick Lin, Keith Abney and George Bekey (eds.), Cambridge, MA: MIT Press, 267–282.

Shoham, Yoav, Perrault Raymond, Brynjolfsson Erik, Jack Clark, James Manyika, Juan Carlos Niebles, … Zoe Bauer, 2018, "The AI Index 2018 Annual Report", 17 December 2018, Stanford, CA: AI Index Steering Committee, Human-Centered AI Initiative, Stanford University. [Shoam et al. 2018 available online]

Silver, David, Thomas Hubert, Julian Schrittwieser, Ioannis Antonoglou, Matthew Lai, Arthur Guez, Marc Lanctot, Laurent Sifre, Dharshan Kumaran, Thore

GRAEPEL, TIMOTHY LILLICRAP, KAREN SIMONYAN, AND DEMIS HASSABIS, 2018, "A GENERAL REINFORCEMENT LEARNING ALGORITHM THAT MASTERS CHESS, SHOGI, AND GO THROUGH SELF-PLAY", SCIENCE, 362(6419): 1140–1144. DOI:10.1126/SCIENCE.AAR6404

SIMON, HERBERT A. AND ALLEN NEWELL, 1958, "HEURISTIC PROBLEM SOLVING: THE NEXT ADVANCE IN OPERATIONS RESEARCH", OPERATIONS RESEARCH, 6(1): 1–10. DOI:10.1287/OPRE.6.1.1

SIMPSON, THOMAS W. AND VINCENT C. MÜLLER, 2016, "JUST WAR AND ROBOTS' KILLINGS", THE PHILOSOPHICAL QUARTERLY, 66(263): 302–322. DOI:10.1093/PQ/PQV075

SMOLAN, SANDY (DIRECTOR), 2016, "THE HUMAN FACE OF BIG DATA", PBS DOCUMENTARY, 24 FEBRUARY 2016, 56 MINS.

SPARROW, ROBERT, 2007, "KILLER ROBOTS", JOURNAL OF APPLIED PHILOSOPHY, 24(1): 62–77. DOI:10.1111/J.1468-5930.2007.00346.X

STAHL, BERND CARSTEN, JOB TIMMERMANS, AND BRENT DANIEL MITTELSTADT, 2016, "THE ETHICS OF COMPUTING: A SURVEY OF THE COMPUTING-ORIENTED LITERATURE", ACM COMPUTING SURVEYS, 48(4): ART. 55. DOI:10.1145/2871196

STAHL, BERND CARSTEN AND DAVID WRIGHT, 2018, "ETHICS AND PRIVACY IN AI AND BIG DATA: IMPLEMENTING RESPONSIBLE RESEARCH AND INNOVATION", IEEE SECURITY PRIVACY, 16(3): 26–33.

STONE, CHRISTOPHER D., 1972, "SHOULD TREES HAVE STANDING - TOWARD LEGAL RIGHTS FOR NATURAL OBJECTS", SOUTHERN CALIFORNIA LAW REVIEW, 45: 450–501.

STONE, PETER, RODNEY BROOKS, ERIK BRYNJOLFSSON, RYAN CALO, OREN ETZIONI, GREG HAGER, JULIA HIRSCHBERG, SHIVARAM KALYANAKRISHNAN, ECE KAMAR, SARIT KRAUS, KEVIN LEYTON-BROWN, DAVID PARKES, WILLIAM PRESS, ANNALEE SAXENIAN, JULIE SHAH, MILIND TAMBE, AND ASTRO TELLER, 2016, "ARTIFICIAL INTELLIGENCE AND LIFE IN 2030", ONE HUNDRED YEAR STUDY ON ARTIFICIAL INTELLIGENCE: REPORT OF THE 2015–2016 STUDY PANEL, STANFORD UNIVERSITY, STANFORD, CA, SEPTEMBER 2016. [STONE ET AL. 2016 AVAILABLE ONLINE]

STRAWSON, GALEN, 1998, "FREE WILL", IN ROUTLEDGE ENCYCLOPEDIA OF PHILOSOPHY, TAYLOR & FRANCIS. DOI:10.4324/9780415249126-V014-1

SULLINS, JOHN P., 2012, "ROBOTS, LOVE, AND SEX: THE ETHICS OF BUILDING A LOVE MACHINE", IEEE TRANSACTIONS ON AFFECTIVE COMPUTING, 3(4): 398–409. DOI:10.1109/T-AFFC.2012.31

SUSSER, DANIEL, BEATE ROESSLER, AND HELEN NISSENBAUM, 2019, "TECHNOLOGY, AUTONOMY, AND MANIPULATION", INTERNET POLICY REVIEW, 8(2): 30 JUNE 2019. [SUSSER, ROESSLER, AND NISSENBAUM 2019 AVAILABLE ONLINE]

TADDEO, MARIAROSARIA AND LUCIANO FLORIDI, 2018, "HOW AI CAN BE A FORCE FOR GOOD", SCIENCE, 361(6404): 751–752. DOI:10.1126/SCIENCE.AAT5991

TAYLOR, LINNET AND NADEZHDA PURTOVA, 2019, "WHAT IS RESPONSIBLE AND SUSTAINABLE DATA SCIENCE?", BIG DATA & SOCIETY, 6(2): ART. 205395171985811. DOI:10.1177/2053951719858114

TAYLOR, STEVE, ET AL., 2018, "RESPONSIBLE AI – KEY THEMES, CONCERNS & RECOMMENDATIONS FOR EUROPEAN RESEARCH AND INNOVATION: SUMMARY OF CONSULTATION WITH MULTIDISCIPLINARY EXPERTS", JUNE. [TAYLOR, ET AL. 2018 AVAILABLE ONLINE]

Tegmark, Max, 2017, Life 3.0: Being Human in the Age of Artificial Intelligence, New York: Knopf.

Thaler, Richard H and Sunstein, Cass, 2008, Nudge: Improving decisions about health, wealth and happiness, New York: Penguin.

Thompson, Nicholas and Ian Bremmer, 2018, "The AI Cold War That Threatens Us All", Wired, 23 November 2018. [Thompson and Bremmer 2018 available online]

Thomson, Judith Jarvis, 1976, "Killing, Letting Die, and the Trolley Problem", Monist, 59(2): 204–217. DOI:10.5840/monist197659224

Torrance, Steve, 2011, "Machine Ethics and the Idea of a More-Than-Human Moral World", in Anderson and Anderson 2011: 115–137. DOI:10.1017/CBO9780511978036.011

Trump, Donald J, 2019, "Executive Order on Maintaining American Leadership in Artificial Intelligence", 11 February 2019. [Trump 2019 available online]

Turner, Jacob, 2019, Robot Rules: Regulating Artificial Intelligence, Berlin: Springer. DOI:10.1007/978-3-319-96235-1

Tzafestas, Spyros G., 2016, Roboethics: A Navigating Overview, (Intelligent Systems, Control and Automation: Science and Engineering 79), Cham: Springer International Publishing. DOI:10.1007/978-3-319-21714-7

Vallor, Shannon, 2017, Technology and the Virtues: A Philosophical Guide to a Future Worth Wanting, Oxford: Oxford University Press. DOI:10.1093/acprof:oso/9780190498511.001.0001

Van Lent, Michael, William Fisher, and Michael Mancuso, 2004, "An Explainable Artificial Intelligence System for Small-Unit Tactical Behavior", in Proceedings of the 16th Conference on Innovative Applications of Artifical Intelligence, (IAAI'04), San Jose, CA: AAAI Press, 900–907.

van Wynsberghe, Aimee, 2016, Healthcare Robots: Ethics, Design and Implementation, London: Routledge. DOI:10.4324/9781315586397

Vanderelst, Dieter and Alan Winfield, 2018, "The Dark Side of Ethical Robots", in Proceedings of the 2018 AAAI/ACM Conference on AI, Ethics, and Society, New Orleans, LA: ACM, 317–322. DOI:10.1145/3278721.3278726

Veale, Michael and Reuben Binns, 2017, "Fairer Machine Learning in the Real World: Mitigating Discrimination without Collecting Sensitive Data", Big Data & Society, 4(2): art. 205395171774353. DOI:10.1177/2053951717743530

Véliz, Carissa, 2019, "Three Things Digital Ethics Can Learn from Medical Ethics", Nature Electronics, 2(8): 316–318. DOI:10.1038/s41928-019-0294-2

Verbeek, Peter-Paul, 2011, Moralizing Technology: Understanding and Designing the Morality of Things, Chicago: University of Chicago Press.

Wachter, Sandra and Brent Daniel Mittelstadt, 2019, "A Right to Reasonable Inferences: Re-Thinking Data Protection Law in the Age of Big Data and AI", Columbia Business Law Review, 2019(2): 494–620.

WACHTER, SANDRA, BRENT MITTELSTADT, AND LUCIANO FLORIDI, 2017, "WHY A RIGHT TO EXPLANATION OF AUTOMATED DECISION-MAKING DOES NOT EXIST IN THE GENERAL DATA PROTECTION REGULATION", INTERNATIONAL DATA PRIVACY LAW, 7(2): 76–99. DOI:10.1093/idpl/ipx005

WACHTER, SANDRA, BRENT MITTELSTADT, AND CHRIS RUSSELL, 2018, "COUNTERFACTUAL EXPLANATIONS WITHOUT OPENING THE BLACK BOX: AUTOMATED DECISIONS AND THE GDPR", HARVARD JOURNAL OF LAW & TECHNOLOGY, 31(2): 842–887. DOI:10.2139/ssrn.3063289

WALLACH, WENDELL AND PETER M. ASARO (EDS.), 2017, MACHINE ETHICS AND ROBOT ETHICS, LONDON: ROUTLEDGE.

WALSH, TOBY, 2018, MACHINES THAT THINK: THE FUTURE OF ARTIFICIAL INTELLIGENCE, AMHERST, MA: PROMETHEUS BOOKS.

WESTLAKE, STIAN (ED.), 2014, OUR WORK HERE IS DONE: VISIONS OF A ROBOT ECONOMY, LONDON: NESTA. [WESTLAKE 2014 AVAILABLE ONLINE]

WHITTAKER, MEREDITH, KATE CRAWFORD, ROEL DOBBE, GENEVIEVE FRIED, ELIZABETH KAZIUNAS, VAROON MATHUR, … JASON SCHULTZ, 2018, "AI NOW REPORT 2018", NEW YORK: AI NOW INSTITUTE, NEW YORK UNIVERSITY. [WHITTAKER ET AL. 2018 AVAILABLE ONLINE]

WHITTLESTONE, JESS, RUNE NYRUP, ANNA ALEXANDROVA, KANTA DIHAL, AND STEPHEN CAVE, 2019, "ETHICAL AND SOCIETAL IMPLICATIONS OF ALGORITHMS, DATA, AND ARTIFICIAL INTELLIGENCE: A ROADMAP FOR RESEARCH", CAMBRIDGE: NUFFIELD FOUNDATION, UNIVERSITY OF CAMBRIDGE. [WHITTLESTONE 2019 AVAILABLE ONLINE]

WINFIELD, ALAN, KATINA MICHAEL, JEREMY PITT, AND VANESSA EVERS (EDS.), 2019, MACHINE ETHICS: THE DESIGN AND GOVERNANCE OF ETHICAL AI AND AUTONOMOUS SYSTEMS, SPECIAL ISSUE OF PROCEEDINGS OF THE IEEE, 107(3): 501–632.

WOOLLARD, FIONA AND FRANCES HOWARD-SNYDER, 2016, "DOING VS. ALLOWING HARM", STANFORD ENCYCLOPEDIA OF PHILOSOPHY (WINTER 2016 EDITION), EDWARD N. ZALTA (ED.), URL = <HTTPS://PLATO.STANFORD.EDU/ARCHIVES/WIN2016/ENTRIES/DOING-ALLOWING/>

WOOLLEY, SAMUEL C. AND PHILIP N. HOWARD (EDS.), 2017, COMPUTATIONAL PROPAGANDA: POLITICAL PARTIES, POLITICIANS, AND POLITICAL MANIPULATION ON SOCIAL MEDIA, OXFORD: OXFORD UNIVERSITY PRESS. DOI:10.1093/OSO/9780190931407.001.0001

YAMPOLSKIY, ROMAN V. (ED.), 2018, ARTIFICIAL INTELLIGENCE SAFETY AND SECURITY, BOCA RATON, FL: CHAPMAN AND HALL/CRC. DOI:10.1201/9781351251389

YEUNG, KAREN AND MARTIN LODGE (EDS.), 2019, ALGORITHMIC REGULATION, OXFORD: OXFORD UNIVERSITY PRESS. DOI:10.1093/OSO/9780198838494.001.0001

ZAYED, YAGO AND PHILIP LOFT, 2019, "AGRICULTURE: HISTORICAL STATISTICS", HOUSE OF COMMONS BRIEFING PAPER, 3339(25 JUNE 2019): 1-19. [ZAYED AND LOFT 2019 AVAILABLE ONLINE]

ZERILLI, JOHN, ALISTAIR KNOTT, JAMES MACLAURIN, AND COLIN GAVAGHAN, 2019, "TRANSPARENCY IN ALGORITHMIC AND HUMAN DECISION-MAKING: IS THERE A DOUBLE STANDARD?", PHILOSOPHY & TECHNOLOGY, 32(4): 661–683. DOI:10.1007/s13347-018-0330-6

ZUBOFF, SHOSHANA, 2019, THE AGE OF SURVEILLANCE CAPITALISM: THE FIGHT FOR A HUMAN FUTURE AT THE NEW FRONTIER OF POWER, NEW YORK: PUBLIC AFFAIRS.

Van Lent, M., Fisher, W., & Mancuso, M. (2004, July). An explainable artificial intelligence system for small-unit tactical behavior. In Proceedings of the national conference on artificial intelligence (pp. 900-907). Menlo Park, CA; Cambridge, MA; London; AAAI Press; MIT Press; 1999.

Lomas, A., Leonardi-Bee, J., & Bath-Hextall, F. (2012). A systematic review of worldwide incidence of nonmelanoma skin cancer. British Journal of Dermatology, 166(5), 1069-1080.

Gunning, D. (2017). Explainable artificial intelligence (xai). Defense Advanced Research Projects Agency (DARPA), nd Web, 2(2).

Diakopoulos, N. (2015). Algorithmic Accountability: Journalistic investigation of computational power structures. Digital Journalism 3, 3 (2015), 398–415.

Kissinger, H. (2018). How the enlightenment ends. The Atlantic, (6).

Danaher, T. S., & Gallan, A. S. (2016). Service research in health care: positively impacting lives.

Cave, A., Kurz, X., & Arlett, P. (2019). Real-world data for regulatory decision making: challenges and possible solutions for Europe. Clinical pharmacology and therapeutics, 106(1), 36.

Yeung, K., & Lodge, M. (Eds.). (2019). Algorithmic regulation. Oxford University Press.

Goodman, B., & Flaxman, S. (2017). European Union regulations on algorithmic decision-making and a "right to explanation". AI magazine, 38(3), 50-57.

Mittelstadt, B. D., Allo, P., Taddeo, M., Wachter, S., & Floridi, L. (2016). The ethics of algorithms: Mapping the debate. Big Data & Society, 3(2), 2053951716679679.

Wachter, S., Mittelstadt, B., & Russell, C. (2017). Counterfactual explanations without opening the black box: Automated decisions and the GDPR. Harv. JL & Tech., 31, 841.

Zerilli, J., Knott, A., Maclaurin, J., & Gavaghan, C. (2019). Transparency in algorithmic and human decision-making: is there a double standard?. Philosophy & Technology, 32(4), 661-683.

ASIRT. (2020, April 13). Road Safety Facts. Retrieved December 05, 2020, from https://www.asirt.org/safe-travel/road-safety-facts/

Legg, Shane (2008). Machine Super Intelligence (PDF) (PhD). Department of Informatics, University of Lugano. Retrieved September 19, 2014.

Chalmers, David (2010). "The Singularity: A Philosophical Analysis" (PDF). Journal of Consciousness Studies. 17: 7–65.

Sagan, Carl (1977). The Dragons of Eden. Random House.

Santos-Lang, Christopher (2014). "Our responsibility to manage evaluative diversity" (PDF). ACM SIGCAS Computers & Society. 44 (2): 16–19. DOI:10.1145/2656870.2656874.

Vinge, Vernor. "The Coming Technological Singularity: How to Survive in the Post-Human Era", in Vision-21: Interdisciplinary Science and Engineering in the Era of Cyberspace, G. A. Landis, ed., NASA Publication CP-10129, pp. 11–22, 1993.

Sparkes, Matthew (13 January 2015). "Top scientists call for caution over artificial intelligence". The Telegraph (UK). Retrieved 24 April 2015.

"Hawking: AI could end human race". BBC. 2 December 2014. Retrieved 11 November 2017.

Ray Kurzweil, The Singularity is Near, pp. 135–136. Penguin Group, 2005.

Müller, V., & Bostrom, N. (1970, January 01). Vincent C. Müller & Nick Bostrom, Future progress in artificial intelligence: A survey of expert opinion. Retrieved December 05, 2020, from https://philpapers.org/rec/MLLFPI

Huebner, Jonathan (2005) "A Possible Declining Trend for Worldwide Innovation", Technological Forecasting & Social Change, October 2005, pp. 980–6

Cem DilmeganiCem founded AIMultiple in 2017. Throughout his career, Says:, K., Says:, M., 23, C., Says:, C., Says:, J., . . . *, N. (2020, September 13). 995 experts opinion: AGI / singularity by 2060 [2020 update]. Retrieved December 05, 2020, from https://research.aimultiple.com/artificial-general-intelligence-singularity-timing/

'Why we should fear the Paperclipper', 2011-02-14 entry of Sandberg's blog 'Andart'

Omohundro, Stephen M., "The Basic AI Drives." Artificial General Intelligence, 2008 proceedings of the First AGI Conference, eds. Pei Wang, Ben Goertzel, and Stan Franklin. Vol. 171. Amsterdam: IOS, 2008.

Kurzweil, R. (2000). The age of spiritual machines: When computers exceed human intelligence. Penguin.

Von Neumann, J., & Kurzweil, R. (2012). The computer and the brain. Yale University Press.

Kurzweil, R. (2005). The singularity is near: When humans transcend biology. Penguin.

Kurzweil, R., Richter, R., Kurzweil, R., & Schneider, M. L. (1990). The age of intelligent machines (Vol. 579). Cambridge: MIT press.

Kurzweil, R. (2013). How to create a mind: The secret of human thought revealed. Penguin.

Kurzweil, R. (2004). The law of accelerating returns. In Alan Turing: Life and legacy of a great thinker (pp. 381-416). Springer, Berlin, Heidelberg.

Good, I. J., & England, C. B. (1965). The estimation of probabilities.

March 2015, The Pharmaceutical Journal6. "Narcotics monitoring board reports 66% increase in global consumption of methylphenidate". Pharmaceutical Journal. Archived from the original on 19 December 2018. Retrieved 19 December 2018.

"The Top 300 of 2020". ClinCalc. Retrieved 11 April 2020.

"Methylphenidate - Drug Usage Statistics". ClinCalc. Retrieved 11 April 2020.

TEGMARK, M. (2017). LIFE 3.0: BEING HUMAN IN THE AGE OF ARTIFICIAL INTELLIGENCE. KNOPF.

CHRISTENSEN, C. M. (2011). THE INNOVATOR'S DILEMMA. NEW YORK, NY: HARPER BUSINESS.

HARARI, Y. N. (2014). SAPIENS: A BRIEF HISTORY OF HUMANKIND. RANDOM HOUSE.

HARARI, Y. N. (2016). HOMO DEUS: A BRIEF HISTORY OF TOMORROW. RANDOM HOUSE.

NEUMANN, J., & LINDGRÉN, S. (1979). GREAT HISTORICAL EVENTS THAT WERE SIGNIFICANTLY AFFECTED BY THE WEATHER: 4, THE GREAT FAMINES IN FINLAND AND ESTONIA, 1695–97. BULLETIN OF THE AMERICAN METEOROLOGICAL SOCIETY, 60(7), 775-787.

DOBBS, R., RAMASWAMY, S., STEPHENSON, E., & VIGUERIE, S. P. (2014). MANAGEMENT INTUITION FOR THE NEXT 50 YEARS. MCKINSEY QUARTERLY, 1, 1-13.

MOKDAD, A. H., FOROUZANFAR, M. H., DAOUD, F., MOKDAD, A. A., EL BCHERAOUI, C., MORADI-LAKEH, M., ... & KRAVITZ, H. (2016). GLOBAL BURDEN OF DISEASES, INJURIES, AND RISK FACTORS FOR YOUNG PEOPLE'S HEALTH DURING 1990–2013: A SYSTEMATIC ANALYSIS FOR THE GLOBAL BURDEN OF DISEASE STUDY 2013. THE LANCET, 387(10036), 2383-2401.

LOPEZ, R. S. (1967). THE BIRTH OF EUROPE. NEW YORK: M. EVANS.

CROSBY, A. W. (2003). THE COLUMBIAN EXCHANGE: BIOLOGICAL AND CULTURAL CONSEQUENCES OF 1492. WESTPORT, CONN: PRAEGER.

THOMAS, H. (2013). CONQUEST: MONTEZUMA, CORTÉS, AND THE FALL OF OLD MEXICO. RIVERSIDE: SIMON & SCHUSTER.

DIAMOND, J. M. (2017). GUNS, GERMS, AND STEEL: THE FATES OF HUMAN SOCIETIES.

TAUBENBERGER, J. K., & MORENS, D. M. (JANUARY 01, 2006). 1918 INFLUENZA: THE MOTHER OF ALL PANDEMICS. EMERGING INFECTIOUS DISEASES, 12, 1, 15-22.

HOFFMAN, B. L., & FOX, D. P. (SEPTEMBER 01, 2019). THE 1918-1920 H1N1 INFLUENZA A PANDEMIC IN KANSAS AND MISSOURI: MORTALITY PATTERNS AND EVIDENCE OF HARVESTING. TRANSACTIONS OF THE KANSAS ACADEMY OF SCIENCE, 122, 173-192.

KNOBLER, S. (2005). THE THREAT OF PANDEMIC INFLUENZA: ARE WE READY? : WORKSHOP SUMMARY. WASHINGTON, D.C: NATIONAL ACADEMIES PRESS.

VAN, R. D. (2015). CONGO: THE EPIC HISTORY OF A PEOPLE.

CHANDRA, S., KULJANIN, G., & WRAY, J. (AUGUST 01, 2012). MORTALITY FROM THE INFLUENZA PANDEMIC OF 1918-1919: THE CASE OF INDIA. DEMOGRAPHY, 49, 3, 857-865.

KOPLOW, D. A. (2004). SMALLPOX: THE FIGHT TO ERADICATE A GLOBAL SCOURGE. BERKELEY, CALIF: UNIVERSITY OF CALIFORNIA PRESS.

Part 5 – The Swell & Epilogue

WILSON, M. M. G. (2004). COMMENTARY: CLASH OF THE TITANS: DEATH, OLD AGE, AND THE DEVIL'S ADVOCATE. THE JOURNALS OF GERONTOLOGY SERIES A: BIOLOGICAL SCIENCES AND MEDICAL SCIENCES, 59(6), M612-M615.

Szreter, S. (2012). Health and Wealth: Studies in History and Policy. Cambridge: Cambridge University Press.

Bostrom, N. (2007). The Future of Humanity. Future of Humanity Institute - Faculty of Philosophy & James Martin 21st Century School Oxford University. doi:https://nickbostrom.com/papers/future.pdf

Floud, R., & National Bureau of Economic Research. (2012). The changing body: Health, nutrition, and human development in the western world since 1700. Cambridge: Cambridge University Press.

Riley, J. C. (2015). Rising life expectancy: A global history.

Alanis, A. J. (November 01, 2005). Resistance to Antibiotics: Are We in the Post-Antibiotic Era?. Archives of Medical Research, 36, 6, 697-705.

Harbarth, Stephan, & Samore, Matthew H. (2005). Antimicrobial Resistance Determinants and Future Control. Centers for Disease Control and Prevention.

Yoneyama, H., & Katsumata, R. (2006). Antibiotic resistance in bacteria and its future for novel antibiotic development. Bioscience, biotechnology, and biochemistry, 70(5), 1060-1075.

Arias, C. A., & Murray, B. E. (2009). Antibiotic-resistant bugs in the 21st century—a clinical super-challenge. New England Journal of Medicine, 360(5), 439-443.

Briggs, H. (2020, December 09). Human-made objects to outweigh living things. Retrieved December 12, 2020, from https://www.bbc.com/news/science-environment-55239668

Spellberg, B., Bartlett, J. G., & Gilbert, D. N. (January 24, 2013). The Future of Antibiotics and Resistance. The New England Journal of Medicine, 368, 4, 299-302.

Gat, A. (2008). War in human civilization. New York [etc.: Oxford University Press.

Pinker, S. (2012). The better angels of our nature: Why violence has declined.

Goldstein, J. S. (2012). Winning the war on war: The decline of armed conflict worldwide. New York, N.Y: Plume.

Walker, R. S., & Bailey, D. H. (January 01, 2013). Body counts in lowland South American violence. Evolution and Human Behavior, 34, 1, 29-34.

Thorpe, I. J. N. (April 01, 2003). Anthropology, archaeology, and the origin of warfare. World Archaeology, 35, 1, 145-165.

Keeley, L. H. (2007). War before civilization: [the myth of the peaceful savage]. New York: Oxford Univ. Press.

Vencl, S. (1999). Stone Age warfare. œ Ancient Warfare. J. Carman.

Global Health Observatory indicator views: Age-standardized suicide rates (per 100 000 population) (Mental health). This indicator is available in the following set of views in the "By topic" section of the Global Health Observatory. https://apps.who.int/gho/data/view.main.MHSUICIDEASDRv

Morris, I. (2011). The patterns of history and what they reveal about the future. London: Profile Books Ltd.

Myers, D. G. (January 01, 2000). The funds, friends, and faith of happy people. The American Psychologist, 55, 1, 56-67.

Inglehart, R., Foa, R., Peterson, C., & Welzel, C. (January 01, 2008). Development, Freedom, and Rising Happiness: A Global Perspective (1981-2007). Perspectives on Psychological Science, 3, 4, 264-285.

Csikszentmihalyi, M. (January 01, 1999). If We Are So Rich, Why Aren't We Happy?. American Psychologist, 54, 10, 821-827.

Easterbrook, G. (2004). The progress paradox: How life gets better while people feel worse. New York: Random House.

Elevating the ridesharing experience - How Uber explain aerial ridesharing will enable rapid, reliable transportation through a network of small, vertical takeoff and landing, all-electric vehicles. See https://www.uber.com/us/en/elevate/uberair/ and https://www.uber.com/us/en/elevate/summit/2019/ and https://www.uber.com/us/en/elevate/summit/2018/

Green, D. (2019, January 17). A survey found that Amazon Prime membership is soaring to new heights - but one trend should worry the company. Retrieved December 06, 2020, from https://www.businessinsider.com.au/amazon-more-than-100-million-prime-members-us-survey-2019-1

Fernholz, T. (2019, December 30). 2020 is the year of the $1 trillion space economy. Retrieved December 06, 2020, from https://qz.com/1774249/2020-is-the-year-of-the-1-trillion-space-economy/

Harris, M. (2018, July 19). Larry Page is quietly amassing a 'flying car' empire. Retrieved December 06, 2020, from https://www.theverge.com/2018/7/19/17586878/larry-page-flying-car-opener-kitty-hawk-cora

Kurzweil, R. (2001, March 7). The Law of Accelerating Returns. Retrieved December 06, 2020, from https://www.kurzweilai.net/the-law-of-accelerating-returns

Kröger, F. (January 01, 2016). Automated Driving in Its Social, Historical and Cultural Contexts.

DARPA. (n.d.). The Grand Challenge. Retrieved December 06, 2020, from https://www.darpa.mil/about-us/timeline/-grand-challenge-for-autonomous-vehicles

Shoup, D., Chamberlain, M., & Gildan Media. (2018). The high cost of free parking, updated edition. New York: Gildan Audio.

Florida, R. (2017, July 24). Parking Has Eaten American Cities A new study documents the huge amount of space taken up by parking, and the astronomical costs it represents, in five U.S. cities. Retrieved December 06, 2020, from https://www.bloomberg.com/news/articles/2018-07-24/the-overparked-states-of-america

Ben-Joseph, E. (2015). Rethinking a Lot: The Design and Culture of Parking. Cambridge, Mass: MIT Press.

Hyperloop Research: https://www.tesla.com/sites/default/files/blog_images/hyperloop-alpha.pdf and http://web.mit.edu/mopg/www/papers/

MITHyperloop_FinalReport_2017_public.pdf and http://spacex.com/sites/spacex/files/hyperloop_alpha.pdf

Death of Sears and how it was worth $14.3 billion: https://www.macrotrends.net/stocks/charts/SHLDQ/sears-holdings/stock-price-history

Target being worth $38.2 billion: Ibid.

Walmart being worth $158 billion: Ibid.

Amazon being worth $17.5 billion: Ibid.

Pélissié, . R. M., McKinsey and Company., & McKinsey Global Institute. (2011). Internet matters: The net's sweeping impact on growth, jobs, and prosperity. Place of publication not identified: McKinsey & Co.

Eeckhout, L. (January 01, 2017). Is Moore's Law Slowing Down? What's Next?. Ieee Micro, 37, 4, 4-5.

Muoio, D. (2016, March 10). Why Go is so much harder for AI to beat than chess. Retrieved December 06, 2020, from https://www.businessinsider.com/why-google-ai-game-go-is-harder-than-chess-2016-3

Dickey, M. (2017, March 01). Facebook brings suicide prevention tools to Live and Messenger. Retrieved December 06, 2020, from https://techcrunch.com/2017/03/01/facebook-brings-suicide-prevention-tools-to-live-and-messenger/

Boyle, A. (2020, July 31). Amazon vows to invest $10B in Kuiper satellites after getting FCC's go-ahead. Retrieved December 06, 2020, from https://www.geekwire.com/2020/fcc-says-amazon-can-proceed-kuiper-satellites-will-accommodate-rivals/

FCC Authorizes SpaceX to Provide Broadband Satellite Services. Available at https://www.fcc.gov/document/fcc-authorizes-spacex-provide-broadband-satellite-services

Koerner, B. (2003, June 1). What Is Smart Dust, Anyway? Retrieved December 06, 2020, from https://www.wired.com/2003/06/what-is-smart-dust-anyway/

Horwitz, J. (2019, August 01). Apple lists AR/VR jobs, reportedly taps executive who finalizes products. Retrieved December 06, 2020, from https://venturebeat.com/2019/08/01/apple-lists-ar-vr-jobs-reportedly-taps-executive-who-finalizes-products/

Augmented reality (AR) and Virtual Reality (VR) bridge the digital and physical worlds. https://arvr.google.com/

Schultz, A. (2018, July 14). Cisco Spark in VR: A Brief Introduction. Retrieved December 06, 2020, from https://ryanschultz.com/2018/07/14/cisco-spark-in-vr-a-brief-introduction/

Needleman, S. (2018, April 03). Virtual Reality, Now With the Sense of Touch. Retrieved December 06, 2020, from https://www.wsj.com/articles/virtual-reality-now-with-the-sense-of-touch-1522764377

Strickland, E. (2017, August 7). Startup Neurable Unveils the World's First Brain-Controlled VR Game. Neurable's brain-computer interfaces

ENABLE HANDS-FREE CONTROL IN VIRTUAL REALITY. Retrieved December 06,
2020, from HTTPS://SPECTRUM.IEEE.ORG/THE-HUMAN-OS/BIOMEDICAL/BIONICS/
BRAINY-STARTUP-NEURABLE-UNVEILS-THE-WORLDS-FIRST-BRAINCONTROLLED-VR-GAME

Mangles, C., Commentator, E., & Chaffey, D. (2016, October 25). Virtual
Reality applications to generate over $35 billion in revenue by 2025
[#ChartoftheDay]. Retrieved December 06, 2020, from HTTPS://WWW.SMARTINSIGHTS.
COM/MANAGING-DIGITAL-MARKETING/MANAGING-MARKETING-TECHNOLOGY/
VIRTUAL-REALITY-APPLICATIONS-GENERATE-35-BILLION-REVENUE-2025-CHARTOFTHEDAY/

Bailenson, J. (2019). Experience on demand: What virtual reality is, how it works, and
what it can do? Publisher: New York : W.W. Norton & Company.

Ganos, L. (2019, July 31). Pokémon GO surpasses the 1 billion downloads milestone.
Retrieved December 06, 2020, from HTTPS://NINTENDOWIRE.COM/NEWS/2019/07/31/
POKEMON-GO-SURPASSES-THE-1-BILLION-DOWNLOADS-MILESTONE/

Bruno, L. (2018, March 13). How AI can stop cybercrime. Retrieved December 12, 2020,
from HTTPS://WWW.CIO.COM/ARTICLE/3262708/HOW-AI-CAN-STOP-CYBERCRIME.HTML

Apple's and Google's platform for building augmented reality experiences HTTPS://
DEVELOPER.APPLE.COM/AUGMENTED-REALITY/ARKIT/ AND HTTPS://DEVELOPERS.GOOGLE.
COM/AR/DISCOVER

Research, Z. (2018, August 31). Augmented Reality Market To Show
Phenomenal Growth And Reach USD 133.78 Billion By 2021. Retrieved
December 06, 2020, from HTTPS://WWW.ZIONMARKETRESEARCH.COM/NEWS/
GLOBAL-AUGMENTED-REALITY-AR-MARKET

Shea, G. (2018, April 10). ISS: Operating an Outpost. Retrieved
December 06, 2020, from HTTPS://WWW.NASA.GOV/CONNECT/EBOOKS/
THE-INTERNATIONAL-SPACE-STATION-OPERATING-AN-OUTPOST/

Goldberg, D., Werthmann, C., & Caballar, R. (2018, December 21). History of 3D
Printing: It's Older Than You Think [Updated]. Retrieved December 06, 2020, from
HTTPS://REDSHIFT.AUTODESK.COM/HISTORY-OF-3D-PRINTING/

Wong J. Y. (2015). On-Site 3D Printing of Functional Custom Mallet Splints for Mars
Analogue Crewmembers. Aerospace medicine and human performance, 86(10),
911–914. HTTPS://DOI.ORG/10.3357/AMHP.4259.2015

ACCENTURE. (2018). COST OF CYBER CRIME STUDY 2017 INSIGHTS ON THE SECURITY
INVESTMENTS THAT MAKE A DIFFERENCE. Retrieved from HTTPS://WWW.
ACCENTURE.COM/T20170926T072837Z__W__/US-EN/_ACNMEDIA/PDF-61/ACCENTURE-2017-
COSTCYBERCRIMESTUDY.PDF

Sevenson, B. (2015, January 22). Shanghai-based WinSun 3D Prints 6-Story Apartment
Building and an Incredible Home - 3DPrint.com: The Voice of 3D Printing /
Additive Manufacturing. Retrieved December 06, 2020, from HTTPS://3DPRINT.
COM/38144/3D-PRINTED-APARTMENT-BUILDING/

Fingas, J. (2020, February 18). 3D-printed wind turbine puts 300W of power in your
backpack. Retrieved December 06, 2020, from HTTPS://WWW.ENGADGET.COM/2014-08-
17-AIRENERGY-3D-WIND-TURBINE.HTML

Watkins, H. (2018, December 10). Doctors Without Borders Hospital in Jordan 3D Print Prostheses for War Victims. Retrieved December 06, 2020, from https://all3dp.com/4/doctors-without-borders-hospital-jordan-3d-print-prostheses-war-victims/

Yandell, K. (2013, August 31). Organs on Demand. Retrieved December 06, 2020, from https://www.the-scientist.com/features/organs-on-demand-38787

Hudson, K. (2010, December 08). First Fully Bioprinted Blood Vessels. Retrieved December 06, 2020, from https://www.businesswire.com/news/home/20101208006587/en/First-Fully-Bioprinted-Blood-Vessels

Bendix, A. (2019, March 12). These 3D-printed homes can be built for less than $4,000 in just 24 hours. Retrieved December 06, 2020, from https://www.businessinsider.com/3d-homes-that-take-24-hours-and-less-than-4000-to-print-2018-9

Griffiths, S. (2014, April 28). 3D printer creates 10 houses in a DAY. Retrieved December 06, 2020, from https://www.dailymail.co.uk/sciencetech/article-2615076/Giant-3D-printer-creates-10-sized-houses-DAY-Bungalows-built-layers-waste-materials-cost-3-000-each.html

Gregurić, L. (2020, January 21). How Much Does a 3D Printed House Cost? Retrieved December 06, 2020, from https://all3dp.com/2/3d-printed-house-cost/

The Guardian. (2015, April 30). Chinese construction firm erects 57-storey skyscraper in 19 days. Retrieved December 06, 2020, from https://www.theguardian.com/world/2015/apr/30/chinese-construction-firm-erects-57-storey-skyscraper-in-19-days

Accenture. (1970, November 10). Banks Have a $380 Billion Market Opportunity in Financial Inclusion, Accenture and CARE International UK Study Find. Retrieved December 06, 2020, from https://newsroom.accenture.com/news/banks-have-a-380-billion-market-opportunity-in-financial-inclusion-accenture-and-care-international-uk-study-find.htm

The World Bank. (2019). Record High Remittances Sent Globally in 2018. Retrieved December 06, 2020, from https://www.worldbank.org/en/news/press-release/2019/04/08/record-high-remittances-sent-globally-in-2018

The World Bank. (2020). ID4D Data: Global Identification Challenge by the Numbers. Retrieved December 06, 2020, from https://id4d.worldbank.org/global-dataset

Casey, M., & Vigna, P. (2019). The truth machine: The blockchain and the future of everything. Publisher: New York, NY : Picador ; St. Martin's Press

Fenech, G. (2019, January 30). Blockchain In Gambling And Betting: Are There Real Advantages? Retrieved December 06, 2020, from https://www.forbes.com/sites/geraldfenech/2019/01/30/blockchain-in-gambling-and-betting-are-there-real-advantages/

Marsh, A. (2018, June 28). Goldman Sachs Explores Creating a Digital Coin Like JPMorgan's. Retrieved December 06, 2020, from https://www.bloomberg.com/news/articles/2019-06-28/goldman-sachs-explores-creating-a-digital-coin-like-jpmorgan-s

Stamford, C. (2019, June 3). Gartner Predicts 90% of Current Enterprise Blockchain Platform Implementations Will Require Replacement by 2021. Retrieved December 06, 2020, from https://www.gartner.com/en/newsroom/press-releases/2019-07-03-gartner-predicts-90--of-current-enterprise-blockchain

Pablo, J., Jackson, N., Webb, M., Chen, L., Moore, J., Morgan, D., . . . Zhao, J. (2019, April 05). New frontiers for the materials genome initiative. Retrieved December 06, 2020, from https://www.nature.com/articles/s41524-019-0173-4

Mouritz, A. P. (2012). Introduction to aerospace materials. Reston, VA: American Institute of Aeronautics and Astronautics.

Physics World. (2019, August 01). Nanotechnology for quantum computers, industry skills for physics students, technologies that make physics happen. Retrieved December 06, 2020, from https://physicsworld.com/a/nanotechnology-for-quantum-computers-industry-skills-for-physics-students-technologies-that-make-physics-happen/

Ferber, D. (2017, January 23). Printing Tiny Batteries. Retrieved December 06, 2020, from https://wyss.harvard.edu/news/printing-tiny-batteries/

Li S;Jiang Q;Liu S;Zhang Y;Tian Y;Song C;Wang J;Zou Y;Anderson GJ;Han JY;Chang Y;Liu Y;Zhang C;Chen L;Zhou G;Nie G;Yan H;Ding B;Zhao Y;. (2018). A DNA nanorobot functions as a cancer therapeutic in response to a molecular trigger in vivo. Retrieved December 06, 2020, from https://pubmed.ncbi.nlm.nih.gov/29431737/

Molteni, M. (2018, July 12). The Rise of DNA Data Storage. Retrieved December 06, 2020, from https://medium.com/@WIRED/the-rise-of-dna-data-storage-284da9d062cd

Shankland, S. (2019, June 29). Startup Catalog has jammed all 16GB of Wikipedia's text onto DNA strands. Retrieved December 06, 2020, from https://www.cnet.com/news/startup-packs-all-16gb-wikipedia-onto-dna-strands-demonstrate-new-storage-tech/

Journal of Clinical Investigation. (2008). Why Gene Therapy Caused Leukemia In Some 'Boy In The Bubble Syndrome' Patients. Retrieved December 06, 2020, from https://www.scribd.com/document/453401503/Wikipedia-pdf

St. Jude Children's Research Hospital. (2019, April 17). St. Jude gene therapy cures babies with 'bubble boy' disease. Retrieved December 06, 2020, from https://www.stjude.org/media-resources/news-releases/2019-medicine-science-news/st-jude-gene-therapy-cures-babies-with-bubble-boy-disease.html

Eveleth, R. (2013, October 24). There are 37.2 Trillion Cells in Your Body. Retrieved December 06, 2020, from https://www.smithsonianmag.com/smart-news/there-are-372-trillion-cells-in-your-body-4941473/

Ayres, R. U. (2020). On Capitalism and Inequality: Progress and Poverty Revisited. Springer.

National Human Genome Research Institute. (n.d.). The Cost of Sequencing a Human Genome. Retrieved December 06, 2020, from https://www.genome.gov/about-genomics/fact-sheets/Sequencing-Human-Genome-cost

HARVARD UNIVERSITY. (2017, NOVEMBER 05). CRISPR 2.0: GENOME ENGINEERING MADE EASY AS A-B-C. RETRIEVED DECEMBER 06, 2020, FROM HTTP://SITN.HMS.HARVARD.EDU/FLASH/2017/CRISPR-2-0-GENOME-ENGINEERING-MADE-EASY-B-C/

LEWIS, T. (2019, OCTOBER 21). NEW GENE-EDITING TOOL COULD FIX GENETIC DEFECTS-WITH FEWER UNWANTED EFFECTS. RETRIEVED DECEMBER 06, 2020, FROM HTTPS://WWW.SCIENTIFICAMERICAN.COM/ARTICLE/NEW-GENE-EDITING-TOOL-COULD-FIX-GENETIC-DEFECTS-WITH-FEWER-UNWANTED-EFFECTS1/

NETBURN, D. (2017, OCTOBER 25). NEW GENE-EDITING TECHNIQUE MAY LEAD TO TREATMENT FOR THOUSANDS OF DISEASES. RETRIEVED DECEMBER 06, 2020, FROM HTTPS://WWW.LATIMES.COM/SCIENCE/SCIENCENOW/LA-SCI-SN-DNA-GENE-EDITING-20171025-STORY.HTML

CYRANOSKI, D. (2019, FEBRUARY 26). THE CRISPR-BABY SCANDAL: WHAT'S NEXT FOR HUMAN GENE-EDITING. RETRIEVED DECEMBER 06, 2020, FROM HTTPS://WWW.NATURE.COM/ARTICLES/D41586-019-00673-1

REGALADO, A. (2020, APRIL 02). EXCLUSIVE: CHINESE SCIENTISTS ARE CREATING CRISPR BABIES. RETRIEVED DECEMBER 06, 2020, FROM HTTPS://WWW.TECHNOLOGYREVIEW.COM/2018/11/25/138962/EXCLUSIVE-CHINESE-SCIENTISTS-ARE-CREATING-CRISPR-BABIES/

CHEN, Y., JEON, G. Y. J., & KIM, Y.-M. (DECEMBER 01, 2014). A DAY WITHOUT A SEARCH ENGINE: AN EXPERIMENTAL STUDY OF ONLINE AND OFFLINE SEARCHES. EXPERIMENTAL ECONOMICS, 17, 4, 512-536.

UNIVERSITY OF MONTREAL. (2009, MARCH 13). FRIDGES AND WASHING MACHINES LIBERATED WOMEN, STUDY SUGGESTS. SCIENCEDAILY. RETRIEVED DECEMBER 6, 2020 FROM WWW.SCIENCEDAILY.COM/RELEASES/2009/03/090312150735.HTM

PERRY, M. (2016). MAP OF CHICAGO TO NEW YORK. HTTPS://WWW.AEI.ORG/CARPE-DIEM/MAPS-OF-THE-DAY-TRAVEL-TIMES-FROM-NYC-IN-1800-1830-1857-AND-1930/

STINE, D. (2011). THE MANHATTAN PROJECT, THE APOLLO PROGRAM, AND FEDERAL ... RETRIEVED DECEMBER 6, 2020, FROM HTTPS://FAS.ORG/SGP/CRS/MISC/RL34645.PDF

PAYNTER, B. (2017, MAY 10). HOW WILL THE RISE OF CROWDFUNDING RESHAPE HOW WE GIVE TO CHARITY? RETRIEVED DECEMBER 06, 2020, FROM HTTPS://WWW.FASTCOMPANY.COM/3068534/HOW-WILL-THE-RISE-OF-CROWDFUNDING-RESHAPE-HOW-WE-GIVE-TO-CHARITY-2

CROWDFUNDING INDUSTRY. (2016, MARCH 21). CROWDFUNDING INDUSTRY STATISTICS 2015 2016. RETRIEVED DECEMBER 06, 2020, FROM HTTP://CROWDEXPERT.COM/CROWDFUNDING-INDUSTRY-STATISTICS/

PRICEWATERHOUSECOOPERS. (2020). PWC MONEYTREE REPORT. RETRIEVED DECEMBER 06, 2020, FROM HTTPS://WWW.PWC.COM/US/EN/INDUSTRIES/TECHNOLOGY/MONEYTREE.HTML

BUSINESS INSIDER. (2017, FEBRUARY 27). THE JAPANESE TECH BILLIONAIRE BEHIND SOFTBANK THINKS THE 'SINGULARITY' WILL OCCUR WITHIN 30 YEARS. RETRIEVED DECEMBER 06, 2020, FROM HTTPS://WWW.INSIDER.COM/SOFTBANK-CEO-MASAYOSHI-SON-THINKS-SINGULARITY-WILL-OCCUR-WITHIN-30-YEARS-2017-2

THE ECONOMIST. (2019, MARCH 23). MASAYOSHI SON PREPARES TO UNLEASH HIS SECOND $100BN TECH FUND. RETRIEVED DECEMBER 06, 2020, FROM HTTPS://WWW.ECONOMIST.COM/BUSINESS/2019/03/23/MASAYOSHI-SON-PREPARES-TO-UNLEASH-HIS-SECOND-100BN-TECH-FUND

Developing ultra high bandwidth brain-machine interfaces to connect humans and computers. https://neuralink.com/

Basulto, D. (2018, October 06). Why Ray Kurzweil's Predictions Are Right 86% of the Time. Retrieved December 06, 2020, from https://bigthink.com/endless-innovation/why-ray-kurzweils-predictions-are-right-86-of-the-time

Ridley, M. (2014). The rational optimist. Place of publication not identified: HarperCollins e-Books.

Lander, E. S. (January 01, 2016). The Heroes of CRISPR. Cell, 16World Bank. (2019). Individuals using the Internet (% of population). Retrieved December 06, 2020, from https://data.worldbank.org/indicator/IT.NET.USER.ZS4, 18-28.

De Jong, Marc, & Van Dijk, Menno. (2016). Disrupting Beliefs: A New Approach to Business Model Innovation. Rotman Management Magazine.

N. Diallo et al. (2018). "eGov-DAO: a Better Government using Blockchain based Decentralized Autonomous Organization," 2018 International Conference on eDemocracy & eGovernment (ICEDEG), Ambato, 2018, pp. 166-171, doi: 10.1109/ICEDEG.2018.8372356.

Korolov, M. (2015, November 11). Second Life GDP totals $500 million. Retrieved December 06, 2020, from https://www.mariakorolov.com/2015/second-life-gdp-totals-500-million/

Pine, B. J., & Gilmore, J. H. (1999). The experience economy: Work is theatre & every business a stage. Boston: Harvard Business School Press.

Levy, S. (2013). Google's Larry Page on Why Moon Shots Matter. Retrieved December 06, 2020, from https://www.wired.com/2013/01/ff-qa-larry-page/

Simpson, C. (2013, October 29). Google Wants to Cheat Death. Retrieved December 06, 2020, from https://www.theatlantic.com/technology/archive/2013/09/google-wants-cheat-death/310943/

van, D. J. M. (January 01, 2019). SENOLYTIC THERAPIES FOR HEALTHY LONGEVITY. Science, 6441, 636-637.

Villeda, S. A., Plambeck, K. E., Middeldorp, J., Castellano, J. M., Mosher, K. I., Luo, J., Smith, L. K., ... Wyss-Coray, T. (June 01, 2014). Young blood reverses age-related impairments in cognitive function and synaptic plasticity in mice. Nature Medicine, 20, 6, 659-663.

Loffredo, F. S., Steinhauser, M. L., Jay, S. M., Gannon, J., Pancoast, J. R., Yalamanchi, P., Sinha, M., Dall'Osso, C., Khong, D., Shadrach, J. L., Miller, C. M., Singer, B. S., Stewart, A., Psychogios, N., Gerszten, R. E., Hartigan, A. J., Kim, M. J., Serwold, T., Wagers, A. J., & Lee, R. T. (2013). Growth differentiation factor 11 is a circulating factor that reverses age-related cardiac hypertrophy. Cell, 153(4), 828–839. https://doi.org/10.1016/j.cell.2013.04.015

Katsimpardi, L., Litterman, N. K., Schein, P. A., Miller, C. M., Loffredo, F. S., Wojtkiewicz, G. R., Chen, J. W., Lee, R. T., Wagers, A. J., & Rubin, L. L. (2014). Vascular and neurogenic rejuvenation of the aging mouse brain by young systemic factors. Science (New York, N.Y.), 344(6184), 630–634. https://doi.org/10.1126/science.1251141

SINHA, M., JANG, Y. C., OH, J., KHONG, D., WU, E. Y., MANOHAR, R., MILLER, C., REGALADO, S. G., LOFFREDO, F. S., PANCOAST, J. R., HIRSHMAN, M. F., LEBOWITZ, J., SHADRACH, J. L., CERLETTI, M., KIM, M. J., SERWOLD, T., GOODYEAR, L. J., ROSNER, B., LEE, R. T., & WAGERS, A. J. (2014). RESTORING SYSTEMIC GDF11 LEVELS REVERSES AGE-RELATED DYSFUNCTION IN MOUSE SKELETAL MUSCLE. SCIENCE (NEW YORK, N.Y.), 344(6184), 649–652. HTTPS://DOI.ORG/10.1126/SCIENCE.1251152

ONODERA, K., SUGIURA, H., YAMADA, M., KOARAI, A., FUJINO, N., YANAGISAWA, S., TANAKA, R., NUMAKURA, T., TOGO, S., SATO, K., KYOGOKU, Y., HASHIMOTO, Y., OKAZAKI, T., TAMADA, T., KOBAYASHI, S., YANAI, M., MIURA, M., HOSHIKAWA, Y., OKADA, Y., SUZUKI, S., ... ICHINOSE, M. (2017). DECREASE IN AN ANTI-AGEING FACTOR, GROWTH DIFFERENTIATION FACTOR 11, IN CHRONIC OBSTRUCTIVE PULMONARY DISEASE. THORAX, 72(10), 893–904. HTTPS://DOI.ORG/10.1136/THORAXJNL-2016-209352

ZHANG, Y., LI, Q., LIU, D., HUANG, Q., CAI, G., CUI, S., SUN, X., & CHEN, X. (2016). GDF11 IMPROVES TUBULAR REGENERATION AFTER ACUTE KIDNEY INJURY IN ELDERLY MICE. SCIENTIFIC REPORTS, 6, 34624. HTTPS://DOI.ORG/10.1038/SREP34624

DELOITTE. (2020, FEBRUARY 13). GLOBAL POWERS OF RETAILING: DELOITTE: CONSUMER BUSINESS INDUSTRY REPORTS. RETRIEVED DECEMBER 06, 2020, FROM HTTPS://WWW2.DELOITTE.COM/GLOBAL/EN/PAGES/CONSUMER-BUSINESS/ARTICLES/GLOBAL-POWERS-OF-RETAILING.HTML

JUNIPER RESEARCH. (2018). DIGITAL VOICE ASSISTANTS IN USE TO TRIPLE TO 8 BILLION BY 2023, DRIVEN BY SMART HOME DEVICES. RETRIEVED DECEMBER 06, 2020, FROM HTTPS://WWW.JUNIPERRESEARCH.COM/PRESS/PRESS-RELEASES/DIGITAL-VOICE-ASSISTANTS-IN-USE-TO-8-MILLION-2023

LEVIATHAN, Y., & MATIAS, Y. (2018, MAY 08). GOOGLE DUPLEX: AN AI SYSTEM FOR ACCOMPLISHING REAL-WORLD TASKS OVER THE PHONE. RETRIEVED DECEMBER 07, 2020, FROM HTTPS://AI.GOOGLEBLOG.COM/2018/05/DUPLEX-AI-SYSTEM-FOR-NATURAL-CONVERSATION.HTML

ABNER, L. (2019). GOOGLER IN CHARGE OF I/O 2019 SAYS IT TAKES 6-9 MONTHS TO PLAN. HTTPS://9TO5GOOGLE.COM/2019/05/06/IO-2019-BEHIND-THE-SCENES/#:~:TEXT=AHEAD%20OF%20I%2FO%202019,TO%20NINE%20MONTHS%20TO%20ORGANIZE.

ZENDESK. (2020, OCTOBER 6). WHAT IS THE IMPACT OF CUSTOMER SERVICE ON LIFETIME CUSTOMER VALUE? RETRIEVED DECEMBER 07, 2020, FROM HTTPS://WWW.ZENDESK.COM/BLOG/CUSTOMER-SERVICE-AND-LIFETIME-CUSTOMER-VALUE/

WOODS, B. (2014, JANUARY 23). EMOTION ANALYTICS COMPANY BEYOND VERBAL RELEASES MOODIES AS STANDALONE IOS APP. RETRIEVED DECEMBER 07, 2020, FROM HTTPS://THENEXTWEB.COM/APPS/2014/01/23/BEYOND-VERBAL-RELEASES-MOODIES-STANDALONE-IOS-APP/

WIGGERS, K. (2020, JANUARY 09). SOUL MACHINES RAISES $40 MILLION FOR AI-POWERED CUSTOMER-FACING DIGITAL AVATARS. RETRIEVED DECEMBER 07, 2020, FROM HTTPS://VENTUREBEAT.COM/2020/01/09/SOUL-MACHINES-RAISES-40-MILLION-FOR-AI-POWERED-CUSTOMER-FACING-DIGITAL-AVATARS/

MEISSNER, M. (2020, DECEMBER 01). SIEMENS SHOWCASES ECO-FRIENDLY TRAVEL ADVISOR USING AI, BLOCKCHAIN AND THE IOT. RETRIEVED DECEMBER 07, 2020, FROM HTTPS://WWW.IBM.COM/BLOGS/CLIENT-VOICES/SIEMENS-AI-BLOCKCHAIN-ECO-FRIENDLY-TRAVEL-ADVISOR/

CROSS, G. (2019, APRIL 24). SOUL MACHINES GIVES AI A HUMAN FACE WITH THE HELP OF WATSON. RETRIEVED DECEMBER 07, 2020, FROM HTTPS://WWW.IBM.COM/BLOGS/CLOUD-COMPUTING/2018/08/02/SOUL-MACHINES-AI-WATSON/

FAHRNI, S., JANSEN, C., JOHN, M., KASAH, T., KOERBER, B., & MOHR, N. (2020, MAY 7). CORONAVIRUS: INDUSTRIAL IOT IN CHALLENGING TIMES. MCKINSEY & COMPANY. HTTPS://WWW.MCKINSEY.COM/INDUSTRIES/ADVANCED-ELECTRONICS/OUR-INSIGHTS/CORONAVIRUS-INDUSTRIAL-IOT-IN-CHALLENGING-TIMES

CB INSIGHTS. (2020, JUNE 26). BEYOND AMAZON GO: THE TECHNOLOGIES AND PLAYERS SHAPING CASHIER-LESS RETAIL. CB INSIGHTS RESEARCH. HTTPS://WWW.CBINSIGHTS.COM/RESEARCH/CASHIERLESS-RETAIL-TECHNOLOGIES-COMPANIES-TRENDS/

MANYIKA, DOBBS, CHUI, BUGHIN, BISSON, WOETZEL. (2015). THE INTERNET OF THINGS: MAPPING THE VALUE BEYOND THE HYPE | INTER AMERICAN DIALOGUE. MCKINSEY GLOBAL INSTITUTE, MCKINSEY & COMPANY - ECONOMICS, TECHNOLOGICAL INNOVATION. HTTP://GLOBALTRENDS.THEDIALOGUE.ORG/PUBLICATION/THE-INTERNET-OF-THINGS-MAPPING-THE-VALUE-BEYOND-THE-HYPE/

THE FUTURE OF RETAIL: SHOPPING AND THE SMART SHELF. (2020). INTEL. HTTPS://WWW.INTEL.COM/CONTENT/WWW/US/EN/RETAIL/DIGITAL-RETAIL-FUTURECASTING-REPORT.HTML

CONSUMER PACKAGED GOODS AND RETAIL IN THE AGE OF INSTINCT. (2020). GENPACT. HTTPS://WWW.GENPACT.COM/INSTINCTIVE-ENTERPRISE/CONSUMER-GOODS-RETAIL?GCLID=CJWKCAIAWRF-BRA9EIWAUWWKXROKNN-M_13BSEZECR-ATL6GV827VP5ZOJNXPU_GPH2B0PLDMTMMLXOCOI4QAVD_BWE

MEOLA, A. (2020, JULY 1). HOW AI AND IOT DEVICES WILL REVOLUTIONIZE SUPPLY CHAIN LOGISTICS AND MANAGEMENT. BUSINESS INSIDER. HTTPS://WWW.BUSINESSINSIDER.COM/IOT-SUPPLY-CHAIN-MANAGEMENT-LOGISTICS?INTERNATIONAL=TRUE&R=US&IR=T

MOON, M. (2017, MARCH 30). DOMINO'S DELIVERY ROBOTS ARE INVADING EUROPE WHICH BEGS THE QUESTION: HOW MUCH DO YOU TIP A ROBOT? ENGADGET. HTTPS://WWW.ENGADGET.COM/2017-03-30-DOMINO-PIZZA-DELIVERY-DRONE-GERMANY-NETHERLANDS.HTML

MATTHEWS, K. (2019, JANUARY 18). RETAIL ROBOTS ARE STARTING TO DISRUPT THE INDUSTRY IN 5 WAYS. ROBOTICS BUSINESS REVIEW. HTTPS://WWW.ROBOTICSBUSINESSREVIEW.COM/RETAIL-HOSPITALITY/RETAIL-ROBOTS-DISRUPT-INDUSTRY/

MURPHY, M. (2019, JUNE 14). NURO WILL DELIVER DOMINO'S PIZZA WITH ITS ROBOTS IN HOUSTON. QUARTZ. HTTPS://QZ.COM/1644476/NURO-WILL-DELIVER-DOMINOS-PIZZA-WITH-ITS-ROBOTS-IN-HOUSTON/

PALMER, A. (2020, AUGUST 31). AMAZON WINS FAA APPROVAL FOR PRIME AIR DRONE DELIVERY FLEET. CNBC. HTTPS://WWW.CNBC.COM/2020/08/31/AMAZON-PRIME-NOW-DRONE-DELIVERY-FLEET-GETS-FAA-APPROVAL.HTML

AMAZON.COM: PRIME AIR. (2020). HTTPS://WWW.AMAZON.COM/AMAZON-PRIME-AIR. HTTPS://WWW.AMAZON.COM/AMAZON-PRIME-AIR/B?IE=UTF8&NODE=8037720011

ETHERINGTON, D. (2016, DECEMBER 20). TECHCRUNCH IS NOW A PART OF VERIZON MEDIA. TECHCRUNCH. HTTPS://TECHCRUNCH.COM/2016/12/20/7-ELEVEN-DELIVERS-77-PACKAGES-VIA-DRONE-IN-FIRST-MONTH-OF-ROUTINE-SERVICE/#:%7E:TEXT=ROUTINE%20SERVICE%20%7C%20TECHCRUNCH-,7%7%2DELEVEN%20DELIVERS%2077%20PACKAGES%20VIA%20DRONE,FIRST%20MONTH%20OF%20ROUTINE%20SERVICE&TEXT=IN%20THE%20MOST%20BRAND%20SYNERGISTIC,AMERICA'S%20OTHER%20BIG%20GAMBLING%20TOWN.

Hanbury, M. (2019, June 18). There's a way Walmart could beat Amazon when it comes to speedy delivery, and new data shows it's going all i. Business Insider. https://www.businessinsider.in/theres-a-way-walmart-could-beat-amazon-when-it-comes-to-speedy-delivery-and-new-data-shows-its-going-all-in/articleshow/69841775.cms

Zaveri, M. (2019, April 24). Wing, Owned by Google's Parent Company, Gets First Approval for Drone Deliveries in U.S. The New York Times. https://www.nytimes.com/2019/04/23/technology/drone-deliveries-google-wing.html#:%7E:text=The%20Federal%20Aviation%20Administration%20said,carry%20and%20deliver%20packages%20commercially.

Lyu, Ramli, and Levin. (2018). Bloomberg - Are you a robot? Bloomberg. https://www.bloomberg.com/tosv2.html?vid=&uuid=64AE0410-38A4-11EB-A66C-1BB919BDC1C9&url=L25LD3MvZmVhdHVyZXMvMjAxOCowNyowMy9jaGluYS1zLW9uLXRoZS1mYXNoLXRvLW1ha2Zy11YXTzTHJvbmUtZGVsaXZlcmLcmllcmw==

Margaritoff, M. (2018, March 14). Drone Deliveries Really Are Coming Soon, Officials Say. The Drive. https://www.thedrive.com/tech/19239/drone-deliveries-really-are-coming-soon-officials-say

Guizzo, E. (2014, December 26). How Aldebaran Robotics Built Its Friendly Humanoid Robot, Pepper. The French company worked in secret for two years to create Pepper. Now Japanese telecom giant SoftBank is ready to sell it to consumers. IEEE Spectrum: Technology, Engineering, and Science News. https://spectrum.ieee.org/robotics/home-robots/how-aldebaran-robotics-built-its-friendly-humanoid-robot-pepper

Nassauer, S., & Cutter, C. (2019, April 9). Walmart Is Rolling Out the Robots. WSJ. https://www.wsj.com/articles/walmart-is-rolling-out-the-robots-11554782460

Kumar, K. (2015, September 26). Best Buy tests robot at New York store. Star Tribune. https://www.startribune.com/best-buy-tests-robot-at-new-york-store/329583301/

Taylor, H. (2016, August 31). Lowe's introduces LoweBot, a new autonomous in-store robot. CNBC. https://www.cnbc.com/2016/08/30/lowes-introduces-lowebot-a-new-autonomous-in-store-robot.html

Rusli, E. M. (2012, March 20). Amazon.com to Acquire Manufacturer of Robotics. DealBook. https://dealbook.nytimes.com/2012/03/19/amazon-com-buys-kiva-systems-for-775-million/

Yarow, J. (2012, December 27). Amazon Was Selling 306 Items Every Second At Its Peak This Year. Business Insider. https://www.businessinsider.com/amazon-holiday-facts-2012-12?international=true&r=US&IR=T

Kestenbaum, R. (2017, April 6). 3D Printing In-Store Is Very Close And Retailers Need To Address It. Forbes. https://www.forbes.com/sites/richardkestenbaum/2017/04/06/3d-printing-in-store-is-very-close-and-retailers-need-to-address-it/?sh=13A2AD8633B4

Entis, L. (2015, October 6). This High-Tech Startup Is Using Science to Hack the Dress Shirt. Entrepreneur. https://www.entrepreneur.com/article/251329

LORD, B. (2018, AUGUST 3). REEBOK'S 3D PRINTED SHOE LINE DASHES INTO PRODUCTION. 3D PRINTING INDUSTRY. HTTPS://3DPRINTINGINDUSTRY.COM/NEWS/REEBOKS-3D-PRINTED-SHOE-LINE-DASHES-INTO-PRODUCTION-137497/#:%7E:TEXT=A%20NEW%20KIND%20OF%20 SHOE,IN%20A%20MATTER%20OF%20HOURS.

ADRIENNE, S. (2019). NEW BALANCE'S LATEST SHOES COME WITH 3D-PRINTED SOLES. 3D PRINTING HAS OTHER BENEFITS BESIDES PERSONALIZATION. IT KEEPS MANUFACTURING IN THE UNITED STATES. WIRED. HTTPS://WWW.WIRED.COM/STORY/ NEW-BALANCE-TRIPLECELL-3D-PRINTED-SHOE/

MOLITCH-HOU, M. (2015, SEPTEMBER 10). STAPLES.COM NOW OFFERING GLOBAL 3D PRINTING SERVICES POWERED BY SCULPTEO. 3D PRINTING INDUSTRY. HTTPS://3DPRINTINGINDUSTRY. COM/NEWS/STAPLES-COM-NOW-OFFERING-GLOBAL-3D-PRINTING-SERVICES-POWERED-BY-SCULPTEO-57264/

KOKOSZKA, P. (2018, JULY 24). IS 3D BODY SCANNING THE FUTURE OF FASHION? VERDICT. HTTPS:// WWW.VERDICT.CO.UK/3D-BODY-SCANNING-FASHION-FUTURE/

BAIN, M. (2015, SEPTEMBER 9). COULD 3D BODY SCANNING MEAN NEVER ENTERING ANOTHER DRESSING ROOM AGAIN? QUARTZ. HTTPS://QZ.COM/497259/ COULD-3D-BODY-SCANNING-MEAN-NEVER-ENTERING-ANOTHER-DRESSING-ROOM-AGAIN/

LAWLER, R. (2012, JUNE 14). TECHCRUNCH IS NOW A PART OF VERIZON MEDIA. TECHCRUNCH IS NOW A PART OF VERIZON MEDIA. HTTPS://TECHCRUNCH.COM/2012/06/14/BOMBFELL/

LOMAS AND CROOK. (2017, OCTOBER 3). AMAZON HAS ACQUIRED 3D BODY MODEL STARTUP, BODY LABS, FOR $50M-$70M. TECHCRUNCH IS NOW A PART OF VERIZON MEDIA. HTTPS://TECHCRUNCH.COM/2017/10/03/ AMAZON-HAS-ACQUIRED-3D-BODY-MODEL-STARTUP-BODY-LABS-FOR-50M-70M/

CHOU, C. (2018, JULY 4). ALIBABA'S FASHIONAI: NEW ALIBABA CONCEPT STORE TEASES FUTURE OF FASHION RETAIL. ALIZILA. HTTPS://WWW.ALIZILA.COM/ NEW-ALIBABA-CONCEPT-STORE-TEASES-FUTURE-OF-FASHION-RETAIL/

MEHTA, P. (2020, JULY 22). ONLINE SHOPPING GETS MORE PERSONAL WITH RECOMMENDATIONS AI. GOOGLE CLOUD BLOG. HTTPS://CLOUD.GOOGLE.COM/BLOG/PRODUCTS/ AI-MACHINE-LEARNING/ONLINE-SHOPPING-GETS-PERSONAL-WITH-RECOMMENDATIONS-AI

STATISTA. (2020, NOVEMBER 4). FACEBOOK: WORLDWIDE QUARTERLY REVENUE 2010-2020, BY SEGMENT. HTTPS://WWW.STATISTA.COM/STATISTICS/277963/FACEBOOKS-QUARTERLY-GLOBAL-REVENUE-BY-SEGMENT/#:%7E:TEXT=FACEBOOK%3A%20WORLDWIDE%20QUARTERLY%20 REVENUE%202010%2D2020%2C%20BY%20SEGMENT&TEXT=IN%20THE%20THIRD%20 QUARTER%20OF,MILLION%20U.S.%20DOLLARS%20IN%20REVENUES.

STATISTA. (2020A, SEPTEMBER 25). GLOBAL ADVERTISING REVENUE 2012-2024. HTTPS://WWW. STATISTA.COM/STATISTICS/236943/GLOBAL-ADVERTISING-SPENDING/

EGAN, M. (2017, JULY 27). FACEBOOK AND AMAZON BOTH HIT $500 BILLION MILESTONE. CNNMONEY. HTTPS://MONEY.CNN.COM/2017/07/27/INVESTING/FACEBOOK-AMAZON-500-BILLION-BEZOS-ZUCKERBERG/INDEX.HTML

LYNLEY, M. (2018, JULY 23). GOOGLE JOINS THE RACE TO $1 TRILLION. TECHCRUNCH. HTTPS:// TECHCRUNCH.COM/2018/07/23/GOOGLE-JOINS-THE-RACE-TO-1-TRILLION/

Carman, A. (2018, September 24). Snapchat is testing a camera feature that lets you easily buy items from Amazon. The Verge. https://www.theverge.com/2018/9/24/17896788/snapchat-amazon-shop-photos-partnership

Harris, J. (2017, November 14). Introducing the next wave of visual search and shopping. Pinterest Newsroom. https://newsroom.pinterest.com/en/post/introducing-the-next-wave-of-visual-search-and-shopping

Wang, L. (2020, May 7). New Google Lens features to help you be more productive at home. Google. https://blog.google/products/google-lens/new-google-lens-features-help-you-be-more-productive-home/

Pardes, A. (2017, September 20). Ikea's New App Flaunts What You'll Love Most About AR. Yahoo!News. https://www.yahoo.com/news/ikea-apos-app-flaunts-apos-161855825.html

Wurmser, Y. (2018, September 26). Visual Search 2018: New Tools from Pinterest, eBay, Google and Amazon Increase Accuracy, Utility. Insider Intelligence. https://www.emarketer.com/content/visual-search-2018

The real danger of deepfake videos is that we may question everything. (2018, August 29). New Scientist. https://www.newscientist.com/article/mg23931933-200-the-real-danger-of-deepfake-videos-is-that-we-may-question-everything/

Schwartz, O. (2019, July 10). You thought fake news was bad? Deep fakes are where truth goes to die. The Guardian. https://www.theguardian.com/technology/2018/nov/12/deep-fakes-fake-news-truth

Hastings, R. (2020, February 6). How I Did It: Reed Hastings, Netflix. Inc.Com. https://www.inc.com/magazine/20051201/qa-hastings.html

Source: Statista. (2020, October 30). Netflix Revenue and Usage Statistics (2020). Business of Apps. https://www.businessofapps.com/data/netflix-statistics/#:%7E:text=Netflix%20subscriber%20growth%20for%20Q4,growth%20declining%20from%200.52%20million.

Netflix Market Cap 2006-2020 | NFLX. (2020). MacroTrends. https://www.macrotrends.net/stocks/charts/NFLX/netflix/market-cap

The Economist. (2018, July 24). Netflix is moving television beyond time-slots and national markets. https://www.economist.com/briefing/2018/06/30/netflix-is-moving-television-beyond-time-slots-and-national-markets

CGMA. (2018, August 13). Amazon, Hulu, and Netflix are looking for artists like you. CGMA Blog. https://blog.cgmasteracademy.com/netflix-is-hiring/

Graser, M. (2013, November 12). Epic Fail: How Blockbuster Could Have Owned Netflix - Blockbuster chiefs lacked the vision to see how the industry was shifting under the video rental chain's feet. Variety. https://variety.com/2013/biz/news/epic-fail-how-blockbuster-could-have-owned-netflix-1200823443/

Mickle, T. (2017, August 17). Apple Readies $1 Billion War Chest for Hollywood Programming. WSJ. https://www.wsj.com/articles/apple-readies-1-billion-war-chest-for-hollywood-programming-1502874004

LEVY, A. (2019, MAY 1). HERE'S EXACTLY HOW MUCH AMAZON IS SPENDING ON VIDEO AND MUSIC CONTENT. THE MOTLEY FOOL. HTTPS://WWW.FOOL.COM/INVESTING/2019/04/30/HERES-HOW-MUCH-AMAZON-IS-SPENDING-ON-VIDEO-MUSIC.ASPX

BROADBAND TV NEWS CORRESPONDENT. (2018, OCTOBER 22). GLOBAL TV REVENUES GROW TO $265 BILLION. BROADBAND TV NEWS. HTTPS://WWW.BROADBANDTVNEWS.COM/2018/10/22/GLOBAL-TV-REVENUES-GROW-TO-265-BILLION/

STATISTA. (2020A, APRIL 24). GLOBAL BOX OFFICE REVENUE FROM 2005 TO 2019. HTTPS://WWW.STATISTA.COM/STATISTICS/271856/GLOBAL-BOX-OFFICE-REVENUE/#:%7E:TEXT=IN%202019%2C%20GLOBAL%20BOX%20OFFICE,INCREASE%20FROM%20THE%20PREVIOUS%20YEAR.

TAKAHASHI, D. (2018, JULY 2). HIGH FIDELITY RAISES $35 MILLION WITH GOAL OF BRINGING VR TO 'A BILLION PEOPLE.' VENTUREBEAT. HTTPS://VENTUREBEAT.COM/2018/06/28/HIGH-FIDELITY-RAISES-35-MILLION-WITH-GOAL-OF-BRINGING-VR-TO-A-BILLION-PEOPLE/

MYXTER, J. (2020, OCTOBER 27). DAVID EAGLEMAN AND CREATING NEW SENSES FOR HUMANS. INSTITUTE FOR SYSTEMS BIOLOGY. HTTPS://ISBSCIENCE.ORG/NEWS/2020/10/23/DAVID-EAGLEMAN-AND-CREATING-NEW-SENSES-FOR-HUMANS/

BISHOP, B. (2019, JANUARY 15). DREAMSCAPE IMMERSIVE IS BRINGING LOCATION-BASED VR TO THE MASSES. THE VERGE. HTTPS://WWW.THEVERGE.COM/2019/1/15/18156854/DREAMSCAPE-IMMERSIVE-VIRTUAL-REALITY-LOS-ANGELES-WALTER-PARKES-BRUCE-VAUGHN

RAMIREZ, G. A., FUENTES, O., JIMENEZ, M., ORDONEZ, J., CRITES, S. L., & 2014 IEEE CONFERENCE ON COMPUTER VISION AND PATTERN RECOGNITION WORKSHOPS, CVPRW 2014. (JANUARY 01, 2014). COLOR ANALYSIS OF FACIAL SKIN: DETECTION OF EMOTIONAL STATE. IEEE COMPUTER SOCIETY CONFERENCE ON COMPUTER VISION AND PATTERN RECOGNITION WORKSHOPS, 474-479.

MARWAN, S. (2018, NOVEMBER 29). RANA EL KALIOUBY CEO OF AFFECTIVA IS TRAINING ROBOTS TO READ FEELINGS. FORBES. HTTPS://WWW.FORBES.COM/SITES/SAMARMARWAN/2018/11/29/AFFECTIVA-EMOTION-AI-CEO-RANA-EL-KALIOUBY/?SH=66AD297E1572

MILLER, N. J., LEON, F. A., EERE PUBLICATION AND PRODUCT LIBRARY, PACIFIC NORTHWEST NATIONAL LAB. (PNNL), RICHLAND, WA (UNITED STATES), & USDOE OFFICE OF ENERGY EFFICIENCY AND RENEWABLE ENERGY (EERE), BUILDING TECHNOLOGIES OFFICE (EE-5B) (SOLID-STATE LIGHTING). (MAY 31, 2016). OLED LIGHTING PRODUCTS: CAPABILITIES, CHALLENGES, POTENTIAL.

AUGMENTED REALITY MARKET BY OFFERING (HARDWARE (SENSOR, DISPLAYS & PROJECTORS, CAMERAS), SOFTWARE), DEVICE TYPE (HEAD-MOUNTED, HEAD-UP), APPLICATION (ENTERPRISE, CONSUMER, COMMERCIAL, HEALTHCARE, AUTOMOTIVE), AND REGION - GLOBAL FORECAST TO 2024. (2020, JANUARY). AUGMENTED REALITY MARKET. HTTPS://WWW.MARKETSANDMARKETS.COM/MARKET-REPORTS/AUGMENTED-REALITY-MARKET-82758548.HTML#:%7E:TEXT=%5B191%20PAGES%20REPORT%5D%20THE%20AUGMENTED,IS%20RISING%20INVESTMENTS%20IN%20MARKET.

PHELAN, D. (2017, FEBRUARY 10). APPLE CEO TIM COOK: AS BREXIT HANGS OVER UK, "TIMES ARE NOT REALLY AWFUL, THERE'S SOME GREAT THINGS HAPPENING." THE INDEPENDENT. HTTPS://WWW.INDEPENDENT.CO.UK/LIFE-STYLE/GADGETS-AND-TECH/FEATURES/APPLE-TIM-COOK-BOSS-BREXIT-UK-THERESA-MAY-NUMBER-10-INTERVIEW-USTWO-A7574086.HTML

RUDOLF. (2020, NOVEMBER 5). POKÉMON GO HITS $1 BILLION IN 2020, SURPASSING $4 BILLION IN LIFETIME REVENUE. POKEMON GO HUB. HTTPS://POKEMONGOHUB.NET/

POST/NEWS/POKEMON-GO-HITS-1-BILLION-IN-2020-SURPASSING-4-BILLION-IN-LIFETIME-REVENUE/#:%7E:TEXT=WHATSAPP-,POK%C3%A9MON%20GO%20HITS%20%241%20BILLION%20IN%202020,A%20NEW%20EARNING%20MILESTONE%20%E2%80%93%20AGAIN.&TEXT=SINCE%20JULY%202016%2C%20THE%20GAME,THE%20END%20OF%20THAT%20YEAR.

STATISTA. (2020C, OCTOBER 30). POKÉMON GO REVENUE AND USAGE STATISTICS (2020). BUSINESS OF APPS. HTTPS://WWW.BUSINESSOFAPPS.COM/DATA/POKEMON-GO-STATISTICS/#:%7E:TEXT=POK%C3%A9MON%20GO%20DAYS%20TO%20%242%20BILLION%20IN%20REVENUE&TEXT=BASED%20ON%20SENSOR%20TOWER%20DATA,TIME%20CAME%20TO%20%2458%20MILLION.

MINKYU AHN, MIJIN LEE, JINYOUNG CHOI, & SUNG CHAN JUN. (JANUARY 01, 2014). A REVIEW OF BRAIN-COMPUTER INTERFACE GAMES AND AN OPINION SURVEY FROM RESEARCHERS, DEVELOPERS AND USERS. SENSORS, 14, 8, 14601-14633.

JIANG, L., STOCCO, A., LOSEY, D. M., ABERNETHY, J. A., PRAT, C. S., & RAO, R. P. N. (DECEMBER 01, 2019). BRAINNET: A MULTI-PERSON BRAIN-TO-BRAIN INTERFACE FOR DIRECT COLLABORATION BETWEEN BRAINS. SCIENTIFIC REPORTS, 9, 1, 1-11.

METZ, R. (2020, APRIL 2). NOW PLAYING: A MOVIE YOU CONTROL WITH YOUR MIND. MIT TECHNOLOGY REVIEW. HTTPS://WWW.TECHNOLOGYREVIEW.COM/2018/05/25/142725/NOW-PLAYING-A-MOVIE-YOU-CONTROL-WITH-YOUR-MIND/#:%7E:TEXT=RICHARD%20RAMCHURN'S%20THE%20MOMENT%20LETS,DIRECTOR%2C%20USING%20JUST%20YOUR%20BRAINWAVES.&TEXT=USUALLY%20WHEN%20YOU%20WATCH%20A,OF%20RICHARD%20RAMCHURN'S%20LATEST%20FILMS.

GARTNER SAYS WORLDWIDE SMARTPHONE SALES WILL GROW 3% IN 2020. (2020, JANUARY 28). GARTNER. HTTPS://WWW.GARTNER.COM/EN/NEWSROOM/PRESS-RELEASES/2020-01-28-GARTNER-SAYS-WORLDWIDE-SMARTPHONE-SALES-WILL-GROW-3--#:%7E:TEXT=WORLDWIDE%20SALES%20OF%20SMARTPHONES%20TO,SMARTPHONE%20MARKET%20EXPERIENCED%20A%20DECLINE.

GLOBAL LEARNING XPRIZE. (2019). EMPOWERING CHILDREN TO TAKE CONTROL OF THEIR OWN LEARNING. XPRIZE. HTTPS://WWW.XPRIZE.ORG/PRIZES/GLOBAL-LEARNING

UNOS. (2018). DATA - TRANSPLANT TRENDS. UNOS.ORG. HTTPS://UNOS.ORG/DATA/

SORVINO, C. (2018, JUNE 20). HOW CEO MARTINE ROTHBLATT TURNS MOONSHOTS INTO EARTHSHOTS. FORBES. HTTPS://WWW.FORBES.COM/SITES/CHLOESORVINO/2018/06/20/HOW-CEO-MARTINE-ROTHBLATT-TURNS-MOONSHOTS-INTO-EARTHSHOTS/?SH=38B2DC2473D3

CLYNES, T. (2018, NOVEMBER 14). 20 AMERICANS DIE EACH DAY WAITING FOR ORGANS. CAN PIGS SAVE THEM? THE NEW YORK TIMES COMPANY. HTTPS://WWW.NYTIMES.COM/INTERACTIVE/2018/11/14/MAGAZINE/TECH-DESIGN-XENOTRANSPLANTATION.HTML

REGALADO, A. (2020, APRIL 2). INSIDE THE EFFORT TO PRINT LUNGS AND BREATHE LIFE INTO THEM WITH STEM CELLS. MIT TECHNOLOGY REVIEW. HTTPS://WWW.TECHNOLOGYREVIEW.COM/2018/06/28/240446/INSIDE-THE-EFFORT-TO-PRINT-LUNGS-AND-BREATHE-LIFE-INTO-THEM-WITH-STEM-CELLS/

ADAMS, E. (2019, JANUARY 11). BETA TECHNOLOGIES, A VERMONT AIR TAXI START-UP, MIGHT BE ABOUT TO CHANGE THE AVIATION WORLD. THE DRIVE. HTTPS://WWW.THEDRIVE.COM/TECH/25914/

BETA-TECHNOLOGIES-A-VERMONT-E-VTOL-AIR-TAXI-START-UP-MIGHT-BE-ABOUT-TO-CHANGE-THE-AVIATION-WORLD

MARSHALL ALLEN, PROPUBLICA, ALLEN, M., & PROPUBLICA. (2017, NOVEMBER 29). UNNECESSARY TESTS AND TREATMENT EXPLAIN WHY HEALTH CARE COSTS SO MUCH. SCIENTIFIC AMERICAN. HTTPS://WWW.SCIENTIFICAMERICAN.COM/ARTICLE/UNNECESSARY-TESTS-AND-TREATMENT-EXPLAIN-WHY-HEALTH-CARE-COSTS-SO-MUCH/

FACT SHEET NEW DRUG DEVELOPMENT PROCESS. (2020, NOVEMBER 24). STUDYLIB.NET. HTTPS://STUDYLIB.NET/DOC/8182066/FACT-SHEET-NEW-DRUG-DEVELOPMENT-PROCESS

NATIONAL HEALTH EXPENDITURE DATA | CMS. (2019, DECEMBER 17). CENTERS FOR MEDICARE & MEDICAID SERVICES. HTTPS://WWW.CMS.GOV/RESEARCH-STATISTICS-DATA-AND-SYSTEMS/STATISTICS-TRENDS-AND-REPORTS/NATIONALHEALTHEXPENDDATA

GURDUS, L. (2019, AUGUST 9). TIM COOK: APPLE'S GREATEST CONTRIBUTION WILL BE "ABOUT HEALTH." CNBC. HTTPS://WWW.CNBC.COM/2019/01/08/TIM-COOK-TEASES-NEW-APPLE-SERVICES-TIED-TO-HEALTH-CARE.HTML

CB INSIGHTS. (2020B, NOVEMBER 30). STATE OF HEALTHCARE Q4'20 PREVIEW: INVESTMENT TRENDS TO WATCH. CB INSIGHTS RESEARCH. HTTPS://WWW.CBINSIGHTS.COM/RESEARCH/REPORT/HEALTHCARE-TRENDS-Q4-2020/

ZION MARKET RESEARCH. (2018, SEPTEMBER 18). MHEALTH MARKET TO BRANCH OUT AND REACH USD 102.43 BILLION BY 2022. HTTPS://WWW.ZIONMARKETRESEARCH.COM/NEWS/GLOBAL-MHEALTH-MARKET

STEIN, R. (2017, JUNE 26). NPR COOKIE CONSENT AND CHOICES. NPR. HTTPS://CHOICE.NPR.ORG/INDEX.HTML?ORIGIN=HTTPS://WWW.NPR.ORG/SECTIONS/HEALTH-SHOTS/2017/06/26/534338576/ROUTINE-DNA-SEQUENCING-MAY-BE-HELPFUL-AND-NOT-AS-SCARY-AS-FEARED#:%7E:TEXT=ROUTINE%20DNA%20SEQUENCING%20MAY%20BE%20HELPFUL%20AND%20NOT%20AS%20SCARY%20AS%20FEARED,-LISTEN%C2%B7%204%3A09&TEXT=WHOLE%20GENOME%20SEQUENCING%20COULD%20BECOME%20PART%20OF%20ROUTINE%20MEDICAL%20CARE.,-RESEARCHERS%20SOUGHT%20TO&TEXT=ADVANCES%20IN%20TECHNOLOGY%20HAVE%20MADE,IN%20A%20PERSON'S%20GENETIC%20CODE.

VASSY, J. L., CHRISTENSEN, K. D., SCHONMAN, E. F., BLOUT, C. L., ROBINSON, J. O., KRIER, J. B., DIAMOND, P. M., ... GREEN, R. C. (AUGUST 01, 2017). THE IMPACT OF WHOLE-GENOME SEQUENCING ON THE PRIMARY CARE AND OUTCOMES OF HEALTHY ADULT PATIENTS: A PILOT RANDOMIZED TRIAL. ANNALS OF INTERNAL MEDICINE, 167, 3, 159-169.

COHEN, J. (2018, FEBRUARY 12). Q&A: GEORGE CHURCH AND COMPANY ON GENOMIC SEQUENCING, BLOCKCHAIN, AND BETTER DRUGS. SCIENCE | AAAS. HTTPS://WWW.SCIENCEMAG.ORG/NEWS/2018/02/Q-GEORGE-CHURCH-AND-COMPANY-GENOMIC-SEQUENCING-BLOCKCHAIN-AND-BETTER-DRUGS

LI, Y., KONG, Q., YUE, J., GOU, X., XU, M., WU, X., & SPRINGERLINK (ONLINE SERVICE). (2018). GENOME-EDITED SKIN EPIDERMAL STEM CELLS PROTECT MICE FROM COCAINE-SEEKING BEHAVIOUR AND COCAINE OVERDOSE. (NATURE BIOMEDICAL ENGINEERING.)

MULLIN, E. (2020, APRIL 2). FDA APPROVES GROUNDBREAKING GENE THERAPY FOR CANCER. MIT TECHNOLOGY REVIEW. HTTPS://WWW.TECHNOLOGYREVIEW.COM/2017/08/30/149399/THE-FDA-HAS-APPROVED-THE-FIRST-GENE-THERAPY-FOR-CANCER/

REUELL, P. (2017, OCTOBER 25). A STEP FORWARD IN DNA BASE EDITING. HARVARD GAZETTE. HTTPS://NEWS.HARVARD.EDU/GAZETTE/ STORY/2017/10/A-STEP-FORWARD-IN-DNA-BASE-EDITING/

HALL, M. J., SCHWARTZMAN, A., ZHANG, J., & LIU, X. (2017). AMBULATORY SURGERY DATA FROM HOSPITALS AND AMBULATORY SURGERY CENTERS: UNITED STATES, 2010. NATIONAL HEALTH STATISTICS REPORTS, (102), 1–15.

ALMUJALHEM, A., & RHA, K. H. (NOVEMBER 01, 2020). SURGICAL ROBOTIC SYSTEMS: WHAT WE HAVE NOW? A UROLOGICAL PERSPECTIVE. BJUI COMPASS, 1, 5, 152-159.

ZHAVORONKOV, A. (OCTOBER 01, 2018). ARTIFICIAL INTELLIGENCE FOR DRUG DISCOVERY, BIOMARKER DEVELOPMENT, AND GENERATION OF NOVEL CHEMISTRY. MOLECULAR PHARMACEUTICS, 15, 10, 4311-4313.

ROCKOFF, J. D. (2018, APRIL 26). THE MILLION-DOLLAR CANCER TREATMENT: WHO WILL PAY? WSJ. HTTPS://WWW.WSJ.COM/ARTICLES/THE-MILLION-DOLLAR-CANCER-TREATMENT-NO-ONE-KNOWS-HOW-TO-PAY-FOR-1524740401

DIMASI, J. A., GRABOWSKI, H. G., & HANSEN, R. W. (JANUARY 01, 2016). INNOVATION IN THE PHARMACEUTICAL INDUSTRY: NEW ESTIMATES OF R&D COSTS. JOURNAL OF HEALTH ECONOMICS, 47, 20-33.

PEIKOFF, K. (2020, SEPTEMBER 25). ANTI-AGING PIONEER AUBREY DE GREY: "PEOPLE IN MIDDLE AGE NOW HAVE A FAIR CHANCE." LEAPSMAG. HTTPS://LEAPSMAG.COM/ ANTI-AGING-PIONEER-AUBREY-DE-GREY-PEOPLE-MIDDLE-AGE-NOW-FAIR-CHANCE/

WRIGHT, D. E., WAGERS, A. J., GULATI, A. P., JOHNSON, F. L., & WEISSMAN, I. L. (2001). PHYSIOLOGICAL MIGRATION OF HEMATOPOIETIC STEM AND PROGENITOR CELLS. SCIENCE (NEW YORK, N.Y.), 294(5548), 1933–1936. HTTPS://DOI.ORG/10.1126/SCIENCE.1064081

SCUDELLARI M. (2015). AGEING RESEARCH: BLOOD TO BLOOD. NATURE, 517(7535), 426–429. HTTPS://DOI.ORG/10.1038/517426A

INSURANCE INFORMATION INSTITUTE. (2020). WHAT DETERMINES THE PRICE OF AN AUTO INSURANCE POLICY? | MANY FACTORS HELP DETERMINE THE COST OF CAR INSURANCE. III.ORG. HTTPS://WWW.III.ORG/ARTICLE/ WHAT-DETERMINES-PRICE-MY-AUTO-INSURANCE-POLICY

A BRIEF STATISTICAL SUMMARY. (2015). CRITICAL REASONS FOR CRASHES INVESTIGATED IN THE NATIONAL MOTOR VEHICLE CRASH CAUSATION SURVEY. U.S. DEPARTMENT OF TRANSPORTATION. HTTPS://CRASHSTATS.NHTSA.DOT.GOV/API/PUBLIC/ VIEWPUBLICATION/812115

ROAD SAFETY. (2020). WORLD HEALTH DATA PLATFORM. HTTPS://WWW.WHO.INT/DATA/GHO/ DATA/THEMES/ROAD-SAFETY

SMARTER CARS, BUT MORE DISTRACTED DRIVERS, TOO. (2019, DECEMBER 19). KPMG. HTTPS:// HOME.KPMG/US/EN/HOME/INSIGHTS/2019/11/2019-ISSUE4-ARTICLE2.HTML

CHAMBERS, LIU, AND MOORE. (2017, MAY 27). DRUNK DRIVING BY THE NUMBERS | BUREAU OF TRANSPORTATION STATISTICS. BUREAU OF TRANSPORTATION STATISTICS. HTTPS://WWW.BTS. GOV/ARCHIVE/PUBLICATIONS/BY_THE_NUMBERS/DRUNK_DRIVING/INDEX

ETHERISC. (2019, JANUARY 17). FIRST BLOCKCHAIN-BASED APP TO INSURE YOUR NEXT FLIGHT AGAINST DELAYS. MEDIUM. HTTPS://BLOG.ETHERISC.COM/FIRST-BLOCKCHAIN-BASED-APP-TO-INSURE-YOUR-NEXT-FLIGHT-AGAINST-DELAYS-10F53B38AD2D

Digital insurance in 2018: Driving real impact with digital and analytics. (2019, November 14). McKinsey & Company. https://www.mckinsey.com/industries/financial-services/our-insights/digital-insurance-in-2018-driving-real-impact-with-digital-and-analytics

Lamagna, M. (2018, March 29). Overdraft fees haven't been this bad since the Great Recession. New York Post. https://nypost.com/2018/03/28/overdraft-fees-havent-been-this-bad-since-the-great-recession/

McCarthy, N. (2018, June 11). 1.7 Billion Adults Worldwide Do Not Have Access To A Bank Account [Infographic]. Forbes. https://www.forbes.com/sites/niallmccarthy/2018/06/08/1-7-billion-adults-worldwide-do-not-have-access-to-a-bank-account-infographic/?sh=754f49354b01

Transparency Market Research. (2018, September 28). Peer-to-peer Lending Market to be Worth US$897.85 Billion by 2024 - TMR. PRNewswire. https://www.prnewswire.com/news-releases/peer-to-peer-lending-market-to-be-worth-us-897-85-billion-by-2024-tmr-883066968.html

Isidore, C. (2018, February 6). Machines are driving Wall Street's wild ride, not humans. CNNMoney. https://money.cnn.com/2018/02/06/investing/wall-street-computers-program-trading/index.html

Marquit, M. (2020, November 22). How To Invest With a Robo-Advisor. Retrieved from https://www.forbes.com/advisor/investing/what-is-robo-advisor/

Levring, P. (2016, December 15). Scandinavia's Disappearing Cash Act. A post-cash society requires trust and an efficient state. Retrieved from https://www.bloomberg.com/news/articles/2016-12-16/scandinavia-s-disappearing-cash-act

Pymnts. (2016, December 18). Denmark Moves Toward No Cash. Retrieved from https://www.pymnts.com/cash/2016/denmark-shutting-down-last-mint-cash/#:~:text=Denmark%20is%20following%20Sweden%20and,shut%20down%20its%20last%20mint.

Rowlatt, J. (2016, November 14). Why India wiped out 86% of its cash overnight. Retrieved from https://www.bbc.com/news/world-asia-india-37974423#:~:text=India%20is%20in%20the%20middle,economy%20would%20be%20effectively%20worthless.

Le, T. H. (2020, April 29). Can Vietnam turn 90% of its transactions into cashless payments? Retrieved from https://kr-asia.com/can-vietnam-turn-90-of-its-transactions-into-cashless-payments

Poon, L. (2020, July 14). Bloomberg CityLab: Coronavirus Hastens the Rise of the Cashless Economy. Cashless transactions have spiked as company policies and consumer habits shift. But protections for people without bank and credit access haven't kept up. Retrieved from https://www.bloomberg.com/news/articles/2020-07-14/the-costs-of-an-increasingly-cashless-economy

Ajmal, A. (2018, July 19). This Billion Dollar Real Estate Company Ditched Physical Offices For A VR Campus. Retrieved from https://wonderfulengineering.com/this-billion-dollar-real-estate-company-ditched-physical-offices-for-a-vr-campus/

Schlosser, K. (2019, June 27). Zillow launches retooled Zestimate that uses AI to analyze photographs and 'see' value in homes. Retrieved from https://www.geekwire.com/2019/zillow-launches-retooled-zestimate-uses-ai-analyze-photographs-see-value-homes/

Condon, S. (2018, September 03). How Trulia tackled machine learning challenges to build an in-house AI platform. Retrieved from https://www.zdnet.com/article/how-trulia-tackled-machine-learning-challenges-to-build-an-in-house-ai-platform/

Armstrong, P. (2019, December 31). How AI Is Really Going To Change Real Estate In 2020 And Beyond. Retrieved from https://www.forbes.com/sites/paularmstrongtech/2020/12/31/how-ai-is-really-going-to-change-real-estate-in-2020-and-beyond/

Written by Robert Muggah, F. (2019, January 16). The world's coastal cities are going under. Here's how some are fighting back. Retrieved December 08, 2020, from https://www.weforum.org/agenda/2019/01/the-world-s-coastal-cities-are-going-under-here-is-how-some-are-fighting-back/

Chadwick, J. (2017). Here's how 3D food printers are changing what we eat. Retrieved December 08, 2020, from https://fabricofdigitallife.com/index.php/Detail/objects/3711

Simon, M. (2018). Lab-Grown Meat Is Coming, Whether You Like It or Not. Retrieved December 08, 2020, from https://www.wired.com/story/lab-grown-meat/

Pirog, R., & Leopold Center for Sustainable Agriculture. (2001). Food, fuel, and freeways: An Iowa perspective on how far food travels, fuel usage, and greenhouse gas emissions. Ames, Iowa: Leopold Center for Sustainable Agriculture.

Move for Hunger. (n.d.). About Food Waste. Retrieved December 08, 2020, from https://moveforhunger.org/food-waste

Khan, A. (2016, November 18). Scientists aim to feed the world by boosting photosynthesis. Retrieved December 08, 2020, from https://www.latimes.com/science/sciencenow/la-sci-sn-boosting-photosynthesis-20161117-story.html

United Nations. (2009). Food Production Must Double by 2050 to Meet Demand from World's Growing Population, Innovative Strategies Needed to Combat Hunger, Experts Tell Second Committee | Meetings Coverage and Press Releases. Retrieved December 08, 2020, from https://www.un.org/press/en/2009/gaef3242.doc.htm

Despommier, D. D., & Carter, M. (2011). The vertical farm: Feeding the world in the 21st century. New York (N.Y.: Picador).

Rabin, R. (2017, November 03). Do Prepackaged Salad Greens Lose Their Nutrients? Retrieved December 08, 2020, from https://www.nytimes.com/2017/11/03/well/eat/do-prepackaged-salad-greens-lose-their-nutrients.html

Ballarte, C. (2017, July 20). Jeff Bezos and other investors raise $200 million for vertical farming startup Plenty. Retrieved December 08, 2020, from https://www.geekwire.com/2017/jeff-bezos-investors-raise-200-million-vertical-farming-startup-plenty/

Tarantola, A. (2018). The future of indoor agriculture is vertical farms run by robots. Retrieved from https://www.engadget.com/2018-10-03-future-indoor-agriculture-vertical-farms-robots.html

Food and Agriculture Organization of United Nations. (2009). 2050: A third more mouths to feed. Retrieved December 08, 2020, from http://www.fao.org/news/story/en/item/35571/icode/

Global meat consumption to rise 73 percent by 2050: FAO. (2011). Retrieved December 08, 2020, from https://www.meatpoultry.com/articles/4395-global-meat-consumption-to-rise-73-percent-by-2050-fao

Ritchie, H., & Roser, M. (2017, August 25). Meat and Dairy Production. Retrieved December 08, 2020, from https://ourworldindata.org/meat-production

Brooks, N. (2018, October 29). Chart Shows What the World's Land Is Used For … and It Explains Exactly Why So Many People Are Going Hungry. Retrieved December 08, 2020, from https://www.onegreenplanet.org/news/chart-shows-worlds-land-used/

Robinson, Timothy P., Wint, William, Conchedda, Giulia, Van Boeckel, Thomas, Ercoli, Valentina, Palamara, Elisa, Cinardi, Giuseppina, … Gilbert, Marius. (2014). Mapping the Global Distribution of Livestock.

Food and Agriculture Organization of United Nations. (2017). Water for Sustainable Food and Agriculture - A report produced for the G20 Presidency of Germany Retrieved December 08, 2020, from http://www.fao.org/3/a-i7959e.pdf

Ebikeme, C. (2013). Water World. Retrieved December 08, 2020, from https://www.nature.com/scitable/blog/eyes-on-environment/water_world/

Carrington, D. (2018, May 31). Avoiding meat and dairy is 'single biggest way' to reduce your impact on Earth. Retrieved December 08, 2020, from https://www.theguardian.com/environment/2018/may/31/avoiding-meat-and-dairy-is-single-biggest-way-to-reduce-your-impact-on-earth

Friedman, L., Pierre-louis, K., & Sengupta, S. (2018, January 25). The Meat Question, by the Numbers. Retrieved December 08, 2020, from https://www.nytimes.com/2018/01/25/climate/cows-global-warming.html

DW: Deutsche Welle. (2019). Will 2019 be the year of lab-grown meat? Retrieved December 08, 2020, from https://www.dw.com/en/will-2019-be-the-year-of-lab-grown-meat/a-46943665

Tuomisto, H. L., & Teixeira, . M. M. J. (July 15, 2011). Environmental Impacts of Cultured Meat Production. Environmental Science & Technology, 45, 14, 6117-6123.

Zaraska, M. (2015, July 27). Is Lab-Grown Meat Good for Us? Retrieved December 08, 2020, from https://www.theatlantic.com/health/archive/2013/08/is-lab-grown-meat-good-for-us/278778/

BBC. (2013). World's first lab-grown burger is eaten in London. Retrieved December 08, 2020, from https://www.bbc.com/news/av/uk-politics-23578179

Sorvino, C. (2018, January 30). Tyson Invests In Lab-Grown Protein Startup Memphis Meats, Joining Bill Gates And Richard Branson. Retrieved December 08, 2020, from https://www.forbes.com/sites/chloesorvino/2018/01/29/

EXCLUSIVE-INTERVIEW-TYSON-INVESTS-IN-LAB-GROWN-PROTEIN-STARTUP-MEMPHIS-MEATS-
JOINING-BILL-GATES-AND-RICHARD-BRANSON/?SH=3E590C1E3351

BACK, L., & COHEN, T. (2019, JULY 15). ON THE MENU SOON: LAB-GROWN STEAK
FOR ECO-CONSCIOUS DINERS. RETRIEVED DECEMBER 08, 2020, FROM HTTPS://
WWW.REUTERS.COM/ARTICLE/US-FOOD-TECH-LABMEAT-ALEPH-FARMS/
ON-THE-MENU-SOON-LAB-GROWN-STEAK-FOR-ECO-CONSCIOUS-DINERS-IDUSKCN1UA1ES

PETERS, A. (2018, MAY 02). LAB-GROWN MEAT IS GETTING CHEAP ENOUGH FOR ANYONE TO
BUY. RETRIEVED DECEMBER 08, 2020, FROM HTTPS://WWW.FASTCOMPANY.COM/40565582/
LAB-GROWN-MEAT-IS-GETTING-CHEAP-ENOUGH-FOR-ANYONE-TO-BUY

BITKER, J. (2020, DECEMBER 02). A SAN FRANCISCO COMPANY IS SET TO BE THE FIRST IN THE
WORLD TO SELL MEAT GROWN IN A LAB. RETRIEVED DECEMBER 08, 2020, FROM HTTPS://
WWW.SFCHRONICLE.COM/FOOD/ARTICLE/A-SAN-FRANCISCO-COMPANY-IS-SET-TO-BE-THE-
FIRST-IN-15767451.PHP

WILSON, A. (2019, FEBRUARY 21). GOT MILK? THIS $40M STARTUP IS CREATING COW-FREE DAIRY
PRODUCTS THAT ACTUALLY TASTE LIKE THE REAL THING. RETRIEVED DECEMBER 08, 2020,
FROM HTTPS://WWW.FORBES.COM/SITES/ALEXANDRAWILSON1/2019/01/09/GOT-MILK-THIS-
40M-STARTUP-IS-CREATING-COW-FREE-DAIRY-PRODUCTS-THAT-ACTUALLY-TASTE-LIKE-THE-
REAL-THING/?SH=1AAFAFFC40DC